The United Nations at Fifty
Retrospect and Prospect

The United Nations at Fifty:
Retrospect and Prospect

Papers from the
Thirtieth Foreign Policy School, 1995
edited by
Ramesh Thakur

University of Otago Press, Dunedin
and the Peace Research Centre,
Research School of Pacific and Asian Studies,
The Australian National University, Canberra

Published by University of Otago Press
PO Box 56, Dunedin, New Zealand
and the Peace Research Centre,
Research School of Pacific and Asian Studies,
The Australian National University,
Canberra, ACT 0200, Australia

ISSN 0111-6177
ISBN 1 877133 03 5

Contents

Acknowledgments *vii*
About the Contributors *ix*
List of Abbreviations *xv*

Ramesh Thakur
Introduction: Past Imperfect, Future UNcertain *1*

Don McKinnon
The United Nations at Fifty: A Performance Appraisal *33*

Malcolm Templeton
The Achievements and Shortcomings of the United Nations *41*

Gareth Evans
Cooperating for Peace *59*

Jacob Bercovitch
The United Nations and the Mediation of International Disputes *73*

Reginald H. F. Austin
The Future of UN Peacekeeping Operations: Cosmetic or
Comprehensive? *89*

Jorge Heine
A UN Agenda for Development: Reflections on the Social Question in
the South *119*

Tom O'Reilly
Peacekeeping in Africa: A New Zealand Defence Force
Perspective *127*

John M. Sanderson
The Lessons Learnt from UNTAC: The Military Component
View *145*

Michael Rose
The Bosnia Experience *167*

John M. Sanderson
Peacekeeping or Peace Enforcement? Global Flux and the Dilemmas of
UN Intervention *179*

Takahiro Shinyo
Reforming The Security Council: A Japanese Perspective *201*

S. K. Singh
An Asian Perspective on the United Nations System *217*

James N. Rosenau
The Adaptation of the United Nations to a Turbulent World *229*

Keith Suter
Reforming the United Nations *241*

Olara A. Otunnu
Promoting Peacemaking and Peacekeeping: The Role and Perspective
of the International Peace Academy *263*

A. J. R. Groom
Global Governance and the United Nations *277*

Bruce Brown
Summary: A Mid-Life Crisis for the UN at Fifty *301*

Index *321*

Tables and Figures

Table 1.1: UN Overreach? *5*
Table 1.2: UN Peacekeeping Operations, December 1994 *6*
Figure 14.1: The United Nations in a Turbulent World *231*

Acknowledgments

That the Otago Foreign Policy School is now into its 30th year is a tribute to those who had the vision to initiate this symposium thirty years ago. As Director of the 30th School and Editor of the resulting proceedings, it is my duty, privilege and pleasure to thank all those involved in making this such a successful occasion and rewarding experience. Pride of place must go to the Academic Committee: Dr William Harris, Dr Terence Hearn, Dr Mohammad Jaforullah, Dr Louis Leland, Dr Robert Patman, Dr Elena Poletti, Dr Roberto Rabel, Professor Ann Trotter, and Profesor G. Antony Wood. Their role was even greater than usual because this year, for the final six months of the two-year planning process, the Director was based in Canberra. Drs Hearn and Poletti in particular had to shoulder much of the logistical burden in the final weeks leading up to the School.

Second, I would like to thank all the speakers. They came from many different corners of the world, some to fulfil a commitment of long standing, others as the result of calls at shorter notice. In the end we assembled a truly distinguished galaxy of eminent persons who are extremely busy in their respective walks of life. All took time off not simply to attend, but to prepare and deliver very substantial and thoughtful papers. The gist of their addresses, and the ensuing debates that were generated, will stay in our minds for years to come as we, no less than the United Nations, struggle to make sense of the cascading world around us. What was remarkable was how on balance, despite the heavy dose of realism that pervaded all discussion, there was a counsel of hope more than despair coming out of the School. Clearly, reports of the death of the United Nations system have been much exaggerated.

Third, I would like to thank all those whose support and sponsorship made it possible to assemble such a sparkling constellation of speakers and a matching group of participants: the UN Association of New Zealand, the NZ Ministry of Foreign Affairs and Trade, the NZ Ministry of Defence, the NZ Defence Force, the NZ Centre for

Strategic Studies, the NZ Institute of International Affairs, the Public Advisory Committee on Disarmament and Arms Control, the British Council, the Embassy of Japan, and the Embassy of the United States of America. Long may their association with the Otago Foreign Policy School continue.

Fourth, a special debt of gratitude is owed to all those who agreed to take on the responsibility of chairing the various sessions. We began, stayed and finished on time: not a small achievement over four days for such a large gathering. The main credit for this must lie with the chairpersons who performed their tasks with diligence, grace and good humour. This can be a difficult task, a delicate task, and often a thankless task at the time. So it is appropriate that I record my and the participants' thanks in this manner.

Finally, and most importantly as far as the School itself is concerned, I would like to thank the participants. There would be no School without them. They came, they stayed, they listened and they contributed. They came in the dozens: at around 150 participants, this was the largest School ever. They came through snow and sleet, and by bus via Invercargill as well as by air, to conquer Dunedin's winter at its best: crisp frosty mornings and bright sunny days after the initial snowstorm.

The editing of the proceedings has been done back in Canberra. I would like to thank Jan Preston-Stanley of the Peace Research Centre for much of the follow-up work that had to be done in getting final copies of papers in reasonable time, and for some re-typing that had to be done. Chris Wilson, also of the Peace Research Centre, assisted with her usual thoroughness in reading through all the manuscripts and compiling the index.

RAMESH THAKUR
Canberra, November 1995

About the Contributors

Reginald H. F. Austin of Zimbabwe has been the Director of the Legal and Constitutional Affairs Division of the Commonwealth Secretariat since 1994. He was educated at the University of Cape Town and University College London and lectured at the latter for several years before moving in 1982 to the University of Zimbabwe as Professor and Dean of the Law Faculty. He has consulted widely both in Zimbabwe and internationally, including being a member of the Zimbabwe Electoral Commission (1984–90), Director of the Electoral Component of UNTAC (1992–93), and Director of the Electoral Component of the UN Observer Mission in South Africa (1994). Professor Austin was also Vice-Chariman of the Zimbabwe Red Cross Society (1983–92).

Jacob Bercovitch is Senior Lecturer in International Relations at the University of Canterbury, Christchurch. He has also taught at the universities of Harvard, London and Jerusalem. He received his Ph.D. from the London School of Economics in 1980. He is the author and editor of eight books and more than 50 articles, his most recent book being *Resolving International Conflicts: The Structure of International Mediation* (Boulder: Lynne Rienner, 1995). His main research interests are international conflict resolution and mediation.

Bruce Brown is in his second term (from 1993) as Director of the New Zealand Institute of International Affairs, having served as the first Director (1969–71). He began his career as Private Secretary to the Rt Hon Walter Nash (Leader of the Opposition 1954–57, Prime Minister 1957–59), and joined the Department of External Affairs in 1959. His postings included the NZ Permanent Mission to the UN in New York (1963–67), Ambassador to Iran (1975–78) and Thailand and Vietnam (1985–88), and High Commissioner to Canada (1988–92). He has written widely on New Zealand Labour Party history and on New Zealand foreign policy.

Senator Gareth Evans has been Australia's Foreign Minister since 1988. A lawyer by profession and a Senator since 1978, he has authored, co-authored and edited a number of books on foreign affairs, public law and politics, including *Australia's Foreign Relations in the World of the 1990s and Beyond* (1991) and *Cooperating for Peace* (1993). He is best known internationally for his work in initiating the UN peace plan for Cambodia, developing the Chemical Weapons Convention, and promoting the idea of Asian–Pacific economic and security communities. In 1995 he was awarded the Grawemeyer Prize for his contributions to international peace and security.

A. J. R. Groom is Professor of International Relations at the University of Kent at Canterbury in the UK. A past chairman of the British International Studies Association, he is the founder and chairman of the European Standing Group for International Relations of the European Consortium for Political Research. He is the Director of the Centre for Conflict Analysis and a Board member of the Academic Council for the UN System. His academic interests include international organisation, integration theory, conflict studies and European international relations, as well as international relations theory. He has published some 16 volumes in these fields and over one hundred papers, including *Contemporary International Relations: A Guide to Theory,* edited with Margot Light (1994).

Jorge Heine (Ph.D., Stanford) is Chile's Ambassador to South Africa and was previously Deputy Minister of Defense, Chilean Air Force. He has held positions at a number of research institutes and universities in the United States, Puerto Rico, Europe and Chile. He has published seven books and over 60 articles in academic journals and symposium volumes. An associate member of the International Institute for Strategic Studies (IISS), he has also been a consultant to the Ford Foundation and the United Nations. A past president of the Caribbean Studies Association and of the Chilean Political Science Association, he has held fellowships from the Social Sciences Research Council, the Guggenheim Foundation and St Antony's College, Oxford.

The Rt Hon. Don McKinnon, having entered parliament in 1978, has been Deputy Prime Minister and Minister for Foreign Affairs and Trade of New Zealand since 1990. He was also appointed

Minister for Pacific Island Affairs in 1991, a member of the Privy Council in 1992 and Leader of the House in 1993.

Colonel Tom O'Reilly has been involved in two peacekeeping operations in Africa. He served with the Commonwealth Monitoring Force sent to Rhodesia in December 1979 to oversee its transition to a democratic Zimbabwe. More recently he spent 16 months with the UN mission in Angola where he was responsible primarily for co-ordinating the planning for the expansion of the verification mission and the necessary military support and input for the peace negotiations then taking place in Zambia. He returned to New Zealand in April 1995.

Olara A. Otunnu is President of the International Peace Academy, an independent international institution based in New York and devoted to promoting peacemaking and peacekeeping. Born in Uganda, Mr Otunnu received his education at Makerere, Oxford and Harvard universities. He practised and taught law before serving successively as member of Uganda National Consultative Council (interim parliament), Uganda's Permanent Representative to the United Nations, and Minister of Foreign Affairs. After the period in diplomacy and government, Mr Otunnu returned to academia, doing research and teaching in Paris before assuming his present position. He is currently a member of the Commission on Global Governance, the Club of Rome, the Carnegie Commission on Preventing Deadly Conflict, and the Council of African Advisers to the World Bank.

General Sir Michael Rose was commissioned into the British Army in 1964. Following 30 years of military service in diverse postings in Britain and overseas, in January 1994 Lt. Gen. Rose was appointed Commander UN Forces Bosnia–Hergovina Command. He was promoted to General and took over as Adjutant General in July 1995. Among other honours, Gen. Rose was awarded the KCB in January 1994 and the DSO in May 1995.

Dr James N. Rosenau is University Professor of International Affairs at the George Washington University. He has taught previously at Ohio State University, Rutgers, the State University of New Jersey, and the University of Southern California. A former President of the International Studies Association, Professor Rosenau is well known for his scholarship on the dynamics of change in world politics and the overlap of domestic and foreign affairs, foci that have resulted in more than 30 books and 140 articles. His most recent publications include *Turbulence in World Politics: A Theory of Change and Continuity* (1990) and *The United Nations in a Turbulent World* (1992).

Lt. Gen. John Murray Sanderson enlisted in the Australian Army in 1958. After a number of regimental, instructional and staff appointments, he was promoted to the rank of Lieutenant General in March 1992 and appointed Commander of the United Nations Transitional Authority in Cambodia (UNTAC). Promoted to Companion in the Military Division of the Order of Australia in 1994, Lt. Gen. Sanderson was appointed Chief of the General Staff, Australia, on 8 July 1995.

Takahiro Shinyo is a Professor in the Osaka School of International Public Policy at Osaka University. He joined Japan's Ministry of Foreign Affairs in 1972 and served as the Director of the Disarmament Division and of the United Nations Policy Division before joining Osaka University in 1993. Among other works, he is the author of *Shin Kokuren Ron* (New United Nations Theory) (1995) and *Kokusai Heiwa Kyoryoku Nyumon* (A Guide to International Peace Cooperation) (1995).

S. K. Singh was educated at St John's College in Agra and Trinity College at Cambridge. He was a member of the Indian Foreign Service from 1954 to 1990 when he retired as Foreign Secretary. As well as having attended 14 UN General Assembly sessions, he was ambassador to Lebanon, Jordan, Cyprus, Afghhanistan, Austria and Pakistan. He has been Visiting Professor at Jawaharlal Nehru University in New Delhi and a contributor to the Indian and international press as well as specialist journals.

Dr Keith Suter, a writer and broadcaster, is the President of the Centre for Peace and Conflict Studies at the University of Sydney. His first doctorate was on the international law of guerrilla warfare and his second on the economics of the arms race. His most recent books are *Global Change: Armageddon and the New World Order* and *Global Agenda: Economics, the Environment and the Nation-State*. He is also President of the UN Association of Australia (New South Wales) and

Chairperson, International Humanitarian Law Committee, Australian Red Cross Society.

Dr Ramesh Thakur, Professor of International Relations and Director of Asian Studies at the University of Otago, is Head of the Peace Research Centre at the Australian National University in Canberra for 1995–96. Among other works he is the author/editor of *Peacekeeping in Vietnam: Canada, India, Poland and the International Commission* (1984), *International Peacekeeping in Lebanon: United Nations Authority and Multinational Force* (1987) and *A Crisis of Expectations: UN Peacekeeping in the 1990s* (1995).

New Zealand armoured personnel carriers (APCs) being loaded at Wellington en route to Bosnia. (Photo: Ministry of Foreign Affairs and Trade, New Zealand)

Abbreviations

ACC	Air Crimes Commission
ACRS	Arms Control and Regional Security working groups
ANZAC	Australia New Zealand Army Corps
APC	armoured personnel carrier
APEC	Asia–Pacific Economic Cooperation
ARF	ASEAN Regional Forum
ASAS	Association of Southern African States
ASEAN	Association of South East Asian Nations
BDLP	Buddhist Liberal Democratic Party
CAMDUN	Campaign for a More Democratic United Nations
CENTO	Central Treaty Organisation
CFE	Conventional Forces in Europe
CIVPOL	Civil Police Component
CPAF	Cambodian People's Armed Forces
CPP	Cambodian People's Party
CTBT	Comprehensive Test Ban Treaty
DPKO	Department of Peacekeeping Operations
EC	European Community
ECAFE	Economic Commission for Asia and the Far East
ECLA	Economic Commission for Latin America
ECOSOC	Economic and Social Council
EEC	European Economic Community
EP5	Expanded Permanent Five (P5 + Australia, Germany, India, Indonesia, Japan, Malaysia, Thailand)
ESCAP	Economic and Social Commission for Asia and the Pacific
EU	European Union
FAO	Food and Agriculture Organisation
FDI	foreign direct investment
FNLA	*Frente Nacional de Libertacao de Angola*

FUNCINPEC	National United Front for an Independent, Neutral, Peaceful and Cooperative Cambodia
G7	Group of Seven industrialised states
GATT	General Agreement on Tariffs and Trade
GDP	Gross Domestic Product
ICJ	International Court of Justice
ICRC	International Committee of the Red Cross
IDEA	Institute for Democracy and Electoral Assistance
ILO	International Labour Organisation
IMF	International Monetary Fund
INSTRAW	International Research and Training Institute for the Advancement of Women
IPSO	International Polling Station Officer
ITU	International Telegraph Union
KMT	Kuomintang
KPNLF	Khmer People's National Liberation Front
MAD	Mutually Assured Destruction
MPLA	*Movimento Popular de Libertacao de Angola*
NADK	National Army of Democratic Kampuchea
NAFTA	North American Free Trade Agreement
NATO	North Atlantic Treaty Organisation
NGO	non-government organisation
NZDF	New Zealand Defence Force
OAU	Organisation of African Unity
OECD	Organisation for Economic Cooperation and Development
OEEC	Organisation for European Economic Cooperation
ONUC	UN Operation in the Congo
OSCE	Organisation on Security and Cooperation in Europe
P5	the five permanent members of the UN Security Council (Britain, China, France, Russia, US)
PDK	Party of Democratic Kampuchea
SADC	Southern African Development Community
SEATO	Southeast Asia Treaty Organisation
SIPRI	Stockholm International Peace Research Institute
SNC	Supreme National Council (Cambodia)
SoC	State of Cambodia
SRSG	Special Representative of the Secretary-General
SWAPO	Southwest African People's Organisation
TNC	transnational corporation

UN	United Nations
UNAMIC	UN Advance Mission in Cambodia
UNAVEM	UN Angola Verification Mission
UNCTAD	UN Conference on Trade and Development
UNDOF	UN Disengagement Observer Force
UNDP	UN Development Programme
UNEF	UN Emergency Force
UNEP	UN Environmental Programme
UNESCO	UN Educational, Scientific and Cultural Organisation
UNHCR	UN High Commissioner for Refugees
UNICEF	UN Children's Fund
UNIDO	UN International Development Organisation
UNIFIL	UN Interim Force in Lebanon
UNITA	*Uniao Nacional para a Independencia Total de Angola*
UNITAR	UN Institute for Training and Research
UNOMSA	UN Observer Mission in South Africa
UNPROFOR	UN Protection Force
UNTAC	UN Transitional Authority in Cambodia
UNTAG	UN Transitional Group
UNV	UN Volunteer
UPU	Universal Postal Union
WEO	Western European and Other group
WHO	World Health Organisation
WMO	World Meteorological Organisation
WTO	World Trade Organisation

Lt. Gen. Sir Michael Rose and Professor Ramesh Thakur at the Otago Foreign Policy School 1995. (Photo: Ian McGibbon)

Ramesh Thakur

Introduction:
Past Imperfect, Future UNcertain

The United Nations opened up large global horizons in 1945. But the steps taken by member states since then have been small, hesitant and limited. The UN Charter begins with the grand words 'We the peoples of the United Nations determined to save succeeding generations from the scourge of war'. It goes on to affirm human rights, justice, social progress and better standards of life. The fine sentiments are yet to be translated into reality. The 1945 dream of a world community equal in rights and united in vision has never come close to being realised. Alexander Solzhenitsyn, in his Nobel Prize acceptance address, described the United Nations as a place where the peoples of the world are served up to the designs of governments.[1] Captured by governments, the UN became increasingly distant from 'We, the peoples'. As Rosemary Righter comments, 'arguments over squared brackets and modifying subclauses have an allure for professional bureaucrats that few politicians, and no layman, can hope to understand'.[2]

The end of the Cold War and the forceful response by the international community to Iraq's invasion and annexation of Kuwait created expectations that the United Nations would change from being a marginal to a central player in world affairs. There is general agreement that the scope for multilateral diplomacy has broadened. There is disagreement on whether the United Nations should be at the centre or the margins of the new multilateral diplomacy. Is the United Nations the best forum for managing the interdependence that we expect to become even more dense over the next fifty years? Or, bedevilled by shoddy machinery, waste accretion and institutional inadequacies, is the United Nations in real danger of a reversal to marginalisation?

---

1   Quoted in Rosemary Righter, *Utopia Lost: The United Nations and World Order* (New York: Twentieth Century Fund Press, 1995), p. 85.
2   Ibid., p. 255.

The Romantics and the Cynics

Observers of the United Nations may be divided into two broad groups: the romantic and the cynical. For the former, the global organisation can do no wrong and is the solution to all the world's problems. They do not deny the reality of the failures of Bosnia, Somalia and Rwanda. Rather, they insist that the failures must be seen in context. First, a lot of good was done even in these 'failed' operations, resulting in the saving of hundreds of thousands of lives. New Zealand Foreign Minister Don McKinnon notes that peacekeepers do make a difference, even in operations that might on the surface appear to be suboptimal in their functioning. Second, there are many other operations that are acknowledged to be overall, if partially flawed, successes, including Namibia and Cambodia. Third, there are other parts of the UN system that are generally efficient and worthwhile. Most importantly, say the ardent supporters of the organisation, the failures of the United Nations are really failures of its member states who find in the UN a convenient scapegoat for their own short-comings and weaknesses. If only the member states had the necessary political will, then the organisation would fulfil its destiny as the global commons, the custodian of the international interest and the conscience of all humanity.

The cynics ask: what has the UN done to justify the respect paid to it by the romantics? Is fifty years not long enough to question the 'potential' of the organisation as the basis for deference? To the cynics the UN seems only too willing to claim credit for any successes while shifting all blame for any failures to the lack of an elusive 'political will' on the part of member states and the major powers. In the cynics' view, the United Nations is itself a symptom of many of the world's problems. It suffers from exaggerated claims, inflammatory rhetoric, inept leadership, a bloated and excessively politicised agenda, bureaucratic sclerosis, uncontrolled expansion of economic and social programmes, agencies' sectoral squabbles, wasteful spending habits, lack of accountability in procedures and programmes and an inability to formulate and implement meaningful reform.

On the basis of its actions and inaction in Somalia, Bosnia and Rwanda, Simon Jenkins concluded that 'the UN has become not a friend of world stability but a menace. Wherever it intervenes, peace is neither made nor kept but postponed'.[3] The UN's credibility has been

3   Simon Jenkins, 'Fanning the Flames of War', *Times* (London), 9 November

seen to be lost, in particular, under tide of human misery, of refugees swarming on the highways and byways of former Yugoslavia. A columnist with the *Economist* mentioned the following as Bosnia's contribution to doublespeak: 'safe area' for a deadly dangerous place; a 'rapid reaction' will occur next month, maybe; a 'protection force' that offers neither.[4] While the cynics might conclude that Bosnia has been the UN's Vietnam, the romantics might respond that it is better explained as the UN's Munich: a failure of collective nerve and will.

When a campaign of heavy but military target-specific air strikes launched by the North Atlantic Treaty Organisation (NATO) lifted the Serbian siege of Sarajevo in September 1995, the romantics were seemingly vindicated. Yet even the earlier record and reality, General Sir Michael Rose points out, are ambiguous. The UN peacekeeping force has performed a massive humanitarian task to save thousands of lives. It is true that in public perception, the UN has abdicated its moral duty as the guardian of the international community's hopes for a better world. Yet the operational failings of the peacekeeping force reflect policy incoherence and vacuum in the major Western capitals.

The United Nations was established in the belief that peace and security cannot be maintained other than by an international organisation prepared to use force if necessary to enforce community edicts. The UN has been doubly flawed in its primary task: it lacks power as a base of authority and it was not designed to make authoritative allocation of values in some of the types of disputes which have arisen since 1945, most notably civil conflicts. As the shroud of the Cold War lifted from the world, the multitude of national, religious and ethnic fault-lines stood out with sharper clarity.

Peace and Security

When faced with a threat to peace, the UN can choose to do nothing. Cynics might say that indeed the organisation is very skilled and experienced in this particular course of action, that the UN exists so that nations who are unable to do anything individually can get together to decide that nothing can be done collectively. Yet previous UN inactivity owed more to rivalry and tensions between the major powers which incapacitated UN ability to deal decisively with crises.

Second, the United Nations can adopt resolutions under Chapter

1994, p. 18.
4 Johnson, 'The injuries of war', *Economist* (London), 29 July 1995, p. 72.

VI for resolving an international dispute peacefully. The normative principle of the primacy of peaceful over forceful means has become firmly entrenched. The UN record in the field of pacific settlement is somewhat qualified. On balance, the organisation has helped states to behave less conflictually, to form habits of cooperation, to develop shared norms and perceptions. The Security Council has played a *peace-influencing* role, and the General Assembly too has undertaken a *peace-shaping* role. UN assets and qualifications for peacemaking remain what they have always been: its authority and impartiality as a third party representing the entire international community.

Jacob Bercovitch draws attention to the fact that often the UN is saddled with conflicts that member states have found too difficult to resolve, and too late in the escalation cycle. While this is a fair comment, it too can be overstated. If member states were permitted to transfer only those cases to the UN which they can resolve among themselves, then they would not need the world body in a peace-maintenance role. Unfortunately, at times the major political organs of the United Nations have given the impression of being more interested in finger-pointing than problem-solving. Until the 1990s, the excessive politicisation of issues produced a plethora of resolutions full of exaggerated rhetoric.

If force is used, the UN can, under Chapter VII, move to graduated shades of escalation. Its third course of action is the imposition of economic sanctions under Article 41: measures 'not involving the use of armed force'. Giving teeth to the implementation of sanctions under Article 42 represents the fourth course of action.

The fifth course is full-fledged military action if the UN decides that sanctions are proving ineffectual and stronger measures are necessary. In the 1990s, Cold War acrimony between the superpowers seemingly gave way to a new world order harmony. As the cohesiveness of the familiar power blocs declined, so the role of the United Nations gained greater coherence and its actions gathered fresh momentum. The most important long-term significance of UN actions in the Gulf (1990–91) lay in the crossing of the conceptual Rubicon by authorising enforcement of sanctions, and then military eviction of the aggressor, by troops not even nominally under UN command (as they had been in Korea in the 1950s). As in Korea, the advantage of the procedure was that it allowed the United Nations to approximate the achievement of collective security within a clear chain of command necessary for large-scale military operations. The cost to the UN was that the Gulf War, like the Korean War, became identified with US policy over which the organisation exercised little real control.

Peacekeeping

The sixth course of UN action is to establish a peacekeeping force. Peacekeeping is the most important UN institutional innovation. It evolved in the grey zone between pacific settlement and military enforcement. Its primary purpose was to bring about and preserve a cessation of hostilities, and it focused on noncoercive and facilitative activities rather than on repelling aggression by armed combat. Peacekeeping operations had no military objectives, were barred from active combat, located between rather than in opposition to hostile elements, and required to negotiate rather than fight. The cardinal distinction between collective security and peacekeeping thus lies in the reliance upon force and consent respectively. In addition, UN peacekeepers were required to be militarily neutral between the belligerents and politically impartial in respect of the issues in conflict.

The jump in the number of peacekeeping operations in the 1990s (Table 1.1) is testimony to the enhanced expectations of the UN in the new order. Of the 35 peacekeeping and observer missions set up by the UN since 1945, no fewer than 20 were set up after 1988. In December 1994, there were 16 UN peacekeeping operations at an annual cost of US $3.4 billion for the total of around 75,000 troops, police and civilian officers involved (Table 1.2). To put this in perspective, Americans spent $3 billion each year on dog food and another $2 billion on cat food, and global defence expenditures in the 1980s averaged one trillion dollars per year.

Table 1.1: UN Overreach?			
	1988	*1992*	*1994*
Security Council resolutions in preceding 12 months	15	53	78
Disputes & conflicts engaging UN attention in preceding 12 months	11	13	28
No. of peacekeeping operations	5	11	17
Military personnel deployed	9 570	11 495	73 393
Civilian police deployed	35	115	2 130
Civilian personnel deployed	1 516	2 206	2 206
No. of contributing countries	26	56	76
Annual peacekeeping budget (US $m)	230	1 690	3 610
Source: *New York Times,* 6 January 1995			

Table 1.2: UN Peacekeeping Operations, December 1994[a]

Force	Location	Starting date	Authorised size[b]	Annual cost ($m)	Fatalities
UNTSO	Middle East	6/1948	220	28.6	28
UNMOGIP	India/Pakistan	1/1949	39	7.2	6
UNFICYP	Cyprus	3/1964	1206	43.9	163
UNDOF	Golan Heights	6/1974	1031	32.2	37
UNIFIL	Lebanon	3/1978	5187	142.3	200
UNIKOM	Iraq–Kuwait	4/1991	1124	68.6	3
UNAVEM II	Angola	6/1991	79	26.3	4
ONUSAL	El Salvador	7/1991	34	29.2	3
MINURSO	Western Sahara	9/1991	334	40.5	4
UNPROFOR	Yugoslavia	3/1992	39 537	1600	129
ONUMOZ	Mozambique	12/1992	5063	294.8	17
UNOSOM II	Somalia	4/1992	14 968	862.2	133
UNOMIG	Georgia	8/1993	126	10.8	0
UNOMIL	Liberia	9/1993	84	36.4	0
UNMIH	Haiti	9/1993	41	5.3	0
UNAMIR	Rwanda	10/1993	5522	197.5[c]	15
TOTAL			**74 592**	**3426**	**742**

a. This list does not include the UN Mission of Observers in Tajikistan established by the Security Council on 16 December 1994. With an authorised strength of 84 personnel, UNMOT was expected to cost about US $442,000 per month.

b. The total size includes the sum of military troops and support personnel, military observers, civilian police, international civilian staff and local staff.

c. The costs of UNAMIR include those of the UN Observer Mission in Uganda–Rwanda (UNOMUR).

Source: *United Nations Peace-keeping* (New York: UN Document DPI/1306/Rev.4, February 1995).

UN peacekeeping operations in the 1990s have expanded not just in numbers but also in the nature and scope of their missions. In the past decade, the UN has assisted the democratic process by providing electoral advice and help to more than 45 countries, including Cambodia, Namibia, Eritrea, Mozambique, El Salvador and Nicaragua. The 'simple emergencies' of yesteryear required the UN to cope with organised violence between states fighting across an international border. As Colonel O'Reilly's discussion of Angola makes clear, today's 'complex emergencies' produce multiple crises all at once: collapsed state structures; humanitarian tragedies caused by starvation, disease or genocide; large-scale fighting and slaughter between rival ethnic or bandit groups; horrific human rights atrocities;

and the risks of competitive intervention by outside powers. Reflecting this, peacekeeping missions in the 1990s have been required to undertake the following nine types of tasks:

* Military, including ceasefire monitoring, cantonment and demobilisation of troops, and ensuring security for elections;
* Policing;
* Human rights monitoring and enforcement;
* Information dissemination;
* Observation, organisation and conduct of elections;
* Rehabilitation and reconstruction of state structures;
* Repatriation and resettlement of large numbers of people;
* Administration either during the transition from one regime to another, or pending the re-establishment of state structures;
* Working with or overseeing the operations of regional or non-UN peacekeeping operations

Peacekeeping in Civil Wars

The United Nations was designed to cope with interstate war. Repelling or reversing a clearcut cross-border aggression of one state by another, such as of Kuwait by Iraq in 1990, is one of the few 'bottom lines' in international affairs. Founded on the principle of national sovereignty, the UN is ill-equipped to cope with civil conflict.[5] Yet the disputes clamouring for UN attention, such as in Cambodia, Somalia and Rwanda, are almost all domestic. This poses particular difficulties, starting with the impossible political question of how the world body committed to maintaining the territorial integrity of member states will decide when to support and when to oppose the 'legitimate' government against attempts at secession. The elemental force of ethnonationalism is more likely to defeat the UN than be tamed by it.

Compared to the relative stability of border conflicts, civil conflicts are characterised by political fluidity. The stakes are higher: the entire territory, not just a border readjustment; and, possibly, life and death, not just victory or defeat in battle. Unlike interstate wars, there is no territorial status quo ante which can be restored after

5 See Paul F. Diehl, 'Peacekeeping in Civil Wars', in Ramesh Thakur and Carlyle A. Thayer, eds., *A Crisis of Expectations: UN Peacekeeping in the 1990s* (Boulder: Westview, 1995), pp. 223–36.

international intervention. Countries in dispute fight each other through uniformed soldiers across an international border. Traditional peace-keeping forces interposed lightly-armed troops to separate consenting combatants after a ceasefire. Civil wars scatter UN troops thinly over a wide geographical area. These are more vulnerable to attack when not deployed at fixed positions in a neutral area. Required to cover an entire national territory instead of just the border, a peacekeeping force will have to undertake frequent travel in unsecured areas. Not only are civil wars not fought by large armies; their weapons too are generally small arms not easily controlled or neutralised by bombings and arms embargoes. The result can be that the UN has to devote more time, resources and personnel to protecting its humanitarian mission than to the mission itself. The conflict entangling the UN operation in Moga-dishu distracted attention from its humanitarian work elsewhere in Somalia towards ending famine, improving security and establishing local administrative, police and judicial structures.

'Second generation' operations have expanded the roles of peace-keeping to include humanitarian assistance and electoral supervision. These require more military personnel, civilian police and technical experts. But humanitarian, electioneering and enforcement measures by the UN face distinctive difficulties in civil wars. Most civil conflicts have deep historical roots and are characterised by broad and mutual suspicion based on past traumatic experience. Objective analyses and rational solutions are meaningless in such contexts. Time is a better solution to historical conflicts. UN intervention in sectarian strife must accordingly acknowledge the prospect of an indefinite commitment.

To be effective in a peacekeeping role, the UN must negotiate with all significant sectarian leaders and so endow them with a degree of legitimacy. In return, however, leaders of ill-disciplined and un-coordinated guerrilla groups may be unable or unwilling to honour the agreements made with the UN. If a viable government is non-existent and the UN is assigned some law-and-order functions, it may face a quandary about future courses of action. It may be required to govern the country until a negotiated settlement is achieved. The alternative may be to tolerate various forms of anarchy that would result in the loss of lives and foreshadow a renewal of full-scale warfare.

Peacekeeping, by freezing a conflict, favours the status quo at the time of its deployment. This makes it more difficult for UN peace-keeping forces to stay neutral in a civil conflict than in an interstate war. Ceasefires 'in-place' might legitimise ethnic cleansing by the militarily most powerful. In 1995 Croatia, fearing that the presence of UN peacekeepers would convert Serb territorial gains into a permanent occupation, asked the peacekeepers to leave. Efforts to delay a ceasefire until territorial gains have been forcibly reversed may drag the UN into the quagmire of an internal war. In Bosnia all sides have committed atrocities, even if the scale differs from one group to another; all have engaged in campaigns of disinformation; and all have tried to subvert the neutral international presence of UN peacekeepers into an instrument of partial propaganda warfare.

In most civil wars today, the distinctions between combatants and civilians are blurred. Fighters from subnational groups are hard to identify and impossible to separate when they live next to one another. UN intervention necessitates measures to protect widely dispersed and highly vulnerable populations that are bitterly hostile towards one another. And if there is no effective government in power, then attempts by the UN to impose its own law and order can provoke fierce backlash from armed bandit groups. This is what happened to the humanitarian peacekeeping mission in Somalia.[6] All this explains why it is difficult to inject UN forces into active civil wars where no government—if one exists—has invited them, the fighting forces are unwilling to cooperate with the UN forces, and there is little possibility of bringing pressure to bear on the several factions.[7]

Peace-enforcement

Should the UN use force against those who would challenge its authority, as in Bosnia and Somalia? Dag Hammarskjöld created the first UN peacekeeping force in 1956 in the Suez. He restricted the use of force to self-defence, defined as the protection of the lives of UN soldiers and of the positions held by them under a UN mandate. In *An Agenda for Peace,* the new Secretary-General Boutros Boutros-Ghali implied that future peacekeeping operations could be organised without the consent of all the parties.[8] *An Agenda for Peace* was a triumph of

6   See Ramesh Thakur, 'From Peacekeeping to Peace-Enforcement: The UN Operation in Somalia', *Journal of Modern African Studies* 32 (September 1994), pp. 387–410.

7   Brian Urquhart, 'Who Can Police the World?', *New York Review of Books,* 12 May 1994, p. 29.

8   Boutros Boutros-Ghali, *An Agenda for Peace: Preventive Diplomacy, Peace-making and Peace-keeping* (New York: UN Department of Public Information, 1992), para. 20.

new world order hopes over Cold War era experience. It was flawed in not paying sufficient heed to the very real differences of interests and perspectives informing the use of force by states in the international arena, nor to the very real constraints upon UN action in the messy conflicts clamouring for world attention today.

The difficulties associated with the organisation, deployment and use of military force do not disappear simply because of UN authorisation. States are reluctant to transfer control over their national armed forces to the UN because of doubts over the its managerial capacity for military operations, scepticism about its institutional capacity to police the world wisely and effectively, and the fear of creating a military monster that might one day turn against them. The inhibitions on the use of UN force are likely to remain in place, including an inoperative Military Staff Committee and non-fulfilment of Articles 42 and 43 requiring national troop contingents to be placed at the disposal of the UN. The promptness and near-unanimity of the Security Council in the Gulf War did not herald a sudden feasibility of collective security.[9]

Alan James makes a useful distinction between a 'peace-restoring response' and a 'peace-enforcement operation'.[10] In the former case, the UN Security Council may have dealt somewhat ambiguously with, or even directly denied, the principle of host-state consent. The mission's mandate and equipment may be more imposing than is usual for peacekeepers, signalling that the force has the right, the ability and, if necessary, the intention to engage in defensive measures of a forceful kind; and that some breaches by the parties of their undertakings may elicit a tough response. James emphasises the word 'response'. Such a force is not meant to take coercive initiatives nor has it been assigned a specific target state or group—which is why it has not been equipped for full-scale battle. As the commander of one UN force with such aspects commented, one does not go to war in white-painted vehicles.[11] Peace-enforcement, by contrast, refers to military activity which is both partial and threatening, and for which the consent of the target state or group is not deemed necessary.

The consensus on traditional peacekeeping was that peacekeepers

---

9   See Inis Claude, 'Collective Security After the Cold War', in Gary L. Guertner, ed., *Collective Security in Europe and Asia* (Carlisle, PA: US Army War College, 1992), pp. 7–28.

10   Alan James, 'Peacekeeping, Peace-Enforcement and National Sovereignty', in Thakur and Thayer, eds., *A Crisis of Expectations,* pp. 263–80.

11   Quoted in ibid., pp. 264–65.

should not have the obligation, the soldiers or the equipment to engage violators in hostilities. International peacekeeping forces express and facilitate the erstwhile belligerents' will to live in peace; they cannot supervise peace in conditions of war. The predicament of peace-keeping soldiers on the ground is that they are unable to move forward into an unwinnable battle, unable to stay put taking casualties for no purpose, and unable to withdraw without repercussions for national foreign policies and UN peacekeeping. Contrary to traditional peace-keeping, peace-enforcement does not work within a broad consensus of all the parties to a conflict, does prejudice the rights of at least one of the parties, and moves beyond a minimalist to a muscular conception of self-defence. Turning a peacekeeping operation into a fighting force erodes international consensus on its function, encourages contributing contingents to withdraw, converts peacekeeprs into factional participants in the internal power struggle, and turns them into targets of attack by rival internal factions. That is, peace-enforcement can lead to 'mission creep', which in turn leads to 'peacekeeping fatigue'.

General Sanderson, Force Commander of an operation that is generally acknowledged to have been a success overall, remarks that enforcement is 'war by another name'. He draws attention in particular to the difficulty of maintaining the neutrality of a peacekeeping operation and the unity of its troop contingents if it slips into peace-enforcement. And without neutrality and unity, he says, 'you either go to war or go home'. General Rose too underscores the point that peace-enforcement is in fact war-fighting.

The alternative viewpoint understands the limitations of traditional peacekeeping, but argues that the world has altered so fundamentally that conventions governing traditional operations are neither appropriate nor practicable any longer. Otunnu lists several scenarios in which UN operations may have to move into a 'grey zone' between traditional peacekeeping and outright war, such as when UN-protected safe areas need to be defended against attackers or UN peacekeepers have been taken hostage. Lightly armed UN peacekeepers in white vehicles operating under restrictions of consent and self-defence are not going to be effective against heavily armed and unruly irregular bands in civil wars. The very meaning of statehood implies a monopoly of the legitimate use of coercion. Where the structures of state have collapsed in complex emergencies requiring the urgent delivery of humanitarian relief assistance by the international community to beleaguered and traumatised populations, a UN peacekeeping mission may need to use force, or a credible threat of force, to be effective. These are complex emergencies because they are multi-dimensional, involving ethnic killings, human suffering and human rights violations on a massive scale, contested legitimacy and national disintegration.

A traditional peacekeeping force is ineffectual in such situations; and the ineffectiveness of the response to the conflicts of Somalia, Rwanda and Bosnia has in turn dangerously diminished the credibility and relevance of many international organisations, not just the UN. Complex emergencies may require comprehensive and integrated responses from several actors. There is scope for a partnership between UN peacekeeping, peace-restoring and peacemaking operations; and between UN operations and the activities of regional and non-government organisation (NGO) actors. Ambassador Otunnu proposes a possible division of labour between the various regional and international actors based on their comparative advantages, while warning of the dangers of a tribalisation of peacekeeping if regional bodies begin to claim ownership of conflicts within their areas of geographic coverage. Wider international participation, he writes, is necessary for reasons of legitimacy, solidarity and capacity. The merits of complementary specialisation among regional and international actors based on comparative advantage are discussed also by Professor Austin.

The 'mode of articulation' of the peoples of the world with the United Nations is consultative status to the NGOs. Their importance is stressed by several contributors, starting with Don McKinnon and including Keith Suter and John Groom. In his discussion, Groom argues that the UN will be a vital component of global governance, but only one component. Others will include NGOs and multinational corporations. In complex emergencies, the NGO actors confronting peacekeepers include guerrillas, terrorists and bands of civilians. In expanded peacekeeping operations set up in response, NGOs like the International Red Cross and Médecins Sans Frontières (MSF) have become increasingly important partners of the United Nations. The office of the UN High Commissioner of Refugees (UNHCR) too works in close coordination with UN peacekeeping operations in complex emergencies, as General Rose notes. But the UNHCR, being part of the formal UN system, suffers from some of the limitations of government organisations.

NGOs can complement UN efforts in several ways. The presence of NGOs in the field could be a vital link in any early warning system that is eventually set up for dealing with humanitarian crises. Their specialised knowledge and contacts could be important components of the post-crisis peace-building process. They can mediate between the peace and security functions of international government organisations, and the needs and wants of local civilian populations. They can exert a positive influence on the restoration of a climate of confidence for rehabilitation and reconstruction to take place.

The role of NGOs is potentially enlarged where UN peacekeeping slides into enforcement operations. NGOs can play a complementary role by coordinating work with UN peacekeepers, but they must be sensitive to perceptions of collusion. In Somalia, for example, as the UN mission succumbed to the pressures to use robust force, the space of humanitarian NGOs contracted. The logic of military action does not easily reconcile with that of humanitarian assistance. Any departure from strict impartiality endangers the work and personnel of humanitarian NGOs, just as it used to imperil the integrity of traditional peacekeeping.

If Cambodia is best described as a flawed success, then Somalia and Bosnia may be said to be mitigated disasters. With regard to Cambodia, General Sanderson highlights the successes while acknowledging the flaws; Professor Austin dwells much more on the deficiencies, especially from a long-term point of view which eschews quick-fix solutions and instant democracy. His detailed analysis underlines the argument that 'peacekeeping' is but a point on the continuum from pre-conflict peace-building to post-conflict peace-reconstruction. The requirements for sustainable peace, Austin argues, are different from those of band-aid or fire-fighting responses. In the case of Bosnia, General Rose notes with pride that two thousand tonnes of food were delivered in the midst of a three-party civil war every single day in 1994. The humanitarian achievements of the UN operation, often overlooked, are emphasised by Foreign Minister McKinnon as well.

In other words, ground realities since the end of the Cold War have highlighted the large gap between the two familiar poles of traditional peacekeeping and Chapter VII enforcement. There is a need for a conceptual and policy bridge for a transition from Chapter VI to VII. At present there is no continuum from consensual peacekeeping to collective enforcement. Because the mechanism for setting up a collective security force under Chapter VII does not exist, the UN has resorted to subcontracting enforcement operations. Modifying the Gulf War precedent somewhat, there seems to be an emerging pattern of UN-authorised military action by a major power or coalition, as by the

US in Somalia and Haiti, France in Rwanda, Russia in Georgia and NATO in Bosnia. UN peacekeepers can take over after the security situation has been stabilised. The danger of this is that major powers take military action only when and where their national interests are engaged. The UN by contrast is the political embodiment of the international community and the custodian of the international interest.

The search for standby arrangements that will provide rapid reaction capability to the UN when confronted with humanitarian crises of horrific proportions is an effort to lessen the reliance on major powers whose national interests may diverge in important ways from the international interest vested in the world organisation. Conversely, if the national interests of the major powers are not at stake, then it is correspondingly more difficult to secure their substantial involvement on purely humanitarian considerations.

A permanent UN force could have the advantages of professional and specialised training, rapid reaction time, organisational efficiency and financial stability. But there are too many difficult issues that would need to be circumvented: of authority, structure, training, administration, logistics and financing.[12] Boutros-Ghali himself concluded subsequently that a standing force would be impractical and inappropriate, and asked instead for more extensive and systematic standby arrangements.[13] Several countries have been prepared to indicate the number and types of troops that can be made available for UN peacekeeping on a response-on-request basis, and the UN is compiling an appropriate database. But in his position paper on 5 January 1995, Boutros-Ghali remarked that even standby arrangements cannot guarantee that troops will be provided for a specific operation. His attention shifted to the idea of a rapid reaction force.

General Sanderson argues further that decisions on the use of military force must only be made after careful consideration of responsible advice that identifies the risks involved and the implications entailed. UN missions derive their legitimacy from the organisation's moral authority. That authority can be rapidly eroded if the initial mandate setting up an operation is flawed. General Sanderson argues in particular for the establishment of a strategic headquarters. In Cambodia, even though force was not used by the UN peacekeeping

---

12   Paul F. Diehl, *International Peacekeeping* (Baltimore: Johns Hopkins University Press, 1993), pp. 108–19.

13   Boutros Boutros-Ghali, 'Empowering the United Nations', *Foreign Affairs* 71 (Winter 1992/1993), p. 93.

operation, a strategic disconnect was evident between those who formulate and those who execute missions. He stresses the different functions and nature of the strategic, operational and tactical levels of military command; and he points to the need for an intelligence capability for UN peacekeeping operations. In short, military effectiveness needs to be combined with collective political control: Bosnia has been a humiliation for NATO and the UN alike.

Humanitarian Intervention

Reading the UN Charter, there is little doubt that a basic premise underpinning the organisation is the notion of inalienable human rights that are universally valid. Governments argue in favour of a relativist interpretation of human rights. Yet there is no society in which individuals do not want adequate food and shelter, the ability to be able to speak freely, to practise their own religion, to avoid torture and imprisonment by the state without first being charged and subjected to a fair trial. None of this is culture-specific.

A steady loss of government control over trans-border exchanges has been accompanied by increased demands and expectations of the United Nations from the peoples of the world. In the case of human rights, this takes the form of people seeking the protection of the international organisation against abuses by their own governments. Governments however continue to be suspicious of claims by international bodies of a qualified right to intervene. But it is not just Afro–Asian governments that are guilty of specious self-serving rhetoric on human rights. Which Western country has elevated the status of women in Saudi Arabia, or the working conditions of foreign maids in the Gulf states, to a priority foreign policy issue?

In practice, the legitimacy of intervention turns upon the answer to questions about the four main elements involved in any act of intervention: actor, act, target and purpose.[14] The most immediately acceptable justification for intervention is the collectivist principle: not *why* intervention was undertaken, but *who* took the decision to intervene. Since 1945, the most widely accepted legitimator of international action has been the UN. It has only a feeble record in enforcement of human rights norms and rules. But the UN has an excellent record in standard-setting and norm-generation. The International Bill of Rights

14   Ramesh Thakur, 'Non-Intervention in International Relations: A Case Study', *Political Science* 42 (July 1990), p. 29.

after all comprises three seminal UN accomplishments: the Universal Declaration of Human Rights of 1948, and the two Covenants on civil–political and social–economic–cultural rights of 1966.

Peace Support Operations and the Laws of War

The use of force by UN peacekeeping units also raises the vexed issue of how the laws of war might be applied to military conduct by troops acting under UN authorisation. A slide into rationalisations of the use of force, as happened with the operation in Somalia,[15] will steadily undermine the authority of the United Nations as the body responsible for moderating the use of force in international relations.

The UN is also committed to setting, promoting and enforcing international human rights standards by member governments. Typically, human rights abuses take place in the context of security operations by national police or military units. Muscular peacekeeping operations raise with particular cogency the question of the applicability of human rights instruments to security operations in the name of the organisation itself. This is especially so because civil society is not a conspicuous feature of many troop-contributing countries. Soldiers from such countries have not been socialised into the gentler norms of dealing with difficult civilians.

The proliferation of UN peacekeeping operations has turned Amnesty International's attention to the accountability and transparency of their human rights record.[16] It argues that the time is overdue for the UN to build measures for human rights promotion and protection into its own peacekeeping activities. Troops serving in peacekeeping operations should be trained in those standards and understand their obligations. Their use of force must satisfy the conditions of *necessity* when less harmful alternatives are not available, *proportionality* in respect to the threat faced and the goal sought, and *discrimination* between combatants and non-combatants.

In the recent past, a number of UN peacekeeping operations have also been criticised for lax standards of social morality. A youth was allegedly tortured to death by Canadian UN soldiers in Somalia in March 1993. Cambodian Minister for Culture Nouth Narang advised the UN to learn from the 'dark side' of its operation in Cambodia in

---

15   See, for example, Sam Kiley, 'UN Gathers Men and Arms for "Final Assault" on Aidid', *Times* (London), 17 August 1993.

16   *Peace-keeping and Human Rights* (London: Amnesty International, 1994).

order 'to avoid detrimental effects on local societies'. The introduction of money had undermined ethical values and disrupted traditional village systems, he said, and Cambodia had suffered from a proliferation of rape and prostitution.[17] Blue-helmeted troops are alleged to have patronised a brothel containing captive Croat and Muslim women in Bosnia,[18] and paid for sex with children in Mozambique.[19] If the UN is to maintain its human rights credibility, then soldiers committing abuses in its name must face investigation and prosecution by credible and effective international machinery.

Traditional peacekeeping lacked coercive or protective power, but was also low-risk. The new burst of vigour multiplies the probability of casualties and failure. That is why it risks stretching the conceptual fabric of UN peacekeeping beyond the point of sustainability. On 18 September 1995, Boutros-Ghali said that the UN troops should be withdrawn from Bosnia regardless of whether the latest peace plan failed or succeeded, and that they should be replaced by NATO troops. The statement was seen as a humiliating admission of the failure of the troubled three-year UN peacekeeping mission in Bosnia.[20]

Withdrawal of UN peacekeeping machinery in the face of armed challenges can of course be cruel in human terms. But it is better in the long run for the organisation to withdraw with its reputation intact and capable of intervention elsewhere with the consent of all parties, than to turn into a factional participant, part of the problem instead of a solution, the object of armed reprisals and street demonstrations. The muscular approach is better left to major powers like the United States.

UN Authority and US Power

The Gulf War was the curtain-raiser to the world organisation being used in a vigorous pursuit of Western interests. This is an especially acute problem for the relationship between the United Nations and the United States. Both have been struggling to learn to coexist in a world in which there is only one superpower and only one general international organisation. The peace of the world may well depend upon the latter's political wisdom and military power. Progress towards a

17   Kyodo News Service report, dated 11 January 1995, on the Internet, *International Peacekeeping News* 5 (January 1995).
18   *Press* (Christchurch), 4 November 1993.
19   *International Herald Tribune*, 26–27 February 1994.
20   Tim Butcher and Robert Fox, 'UN signals end of mission in Bosnia', *Daily Telegraph* (London), 19 September 1995.

world order based on justice and law requires that US power be harnessed to UN authority. There is wisdom and virtue in imposing the international discipline and moderating influence of the UN upon the exercise of US power.[21] Conversely, there is danger in permitting American power calculations to be cloaked uncritically in the UN flag. This would not represent progress towards a world where force is ruled by law. Instead it would be a reversion to a world where law is put to the service of the mighty. UN decisions should be based on a mix of calculations about past legalities, present political alignments and future community needs.

The United Nations is a political institution. Its decisions are the resultants not of judicial but political processes of calculations and reconciliations of national interests. Across Asia and Africa there is a gathering under-current of unease and trepidation that the UN, led by a US-dominated Security Council, is being used as an instrument of Western interests. Madeleine Albright, US Ambassador to the United Nations, testified before a Congressional subcommittee on 5 May 1994 that UN peacekeeping is 'a contributor, not the centerpiece of, our national strategy'. The UN, in order to retain diplomatic credibility, has to remain impartial between belligerents. But impartiality may be less useful for military credibility. Consequently, UN peacekeeping 'is not...a substitute for vigorous alliances and a strong national defense'.[22] In an address to the Security Council itself on 19 January 1995, she outlined the lessons learned from the peacekeeping operations launched since 1988, including:

- Missions should not begin until the warring parties accept and observe military–political steps towards a negotiated settlement;
- Rigorous standards should be used to ensure that UN missions have clear and realistic objectives, peacekeepers are properly equipped, and money is not wasted;
- The challenge of keeping peace is quite different from creating a

---

21   In US English, in the words of Secretary of State Warren Christopher, 'leveraging our power and leading through alliances and institutions'; in testimony before the House International Affairs Committee on 26 January 1995, *USIS Wireless File* EPF402, 01/26/95.

22   Madeleine K. Albright, 'The Clinton Administration's Policy on Reforming Multilateral Peace Operations', *U.S. Department of State Dispatch* 5 (16 May 1994), p. 315.

secure environment during an ongoing conflict.[23]

Most of these lessons are drawn by Colonel O'Reilly. Nor is this list dissimilar to Senator Evans's criteria for future use of preventive deployment: clear objectives, clear mandates, high probability of objectives being met, and clear linkage to a broader conflict resolution process.[24] Congressional critics have not been appeased. The new Republican Congress pared US contributions to UN peacekeeping operations from 32 to 25 percent of the costs from 1 October 1995, and proscribed participation by US troops in military missions under non-US commanders. The anti-UN sentiment in the US media and Congress has been fed by such misadventures as Somalia. The tragedy is that this is a predictable, and therefore avoidable, cost of a resort to force by UN peacekeeping operations.

A paring back of the US financial contribution could have a crippling effect on an organisation that is already in large arrears. The financial insecurity and military impotence afflicting the UN have been almost as striking as the institutional innovation and political resilience of the organisation. As well as being the UN's biggest paymaster, the US is also its biggest debtor. As of September 1995, the US share of the total of US $3.7 billion owed to the world body for its regular and peacekeeping budget combined, was US $1.6 billion.[25]

Reforms

Professor Rosenau makes the important point that all discussion of the future of the United Nations is subject to 'path dependence'. That is, the UN system today is a resultant of critical choices made in the past. In turn, all future choices are circumscribed by choices already made in previous years. Rosenau's claim that the UN will be around for centuries is open to debate. Nevertheless, the future course of the organisation—including its very future itself—is conditioned by the moment of inertia of time and history: international organisation does not begin on a *tabula rasa*.

The UN Charter was a triumph of hope rooted in idealism over the experience of two world wars. These inherent tensions were buried in a formulaic unreality that enveloped debate in the world's great

23   *USIS Wireless File* EPF406, 01/19/95.
24   Gareth Evans, *Cooperating for Peace: The Global Agenda for the 1990s and Beyond* (Sydney: Allen & Unwin, 1993), p. 85.
25   *Independent* (London), 16 September 1995.

talking chamber. At the height of the Ethiopian famine, the General Assembly voted to build a US $73 million conference centre in Addis Ababa.[26] Ideological confrontation between the East and the West jostled for agenda space with that between the North and the South. Successive attempts at reforming an increasingly inefficient, as well as irrelevant, organisation have failed to shake the UN out of a stifling bureaucratic sclerosis. The UN is too heavily involved in micromanaging too many field programmes. There is too much UN machinery, each bit with powerful vested interests to protect in jurisdictional turf battles. Most of it is glacially slow and unaccountable to any outsider.

UN operations are conducted essentially within the framework of a Charter signed almost half a century ago. The time is long overdue to consider substantial reforms which would realign the organisation with present-day realities. The Security Council reflects the power realities of 1945, the General Assembly is wordy, tedious and ineffective, and the Secretariat is demoralised and dogged by outdated personnel and management practices.[27] Patronage rules, quality suffers. Keith Suter introduces a useful distinction between micro- and macro-reforms, depending on whether or not Charter amendment is required. The problem, he writes, is less an inadequate Charter than an insufficiently honoured Charter. More broadly, both Groom and Suter draw attention to the need to enfranchise non-government organisations and multinational corporations (MNCs) in the UN system so that it more accurately reflects the world of today. At present MNCs have no formal status, while NGOs have only consultative status. While right and left might differ on the merits and consequences, they agree that multinational firms are major players in international affairs. Yet they remain disenfranchised in the UN system. Such detachment from the realities of political and economic power undermines the credibility and effectiveness of the organisation.

Has the UN cocooned itself in reform-proof procedures and structures? One recent commentator believes that no further effort should be invested in reforming the UN as such. Where the rapidity of changes in the world places a premium on flexibility and ability to improvise, the UN is hopelessly fossilised and incapable of adaptation. Instead, its worst-performing parts should simply be allowed to

26   Righter, *Utopia Lost,* p. 231.
27   Peter Wilenski, 'Reforming the United Nations for the Post-Cold War Era', in Mara Bustello and Philip Alston, eds., *Whose New World Order?* (Sydney: Federation Press, 1991), pp. 123–24.

wither. The UN is an instrument, not an end in itself. Righter argues that we would be much better off to identity those parts of the UN that do work well, and concentrate our money and efforts on them.[28] Her argument might conceivably be reinforced by Professor Austin's lament of the lack of a culture of learning in the United Nations.

Such demand-led reform would require Western governments to be more selective in the choice of goals to be pursued through multilateral efforts, and then more rigorous in identifying those institutions—in the UN and outside—that can best serve these interests. In a sense this is a market model of international organisations where if the UN fails to deliver services required by its members, the biggest paymasters (meaning the industrialised Western democracies) should feel free to contract out elsewhere for those services.

Yet the critique is overdone. The ideals and workings of the UN were subverted by the major Western powers in the first decade of the organisation's existence, when the West held a commanding majority of votes. The larger relevance of this lies in widespread scepticism that the major Western powers approach the UN in other than a self-interested manner. Hypocrisy and overblown rhetoric are no monopoly of the Third World.

Security Council

The five permanent members of the Security Council (P5) are a self-appointed oligarchy who wrote their own exalted status into the Charter. This needs addressing for two reasons. Firstly in terms of the logic of permanent membership: international stratification is never rigid, and states are upwardly and downwardly mobile. A static permanent membership of the Security Council will undermine the logic of the status, thereby diminish the authority of the organisation and breed resentment in the claimants to the ranks of the great powers.

Secondly, it is unfortunate that the permanent membership is co-terminous with the five nuclear-weapons powers. This gives rise to the mistaken but understandable perception that the possession of nuclear weapons confers the status of great power. If non-nuclear-weapon states like Germany and Japan—whose claims to permanent membership of the Security Council cannot be regarded as less worthy than those of Britain, China and France—could be admitted to the hallowed ranks of permanent membership of the Security Council, then the international community would effectively divorce the status of great power from the possession of nuclear weapons. Takahiro Shinyo presents a Japanese viewpoint on the desirability of Japan as a non-nuclear, civilian permanent member of the Security Council. He further argues that for Japan to continue to bear a heavy financial burden in the UN system without permanent Security Council membership would be tantamount to taxation without representation.

Representation can have at least eight different meanings. One can represent the interests of one's constituents, as parliamentarians do. In this case, a country need not be a member of a group or region in order to represent its interests. During its two years on the Security Council in 1993–94, for example, New Zealand acted more as a representative of Asian–Pacific and smaller states than of 'Western Europe' to which it is attached in the UN system of groupings. Or the Council could be so composed as to represent accurately population distributions in the countries of the world, in which case India's claim to permanent membership would be greater than that of any other save China. A third possible meaning would be in terms of economic weight, the argument on which Germany and Japan are included in most lists. Fourth, it could refer to the need for the Council to reflect the major cultures, religions and civilisations of the world. There is, for example, no Islamic permanent member at present.

The most common meaning given to representation is in terms of the different regions of the world: Asia is under-represented, Africa and Latin America are not represented at all. Sixth, one could argue for the need to represent the most dynamic regions in world affairs, which today are East Asia and Latin America. Or should the Council's permanent membership, in terms of its original logic, reflect the military size and roles of states in world affairs? Eighth, should permanent membership be a reward for or conditional upon sizeable contributions to the military activities of the UN, principally participation in peace-keeping; that is, representation on the frontline? On this criterion, India and Sweden might have better claims than Germany and Japan.

With regard to reforming the procedures, Otunnu draws attention to the need to provide a platform for the views of NGOs in the Security Council as well as in the General Assembly. NGOs make up one important layer of international civil society. Yet there is no official or informal channel of communication between them and the Council.

Defenders of the status quo might respond that the Security Council is organised on the principles of responsibility and capacity, not representativeness. The principle of equitable geographical representation is essential to the philosophy of the organisation and adds to its legitimacy. S. K. Singh—whose views must be heeded because of the positions he has held in the Indian government—is less than complimentary about the UN's contributions to Asia in its first fifty years. The continent's dramatic economic dynamism means that its due representation in the structures of the UN acquire greater urgency.

The world community may have to address the question of the unit of UN membership. Perhaps regional organisations like the EU and the OAU could be given permanent membership of the Security Council instead of three European and no African states. An alternative would be to create a third tier of permanent but veto-less Security Council membership. Or the prohibition on immediate re-election could be lifted. And, as Olara Otunnu commented, the United Nations, if it is to remain true to its soul, must be a place where ideas matter as much as *realpolitik*. On the criteria of permanent or continuing membership, an important attribute ought to be good UN citizenship. Yet this is a criterion that seems to be totally ignored. Countries like India, Indonesia, Nigeria, South Africa and Brazil are important middle and regional powers with claims to longer terms on the Security Council on grounds of representation. But what of Scandinavian and Australasian countries who are exemplars of good international citizenship in terms of their contributions to making the UN system work, who pay their dues on time and in full, contribute diligently to peacekeeping operations, and in myriads of other ways work hard to keep the UN system ticking?

Whatever formula is adopted, the challenge will be to combine the efficiency, representational and value-order arguments. Membership of the Council must reflect current global power relationships but not be so large as to make it an unwieldy executive body. If the Council's membership is reformed, then care must also be taken to ensure that the new structure is subject to built-in reviews at fixed intervals of ten, fifteen or twenty years. Otherwise the same problem will recur.

In regard to the wide range of action permitted to and possible for the Security Council in the new order, one of the most important measures was Resolution 687 of 3 April 1991 (the Gulf ceasefire resolution). Imposing binding and unilaterally defined restrictions on Iraq after the Gulf War, it was testimony to the Security Council's ambitions as the guarantor of international peace and security and affirmed its juridical and operational resurgence.

The United Nations is usually attacked for doing too little, too late. It is equally possible that the organisation, or at least the Security Council, infected by the US virus, may have been doing too much and too soon.[29] Founded on the principle of the separation of powers as the means to avoiding tyranny of government, the United States employs the most concentrated power in its dealings abroad.[30] In recent times the UN Security Council has been similarly co-opting functions that belong properly to legislative and judicial spheres. Iraq has been put under international receivership by means of time-unlimited sanctions. The Security Council has determined the borders of a supposedly sovereign state; told it how much of its export earnings it may keep; how many observers it must admit, as well as where and when; and what weapons it may keep and develop. On the first point, for example, would it not have been more appropriate for the Council to have told Iraq (and therefore Kuwait as well) that it must submit the border dispute to binding international adjudication?

Similarly, in Resolution 748 (31 March 1992), the Security Council imposed sanctions on Libya for its failure to extradite two citizens accused (not convicted) of being the brains behind the Lockerbie bombing. That is, without even the pretence of a trial, the Council was bent on compelling one sovereign state to hand over its citizens to another sovereign state on the basis of allegations from the latter—which had itself, just a few years earlier, defied the World Court's verdict in a case brought against it by Nicaragua. If and when the UN Charter is reformed, one item on the agenda should be curbs on untrammelled authority in the Security Council that is presently subject to no countervailing political check or judicial review.

The setting-up and procedures of the war crimes tribunal in Bosnia were dictated more by the need-to-do-something factor than by legal considerations. The tribunal, set up by the Security Council, 'does not always respect the rights of the criminal defendant in ways consistent with international human rights norms or national constitutions'.[31] Similarly troubling was the rush to judgment on who had

---

29   See Jose Alvarez, 'The U.N. Security Council: Are there checks to provide balance?', *Law Quadangle Notes* (University of Michigan Law School) (Fall 1994), pp. 40–45.

30   Ali Mazrui, 'The Moral Paradigms of the Superpowers: A Third World Perspective', in Ramesh Thakur, ed., *International Conflict Resolution* (Boulder/Dunedin: Westview/University of Otago Press, 1987), pp. 200–01.

31   Alvarez, 'The U.N. Security Council', p. 43.

fired the shells on Sarajevo on 28 August 1995 that killed about 40 and wounded some 90 people. The UN issued a statement declaring that Serbian responsibility was indisputable. Yet it seems that British and French crater analysis experts who examined the scene of the market massacre had concluded that there was no evidence that the lethal mortar round had been fired by Bosnian Serbs. Four mortars that caused no carnage had indeed come from the Serbian positions. But the fifth, which caused the bloodshed, had most likely come from a position held by Bosnian government forces. These doubts were overruled by a senior US military officer.[32] The 'Serbian atrocity' was then used as the excuse to intervene decisively in the internal Bosnian war through massive and sustained NATO air strikes against the Serbs. This turned the tide of the war—an outcome that the Bosnian government had been manoeuvring for for more than three years. To what extent had the Clinton Administration been motivated by calculations of re-election? To what extent had the UN Security Council allowed itself to be subverted into serving the political interests of the incumbent US president?

Secretary-General

One matter that the Secretary-General himself has raised recently is that of the appropriate relationship between the Security Council and his office. He accused the Council of 'micromanaging' peacekeeping operations at the expense of his authority and that of ground commanders.[33] The discretionary authority vested in the Secretary-General by Article 99 linked the chief executive of the UN constitutionally and symbolically to its central ideal. The failure of the principal political organs to function as originally envisaged placed a disproportionate burden on the shoulders of the Secretary-General. As a result the office became one with little power but considerable influence.

The chief executive of the organisation came to symbolise as well as represent the United Nations. In turn this enhanced the importance of the qualities required of Secretaries-General: integrity, independence of mind and the ability and willingness to set the collective interest of the United Nations above the partisan interests of member states. The Secretary-General is looked to to provide intellectual leadership,

---

32 *Australian,* 2 October 1995, quoting the *Sunday Times* (London). UN officials rejected this account of the event.

33 Barbara Crossette, 'U.N. Chief Chides Security Council on Military Missions', *New York Times,* 6 January 1995.

managerial ability, negotiating skill and, in an age of mass communications, the ability to establish a rapport with an international audience. He or she must know when to take the initiative in order to force an issue and when to maintain a tactful silence; when courage is required and when discretion is advised; and when commitment to the UN vision must be balanced by a sense of proportion and humour.

The process of selecting Secretaries-General has been haphazard and ad hoc. The General Assembly appoints a Secretary-General on the advice of the Security Council; 'appointment' supposedly stresses the administrative, while 'election' would have suggested a more clearly political role. The Council vote is subject to veto by a permanent member. This immediately changes the thrust from selecting someone who commands the widest following to someone who is least unacceptable to the major powers. The permanent members do not look with favour on activist candidates for fear of too vigorous a scrutiny of their own actions in world affairs. Undue deference to the major powers by a Secretary-General is reinforced if the incumbent should be interested in re-election. Even other governments would not generally wish a Secretary-General to oppose them publicly. Righter notes that 'In the history of the United Nations, not one UN secretary-general has been appointed because he was expected to provide outstanding leadership.... In Dag Hammarskjöld, the five permanent members simply made a mistake of judgment'.[34] Shirley Hazzard remarked of Kurt Waldheim that he would be 'proof against every occasion of a larger kind'.[35] As US Ambassador Max Finger put it, member states want 'excellence within the parameters of political reality' of their Secretary-General.[36]

'We the people' would probably prefer excellence within the parameters of human reality. The Secretary-General is the chief symbol of the international interest, advocate of law and rights, general manager of the global agenda and a focal point in setting the direction of world affairs. Some of the built-in disadvantages of the office can be overcome by altering the term from five to seven years and making it non-renewable. The procedure could also be exempted from the veto.

34   Righter, *Utopia Lost,* p. 270.
35   Shirley Hazzard, *Countenance of Truth: The United Nations and the Waldheim Case* (New York: Viking, 1990), p. 73.
36   Brian Urquhart and Erskine Childers, *A World in Need of Leadership: Tomorrow's United Nations* (Uppsala: Dag Hammarsköld Foundation, 1990), p. 18.

Parochial considerations will always shape the choice of a Secretary-General. But political calculations should not dominate the process of selecting someone for the only truly representative office of the world.

In some respects a more crucial change concerns the relationship between the Secretariat and the various specialised agencies. The UN structure is built around a sectoral division of tasks and responsibilities: nuclear energy, trusteeship, health, etc. Yet the contemporary international system is required to cope with problems which are global and deeply interconnected: ecological degradation, international drug trafficking, AIDS and the international trade in arms. In order to avoid becoming irrelevant to contemporary needs and to the demands being placed on it, the organisation needs to strengthen its institutional capacity to manage the global commons. Perhaps the Secretary-General should delegate sectoral responsibilities to newly-created deputies in a cohesive 'cabinet' type of team. The deputies would have expanded powers and enhanced authority; the Secretary-General would remain the focal point of coordination without being overwhelmed by the requirements of executive leadership.

Development

Senator Evans has been at the forefront, more so even than the Secretary-General, in arguing for the need for and cost-effectiveness of preventive measures before situations spin out of control. He has changed the meaning of preventive diplomacy from the days of Dag Hammarskjöld, when the concept was the twin of traditional peace-keeping. Evans presents a convincing and forceful argument for developing mechanisms and institutions for solving disputes before they degenerate into violence. We cannot have peace without development; but we cannot have development without peace. The relationship between the two is both competitive, in terms of the opportunity costs of resources expended, and symbiotic between them. Peace is meaningless without development, akin to the peace of the dead. Equally, the fruits of development cannot be enjoyed in the absence of peace.

Western governments have regarded the International Monetary Fund (IMF) and the World Bank as more important to the maintenance of international order than any other part of the UN system after the Security Council. They compared the inefficient universalism of the UN unflatteringly with the market efficiency epitomised in the two Bretton Woods institutions. Even UN expertise in education and the environment is exceeded by that of the World Bank.

Conversely, many in the Third World (as well as some in the West) have viewed them with deep suspicion as agents of neocolonialism imposing alien models that are as severe as they are inappropriate. In recent years much greater attention has been paid by these institutions to the *rentier* policy environment in recipient countries: corrupt and incompetent rulers, power- and rent-maximising bureaucrats, and growth-stunting state enterprises. The *rentier* state in military hands had led to the cycle of military spending, luxury consumption and capital flight. Some African countries, for example, ran their national economies as a spoils system for their relatives, clans or armies.

Mutual disillusionment led to the crisis of the triple fatigue: donor fatigue among Western governments, debt fatigue among Western bankers, and adjustment fatigue among developing countries. For years, most Western governments had taken the line of least resistance at the UN and tried to soften the harsher edges of anti-Western rhetoric by Third World radicals. Washington decided it was time to end such preemptive capitulation, and launched a counter-offensive. The most extreme of this was withdrawal from UNESCO.

Nitpicking critics of UN finances could be faulted for knowing the price of everything and the value of nothing. The accountants' approach to the organisation risked putting it into intellectual receivership. Human beings are engaged in transactions and exchanges in the local, national and international economy. But they live in society. If there is an international society, then the UN is surely its normative centre. Boutros-Ghali recently lamented the fact that 70 percent of his time had to be spent on the one issue of peacekeeping. Issues of the environment, under-development and overpopulation were huge human challenges and long-term problems. Peacekeeping operations should essentially be short-term preoccupations, he said.[37]

Olara Otunnu too draws attention to the growing imbalance of the peace and security agenda of the UN and that of development, producing disequilibrium between resource allocations for peacekeeping and relief operations and long-term peace-building. Expenditure on social and economic development is a long-term investment in the foundations of peace, a point of view also stressed by Senator Evans.

37   Barbara Crossette, 'U.N. Leader to Seek Changes in Peacekeeping', *New York Times*, 3 January 1995. Somewhat disconcertingly, and 'not entirely in jest', Boutros-Ghali proposed that the UN could sponsor advertisements featuring a beautiful woman in a flashy car driving up to the glass box on First Avenue and saying, 'Ah, the United Nations!'; ibid.

Both agree too on the need for more prophylactic action by the UN, where the organisation becomes involved before disputes have flared into conflict. But both acknowledge the philosophical and practical problems posed to early UN involvement by the vexed issue of national sovereignty.

Ambassador Jorge Heine accepts economic growth as a necessary condition of development, but not a sufficient one. Economic growth gives policy options to governments. These must include efforts to alleviate, if not eradicate, poverty; and to integrate the growing numbers of social actors into the processes of investment, production and technological change. The gap between the modern and informal sectors of society must be progressively narrowed by government policy; the market will not solve this social problem by itself. Otherwise the sources of social dislocation will multiply. Human capital formation is the key to the progressive incorporation of all sectors of society into the mainstream of productive activities. For example, the single best correlate of economic development is female literacy. This does not mean embracing discredited welfarism, for a bankrupted public sector cannot underwrite social welfare, let alone alleviate or eradicate poverty. Only a productive economy can.

This draws our attention to a related consideration. Preventive diplomacy could be broadened still further to include the fight against poverty, disease and ignorance. While the world correctly judges the United Nations ultimately with regard to its primary function of maintaining international peace and security, there are many other tasks that the UN system performs. It has been at the vanguard of efforts to improve the physical quality of life index of millions of people:

- Leading a global effort to bring safe drinking water to over one billion people in the past decade;
- Eradicating smallpox in 1980;
- Immunising 80 percent of the world's children (up from 5 percent in 1974) against polio, tetanus, measles, whooping cough, diphtheria and tuberculosis.[38]

Community of Values

It is interesting that a military officer, namely General Sanderson,

---

38   Fiftieth Anniversary Secretariat, *UN 50 Information* (New York: United Nations, S-3161, 1995).

should dwell on the importance of safeguarding the moral authority of the UN. Ambassador Otunnu too writes of the normative underpinnings of the UN and of a community of values. Today we use the phrase 'international community' by habit and without thinking. The UN deserves some credit for this revolutionary situation. It has been at the centre of the transformation of an essentially Eurocentric system of diplomacy into a truly global and universal system, where even the weakest and the poorest do feel that they are part of the world community.

Decolonisation produced not just a proliferation in new UN members. It led to the voting dominance of the UN system by new kinds of members who suffered from institutional fragility and diplomatic inexperience. The era of Third World solidarity at the UN made its formal start with the UN Conference on Trade and Development (UNCTAD) in 1964 and the formation of the Group of 77 nonaligned developing countries. The G-77 progressively radicalised the agenda of international economic relations.

In the 1970s and the 1980s, efforts by an assertive Third World majority coalition to transform and dominate the agenda of the United Nations initially put the West on the defensive. But over time there was a backlash in the countries that pay most of the organisation's money, and the net result was to snap the moral consensus necessary for international 'community' action. The Reagan Administration in particular lost patience with the increasing stridency and expanding *dirigisme* of UN resolutions and activities, and sharply curtailed its financial support for many of the more outrageous programmes.

The normative and political claims of the new economic and information orders challenged the liberal view of the proper relationship between citizen and state, state and market, and state and state. In response to mounting Western criticisms, the 'solution' of UN bodies was to adopt resolutions that masked disagreements. The search for the most efficient solution gave way to that for the most acceptable wording. The ritual passage of resolutions fundamentally inimical to Western values, and frequently critical of Western countries, led to a taxpayer revolt in Washington born of accumulated exasperation.

The collapse of communism and the seeming triumph of liberal internationalism highlighted the inexorable globalisation of so many aspects of our lives. Previously, the sovereignty principle meant that international observers and monitors were regarded as an unacceptable intrusion in national affairs. In Cambodia, General Sanderson notes,

UNTAC forged a winning coalition with the *people* against both the State of Cambodia and the Khmer Rouge. As a result, elections organised, supervised and conducted under UN auspices were regarded by the international community as the most authentic expression of Cambodian popular sovereignty.

Yet the notion and sentiment of sovereignty has proven surprisingly resistant to emasculation. The United Nations was conceived as the centre for harmonising national action in the international arena. It is a forum for the articulation *and* reconciliation of national interests. Unfortunately, the second part tends to be forgotten, and the international interest overlooked. Dragoljub Najman, Assistant Director-General of UNESCO, remarked that 'States are losing sovereignty, but they are reluctant to yield it. The UN, instead of guiding the transition, is the last refuge of their illusions'.[39]

Conclusion

Without the United Nations, in the last fifty years the world would have been a more, not less, dangerous place. Yet with the UN remaining essentially unchanged in structure, authority and powers, the world is unlikely to be a mainly free, healthy, prosperous and peaceful place in the next fifty years.

The romantics point out that the UN system has been awarded the Nobel Peace Prize no fewer than five times: the UNHCR in 1954 and 1981; the UN Children's Fund in 1965; the ILO in 1965; and UN peacekeeping forces in 1988. Even in the peace and security field directly, demining lies at the intersection of peacemaking and peace-building.[40] The UN has been engaged in a campaign to clear landmines that kill and maim tens of thousands of civilians each year in former and continuing battlefields of Cambodia, Afghanistan, Angola and other places. There are about one hundred million mines scattered through more than sixty countries. In Cambodia alone there are 30,000 amputees. This has led to a new offshoot of peacekeeping where some countries have a particular role to play in such specialised and highly dangerous tasks. Australia and New Zealand have provided skilled mine-clearance personnel for UN duty in many parts of the world, a point mentioned by Colonel O'Reilly.

39   Quoted by Righter, *Utopia Lost*, p. 345.
40   Don McKinnon, 'Address to the United Nations General Assembly', 27 September 1994, p. 10.

In the past, the UN has emphasised abortion to the neglect of prophylaxis. It needs to sharpen its skills at identifying potential conflicts before the fact so that parties to disputes can be brought together during the period of infancy. The UN also needs to become involved in post-conflict peace-building by identifying, supporting and deepening the structures which will consolidate peace and enhance people's sense of confidence and well-being.[41] Peacekeeping is a circuit-breaker in a spiralling cycle of violence. The problem with traditional peacekeeping was that it could at best localise the impact of conflicts and then freeze them. Rarely did the UN prevent conflicts from breaking out or resolve them after they did.

Where the UN suffered from a lack of credibility during the Cold War, it has been afflicted by a crisis of expectations since the end of the Cold War. It will have to address the resulting problem of overload. The zeal to intervene everywhere will have to be tempered with caution about entering into entangling commitments. The UN's dilemma is that it must avoid deploying forces into situations where the risk of failure is high; yet not be so timid as to transform every difficulty into an alibi for inaction.

The romantics, their eye firmly on the prized UN ideal of a just and humane world without borders, fail to see the sordid wheeling and dealing driven by personal ambition, venality and naked power politics. The cynical, overwhelmed by the reality of waste, corruption and inefficiency that pervades much of the UN system, fail to raise their eye to the prize of a better world that beckons over the horizon. The United Nations must meet the challenge of a balance between the desirable and the possible. In Hammarskjöld's words, 'the constant struggle to close the gap between aspiration and performance...makes the difference between civilization and chaos'.[42] Echoing these words, Senator Evans describes peacekeeping as a means of 'bridging the gap between the will to peace and the achievement of peace'.[43] The greatest strength of the United Nations is that it is the only universal forum for international cooperation and management. It must continue to play a central role in establishing a normative order which strikes a balance between the competing demands of equity and political reality; that is, between its soul and its member governments.

41   This was recognised by Boutros-Ghali in *An Agenda for Peace,* paras. 55–59.
42   Quoted in Brian Urquhart, *A Life in Peace and War* (London: Weidenfeld and Nicolson, 1987), p. 378.
43   Evans, *Cooperating for Peace,* p. 99.

Don McKinnon

The United Nations at Fifty:
A Performance Appraisal

Writing in 1975 Andy Warhol said "They always say that time changes things, but you actually have to change them yourself". One of the preoccupations of this, the UN's fiftieth year, has been the need for the organisation to change, to be reformed. I want to look at this. But I also want to focus on the 'you' part of Andy Warhol's quote—the role of the individual in the United Nations, both in terms of bringing about the reform and in terms of the individual's contribution.

In Wellington on 26 June we celebrated the fiftieth anniversary of the signing of the UN Charter by launching a book called *New Zealand as an International Citizen: Fifty Years of United Nations Membership.*[1] The occasion brought together many New Zealanders who have been involved or who are now involved in UN work.

One of those who could not be in Wellington was Colin Aikman. Colin was in San Francisco for the celebrations there. He is a great example of the role an individual can play. He was on New Zealand's delegation to San Francisco in 1945 when the Charter was being drafted. I wonder if he realised at the time the significance of the event he was playing a part in.

In looking back over the papers documenting New Zealand's stance at those negotiations, I have noted something particularly relevant to this enterprise. That is, that we worked very closely with the Australian delegation. The Australians had similar goals to ours for the type of global organisation they wanted to see established. Because of their persistence and our collaboration, many of these aims were realised in the document that was signed.

It is therefore great to have a contingent of Australians and to have

---

1   Malcolm Templeton, ed., *New Zealand as an International Citizen: Fifty Years of United Nations Membership* (Wellington: Ministry of Foreign Affairs and Trade, 1995). Copies were distributed at the Otago Foreign Policy School.

had Senator Gareth Evans as the first speaker.[2] I am delighted that he was able to accept the invitation. It was particularly appropriate that he should be the signature speaker because he takes a very sincere and close interest in UN work, especially issues concerning peace.

It is perhaps inevitable that peacekeeping should be one of the big issues being scrutinised in the UN's fiftieth year. Gareth has just given an excellent address on this subject and under the general themes of change and the role of the individual I outlined initially I also want to look at this subject. The other subjects I want to examine tonight are the role non-government organisations (NGOs) play in the United Nations and the part we as New Zealanders play.

Peacekeeping

The maintenance of international peace and security has always been one of the core purposes of the United Nations. 'To maintain international peace and security' are the first substantive words of the Charter. Today there some 65,000 peacekeepers deployed on 16 missions around the world and the United Nations is spending about US $3 billion to support them. This may seem like a tremendous amount. But it is a small price to pay when compared to some national defence expenditures or indeed the costs of war, and we have all made the comparison with the New York Police Department and others responsible for security.

New Zealand has a proud record of support for UN peacekeeping. There are over 300 New Zealanders serving on peace support missions at present—from Africa to the Balkans. They are all individuals actually helping to bring about change, to bring about the environment for peaceful solutions to conflict.

One of the really basic necessities of peacekeeping is funds. We have always been scrupulous in paying our assessed contributions to the United Nations in full and on time. Unfortunately the same cannot be said for many members of the United Nations, including some of those who occupy permanent seats in the Security Council.

The Secretary-General said in June 1995 that the financial crisis will force him to stop virtually all payments to troop contributors for troops and equipment. This crisis has been caused by delinquent payers. This is appalling, and I said as much in my speech to the General Assembly in September 1994. The foot-dragging over who

2   See chapter 4 below.

will pay the bill for the Rapid Reaction Force for Bosnia is tragic. Voluntary contributions can *never* offer a stable base for large-scale operations of the complexity and importance of the UN Protection Force in former Yugoslavia (UNPROFOR). The concerns I articulated in September 1994 are now being addressed by a high-level working group in which New Zealand is participating vigorously.

So why does a country like New Zealand bother about its responsibilities when some of the major powers fail to show leadership in these matters? Quite simply because of self-interest and domestic politics. Small countries have to believe in the rule of international law, in collective security, in mechanisms for the peaceful settlement of disputes. These things are all that stand between us and a reversion to the law of the jungle. This was our position at San Francisco fifty years ago. It remains our position today.

Sadly the law of the jungle seems to be playing a role in former Yugoslavia. It is challenging all the notions we hold dear about civilisation in the late twentieth century. Ethnic conflict produces some of the greatest horrors imaginable. More than half of the total number of UN peacekeepers, about 40,000 of them, are currently deployed in former Yugoslavia. About 1000 are serving on an experimental, and so far highly successful, preventive deployment mission in the Former Yugoslav Republic of Macedonia. About 15,000 are serving in Croatia and nearly 25,000 are in Bosnia, including the 'Kiwi Company' in central Bosnia—Sector Southwest as the military call it.

That sector was the scene of some of the most vicious fighting in Bosnia. It took place principally between the Muslim and Croat communities. Whole villages were wiped out. Gangs of extremists massacred women and children and their menfolk. I was there in December 1994 and the destruction was ferocious and sobering to see. The sight of the ghost town of Amici, and its toppled minaret, was a stark reminder of the atrocities that were carried out there in the name of 'ethnic cleansing'.

Kiwi Company's camp at Santici lies smack on the old confrontation line. If you walk down the main street of the nearby, principally Croat town of Vitez you soon come to the old quarter where the Muslims live. Until February 1994 these people were subject to 'ethnic cleansing'. Today a Kiwi armoured personnel carrier (APC), painted in the white livery of the United Nations, keeps checkpoint duty on the main route into the Muslim quarter. New Zealand soldiers do seven-day shifts and liaise with the Croat and

Bosnian policemen assigned to the checkpoint. Together they ensure the freedom of movement of the inhabitants. They also check what goes in and what comes out.

The faces you see watching nervously from behind curtains in darkened windows of apartment buildings pock-marked by bullets see the APCs as their insurance against the political gangsters from out of town. At the end of the day much of the Kiwi Company's role is essentially civil and political in character, providing an envelope of confidence to enable ordinary people to go about their lives again. Kiwi personnel help build peace, liaising between the two communities on issues like the restoration of services and the reopening of schools.

But in wider Bosnia the fighting continues. I believe that UN-PROFOR nevertheless plays a crucial role. It has assured the delivery of tonnes of food. It saves lives. US President Bill Clinton highlighted some impressive figures recently—in 1992, 130,000 deaths; in 1994, less than 3000.

I hope that those who advocate the lifting of the arms embargo to salve their consciences understand fully the responsibility they would bear for the enormous suffering which would be unleashed by that policy. Bosnia without UNPROFOR would be a bloodbath. That is the core of our essentially humanitarian purpose for being in Bosnia, that and providing a platform for the resolution of the conflict. Despite the often facile criticism of the international media these are two very valid reasons for being there.

The international community must continue to pursue a sustainable political solution. I think the latest initiative, having as it does the support of the United Nations, the US, the European Union (EU) and Russia, has as good a chance as any of succeeding. Former Swedish Prime Minister Carl Bildt has only recently taken up his role as Co-Chair of the International Conference on Former Yugoslavia, but he has already displayed commendable energy and fortitude as he sets out to talk to the various parties. For a period of time there were too many negotiators and mediators each being played off against each other.

This may be the last chance for the outside players to be part of a meaningful role in encouraging all the protagonists to want that elusive political settlement. Bildt is a good strategic thinker. We all hope that he will revitalise the peace process and succeed, where so many others have failed, to find a formula for a political settlement acceptable to all.

The Role of NGOs in the United Nations

The seemingly insoluble nature of the conflict in the Balkans has been one of the main reasons for criticism of the United Nations. But there have also been many successes by the United Nations. Ironically, these tend to be overlooked.

NGOs and their participation in the United Nations is a subject of growing interest. As I say in the introduction to *New Zealand as an International Citizen,* the United Nations is becoming more than just a government-to-government organisation.[3] While it was envisaged from the start that accommodation should be made for such groups, the burgeoning of activity within the NGO field over recent years must be far greater than the founding delegates would have ever envisaged.

To me the NGOs are a reflection of the UN working at a much more practical and hands-on level. The UN Conference on Environment and Development was perhaps the first to attract enormous NGO attention and involvement. It was held in 1992 in Rio de Janeiro and over 4000 NGOs attended. The total New Zealand delegation was one of the largest ever. More recently the population conference was held in Cairo and the social development conference was held in Copenhagen. Each conference has dealt with issues that are contentious but that really matter in terms of the world's ability to deal with its rapidly growing population. The next large conference is the Women's Conference in Beijing, to be held in September 1995. About 30,000 non-government delegates are expected to attend.

This sort of activity and the greater direct involvement that it is creating for NGOs in the UN processes is going to lead to huge challenges of both political and organisational dimensions. Nevertheless, I believe that it is important to ensure this great outpouring, of what is essentially a great collection of individual energies, is creatively used by the UN and its member governments. It is all part of the challenge that the UN is facing to change and reform.

New Zealanders' Role in the United Nations

Individual energies bring me to the last part of my speech—the role of New Zealand individuals. In our two years on the Security Council we were known for our pragmatic, principled and practical approach to problems.

3   Don McKinnon, 'Introduction', in Templeton, ed., *New Zealand as an International Citizen,* p. 12.

I believe that these qualities are inherent in all the New Zealanders who are working with the United Nations. Many are in New York, but an equal number are working in countries all over the world. They are working as lawyers, advisers, heads of UN bodies, documentary producers, deminers, and of course peacekeepers.

In New York there are people like Jan Beagle who is working in the Secretary-General's Office; Steve Whitehouse, who is producing documentaries on the work of the United Nations; and Jennifer Lake who is in the UN legal division. New Zealanders have worked as election observers in places like Nicaragua and Cambodia. Ros Mountain, an energetic New Zealander, works for the UN Development Programme (UNDP) and has had assignments in some of the toughest places at the toughest times, including Afghanistan, Liberia and Haiti. And of course one must not forget those many military observers from each of the three services watching over fragile lives in many countries far from their homes.

Well-known New Zealand women have also played important roles in organisations like the International Research and Training Institute for the Advancement of Women (INSTRAW). This is where Margaret Shields was probably the most senior New Zealand representative we have had in the United Nations. She was director of INSTRAW for two years. Dame Ann Hercus was for several years the Permanent Representative at our Mission and has continued her association with the United Nations through UN agencies. Dame Silvia Cartwright was elected for a four-year term as a member of the Committee on the Elimination of Discrimination Against Women. In other parts of the world women are also playing a part. Caroline Bilkey and Helen McNaught have both taken leave from the Ministry of Foreign Affairs and are working in Rwanda with the UN high commissioners for human rights and refugees.

All these people have contributed to the United Nations, they have all played a part in its developing role in the world.

In the last ten or fifteen years the world has seen tremendous change, especially in terms of the end of the cold war. This is placing fundamental challenges before the United Nations. To pull all the strands together, the United Nations has to change and reform if it is to maintain its credibility. Without credibility it will be ignored. For reform to come about we actually have to change the United Nations ourselves, to paraphrase Andy Warhol. *We* have to provide the effort.

The enormity of the task should not put us off. The power of the individual—a trite cliche though it is—is real. It can be seen in the difference peacekeepers are making, it can be seen in the role that NGOs are playing, and it can be seen in the role that New Zealanders are playing.

The challenge I am issuing, especially to students, is be positive, be confident about your ability to make a difference, see what you can do to bring about change. The United Nations is a worthwhile organisation. How about channelling your energies into it? We each have the ability to contribute to its future.

Secretary-General Dr Boutros Boutros-Ghali and Mr Don McKinnon (presiding over the UN Security Council, April 1994). (Photo: Ministry of Foreign Affairs and Trade, New Zealand)

Malcolm Templeton

The Achievements and Shortcomings of the United Nations

I am very conscious that the kind of assessment I have been asked to make must be greatly influenced by my own background and experience. My perceptions might have been very different if I had been a politician, a political scientist, a peace activist or an international civil servant. But I have been none of these. My experience for 38 years was as a New Zealand public servant who for much of his working life was required to deal with UN affairs in one capacity or another, whether in Wellington or in New York. I have now been long enough away from the diplomatic coal face, I hope, to have broadened my perceptions and positioned myself to be able to make a more detached, a more balanced, appraisal of the UN's record of achievements and shortcomings than might have been the case a decade ago. But then, I suppose we all think like that.

The point I want to underline is that there is even more than the usual room for disagreement about the past and present performance of the United Nations. I have been saddened by some of the negative views about the organisation expressed by prominent personages in this country in recent months. I have my own criticisms, and I fully expect that some others will disagree in turn.

Achievements

Longevity

I want to begin by talking for a few minutes about what a world without the United Nations would be like, or rather what it was like until not so long ago. Many will not remember a world when we did not have the United Nations, but fifty years is, after all, no more than a moment in history. The United Nations' ill-fated precursor, the League of Nations, was only four years old when I was born, it collapsed with the outbreak of war when I was still at high school, and the

United Nations was established just after my 21st birthday. It has thus already lasted more than twice as long as the League, and that in itself must be set on the credit side of the UN balance sheet. Let us put this down as its first, admittedly modest, achievement.

Universality

Before the League, its historian says, 'it was held both in theory and practice that every state was the sole and sovereign judge of its own acts, owing no allegiance to any higher authority, entitled to resent criticism or even questioning by other states'.[1] On what basis, then, were relations among civilised states conducted? Three phrases in common historian's usage, offer clues: *raison d'Ètat, realpolitik,* and the balance of power. *Raison d'Ètat* was invented by Cardinal Richelieu in the seventeenth century, presumably to justify his putting national aggrandisement before the Christian principles which a Prince of the Church might have been expected to uphold. It should not be translated as 'national interest', since an enlightened pursuit of national interest requires recognition of the legitimate national interests of others: *raison d'Ètat* accepted no such restriction. *Realpolitik,* similarly, based foreign policy on the realities of power, with no regard for moral considerations. In its heyday last century Bismarck, if not its inventor, was its most successful practitioner. *Realpolitik,* according to another prominent diplomatic practitioner, Henry Kissinger, brought about the unification of Germany. In the eighteenth century, again according to Kissinger, Britain elaborated the concept of the balance of power, which dominated European diplomacy for the next two hundred years. British policy in essence was to shift its weight to the weaker side among the contending European powers in order to prevent domination of the continent by any one of them. In 1815, after the defeat of Napoleon, the Congress of Vienna stabilised the balance of power sufficiently, says Kissinger, to secure 'a century of international order uninterrupted by a general war'. It did not, one must add, prevent the outbreak of several major conflicts, the Crimean and Franco–Prussian wars among them. By 1890 'the concept of the balance of power had reached the end of its potential'.[2]

Students of international affairs will have deduced by now that I

---

1   F. P. Walters, *A History of the League of Nations* (Oxford: Oxford University Press, 1952), Vol. I, pp. 1–2.
2   Henry Kissinger, *Diplomacy* (New York: Simon and Schuster, 1994), pp. 58–79, 165–67.

have been reading Kissinger's latest book, grandly entitled *Diplomacy*. It is a fascinating book, but with a curiously old-fashioned air about it, determinedly Atlantic-centred, with a vision largely limited to the northern hemisphere. Indeed if the earth were sawed in half at the equator and the bottom fell away, Kissinger might perhaps notice it but he would scarcely need to revise his book.

To Kissinger, the principle of collective security, a concept embraced successively by Presidents Woodrow Wilson, Franklin D. Roosevelt and Harry S. Truman, and the foundation stone of both the League and the United Nations, is totally flawed. It is based, he says, on the premise that all nations would view every threat to security in the same way and be prepared to run the same risks in resisting it: and this, he says, has never happened and is never likely to.[3] The disappointing aspect of the Kissinger analysis, and this also applies to some critics of the United Nations in New Zealand, is that he offers no coherent alternative, either to the principle or to the organisation that was established to uphold it. Kissinger acknowledges that 'American policy makers have generally preferred multilateral approaches to national ones: the agendas of disarmament, non-proliferation and human rights rather than essentially national, geopolitical or strategic issues'. Yet it is the latter that clearly engage his attention: the United States has the capacity, he suggests, though not necessarily the philosophy, to function as Britain did in Europe before the two world wars in maintaining a balance of power.[4]

Perhaps I am giving undue attention to the views of a former Secretary of State who seems out of sympathy with what he himself describes as traditional American idealism. I have done so in order to underline the fact that there still exists a so-called realist school of strategic thinkers which tends to reject collective security, and such latter-day variants as common security and comprehensive security, in favour of an updated version of the balance of power. In the United States, the sole remaining superpower, there are those who see their country as this time holding the balance. Others favour a return to the non-interventionism of the past. Neither approach is calculated to strengthen the peacemaking or peacekeeping capacity of the UN.

The attempt to maintain a balance of power signally failed to prevent the First World War. The realist school will of course point out that the League of Nations, founded on the principle of collective

3   Ibid., pp. 52–53.
4   Ibid., pp. 826 and 833.

security espoused by President Wilson in the last of his Fourteen Points, signally failed to prevent the Second. My reply is that it was not the principle that failed, but the will of its founders to uphold the principle and to carry out the undertakings set out in the Covenant. Notably the United States, thanks to an isolationist minority in the Senate, rejected the Covenant, and under a Republican successor to President Wilson, ostentatiously turned its back on the League. That in itself was likely to prove a major stumbling block in the way of the effective application of sanctions. The League had a peak membership of 63. Of these, no less than 16 had withdrawn or given notice of withdrawal by the time war broke out again in 1939; four more had been invaded and swallowed up by other members; and another (the Soviet Union) had been expelled. Ominously, the withdrawers had included Germany and Japan.

By contrast, the United Nations has achieved virtual universality of membership, with Switzerland the only significant holdout. Wisely, the authors of the Charter did not repeat the mistake of the authors of the Covenant by including a formal provision for withdrawal. In fact only one member, Indonesia, has tried to withdraw, but quickly returned to the fold. Membership of the United Nations is now regarded as a sort of certificate of statehood, and that certificate is displayed by entities so small that a few years ago one would scarcely have believed them capable of sustaining even a nominal independence. Universality then is the organisation's second achievement.

Human Rights

I should now like to discuss some major innovations in the Charter, which have laid the groundwork for what I regard as its most important achievements—achievements which tend perhaps to be overlooked amid current preoccupations with the peacekeeping and peacemaking functions of the organisation.

The first innovation was to treat human rights as a proper subject for international concern and for eventual incorporation into international law. The expression 'human rights' did not feature in the Covenant. Efforts to include mention of certain specific rights proved abortive. Reference to religious freedom was opposed by France. Japan proposed that the Covenant should proclaim the equality of nations and call for the just treatment of their nationals. This was opposed by New Zealand, and also by Australia and the United States, who feared that it could become the basis for an attack on their discriminatory immigration laws. The Japanese argument, said the League's historian, combined disconcertingly the qualities of being unanswerable and unacceptable.[5]

What survived in the Covenant, without reference to rights, were provisions requiring the League to promote fair conditions of labour and just treatment of the inhabitants of colonial territories, and to supervise agreements dealing with the traffic in women and children and dangerous drugs.

Both the Covenant and the Charter contain provisions which were designed to prevent the League and the United Nations from intervening in matters within the domestic jurisdiction of a member state.[6] For some years a few members of the United Nations, including New Zealand, were disposed to argue that charges of racial discrimination fell within the ambit of that clause; but eventually it came to be accepted that, by virtue of the Charter provisions, human rights were an appropriate subject for international consideration. Their elaboration in the Universal Declaration and the International Covenants of Human Rights should have put the issue beyond argument. Disconcertingly, I notice a tendency among some New Zealanders to regard our own Bill of Rights as a rather irritating piece of domestic legislation which the judiciary is taking too literally and which might even stand in the way of the implementation of government policy. I was mildly astonished a few months ago to read an article, by a member of the Law Faculty of the University of Otago, which trenchantly criticised the New Zealand Bill without once mentioning the fact that it represented no more than a rather belated spelling out, in New Zealand law, of international obligations in respect of human rights assumed by New Zealand some twelve years earlier.[7]

It will of course be said that the practice of many members of the United Nations falls far short of the standards set in the Charter and the Human Rights Covenants. Nevertheless the embodiment of those standards in international law is a giant step forward. Countries of the European Community (EC) have gone a stage further and established their own European Court of Human Rights. New Zealanders, for their part, may now have recourse to the Human Rights Committee of the Political and Civil Rights Covenant in accordance with the Optional

5   Walters, *History of the League of Nations,* pp. 63–64.
6   Articles 15(8) of the League Covenant and 2(7) of the UN Charter.
7   James Allan, 'Harm from the Bill of Rights Act', *Press* (Christchurch), 1 March 1995.

Protocol to that Covenant. As the Court of Appeal has recently pointed out, New Zealand's accession to that Protocol means that the UN Human Rights Committee is now in a sense part of New Zealand's judicial structure.[8]

No one would pretend that there have not been or continue to be glaring breaches of human rights in many parts of the world since the United Nations was founded, or that such breaches have been invariably dealt with by the United Nations in an effective and even-handed way. Until recently there was a felt absence of a senior UN official, corresponding to, say, the High Commissioner for Refugees, with the sole task of promoting human rights and seeking to prevent their violation. For many years there was resistance to such an appointment, but it was overcome at the end of 1993, and a High Commissioner for Human Rights (Jose Lasso of Ecuador) is now active.[9] It is too early to judge how effective a role he can play. But he has already sought to assist in stemming human rights violations in countries such as Rwanda, by sending special rapporteurs and human rights monitors to focus attention on the human rights situation in those countries. Other special rapporteurs have been appointed to work on specific human rights themes. There are now some twenty in all.

New Zealanders have tended to take a rather complacent attitude to human rights breaches as being the sort of things that happen in other places, such as East Timor, rather than at home. The increasing attention now being paid in the United Nations to the concerns of indigenous peoples may serve to prick that complacency.

Decolonisation

I have no hesitation in listing the internationalisation of human rights among the United Nations' major achievements. The decolonisation process too can be classed as one of the organisation's most important achievements. New Zealand played an active part at San Francisco in strengthening the economic and social provisions of the Charter, including its emphasis on human rights. It played an even more signi-ficant role, through Peter Fraser's chairmanship of a key committee, in

8   Tavita v Minister of Immigration (1994]) 1 *New Zealand Law Review* 257. Helen Fawthorpe, 'Human Rights', in Malcolm Templeton, ed., *New Zealand as an International Citizen* (Wellington: Ministry of Foreign Affairs and Trade, 1995), p. 101.

9   UN General Assembly Resolution 48/141 of 29 December 1993 established the post.

developing the Charter provisions relating to the welfare and political development of colonial peoples.

In 1945, it must be remembered, most of Africa, a large part of Asia, and most island countries in the Pacific and the Caribbean, remained under the colonial rule of a handful of metropolitan powers. Only four African countries, three of them enjoying a rather precarious independence, were founder members of the United Nations: now there are fifty-two.

For the first time, the UN Charter recognised the principle of equal rights and self-determination of peoples, and declared that the Organisation was based on the sovereign equality of all its members.[10] New Zealand, as I have said, worked hard at San Francisco to ensure that the colonial powers, of which it was itself one, assumed an obligation to develop free political institutions in their non-self-governing territories, and to take account of the political aspirations of their peoples.

In 1960 the General Assembly took a giant step forward by adopting a Declaration on Colonialism which called for the granting of independence to all colonial territories. New Zealand was the only administering power to vote for the Declaration. Since that time all the trust territories and the vast majority of territories under colonial rule at the end of World War II have completed an act of self-determination acceptable to the UN General Assembly, and most of them have been admitted to membership, in numbers and at a pace that could never have been contemplated in 1945.

Shortcomings

The achievements that I have described by no means constitute an exclusive list. There is much more that could be said about the work of the United Nations and its specialised agencies in economic and social development and in such fields as education, health, agriculture, the environment, and in the elaboration and codification of international law. But I think it is time to say something about the principal areas in which the United Nations may be said to have fallen short of the aspirations and expectations of its founders. Let me assert at the outset my general theme that the failings of the organisation derive, for the most part, not so much from defects in its constitution and structure as from the failure of its members to accept the limitations on their

10   Articles 1(2) and 2(1).

sovereignty implicit in the Charter and to fulfil conscientiously the obligations it imposes. It follows from this that whatever defects there may be in the Charter itself or in the organisation as it has developed since 1945, they cannot be remedied by constitutional reform alone. I shall come back to this thesis later on.

Maintenance of International Peace and Security

There is no escaping the fact that when most people seek to measure the success or failure of the United Nations, the measuring stick they apply is its ability to restore or keep the peace. I have tried to show that the United Nations has had important successes in other fields, that it has done much to change the face of the world and change it for the better. But I have no illusions that to talk of these achievements will alter public perceptions. The Secretary-General, a politician, recognised this, I think, during his recent visit, when he spoke publicly of little else than the peacemaking and peacekeeping operations in which the organisation is engaged. It was understandable, but perhaps unfortunate that more emphasis was not placed on what the United Nations has achieved and is achieving in other fields. New Zealand critics of the United Nations, when they speak of the organisation as 'bankrupt' or 'wallowing in ineffectiveness',[11] focus their attention on the current inability of the United Nations to restore the peace in what used to be Yugoslavia.

An historical review will, I hope, provide something of a corrective. A distinction needs to be kept in mind between enforcement actions, peacemaking, and peacekeeping. Effective action against aggression was always going to pose a problem, given the veto. The constitutional defect was magnified by the outbreak and intensification of the Cold War. Yet there were successes. Had it not been for UN intervention, South Korea, one of New Zealand's most important trading partners, would today be ruled by the world's most regressive communist regime. The end of the Cold War facilitated UN action to free Kuwait, which would otherwise be part of Saddam Hussein's Iraq. It is true that both these actions were made possible by the willingness of the United States to provide the bulk of the military forces required to repel the aggression, but that is beside the point. In the mid-1950s, in another development, the United Nations forced

11   David Lange, *Dominion* (Wellington), 15 January 1995 and the *Press* (Christchurch), 28 April 1995.

Britain, France and Israel to desist from their invasion of Egypt and established the UN Emergency Force (UNEF I), the first of a series of UN peacekeeping forces, to keep the peace between Israel and its neighbours. More recently it has applied sufficient pressure to the South African Government to force it to abandon the policy of apartheid, which it had declared a threat to international peace.

There is an important difference between the functions of peacemaking and peacekeeping, even though the distinction has sometimes become blurred in practice. Successful peacekeeping requires the acquiescence, if not the cooperation, of the parties. In the former Yugoslavia, forces originally designated and equipped to keep the peace have been forced by circumstances to try to stop continuing hostilities. It is not surprising that they have been less than successful. As Ramesh Thakur has remarked, peacekeepers cannot be expected to supervise peace in conditions of war.[12]

In the case of Yugoslavia, there has been a notable reluctance on the part of the governments which have the military capacity to undertake effective peacemaking action to accept that level of involvement. It is not good enough to say that intervention in a civil war presents insuperable difficulties. There are now five states in what was once Yugoslavia, four of them already members of the United Nations. The situation is not simply one of civil conflict within a state, and is eminently one which the United Nations was intended and has a duty to try to resolve. In that regard the permanent members of the Security Council have a special responsibility which goes with their privileged position.

I do not have any doubt that New Zealand was right to send troops to Bosnia. Our obligations under the Charter are global in character. The New Zealand Government that ratified the Charter was opposed to the regionalisation of responsibilities for maintaining international peace. We must wait to see whether the collective will of the governments taking part in the UN operation in former Yugoslavia is sufficiently resolute to bring it to a successful conclusion.

Arms Control and Disarmament

Another field in which the UN has not met the expectations of peoples

---

12 Ramesh Thakur, 'Peace-keeping', in Malcolm Templeton, ed., *New Zealand as an International Citizen: Fifty Years of United Nations Membership* (Wellington: Ministry of Foreign Affairs and Trade, 1995), p. 73.

is that of disarmament. It was without doubt the most frustrating topic with which I had to deal during my time in New York.

The Charter is, of course, a pre-nuclear treaty. Disarmament does not feature in the purposes and principles set out in Articles 1 and 2, and is not mentioned until Article 11, which states that the General Assembly may make recommendations to members and to the Security Council about the principles governing disarmament. In Article 26 the Security Council is given the task of establishing a system for the regulation of armaments. It has never come within even measurable distance of achieving this goal, although at an early stage it established a Disarmament Commission of parallel membership for that purpose.

In practice, consideration of disarmament proposals in a UN context has taken place in the General Assembly, where they have been the subject of interminable debate and innumerable resolutions, with remarkably little to show by way of concrete results. The reasons are not far to seek. The early sessions of the Assembly coincided with the onset of the Cold War. Proposals for the international control of atomic energy, including its military applications, soon stalled: the United States and its allies insisted that the control organ to be established by the Security Council must be free of the veto, while the Soviet Union was equally insistent that it must apply. There followed a kind of ritual dance among the great powers, with each side in turn putting forward proposals designed to improve its own strategic position. The West sought to reduce what it saw as the preponderant conventional military forces which the Soviet Union was able to deploy, while the Soviet Union, at a time when it was well behind the West in the development of its own nuclear capacity, proposed the immediate prohibition of the manufacture of atomic weapons and the destruction of stocks. Later, when the Soviet Union had largely caught up with the West in the development of nuclear weapons, and even taken a lead in missile development, the emphasis shifted to the vexed question of inspection, with the West insisting that in any agreement relating to nuclear weapons on-site inspection was essential, and the Soviet Union as vehemently opposed to any inspectorial presence on their territory.

Most substantive negotiations on disarmament have been conducted directly among the great powers, and most of such significant agreements as have been achieved have emerged from these negotiations. In 1961 a committee of limited membership, linked very loosely with the United Nations, was established to seek agreement on general and complete disarmament. This committee has been progressively enlarged and was strengthened in 1978 when China and France agreed to join the other principal nuclear powers in its work. It has achieved some limited successes, including the conclusion of a convention prohibiting chemical weapons.

The most important disarmament treaties so far concluded have affected the armouries of the major nuclear powers. The armaments and armed forces of other countries have been largely unaffected by global agreements: the major exceptions have been regional agreements such as the Conventional Forces in Europe Treaty (CFE) and the various nuclear-free zones such as Tlatelolco and the South Pacific Nuclear Free Zone, under which parties have forsworn the possession of nuclear weapons and their stationing on their territories.

New Zealand for many years gave faithful support to Western positions on disarmament. In the 1950s, for example, it supported the view that nuclear disarmament should form part of a wider disarmament agreement, and also supported the continued testing of nuclear weapons in the absence of a foolproof system of detecting nuclear explosions to permit verification of any cessation agreement. It supported the British in their wish to develop their own independent nuclear deterrent, and assisted them in conducting atmospheric tests at Christmas Island by making ships and aircraft available to help in monitoring them.

Nevertheless, it was the perceived potential danger from radioactive fallout in our own part of the world that sensitised New Zealand public opinion to the nuclear threat and led New Zealand governments to adopt their own policy on nuclear-weapons issues. In 1959 New Zealand parted company from most of its Western allies in voting for an Assembly resolution which called on France to stop its nuclear test programme in the Sahara.[13] In 1963 the Prime Minister, without attracting much attention, proclaimed New Zealand's own nuclear-free status: New Zealand, he said, had no nuclear weapons, no intention of acquiring any, and no nuclear bases on its territory.[14]

To New Zealand's dismay, France responded to African opposition to its Saharan tests by transferring the operation to French Polynesia. From then on opposition among New Zealanders to nuclear testing, mainly directed to the French programme, mounted steadily.

13   Resolution 1379(XIV) of 20 November 1959.
14   K. J. Holyoake, 'The Problem of Nuclear Weapons', statement of 31 May 1963, *External Affairs Review* 13 (May 1963), pp. 30–31.

Torn between public concern and a desire not to offend France unduly while access for our agricultural products to the European Economic Community (EEC) was at issue, New Zealand governments nevertheless felt obliged to take a more active stand against nuclear testing.

The most logical approach to the problem, it was felt, was to promote a comprehensive test ban treaty (CTBT). This would prevent both the further development of more sophisticated weapons by the nuclear powers and the spread of nuclear weaponry to other countries. If the superpowers would accept a ban, there would be great pressure on France and China to accede.

This is where the frustration has come in. For more than twenty years New Zealand has taken a leading part in promoting General Assembly resolutions calling for a CTBT. These are passed each year by large majorities. But until very recently the superpowers, despite their enormous arsenals, have been unwilling to forgo the right to develop and test new types of nuclear weaponry. Thus there was little effective pressure on France to stop its testing programme in the South Pacific, and indeed there is every reason to believe that France received tacit support from the other Western nuclear powers.

Now at last there seems to be a reasonable prospect that a CTBT will be signed next year by all five of the acknowledged nuclear powers. But this does not necessarily mean that nuclear weapons will no longer be manufactured—simply that they will no longer be exploded as part of the testing process.

In the face of French intransigence, New Zealand decided in 1973 to take a more directly focused stand against French testing. A frigate was deployed at Moruroa during France's testing programme that year, and New Zealand joined with Australia in taking France to the International Court of Justice. Although France rejected the Court's jurisdiction, it ceased thereafter to conduct its tests in the atmosphere, but has continued to do so underground, and now, after several years of moratorium, has decided to resume them. The most discouraging aspect of this decision, in my opinion, is its destabilising effect on the negotiations which have still to be concluded to ensure a truly comprehensive test ban treaty.

In another approach to the problem, New Zealand asked the UN Assembly in 1975 to endorse the concept of a nuclear-weapon-free zone in the South Pacific. The Assembly did so by a large majority,[15] but after a change of government New Zealand failed to pursue the

15   Resolution 3477 (XXX) of 11 December 1975.

idea until 1983, when it was resuscitated by a newly-elected Labor Government in Australia. The zone is not observed by France, which not only has continued to test its nuclear weapons in the zone but in 1985 committed an act of terrorism against the protest vessel *Rainbow Warrior* in a New Zealand port.

In April–May 1995 the Nuclear Non-Proliferation Treaty, the most important existing agreement limiting the spread of nuclear weapons, came up for renewal. Some anti-nuclear campaigners in New Zealand were in favour of scrapping the treaty or of putting a time limit on its continuance, with a view to putting pressure on the nuclear-weapon states to get rid of their weapons. In the end there was a consensus among the parties to the treaty which New Zealand supported,[16] for its indefinite continuance. Countries which favoured a series of short-term renewals could not get their act together.

It is to be hoped that the nuclear-weapon states do not feel that they have been let off the hook in the treaty which requires them to work for complete nuclear disarmament. For the end of the Cold War has not removed the danger. Even if the United States and Russia have reduced their stockpiles under bilateral agreements by two-thirds at the end of the millennium, they will still have enough nuclear capacity to blow the world up several times over.

New Zealand has joined in an approach to have the World Court consider whether nuclear weapons are lawful, and it has committed itself to making a submission to the Court.[17] I don't see this as a particularly promising approach. The Court is not a legislative body. It seems unlikely that it will produce a clear-cut ruling, and if the judges who are nationals of nuclear-weapon states come out in favour of the legality of nuclear weapons, I doubt whether their governments, from which they are of course independent, will disagree with them.

There therefore remains much to be done. I believe that the road to success, however painfully slow, lies in the conclusion of more multilateral agreements along the lines of the CTBT, and in a more urgent approach to nuclear disarmament among the governments that own the

16 Statement by Douglas Graham, the Minister for Disarmament, at the Nuclear Non-Proliferation Treaty Review and Extension Conference, 21 April 1995; *New Zealand Foreign Affairs and Trade Record* 3 (April 1995). See also the press statement by Graham at the conclusion of the Conference, 12 May 1995.

17 Press statement by Messrs Don McKinnon and Douglas Graham on 9 May 1995 stated that a submission would be made before 20 June.

weapons. I hope that New Zealand's efforts to secure membership of the Committee on Disarmament will eventually prove successful, and that it will make good use of that membership.

Inefficiency and Insolvency

The last shortcoming of the United Nations on which I propose to comment—this is not meant to be a comprehensive list—is its reputation for bureaucratic inefficiency and its admitted near-bankruptcy. The latter shortcoming I have no hesitation in pinning on the failure of a good number of members to pay their dues promptly, or in some cases at all. The attitude of some of the major contributors, and I do not think it unfair to single out the United States, is especially disappointing.

The charge of inefficiency is more difficult to adjudicate. The Secretariat is, by the standards expected of an efficient national public service, indeed a bloated bureaucracy. There are a number of factors contributing to this state of affairs. The first is the requirement for equitable geographical representation. A second is the disposition of some states to treat the Secretariat as a repository for politicians and officials whose usefulness to their own governments has, for whatever reason, been seen to have diminished. These two factors taken together militate against the appointment to vacancies of the most meritorious candidate. There are devoted hardworking officials in the Secretariat, but there are also passengers. The third and perhaps the most important reason for the excessive growth of the Secretariat is the tendency of the General Assembly and other organs, year after year, to load it with new tasks, as a rule without counting the cost.

Reforms

I should like to finish with a few comments about the vexed subject of reform. I know that this is going to be dealt with in much more detail by others, but my excuse is that I want to underline my belief that endless discussion about constitutional reform is not in itself going to remedy the shortcomings I have been attempting to describe. Only a change of attitude among the members can do that. I cannot help recalling that the League spent from 1936 to 1938 discussing reform (New Zealand made a major submission[18]) only a year before World

18   See Bruce S. Bennett, *New Zealand's Moral Foreign Policy 1935–39: The Promotion of Collective Security through the League of Nations*

War II brought the organisation effectively to an end.

The structural defects in the Charter are easy enough to see. The veto sticks out like a sore thumb. I had been going to say that fortunately there seemed to have developed in the last year or two an unspoken agreement among the permanent members not to invoke it except in cases of the direst necessity. Unfortunately the other day the United States chose to veto a resolution which all the other Council members supported,[19] a resolution which was critical of Israel but which could scarcely be interpreted as affecting any vital American interest, and which was fully justified when Israel shortly afterwards complied with it—even if for the wrong reasons. Certainly it would be good if something could be done about the veto, especially as at present it can be used to prevent any amendment of the Charter at all. But don't hold your breath.

An allied issue is that of the composition of the Council. An argument can plausibly be made that the present permanent membership is anomalous, and that (for example) apart from their nuclear-weapons capability, Britain and France can no longer be distinguished from a number of other states, for example Germany and Japan, which are larger, more populous and/or more wealthy than they. But what are the criteria? Britain and France may well argue that next to the United States they have the best record as contributors to peacemaking and peacekeeping operations. Is economic clout an appropriate criterion? Should a state which is constitutionally inhibited from military activity outside its borders be regarded as an appropriate candidate for permanent membership of the body which is dedicated to keeping and if necessary enforcing the peace? What of the claims of India, Brazil or Nigeria? And what of the reaction of neighbouring states to the recognition of those claims?

There may be a case for increasing the size of the Council, but surely not for giving more of its members the power of veto. And the more members, the more cumbersome and the slower, in all probability, will be the ability of the Council to act.

A case can also be made for reform of the regional group system on which elections are based. This at least can be done without amending the Charter. New Zealand is in an odd position, along with Australia and Canada, tacked on to the Western European Group. It is

(Wellington: New Zealand Institute of International Affairs, 1988) pp. 40–42 and 68–71.

19   *Dominion* (Wellington), 19 May 1995.

not easy for us to get elected to major UN organs. Yet from a purely selfish point of view we could be better off where we are than in a more geographically logical grouping. We have not had a bad run on the Security Council—three terms so far, as many as the two Germanies put together. On the other hand, how would we fare in a Pacific Grouping along with large countries such as Japan and Indonesia? (Japan has had seven terms on the Council so far.)

The effectiveness of the United Nations as a collective security organisation depends on the willingness of its members to accept and comply with decisions of its organs reached by duly constituted majorities. By ratifying the Charter UN members accepted the limitation of their sovereignty that compliance with such decisions implies. To strengthen the decision-making powers of the organisation through constitutional reform would require members to concede more of their sovereignty—a course which most members, and notably the permanent members of the Security Council, do not seem disposed to contemplate.

It must be recognised that it took two world wars to persuade governments to make even the concessions of sovereignty embodied in the Charter. It is not too much to say, in fact, that those concessions represented a high point from which member states have in practice retreated quite a long way. Article 43 of the Charter envisages the conclusion of agreements between member states and the Security Council requiring members to hold in readiness units of their armed forces to take part in enforcement actions decided upon by the Council. That article has never been implemented. Would any New Zealand government now be prepared to earmark elements of its armed forces to go automatically into combat on the call of the Security Council? Proposals for the creation of a standing UN ready reaction force are modest by comparison.

The determination of members to guard their sovereignty, particularly in regard to their internal affairs, has not decreased. Do not imagine that New Zealand is an exception. When there was some suggestion that the International Labour Organisation (ILO) might issue a critical report about the New Zealand government's labour legislation, there was an outraged response: if New Zealand was in breach of its obligations under ILO conventions, the conventions must be outdated and the ILO a dinosaur.

This was, I hope, an aberration. New Zealand's record in the United Nations over the past half century, from its support of decolonisation to nuclear disarmament, from its reputation for prompt payment of its financial contributions to its active participation in peacekeeping, has been more than respectable. Its most recent term on the Security Council has raised its international profile. It is a record, however, that needs to be sustained and not eroded by unconstructive criticism.

The last word about the future of the United Nations may be left to the Secretary-General. As he said to Stuart McMillan recently:

> If the member states want a strong UN they can have a strong UN. The UN is an instrument at the disposal of member states. If the member states want a marginal organisation and they want to continue their own bilateral policy, then the UN will be ... a marginal organisation.[20]

What, I wonder, do the member states want? Domestic pressures to pull back from painful international commitments are strong, even, indeed especially, in the US, the UN's most powerful member. Both George Kennan and Henry Kissinger have recently resurrected the famous assertion of John Quincy Adams that 'America goes not abroad in search of monsters to destroy. She is the well wisher to the freedom and independence of all. She is the champion and vindicator only of her own'. Kennan suggests that the United States should for the future deviate from Adams's principle of non-intervention only where vital US interests are clearly threatened. Beyond that America should confine itself to giving, in Adams's words 'the benign sympathy of our example'.[21] But does the highminded isolationism of 1821 fit the circumstances of today? Kissinger acknowledges that 'some monsters need to be, if not slain, at least resisted'.[22]

For New Zealand, a small country for which policies of *realpolitik* and balance of power have no relevance, and whose economic vulnerability militates against any disposition to isolationism, the choice from Boutros Boutros-Ghali's alternatives should surely be clear.

---

20   *Press,* (Christchurch), 5 May 1995.
21   George F. Kennan, 'On American Principles', *Foreign Affairs* 74 (March/April 1995), p. 125.
22   Kissinger, *Diplomacy,* p. 833.

Senator Gareth Evans presenting a copy of his book to Secretary-General Boutros Boutros-Ghali, United Nations, 1993. (Photo: Department of Foreign Affairs and Trade, Australia)

Gareth Evans

Cooperating for Peace

It is particularly appropriate to address this topic in New Zealand, a country which has demonstrated so clearly its commitment to improving cooperative security mechanisms and which has contributed so much to tangible progress in this field within the United Nations system. New Zealand expressed that commitment during its highly active term on the Security Council in 1993–94 with its initiative to establish a Convention on the Safety of United Nations and Associated Personnel. That was multilateral diplomacy at its most effective, not least because the Convention was proposed, drafted and adopted in little more than a year, an astounding feat in UN terms. The Convention is important both because of the added protection it will confer on personnel and because it will add to the confidence that troop-contributing nations can have in reaching decisions to participate in UN peacekeeping operations.

New Zealand has made another contribution with its work with Argentina in the UN Security Council to give troop-contributing nations a greater say in the decision-making process for UN peace-keeping operations. These efforts resulted in a Security Council Presidential Statement in November 1994 which introduced improved consultative arrangements between the Security Council, the UN Secretariat and troop-contributing nations.

Such activity has become increasingly important. In place of the new era of international peace and cooperation which many thought would follow the end of the Cold War, the last few years have brought new uncertainties and ambiguities to international relations, new and savage conflicts within states and new challenges to the UN's central, historical responsibility for ensuring peace. It can easily be asserted from the troubled history of its involvement in places such as Bosnia, Somalia and Rwanda, that the United Nations is failing to meet this responsibility—failing to live up to the promises implicit in its 1945

Charter. In this fiftieth anniversary year I believe the need has never been greater for the international community to devote all its intellectual resources and creativity to solving these problems and to fitting the United Nations for the challenges of the next fifty years. I want to address some approaches to this issue which I believe hold out particular promise.

Cooperative Security

There is a central sustaining concept for international efforts to maintain peace and security, both in the United Nations and outside it, which I believe is best expressed in the term 'cooperative security'. This embraces three separate ideas—collective security, common security and comprehensive security—which have been current in thinking about international security cooperation for some time.

The first of these, collective security, has a long tradition in the United Nations and other groups of states: it involves the notion of member states in a group agreeing to renounce the use of force among themselves and collectively coming to the aid of any member attacked by an outside state (or a renegade member).

The idea of common security was first clearly articulated in the 1980s, and has become ever more prominent with the end of the Cold War: essentially it is the notion of states finding security by working with others, rather than against them.

Comprehensive security is simply the notion that security is multidimensional in character, encompassing a range of political, economic, social and other non-military considerations as well as military capability.

Cooperative security is a useful term. Not only does it bring these three familiar approaches together, but it does so in a way which emphasises prevention and encompasses the whole range of responses to security concerns, both before and after the threshold of armed conflict has been crossed: at one extreme this would involve long-term programmes to improve economic and social conditions which are likely to give rise to future tensions, and at the other it includes enforcement of peace by full-scale military means.

The real world in which these approaches must be tested is changing quickly. Traditional warfare between states, with its relative simplicities and certitudes, is now conspicuously rare, and the new problems are overwhelmingly to do with intra-state conflict. According to SIPRI's 1994 *Yearbook*, all the 34 major armed conflicts waged in

1993 were intra-state in character.[1] They are a characteristic of a 'zone of conflict' including the former communist states, much of Africa, and parts of Central and Latin America and South Asia, where all too many states seem caught in a downward spiral of economic decline, often exacerbated by official corruption and mismanagement, creating governments which are at or near collapse and which are being challenged, often violently, by their own citizens. Economic decline has hastened the process of national disintegration, and vice versa.

The collapse of the Soviet empire has brought extraordinary social, political and economic change to all of the former communist states. The transition from state repression to relative political licence has permitted the emergence of long-suppressed ethnic, religious and political hatreds and created new ones. In the former Soviet Union, the fighting in Chechnya—and the backlash of Chechen terrorist reprisals—is only the latest in a string of more than twenty violent conflicts which have resulted in thousands of deaths and over a million people displaced. The potential for still greater conflict is considerable. The vulnerabilities of the 25 million ethnic Russians who still live in non-Russian republics constitute a major potential security problem, as does the presence of 35 million non-ethnic Russians living in the Russian Federation. In the face of discrimination in the new non-Russian republics, some ethnic Russian minorities are demanding autonomy or even secession, while hundreds of thousands of others have voted with their feet and migrated back to Russian to swell the ranks of the unemployed and homeless. Protecting these Russian minorities has become a major strategic preoccupation for Moscow.

In states where economically and politically bankrupt governments can no longer provide vital social and economic services, citizens have increasingly been turning to other religious, ethnic and private economic organisations. Ethnic and religious differences are not in themselves usually the causes of conflict, but they are easily capable of being exploited by unscrupulous political leaders. This is particularly so in periods of economic decline, which provides fertile ground for the rise of demagogic politics and the intensification of chauvinistic myth-making.

Emerging ethnic and religious movements in the 'zone of conflict' offer an increasingly serious challenge to sovereign states which fail to

---

1   Peter Wallensteen and Karin Axell, 'Major armed conflicts', *SIPRI Yearbook 1994* (Oxford: Oxford University Press for the Stockholm International Peace Research Institute, 1994), p. 81.

meet the basic needs of their citizens. Some movements seek to secede and create their own states; some seek to overthrow existing regimes; and others seek some form of autonomy. The desire to achieve ethnic 'purity' out of the ethnically intermingled populations of most states leads in many cases to intra-communal atrocities.

The available evidence strongly suggests, in fact, that violent intra-state conflict is unlikely to decrease of its own accord in the near or mid-term future. The decline in individual living standards, and the erosion of good governance, with which civil strife is so closely linked, will not be quickly reversed anywhere in the zone of conflict, although the states of Eastern Europe and the former Soviet Union are at least able to build on already established infrastructures and systems of education and administration which are lacking, for example, in most African states.

These new forms of conflict have thrown up fresh complications for effective United Nations action. There are new tasks to be under-taken in what has come to be known as 'expanded' peacekeeping, in which UN operations have moved beyond a more or less passive observation and monitoring role to full-scale election organisation, refugee resettlement, human rights development and civil adminis-tration. There are new questions of political acceptance to be faced, including developing-world sensitivities about the perceived readiness of the West to ignore the principle of sovereignty. Ironically, these have taken the place of the major political constraint that used to circumscribe UN action during the Cold War—the use of the veto power by the permanent members of the Security Council—which has for most purposes now disappeared.

If we are to meet these challenges we will clearly need to devote more resources to prevention. In a world where commitment and resources are always likely to fall short of aspirations, it makes far more sense to concentrate efforts on peace-building and other preven-tive strategies than on after-the-event peace restoration. That holds as much for intra- as for inter-state conflicts: violent conflicts are always far more difficult and costly to manage and resolve than non-violent disputes, and failed states are extremely difficult to put back together again. That is not such an attractive approach in strict political terms, of course, because if it works nobody notices. It is an iron law of politics—national or international—that everyone likes to be *seen* to be doing something: the notion of taking action behind the scenes that might be inherently worth doing, or worth doing as an insurance premium to avoid a larger payout later, tends to be foreign to the political psyche. But we must get more people to see the point of that splendid observation attributed to Jean-Marie Lehn, who won the Nobel Prize for Chemistry in 1987: 'Only those who can see the invisible can do the impossible'.

Building Peace

Peace-building is the most important preventive strategy because it goes to the fundamental underlying causes of disputes and conflicts— to ensure that they do not occur in the first place, or if they do arise, that they will not recur. I have always thought it a waste of a good phrase to confine the idea of peace-building to situations of post-conflict reconstruction, as the Secretary-General has been inclined to: the idea has much wider potential reach, it is intuitively easy to understand, and in fact it is central to my earlier reintegration theme.

At the international level, peace-building strategies centre on building or strengthening a range of international structures or regimes aimed at minimising threats to security, building confidence and trust and operating as forums for dialogue and cooperation. Multilateral arms control and disarmament regimes; treaties governing issues like the Law of the Sea; forums like the International Court of Justice and other international bodies for resolving disputes; and multilateral dialogue and cooperation forums are all examples of these structures. The ASEAN Regional Forum (ARF) is a prime example in our own region.

Peace-building within states, by contrast, seeks to encourage equitable economic development in order to enhance human rights, broadly defined, and to facilitate good governance. These are goals we should pursue for their own sakes, but also because advancing them contributes directly to national and international security. Policies which enhance economic development and distributive justice, en-courage the rule of law, protect fundamental human rights and foster the growth of democratic institutions are also *security* policies. They should be recognised as such, and receive a share of current security budgets and future peace dividends.

Economic development, human rights, good governance and peace are, in fact, inextricably connected and mutually reinforcing. Peace is a necessary precondition for development; and equitable development eradicates many of the socio-political conditions which threaten peace. It comes as no surprise to find that those countries whose economies are declining, whose political institutions are failing and where human rights are abused, should also be the ones experiencing the greatest amounts of violence and turmoil.

There are some reasons for long-term optimism about the future of peace-building. The proportion of the world's population living in abject poverty fell from 70 percent in 1960 to 32 percent in 1992. The world is slowly becoming more democratic, with more than half its population now living under relatively pluralistic governments.

But unfortunately—perhaps almost inevitably—the areas which suffer the greatest levels of intra-state violence are also those in which economic conditions are declining and governments are failing. National governments in the zone of conflict must bear much of the blame for the deteriorating economic and political conditions which exacerbate internal conflicts. Persuading such governments to change security-eroding policies will always be difficult, but the international community does have some levers of influence. International financial institutions such as the World Bank and the International Monetary Fund (IMF) have long applied economic management conditionality to their aid programmes, with loans contingent on recipients' willingness to adopt far-reaching structural adjustment measures. They are now considering applying conditionality more widely to embrace other aspects of good governance. Similarly, individual donor countries have begun linking their assistance programmes to human rights observance in recipient countries. These developments, although in an embryonic stage so far, raise the possibility that more systematic approaches may be developed to apply conditionality specifically to the problems of intra-state conflict.

The relationship between democracy and security is a very direct one, and it is a striking fact that democracies—at least mature ones—seem never to go to war with each other. There is also a strong relationship between democracy and violence within states. From the beginning of this century to 1987, according to one estimate, some 151 million persons have been killed by governments over and above the death toll from war and civil war (which accounted for an additional 39 million).[2] The overwhelming majority of these deaths were perpetrated by governments against their own citizens. Totalitarian states were responsible for 84 percent of the deaths, authoritarian states for most of the rest. Democracies were responsible

2   Rudolph J. Rummel, 'Power, Genocide and Mass Murder', *Journal of Peace Research* 31 (February 1994), p. 2.

for a tiny proportion of the deaths, although the absolute numbers were large.[3] Democratic states are thus not only less warlike, they are also less prone to violence against their own citizens.

One of the principal underpinnings of a strong democracy is an effective system of law and order and a viable legal system. So-called 'justice packages' could be developed to assist nations in institution-building in both pre- and post-conflict situations. Some examples of this type of assistance would be creating a body of criminal law and procedure; establishing police forces; training judges, prosecutors and defenders; and developing adequate correctional facilities.

The International Institute for Democracy and Electoral Assistance (IDEA) recently established in Sweden, of which Australia is a founding member, aims to bring coordination to existing forms of electoral cooperation, institution-building and development of democratic norms. The coordination and research role of the new institute provides examples of practical peace-building activities which can be undertaken by the international community, largely drawing on existing bilateral and regional linkages.

Maintaining Peace

Preventive strategies must also address actual disputes which may deteriorate into armed conflict if they are not resolved. Hence, peace-building must be accompanied by strategics of peace maintenance, the major strand of which is preventive diplomacy. One perhaps normally thinks of this as something done to resolve or contain disputes occurring between states. But it has equal application to many situations of internal ethno-nationalist and religious squabbling: the Organisation on Security and Cooperation in Europe (OSCE) already has shown, both through its own direct missions, and through the role of the High Commissioner on National Minorities, how this might work in countries like Albania, Estonia, Latvia, the Former Yugoslav Republic of Macedonia, Hungary and Slovakia. Creative political solutions, involving power-sharing strategies and the like, can be found and negotiated to many problems involving disaffected national minorities.

Like peace-building, preventive diplomacy tends by its nature to be a low profile activity, lacking the obvious media impact of blue helmet peacekeeping and peace-enforcement operations. Preventive diplomacy succeeds when things do not happen. It is most successful

3   Ibid., pp. 1–10.

when it is applied early, well before armed conflict is likely, but it has unfortunately been the case too often in the UN system, that preventive diplomacy efforts have been attempted too late, when the dynamics of escalation are so advanced that a slide into hostilities is almost inevitable.

Despite the importance of this activity, the United Nations devotes relatively few resources to it, even though it is now universally acknowledged to be the most cost-effective means of dealing with potential conflict. There are only some forty UN officials assigned to tasks immediately relevant to preventive diplomacy. This compares with nearly 65,000 UN peacekeepers in place at the end of May and approximately 30 million armed service personnel worldwide. Some reforms to UN practice have been implemented but far more needs to be done.

If the United Nations is to play its rightful role as the preeminent cooperative security institution in the post-Cold War era, it must upgrade its capacity to the point where it can offer an effective dispute resolution service to its members, providing low-profile, skilled, third party assistance through good offices, mediation and the like. In my book *Cooperating for Peace,*[4] I proposed that regionally focused UN preventive diplomacy units should be established. Staffed by senior professionals expert in dispute resolution, closely familiar with the areas and issues on which they work, and with the experience and stature to be able to negotiate at the highest levels, preventive diplomacy units could operate not only at UN headquarters, but also in the field, in regional centres. They would require adequate resources and infrastructure, with appropriate back-up personnel and equipment, and close consultative links with regional organisations, specialist scholars, peace research and other academic institutes. Because preventive diplomacy is so cost-effective, a large increase in the UN's capability could be achieved at minimal cost. The creation of, say, six regional preventive diplomacy centres, of the kind I have described, with a total staff of one hundred and the necessary support funding, would cost little more than US $20 million a year. By comparison, the UN's peacekeeping budget for 1994 was US $3.5 billion (with the cost of its operation in Mozambique alone being over US $1 million each day). And the cost to the UN coalition of fighting the Gulf War against Saddam Hussein was fully $70 billion!

4   Gareth Evans, *Cooperating for Peace: The Global Agenda for the 1990s and Beyond* (Sydney: Allen & Unwin, 1993).

It is not only the United Nations which has a preventive diplomacy role to play. Many successes in this area have been achieved by individual states, regional organisations and non-government organisations (NGOs). The Vatican successfully mediated in the Beagle Channel dispute between Chile and Argentina. The Carter Center operated to help defuse the nuclear impasse with North Korea and the removal of the military government in Haiti. And 'second track' diplomacy has been an important aspect of dialogue on security issues in East Asia, such as the Indonesian-sponsored workshops on the South China Sea problem.

Regional organisations, too, have a special role in preventive diplomacy. Being close to the conflicts and with obvious interests in their resolution, they are often (although not always) better placed to act than the United Nations. The role of the OSCE High Commissioner on National Minorities, mentioned above, is one example, and the ARF is another. Regional mechanisms for conflict prevention have begun to emerge in Africa and the Middle East. For example, the Association of Southern African States (ASAS) has recently been formed as a part of the Southern African Development Community (SADC) with a strong conflict prevention objective. As part of the Middle East peace process, the proposed Regional Security Centre in Jordan and two related centres in Qatar and Tunis to be established through the Arms Control and Regional Security (ACRS) working group should also contribute to enhancing preventive diplomacy. There is, as well, discussion in the ARF context of a possible centre in East Asia.

Restoring Peace

While prevention is always better than cure, it remains important that there be some credible international capacity to deal collectively, and if necessary forcefully, with deadly conflicts, including humanitarian crises, that cannot be prevented or resolved by other means.

While political constraints on decision-making by the Security Council have lessened significantly with the passing of the Cold War, the experience of more UN peace operations, and of more ambitious operations, has exposed important constraints on the effectiveness of military responses under the UN flag. In the last few years, we have tested the limits of how far the UN's secretariat resources can stretch, and of how much member states are willing to contribute in troops and finance. We have discovered that, even with generous arrangements for seconding military staff into UN headquarters—the Australian Defence Force, for example, has seven staff seconded into the Department of Peace-keeping Operations (DPKO)—there are serious limits to the capacity of the UN Secretariat to act as a strategic headquarters handling, as is now the case, seventeen operations around the world. Our defence ministers have come to focus with greater preoccupation on the limited headquarters capacity for planning and administration.

It appears to be the case that, at least for the moment, there is a ceiling of around 70–80,000 troops which member states will collectively make available to the Secretary-General at any one time, and that there is often a considerable lag before these forces can be deployed to the field. The budget for peace operations has risen tenfold in three years, and we are now seeing that the largest contributor has decided unilaterally to cut its share of that budget. Many developing countries fear that the expansion in payments for such operations will be at the expense of funding for their priority concern of economic and social development.

We have also observed the limitations on Security Council mandates for many operations. The last few years have given us all too many examples—especially in the former Yugoslavia—of politically-influenced mandates which have not been achievable in the field, or which have lacked the clarity about goals and time-frames which commanders could reasonably expect. There is a need to better integrate the Security Council's process of formulating mandates for operations with the Secretariat's planning processes. One suggestion for achieving this could be to begin institutionalisation of the two sets of parallel processes. This need not impinge on traditional Security Council prerogatives, but rather ensure that the Council has more direct access to high quality military advice and militarily viable concepts of operations.

Similarly, we have seen missions undertaken without provision for the necessary resources, and the United Nations assuming a role in complex situations without sufficient thought given to how blue helmeted forces should interact with other international actors, whether these be non-governmental aid bodies, major UN organs, or agencies such as the UN High Commissioner for Refugees (UNHCR).

There has been a flurry of recent proposals and studies to consider how the United Nations could do better to deploy forces to crises more rapidly. Several foreign ministers, including me, have commented that the UN's tardiness in mounting an effective operation in Rwanda in time to halt the genocidal killings there twelve months ago has confronted us squarely with the need to reconsider the options, including the idea of a standing volunteer force. The proposals range from Dutch Foreign Minister Hans Van Mierlo's idea of a 'UN fire brigade'—a variation on a theme long advanced by Sir Brian Urquhart—to suggestions for enhanced standby arrangements put forward by the Secretary-General and the Danish Government. Canada is conducting an intensive study on how the UN's rapid deployment capacity could be improved which will cover early warning, integrated planning, logistics, command and control systems, doctrine and interoperability.

My own instinct on all this, after devoting many hours of discussion to the subject around Europe and in New York and Washington in recent months, is that it would make most sense in the immediate future for us all to concentrate our efforts on building the UN's headquarters capacity—to enable it to conceptualise operations better, construct their mandates, plan and organise them, and rapidly set them in train on the ground. More professional oversight and support is necessary at both the strategic and operational level. Although a great deal has been done to improve that capacity in recent times there are still major inadequacies, both quantitative and qualitative. I believe that if member states had more confidence in the role and competence of the headquarters military general staff, then the 'stand by' option would be likely to be much more effectively utilised in practice, and there would be less need to pursue what increasingly seems like the will-o'-the-wisp of a standing volunteer force. The UN's standby arrangements, to which New Zealand has signed up and Australia has also recently agreed, is a useful tool to assist the UN's planning of peacekeeping operations without ceding member states' autonomy of decision-making or affecting the way they structure their defence forces.

Enforcing Peace

We have seen the problems caused when peacekeeping operations, which are premised upon the consent of the parties to the UN's presence and should be inherently peaceful, are mixed with peace-enforcement missions which presume resistance by one or more of the parties and are mandated to apply whatever force is needed to meet the operation's objectives.

The use of force in peace operations was the subject of a recent workshop in Stockholm held jointly by the Stockholm International Peace Research Institute (SIPRI) and the Australian Department of Foreign Affairs and Trade. It was attended by a group of former and current UN Force Commanders, academics and policy makers, and Lt. Gen. Sanderson and I represented Australia. The meeting's key conclusions were that there should be a sharp distinction—in mandates, force levels and command and control arrangements—between Chapter VI and Chapter VII operations; that 'mixed' mandates should be avoided; and that, in certain situations, the UN Security Council should consider authorising operations under Chapter VII which fall short of unrestrained use of force but give force commanders scope for resort to force beyond the confines of self-defence and defence of the mission.

Most participants argued that there is no continuum between peacekeeping operations (that is, those that have evolved under Chapter VI of the Charter—to do with the 'pacific settlement of disputes') and enforcement operations under Chapter VII—certain provisions of which authorise use of force. As Lt. Gen. Sanderson has said, peacekeepers, as opposed to peace enforcers, are 'instruments of diplomacy, not war'. In peacekeeping operations there is a need to maintain consent and acceptance of the process. The UN Secretary-General commented in his supplement to *An Agenda for Peace* of January this year that the experiences of the last few years have confirmed the importance of some basic principles of peacekeeping: consent of the parties, impartiality of the peacekeepers and the non-use of force except in self-defence. Use of force other than in self-defence—or in some instances, perhaps, defence of the operation's mandate—runs the risk of forfeiting the consent of the parties and compromising the neutrality of the peacekeepers.

There is also the need for an unambiguous legal basis for peace operations, including any authority to use force. Consent should be made concrete wherever possible through specific host agreements and, in the case of intra-state conflicts, by the express commitment of all sides—to the maximum extent possible—to the UN's presence. Consent of the parties to the conflict to the UN's role is a precondition for the success of a peacekeeping operation: 'operational consent' is the dividing line between operating under Chapter VI and Chapter VII. Peacekeeping personnel should not be converted to peace enforcers. At the very least, any attempt to change the mandate of a peacekeeping operation to enforcement requires a significant period of transition, in which forces could be retrained or substituted.

The experiences of the United Nations in Somalia and Bosnia have raised the question of whether traditional ideas of peacekeeping are appropriate. It has been argued that the notion that there are no options between consent-based peacekeeping and waging war puts the United Nations and the international community in the untenable position of having no viable response in such situations. According to this line of argument, there should be an option short of peace enforcement whereby a multinational force could operate without operational consent and with the option of resort to force (albeit wherever possible using non-forceful means) authorised by the Security Council acting under relevant provisions of Chapter VII.

The purpose of such operations would be to shape an environment in which consent-based operations would be possible. I would argue, however, that it is preferable to establish a Chapter VII mandate from the outset, or in response to loss of 'operational consent', rather than tack elements of Chapter VII enforcement authority onto a Chapter VI operation. I fully recognise the organisational and other limitations on the United Nations acting as the strategic headquarters for Chapter VII operations, but it is better to be clear from the start about what the international community proposes to undertake—so if it lacks the will and resources, it will not take on tasks that the United Nations is not capable of carrying out.

Conclusion

I am realistic enough to accept that many of the problems the United Nations faces in ensuring peace cannot be solved in the short term. The international community has probably still not fully grasped the magnitude of these difficulties, and is not ready for the hard decisions it will need to make. This is in part due to the increasingly isolationist mood of the US Congress since the elections last November, which quite clearly swung away from support for UN reform. But we cannot allow the difficulty of achieving everything to prevent us from trying to do anything. The first step is simply to achieve recognition of the problem, and to get consensus on what is to be done. That in itself will be a huge advance.

UN peacekeepers engaged in conversation with locals, Somalia, 1993.
(Photo: Australian Defence Force)

Jacob Bercovitch

The United Nations and the Mediation of International Disputes

Only a few years ago it seemed that the widespread euphoria which greeted the end of the Cold War and the demise of communism was going to invigorate the UN system and enhance its role in executing its central function; that of maintaining international peace and security and dealing with threats to peace. Initial success in ending the fighting between Iran and Iraq, and facilitating the withdrawal of Soviet forces from Afghanistan, created an optimistic perception about the continuing and increasing relevance of the United Nations in meeting the challenge of creating order in an anarchic system of states, all of whom still jealously guard their sovereignty and freedom of action.

Such was the feeling in the heady days of 1989–90 that President George Bush was able, in his address to Congress on 11 September 1990, to talk of a 'new world order struggling to be born, a world quite different from the one we have known, a world where the rule of law supplants the rule of the jungle'.[1] The group of seven industrialised states (G-7), not to be outdone, issued a declaration on 16 July 1991 which stated that 'the conditions now exist for the United Nations to fulfil completely the promise and vision of its founders. A revitalised United Nations will have a central role in strengthening the international order'. It seemed then that the international momentum towards peace and stability could not but gather further pace.

The initial optimism regarding the birth of a new United Nations quickly proved to be misplaced. Subsequent UN efforts at dealing with an increasing number of brutal conflicts seemed quixotic at best, and palpably irrelevant at worst. The dream of an effective international organisation mediating conflicts, ending wars and producing settlements may be deferred for a while longer. As the UN enters its 51st year, it seems time to take stock of how to make the organisation

1   *Weekly Compilation of Presidential Documents* 26(37), 17 September 1990.

more effective, and how best it can respond to the myriad of problems brought about by the changes in the pattern of international relations. Where are we then on the anniversary of the United Nations? Right now there is much confusion and uncertainty about the United Nations and little public support of it. Many are prepared to stamp an icon of failure on the organisation. The ad hoc response to the conflicts in Bosnia, Croatia and Somalia, and the failure to avoid tragedy in Chechnya, generated a wave of public disappointment with the United Nations and raised questions about its continued relevance in a hostile and anarchic environment of states.

The purpose of this paper is to assess the strengths and weaknesses of the United Nations as a mediator of international conflicts in the post-Cold War era. Such an assessment can only take place within a wider structural framework, and against the background of two dominant trends: a strong demand and burgeoning expectations for the United Nations to take a more useful role in responding to international conflicts; and a widespread disappointment and reluctance to support an effective and autonomous United Nations.

The Changing Nature of Conflict

For more than four decades the Cold War cast a heavy shadow over any multilateral attempt to manage or resolve international conflicts. Regional conflicts in most parts of the world were seen as reflection of the rivalry between the superpowers. No state or organisation was going to risk a major confrontation between the US and the Soviet Union, so most serious conflicts were dealt with by direct negotiations, arms control arrangements or were simply allowed to simmer for many years. An international organisation such as the UN could only act as a third party in a conflict when neither of the great powers had any interest in the conflict (and there were few areas where neither had, nor claimed to have, an interest). Most of these conflicts took on a life of their own and resisted any attempts at resolution.

Most international conflict from 1945–89 was of the traditional interstate kind resulting from incompatible interests over economic, military or territorial issues. The overwhelming majority of conflict in the period took place between Third World countries where the great powers had been involved on opposite sides and often encouraged and supported the continuation of a conflict. These conflicts were exacerbated by the ideological divide that for decades gave rise to so much distrust and hostility and prevented any effective international steps from being taken. Bipolarity, a system of competing alliances, a strategy of deterrence and an overwhelming desire to win at the expense of the other side maintained a precarious semblance of world order.

The Cold War system of international relations was just plainly inhospitable to any serious attempts at conflict resolution. It was a system based on the assumption that all politics, domestic as well as international, is essentially a struggle for power. The Hobbesian vision of pernicious individuals and wicked states, all motivated by insecurity and a desire to prevail over their opponents, exercised a powerful image on decision-makers in Moscow and Washington. In such a system a global organisation dedicated to the pursuit of peace and security through non-violent means could not but be highly marginal.

All this has changed since 1989. The pent-up violence unleashed by the dissolution of the Soviet Union created anything but a more secure world. The dream of 'the end of history' turned somewhat sour. The new pattern of conflict occurred typically within a state. Of the 33 major conflicts that occurred in 1992, only one was an interstate conflict, and all the 34 major conflicts that occurred in 1993 were intra-state conflicts.[2]

Intra-state conflicts are mostly ethnic or religious in character. They usually entail high human costs, much of it borne by the civilian population. They have dire consequences, they are fought by non-traditional means, they are usually protracted, and can only be resolved by concerted action and the consent of the parties. Techniques of power and deterrence are plainly inapplicable where ethnic groups and other minorities wish to assert their basic needs and give expression to their collective will. Different strategies of conflict management and accommodation between the interests of ethnic groups and their states have to be devised if conflicts, of the sort we have had recently in Ethiopia, Somalia, Iraq, Sri Lanka and others, are to be transformed peacefully while promoting the collective interests of those involved. The shift from interstate to intra-state conflict raised expectations about a more significant, and innovative, conflict management role for the United Nations in the 'new era of cooperation'.

The withering away of the Cold War and the proliferation of ethnic–communal conflicts have created an entirely new international environment; an environment where the tasks of conflict management

2   Peter Wallensteen and Karin Axell, 'Major armed conflicts', *SIPRI Yearbook 1994* (Oxford: Oxford University Press for the Stockholm International Peace Research Institute, 1994), p. 81.

have become more complex, more diverse and more urgent. If conflict management, by states or the international community, is to succeed, it must be part of a coherent plan. One cannot respond to conflicts in an ad hoc manner, nor move from one conflict situation to another through fits and starts. Ill-fated responses to conflict, or publicised acts of ill thought out peacekeeping operations, produce not only policy reversals, but in addition do considerable damage to the institutions of the international community. Consistent and effective policies require a framework to suggest when the international community, operating through the United Nations, should respond to conflict and determine the appropriate responses.

Defining Possible Responses to Conflict

Basically one can respond to any conflict situation in three quite different ways: through the use of violence, force and coercion; by direct or indirect negotiations between those involved; and through the involvement of a third party.[3] These approaches are of course quite distinct; each suits different circumstances and each leads to different outcomes. Clearly, the least preferred response is that of violence and coercion.

Another possible framework for thinking about the response to conflict is suggested by Gareth Evans.[4] He suggests four possible responses to conflict: peace-building strategies, such as economic development and institution building; peace-maintenance strategies, such as the range of methods outlined in Article 33 of the UN Charter; peace-restoration strategies, for example traditional peacekeeping activities to assist the parties in the implementation of an agreement; and peace-enforcement strategies, for example sanctions. Each conflict should ideally be matched with a different response.

In examining the range of possible responses to conflict situations, we can do no better than adopt the ideas and terminology of the Secretary-General's *Agenda for Peace*.[5] In that document, which generated considerable discussion and offered many useful sug-

---

3   Jacob Bercovitch, 'International Mediation: A Study of the Incidence, Strategies and Conditions of Successful Outcomes', *Cooperation and Conflict* 21 (July 1986), pp. 2155–68.

4   Gareth Evans, *Cooperating for Peace: The Global Agenda for the 1990s and Beyond* (Sydney: Allen & Unwin, 1993).

5   Boutros Boutros-Ghali, *An Agenda for Peace: Preventive Diplomacy, Peacemaking, and Peace-keeping* (New York: United Nations, 1992).

gestions, the then newly installed Secretary-General framed the debate—both conceptually and practically—on possible responses to conflict, especially as they affect the United Nations. It remains the most ambitious document in defining the UN role in resolving conflicts in the post-Cold War era.

The focus of the document is on international responses to, or interventions in, conflict situations. The term intervention here suggests that we are talking about an organisation, or a party, that is external to the conflict, but that, for a variety of reasons, is expected, asked or invited to do something about the conflict, lest it threaten international peace and security. An intervention by an outsider, or a third party, may be coercive and binding, or non-coercive and facilitative. It may range from using an emissary to convey information, to the dispatch of UN troops. In between there is a whole spectrum of possible actions by a third party to influence the behaviour of those in conflict. Conceptual clarity, when speaking of international responses to conflict, is a prerequisite if such responses are to be effective.

Whichever response to conflict is undertaken, at the micro or macro level, the main objective is to achieve an effective conflict management. By this we mean:

1. To prevent the spread or escalation of conflict;
2. To achieve an early resolution of the conflict;
3. To minimise human suffering; and
4. To uphold international law and norms.

These objectives are as relevant to the international community as they are for individuals or groups. Clarity of objectives together with an understanding of the range of responses can lead to the development of more effective politics of conflict management.

Multilateral responses to conflict can be divided into four main categories. They are: preventive diplomacy; peacemaking; peace-keeping; and peace-building. Each response represents a distinct category of intervention in conflict situations. Each may be suitable for different circumstances, though each should ideally build on the work of the other. Let us examine each in brief.

Preventive Diplomacy

Preventive diplomacy refers to the development of effective international policies for the prevention of conflict. Once a conflict has escalated, opinions harden, loss of life is experienced, and the difficulty of resolving the conflict increases immensely. When that happens, the international community may face the prospect of inaction or costly intervention with further loss of life.

Preventing conflict is undoubtedly the most desirable, efficient and cost-effective policy for the international community. Policies of conflict prevention are activated when a potential crisis threatens to explode into an armed conflict. A variety of policies and tools may be used by the international community to resolve conflict at an early stage of their evolution. These include:

- Mediation;
- Fact-finding;
- Official or non-official diplomatic missions;
- Monitoring individual and minority group rights and reporting violations to the United Nations;
- Encouraging confidence-building measures to alleviate reciprocal fears;
- The preventive deployment, with the consent of the states involved, of an international military force; and
- The development of a network of early warning systems to warn the international community of impending environmental threats, abuses of human rights, nuclear risks, or the spread of disease or natural disaster.

Peacemaking

Peacemaking is related to preventive diplomacy, but is applied *after* a dispute has turned into an armed conflict. It represents an attempt by the international community to bring hostile parties to an agreement by peaceful means. The main thrust of this kind of response is to get parties engaged in armed conflict to use alternative tools of conflict management. These tools are set out in Article 33 of the UN Charter which asks parties to a conflict to 'seek a solution by negotiation, enquiry, mediation, conciliation, arbitration, judicial settlements, resort to regional agencies or arrangements, or other peaceful means of their own choice'.

Although the United Nations has had wide experience with peacemaking activities, its track record in this area was, for many years, lacklustre at best. *An Agenda for Peace* called for a revamp of UN peacemaking efforts by using such efforts in tandem with preventive diplomacy and peace-building, and developing machinery for the early referral of conflicts to the United Nations. A revived United Nations can utilise peacemaking tools to bring about cessation of hostilities, and, when this has been achieved, to secure a long-term settlement.

Peacekeeping

Peacekeeping responses to conflict have been the most numerous and visible manifestation of the UN engagement in conflict situations. Peacekeeping has developed on an ad hoc basis, and represents an innovative form of multilateral international action in which the United Nations, acting as an impartial third party, undertakes, with the consent of the parties to a conflict, the deployment of multinational military or civilian forces to assist in the settlement of a conflict between two or more parties. Peacekeeping is used to prevent the resumption of conflict, contain conflicts, facilitate troop withdrawals, verify and supervise a ceasefire, and generally act as a physical barrier against further conflict.

Of the possible international community's responses to conflict, peacekeeping has undoubtedly been the most costly and controversial. Peacekeeping operations may involve only a few lightly armed soldiers engaged in monitoring or verifying a ceasefire or other arrangement, or they may involve a much larger contingent of military personnel and civilian administrators, all engaged in trying to create the conditions for order, stability and conflict resolution. In 1994 the United Nations had more than 75,000 troops deployed in peacekeeping operations throughout the world, at a cost to the organisation of almost US $4 billion (see Table 1.1 above).

Wherever it occurs, the deployment of military personnel in a peacekeeping role constitutes a multilateral response to, or intervention in, conflict that can best succeed if the role and objectives of intervention are clearly articulated, and if such intervention is undertaken as part of a broader approach to conflict management. Peacekeeping *must* include elements of peacemaking and peace-building.

Peace-building

The fourth possible international response to conflict is that of peace-building. Here the emphasis is on post-conflict interventions and on policies and practices that prevent the recurrence of hostilities, and the focus is on economic development and institution building, co-operative projects, promoting efforts to protect human rights, and reforming and strengthening government institutions. Peace-building is designed to ensure that a settled conflict will not again relapse into an armed clash. If peace-building policies are not pursued with vigour, a conflict may re-emerge with even more tragic consequences, as in Angola.

A number of specific peace-building policies for strengthening and solidifying peace and rebuilding the infrastructure and institutions of nations torn by conflict can be envisaged. These may include policies of long-term mediation to deal with the underlying political issues in conflict, the deployment of a military force to prevent a return to violence, encouraging strategies of arms control and demobilisation, channelling economic aid and development and linking it to continuous cooperative behaviour, and providing training and resources for the local people to take on political and administrative roles.

All these possible responses to conflict are separate, but in many ways interdependent and complementary. It would be naive to assume that peacekeeping and peace-building strategies do not complement each other, and together provide a comprehensive range of responses to any given conflict situation. Central to the initiation of a successful response is an understanding of an agreed objective, a definition of a coherent policy, and the choice of policy instruments that are most likely to succeed in that conflict situation. If we have learnt anything from the recent ad hoc use of different responses by the United Nations, it is that we need to be clear about our objectives, recognise the nature of our response to conflict, accept the costs involved, but also appreciate the limitations of different policies and responses.

International Mediation and the United Nations

One of the most effective and least costly multilateral responses to conflict is that of mediation. As a tool of conflict management, mediation is the only strategy that may be used as a part of an overall strategy of preventive diplomacy, peacemaking, peacekeeping or peace-building. Its voluntary and diplomatic nature, non-coercive character, and reliance on impartiality and the parties' consent, mean that mediation can be, in many ways, an ideal response to conflict by the international community. To what extent, then, has the United Nations been an effective mediator of international conflicts?

To start with we must recognise that the practice of settling disputes through intermediaries is universal and timeless, with a rich history in all cultures, both Western and non-Western.[6] In the international arena—with its perennial challenges of escalating conflicts, an anarchical society, and the absence of generally accepted 'rules of the game'—third-party mediation is about as common as conflict itself. As a form of multilateral conflict management, third-party mediation is particularly likely to take place when:

a. Disputes are long, drawn out and complex;
b. The disputants' own conflict management efforts have reached an impasse;
c. Neither side is prepared to countenance further costs or escalation of the dispute; and
d. The disputants are prepared to break their stalemate by co-operating with each other and engaging in some contact and communication.[7]

All these conditions apply to the new breed of conflicts we have been experiencing since 1989.

Mediation, the most common form of third-party intervention, is not a single discrete activity. Rather, it is a continuous process that falls on a spectrum of behaviour ranging from highly passive (e.g., go-between) to highly active (e.g., putting pressure on disputants). The form and character of mediation in a particular international dispute are determined by many factors, including the nature of the dispute, the nature of the mediator, and a number of other cultural and contextual variables. In this paper, mediation is broadly defined as a process of conflict management where disputants seek the assistance of, or accept an offer of help from, an individual, group, or organisation to settle their conflict or resolve their basic differences without resorting to physical force or invoking the authority of the law.

Mediation by the United Nations (in effect a UN representative) may denote a form of activity which includes the facilitation of communication, for example Gunnar Jarring's mediation in the Arab–Israeli conflict in 1967–68. Or it may go beyond that and involve the drafting and promotion of specific plans for conflict resolution, for

6   P. H. Gulliver, *Disputes and Negotiations* (New York: Academic Press, 1979).
7   Jacob Bercovitch, *Social Conflict and Third Parties* (Boulder: Westview, 1984).

example Count Folk Bernadotte's plans for settling the Arab-Israeli conflict in 1947. In most conflicts mediators may perform basic service functions (e.g. acting as a channel of communication) or more substantive functions (e.g. guiding the parties towards a settlement). Given the dynamics of any conflict situation, and the changing circumstances of each mediation, it seems appropriate to examine how each mediation *event* unfolds, rather than stipulate and discuss a mediation *role*. In particular, we wish to examine the conditions that are conducive to successful mediation.

To appreciate the effectiveness and limitations of the United Nations as a mediator in international conflict, we need to shift our focus slightly and undertake a quantitative analysis of the correlates of success and failure of United Nations mediation. In what follows I utilise a unique data set, developed over the last decade or so, which contains more than 1500 different mediation events since 1945. Each mediation event was coded for many contextual features such as time, intensity, power, and so on, so that we have as complete a picture of each mediation as we are likely to get.

As to the consequences or outcomes of these mediations, I define those mediation efforts as successful that demonstrably contributed to a cessation or reduction of violence, the signing of an agreement or the settlement of a conflict. I define mediations which had no impact at all on the conflict as unsuccessful. Others may define success differently, but for our purposes these definitions serve a useful function. In Table 5.1 I provide information on the mediation behaviour of various actors in international relations and their relative degree of success.

Table 5.1: Mediators and their Effectiveness				
Mediators	*Number of mediations*	*Percent of total*	*Successful mediation* Number	Percent
Individual	55	3.6	16	29
Regional organisations	174	11.3	78	44
United Nations	355	23.1	127	35
NGOs	97	6.3	25	25
State	722	46.9	244	33
Mixed	135	8.8	54	40
Total	1538	100	544	

To observe that the UN has had a positive impact (which I define as success) at all in over a third of its mediation efforts may, at first sight, not inspire much hope in the international community's ability to mediate complex conflicts. Further explorations may well reveal that such perceptions are not fully warranted. The correlates of success and failure of UN mediation may have more to do with the kind of conflicts it is asked to mediate than with its own shortcomings.

Contextual Factors

The United Nations is often asked to mediate conflict as a last resort, when all other efforts have failed. To blame the UN for failing to resolve what is apparently an intractable or insoluble conflict may seem less than fair. In examining our universe of cases, we find that most UN mediation efforts took place between two states with a previous history of antagonism, or states that had already experienced one or two conflicts in the past (295 cases out of 355 mediations by the United Nations were in this category). Mediation between states with a previous history of conflict is as unlikely to accomplish anything significant as any other conflict management strategy.

Furthermore, many of the recent conflicts which the United Nations has been asked to mediate, such as Haiti, Somalia, the former Yugoslavia, Rwanda, Liberia, Nagorno–Karabakh and others, involve societies that are deeply disunited, with no recognised leadership and with competing claims to authoritative decision-making. Disunity, or lack of cohesion, which are so typical of the new breed of ethnic conflicts, make any attempt at mediation a precarious effort at best.[8] Thus, while most actors in international relations shy away from such conflicts, the United Nations is saddled with the task of managing them. That its record in dealing with such conflicts is so poor may have as much to do with the intractable nature of the conflict as with the behaviour and performance of the United Nations.

Pursuing mediation through the United Nations or any other organisation requires that mediation be initiated at a propitious moment. Recognising what precisely constitutes a propitious moment may be somewhat difficult in practice, but there is a growing body of opinion which claims that mediation is more likely to succeed if it is

8   D. Frei, 'Factors Affecting the Effectiveness of International Mediation', *Peace Science Society (International) Papers* 26 (October 1976), pp. 67–84.

attempted at an early stage in the conflict.[9] Once a conflict has been in existence for some time, human losses may be incurred, attitudes are hardened, each party's position becomes more entrenched, and their disposition to win at all costs rather than settle becomes more pronounced. The longer a conflict goes on, the more will mediation's chances be hindered.

A glance at the UN record of mediation reveals that most UN mediations are initiated once a conflict has been in existence for three years or more (203 cases out of 355). By the time a conflict is submitted to the United Nations it may well have spread and escalated beyond the capacity of any conflict manager. When states will not mediate on their own, but will instead wait and see how costly a conflict may become, and which way will it evolve, and only then expect the United Nations to come in and clean up the mess, it is hard to explain the outcome as a failure of UN mediation.

Closely related to conflict duration is the notion of conflict intensity. Any discussion on the relative success or failure of the United Nations in conflict management must take note of the fact that intense conflicts are more difficult to manage.[10] A number of dimensions, both 'objective' and 'subjective', may be used to assess conflict intensity. Here I have chosen two 'objective' dimensions and combined them into a measure of intensity. The two dimensions are the presence of actual violence, and the number of fatalities suffered by each party.

Initiating and pursuing mediation through the United Nations, or any other international actor, while hostilities actually take place, or conflicts are escalating, carries serious disadvantages. We find that fully 234 (out of 355) cases of UN mediation were undertaken when military confrontation took place between the parties. We also find that over 70 percent (253) of all UN mediation efforts were undertaken in conflicts where the level of fatalities exceeded 10,000 people. It is somewhat surprising that the organisation, which is used by states as a last-ditch, last resort, should be blamed for failing to manage the most intractable of conflicts that have been found to be insoluble by states. When conflicts are deadly, when hostilities escalate and spread widely, the disputing parties may be wary of mediation or any other

9   F. Edmead, *Analysis and Prediction in International Mediation* (New York: UN Institute for Training and Research, 1971).

10   F. Northedge and M. Donelan, *International Disputes: The Political Aspects* (London: Europa, 1971).

opportunities to participate in conflict management.

There is general agreement in the literature that the success or failure of conflict management and mediation is largely determined by the nature of the issue in conflict.[11] Clearly, where issues of vital interests are involved, the likelihood of a successful third-party intervention is quite limited. What precisely do we mean by 'issues' in conflict, and how can the relationship between issues and successful outcomes be unravelled?

Issues refer to the underlying causes of a conflict. Although they may not always be clear, it has become customary to divide issues in conflicts into issues of sovereignty, ideology, independence (or decolonisation), territory, Cold War issues, and internal conflict issues. When we examine the record of the United Nations in conflict, we find that nearly a third (116 attempts) of all UN mediations took place in decolonisation conflicts, where they had a success rate of just over 45 percent. Seventy-four UN mediation attempts (22 percent of the total) involved Cold War issues, and here the overall success rate was only 24 percent. Sixty-three UN mediations took place in conflicts where the main issue was internal, and here their overall success rate was just 21 percent.

The United Nations is capable of intervening in, and managing, conflicts that do not involve Cold War issues, or internal (ethnic) issues. The global division into two superpowers, each determined to forestall any interference with its own affairs, and the emergence of ethnicity as a major conflict issue in the last few years, have both had serious implications for the UN's capacity to manage international conflicts. With other issues, such as decolonisation, the United Nations has had an impressive record of dealing with conflict.

Organisational Factors

For any mediator to use their good offices, they must be seen as impartial, acceptable, legitimate and credible. These attributes are undoubtedly associated with the United Nations. To achieve success in mediation, however, a mediator needs to persuade each party to change its image of the adversary, or influence both parties to modify their position. All too often we emphasise the first set of attributes, but tend to forget that the essence of mediation is to create, or bring about,

---

11   Robert F. Randle, *The Origins of Peace: A Study of Peacemaking and the Structure of Peace Settlements* (New York: Free Press, 1973).

change, to influence, persuade and to induce a change in motivations. To engage in such behaviour requires resources or some leverage.

Some of the UN leverage derives from its institutional standing and the kind of norms it exemplifies, but beyond that UN mediation is hampered considerably by lack of resources. The UN has no readily accessible resources of its own. It is dependent on the goodwill of its members in every respect. Whereas states might use financial credits, economic promises or diplomatic gestures to change parties' positions and induce cooperation, the UN has no resources to pool behind its mediation efforts. It can offer no promises, nor make any threats. Its only resource is its aura of legitimacy, and that may not always be perceived as a sufficiently strong asset by the disputing parties.

Mediation, and other aspects of international conflict management, are pursued in a dynamic environment, where success is achieved when mediators have the necessary flexibility to make quick decisions and utilise resources to change positions as the situation unfolds. The United Nations, with its many layers of bureaucracy, and the need to gain empowerment from various states and to build up a strong consensus, has the most cumbersome machinery for decision-making. When decisions are finally reached, they are likely to be hedged by too many qualifications or ambiguities. Such a structure, lacking coherence and direction, and bound by specific resolutions, does not lend itself to effective mediation.

In comparison with most states, the United Nations, like other inter-governmental organisations, is encumbered with slow decision-making procedures; it can change a course of action only gingerly; and it cannot harness any significant resources to be used as sticks and carrots in conflict management. Moreover, the independent latitude of action of the United Nations, and its ability to speak with one voice, are minimal at best. Such a body is not the most suited to perform mediatory functions. That the UN, with all its ingrained limitations and embedded difficulties, does after all have a far from lamentable record of success in dealing with some of the most intractable conflicts of all, is a tribute to the resilience of the organisation.

Conclusion

The United Nations is poised today between the Cold War and an embryonic new order—one of whose most visible characteristics is the proliferation of crises and conflicts that threaten the state from within. To achieve any degree of success (however one wishes to define it),

UN responses must be better defined and better integrated. Drifting from one response to another, being hindered by complex decision-making procedures, and an inability to commit even scant resources, often demonstrate the UN's less than successful experience in conflict management.

Rather than stumble from one chaotic experience to the next, the United Nations would do better to recognise that any successful response to conflict requires clarity of objectives, a guiding framework, and a matching of responses to different conflict situations. Responses to conflict should be part of an overall, coordinated and well-thought out series of steps. Before taking action, the United Nations must ask itself what is the nature of the conflict, how best to respond to it, and how should the response be implemented? Conceptual clarity, careful attention to a guiding framework, and training in conflict resolution, can help the United Nations to develop even more viable intervention strategies.

In this regard UN mediation may be seen as one of the most effective forms of intervention. It can be applied to most, but not all, conflicts; it can be part of a graduated and flexible response; it can be used as an aspect of preventive diplomacy, peacemaking, peace-keeping or peace-building; and it entails the minimum of costs. Multilateral mediation is not, however, a panacea for all the world's ills. It cannot deal effectively with the exploding power of ethno-nationalism, nor can it cure all intractable conflicts. And yet, these are precisely the kind of conflicts in which the United Nations is asked to intervene. For the UN the dilemma is stark; non-intervention could be even more perilous than a failed intervention.

If the United Nations can, as Touval suggests,[12] reallocate the task of mediation to its member states or regional organisations, and energise their efforts, rather than await patiently for a conflict to be submitted to it; if the United Nations could but be used more as an *actor* rather than merely as an *arena;* if the United Nations could mandate states to mediate, and support them when they do so: then the organisation may still, in the words of Dag Hammarskjöld, 'not take us to heaven, but save us from going to hell'.[13]

---

12   S. Touval, 'Why the U.N. Fails', *Foreign Affairs* 73 (September/October 1994), pp. 44–57.
13   Brian Urquhart, *Hammarskjöld* (London: Bodley Head, 1973), p. 27.

New Zealand army experts teaching mine-clearing techniques to a Cambodian soldier with the help of an interpreter. (Photo: Ministry of Foreign Affairs and Trade, New Zealand)

Reginald H. F. Austin

The Future of UN Peacekeeping Operations: Cosmetic or Comprehensive?

I am grateful for the opportunity to contribute to the discussion of the peacemaking role of the United Nations in the fiftieth anniversary of the organisation. For me, as a Zimbabwean, Otago has a particular relevance to my topic: it was from this part of New Zealand that Garfield and Edith Todd went to what was Southern Rhodesia. He has spent an inspiring lifetime there, working for first, the transformation from minority to non-racial government in what is now Zimbabwe, and still today, for democratic and accountable government.

It is worth recalling that the achievement of peace is in the first place an intensely personal, family and national responsibility. The tendency to shift this responsibility to the international community may be inevitable. Perhaps, as Professor Rosenau has suggested, on a 'path' from which we cannot, and should not, seek to escape. But we should also be conscious of the role which these more intimate units, the family and the nation, have to play, and the fact that sovereignty is still an important concomitant of responsibility. We need to be wary of the temptation to regard international wisdom and power as somehow superior, especially when it is visited upon weaker sovereigns by their stronger counterparts.

Awareness of this was seen as a very important aspect of the electoral project of the UN Transitional Authority in Cambodia (UNTAC). My first and repeated message, as Chief Electoral Officer, to the 80 odd Provincial Electoral Officials, the 420 UN Volunteers (UNVs) who served for the entire mission as the backbone of the international electoral machine throughout Cambodia, and to the 1000 International Polling Station Officers (IPSOs) deployed for the last three weeks of the operation was: be constantly aware that we were involving ourselves in the most intimate act of national politics—the choosing of Cambodia's constitution-makers and future governors. As such we had all to avoid being arrogant. We needed to act in accordance with the democratic principles we were 'bringing' to Cambodia, to demonstrate their supremacy over the arbitrary use of power, by practical example rather than arrogant assertion.

UNTAC, Peace and Democracy in Cambodia

The UNTAC-administered elections in Cambodia in May 1993, produced a clear result. The FUNCINPEC (the National United Front for an Independent, Neutral, Peaceful and Cooperative Cambodia) party led by Prince Norodom Ranariddh won 58 of the 120 seats in the Constituent Assembly with 45 percent of the votes in a provincially based proportional representation election. The former incumbent government in the State of Cambodia (SoC), the Cambodian People's Party (CPP) led by Hun Sen, gained a substantial minority, 51 seats and 38 percent of the votes. FUNCINPEC, in an alliance with the Khmer People's National Liberation Front (KPNLF), renamed for electoral politics, the Buddhist Liberal Democratic Party (BLDP), and the Party of Democratic Kampuchea (PDK)—often referred to as the Khmer Rouge—had fought a bitter civil war against the CPP since the early 1980s.

The election campaign turned out to be essentially a competition between FUNCINPEC and the CPP, in a campaign that was both orally and, especially on the part of the CPP, physically violent. As such, the CPP was the obvious candidate to become the Opposition in a Westminster system, if that were the constitutional model chosen by the Constituent Assembly. In the event the system of government was not chosen by the Assembly, but forced upon it before it commenced the democratic task which the electorate had delegated to it.

The BLDP had gained four percent of the votes and a small but strategically important block of 10 seats. It was predictable that FUNCINPEC would continue its alliance with its anti-communist ally should it wish eventually to form a government. It was however equally clear that a mutually agreeable constitution could be hammered out only on the basis of the active cooperation of these three elected parties. This was because the Paris Agreements which, with Security Council Resolutions, was the legal basis of the entire Cambodian Peace operation, provided that the adoption of the new constitution would require a two-thirds majority. This gave the CPP the necessary veto and bargaining position in the new democratic politics where votes rather than guns were to be the basis of power and compromise, to obtain a place for itself in the government. The Paris Agreements required that the government should be set up from the Assembly after the adoption of the constitution, and before UNTAC left Cambodia.

Thus a foundation for serious democratic politics seemed to have been laid, almost miraculously, by the UNTAC elections. The FUN-CINPEC victory was clear, but at the same time the former incumbent had by no means been humiliated at the polls and would be ideally placed to practice the art, previously unknown to Cambodia, of loyal opposition to a democratically elected government, which in time it might replace.

The desire for unity was generally regarded as vital for peace and the prospect of building democracy in Cambodia. The people had been subjected, under the Khmer Rouge regime, to a uniquely horrific form of internecine conflict amounting to auto-genocide. This had been followed by over a decade of war which saw the country divided into zones under the control of four separate factions. But the UNTAC presence, and in particular its military and electoral activities with the Cambodians, had reduced those divisions to two: those who agreed to follow a peaceful, democratic path to the future, (essentially the three major parties who committed themselves to and fought the electoral campaign), and the PDK which rejected the elections and maintained its right to seek victory through violence and the threat or use of arms. The PDK had seriously miscalculated the potential of the election process and had excluded itself from the new politics of Cambodia. This meant that the elected parties, whether majority or minority, now had a powerful common interest in making plural democratic government work and proving finally, and through their own rather than the UN's actions, that they rejected violence, murder and intimidation as the chosen instrument to gain or keep political power. In these circumstances, the prospect of a government of national unity (also a major stated aim of the acknowledged 'father of the nation' Prince Norodom Sihanouk) made possible by the bargaining position given to the CPP by the 'two-thirds' rule, and by 1993 a well tried tool in other post-conflict peace and nation building exercises, looked very good indeed.

Democracy Destabilised

The reality was to be otherwise. A Government of National Unity was indeed created. However, it was not the product of political compromise and negotiation in the context of respect for the principle that the democratic choice of the people of Cambodia was inviolable. Instead it was the result of a reversion to the worst of the Cambodian 'practices of the past': brute force and military intimidation. The new reality was that FUNCINPEC's electoral victory was first debased— in a matter of days after it was celebrated, certified and endorsed by the UN before the assembled world press and other international observers—from the clear and convincing result of an election which was palpably 'free and fair', to the discredited and dubious outcome of an electoral exercise of doubtful integrity; and then crudely amended to a 'draw' with the CPP.

The CPP had won fewer votes, but it had many more guns and troops at its disposal, and it was prepared, successfully as it turned out, to threaten and actually use them to overturn the result.

What made this reversal of democracy more remarkable, and also gave the impression that democracy and peace had been success-fully introduced to Cambodia, was that the entire process was sanc-tioned, and ultimately sanctified, by UNTAC itself. For this reason, if no other, the UNTAC operation in Cambodia deserves further atten-tion and analysis. This is all the more so because UNTAC has been described by the UN Secretary-General as a flagship and model for future UN comprehensive peacemaking operations:

> The United Nations is leading the way into a new era. To the role of peace-keeping as created and defined by the world organisation during the Cold War decades have been added vast new responsibilites in peace operations. In this second generation of peacekeeping every mission is unique, yet each has in common a greater scale, more extensive civilian participation, and a far more comprehensive approach to address the problems which at times afflict an entire society and state. The United Nations mission in Cambodia over the past few years has served as the flag-ship for the UN-led voyage to the future.[1]

The point might be made, quite fairly, that the task of making peace in Cambodia in the 14 months between March 1992 and October 1993 is not to be equated with implanting even the begin-nings of democracy there. The validity of that argument needs to be considered in the light of the following observations.

First, the Paris Agreements adopted by the Security Council

1   Boutros Boutros-Ghali, 'Message to the Institute of Policy Studies/UNITAR Conference on UNTAC: Debriefing and Lessons', Singapore, 2–4 August 1994 (Geneva: UN Institute for Training and Research, 1995).

purported to offer, specifically, a comprehensive settlement to the violence which had plagued Cambodia for decades. The centrepiece of the solution was democracy, and the most fundamental expression of that idea, brought at enormous trouble and expense for every Cambodian to see and experience, was an election process, in all its stages, which should serve them as a model. That was what the ordinary Cambodian expected of the UN, however imperfectly she or he understood the concept. Democratic government based upon respect for the integrity of the secret vote of ordinary citizens would replace totalitarian, authoritarian rule based upon terror and fire-power. Thus democracy, in that basic sense, was integral to the peacemaking for Cambodia as seen by both the international community and the people of Cambodia.

Second, and more generally, the concept of comprehensive peacemaking had achieved a considerable history and a recognisable and substantial meaning by 1992. It involves typically, as was the case in Cambodia: ceasefire monitoring, troop cantonment, disarmament and demobilisation, followed by the international supervision of, monitoring of, or uniquely to Cambodia, the UN actually legislating for and wholly implementing, a credible democratic election. The objective of these 'comprehensive' peace/electoral exercises, going back to their origins in the decolonising plebiscites conducted by the UN and developed through experiences such as those which helped to end the conflicts in Zimbabwe, Nicaragua and Namibia, has not been merely to provide 'a catalyst for the attainment of democracy'. Rather, it has been to provide a real model and foundation for a new direction in government, that new direction being specifically democratic. This objective requires not only that the UN should act consistently with the democratic ideal it purports to be promoting, but that it takes the comprehensive dimension of the task seriously.

Comprehensive or Cosmetic Peace?

In both regards the UNTAC operation was imperfect. The management of the electoral process, as will be argued below, was often distorted by short-term political considerations, culminating in UNTAC's readiness to question the essential credibility of its own election to avoid a political confrontation. This has meant that the UN model of a 'free election' will now have as little to do with the normal understanding of this term as the UN 'safe havens' have been shown to do with safety. But this tendency to choose short-term or cosmetic solutions is connected with the problem of taking the comprehensive task seriously. As has been spelt out elsewhere, the various critical preparatory tasks—the ceasefire, cantonment, disarmament and demobilisation of the armies; the controlling of the arbitrary use of civilian power; the establishment of a minimum human rights regime and a credible start to rehabilitation and reconstruction—were not achieved by UNTAC. The operation was reduced to a one-dimensional effort to hold an election, as if that alone could bring peace.

This is not to argue that an election can only be held in circumstances of perfect stability. 'Peace Elections' are almost inevitably conducted in imperfect, risky and insecure situations. The point is that there must be a more comprehensive commitment, preferably before and after the election, to support for democracy. 'Instant democracy', on the basis of an election alone, is unlikely to last.

UNTAC was a first in many ways, and it is no surprise that it was less than perfect. But it is vital that the imperfections are not glossed over, or worse, presented as models for the future. The purpose of this paper is:

1. To revisit, and draw some lessons from earlier efforts at peacemaking; and
2. To note and discuss some of those aspects of UNTAC's activities in Cambodia which might be avoided in future comparable, though inevitably different, exercises. It comes, without apology, from the perspective of one who has been involved, personally, politically and professionally, with the difficult task of achieving workable and sustainable democratic government through credible elections, in post-civil conflict or post-one party government situations. One is aware that the task of comprehensive peacemaking, which has in the past been exclusively and often imperfectly undertaken by sovereign states, is being increasingly thrust upon international organisations. As such it is a learning, as well as a 'doing' process. The dangers of this novel situation are considerable, which makes it the more necessary to confront rather than avoid the problems as they emerge.

The New Dimensions of Peacemaking

As the Secretary-General stressed, the scope of peacekeeping has clearly expanded since the earliest UN operations were set up to deal with inter-state conflicts. It is obvious that sustainable peace rather than band-aid, fire-fighting action is what is needed, at both national and international levels. The objective must be to create a peace which will survive the withdrawal of the peacekeepers, to put in place solutions and institutions which will discourage and eventually override the 'known disposition' of humanity to war. Thus peace-keeping must of necessity include peacemaking and peace-building. Substantial democracy is now generally recognised as being a fundamental means of achieving such a peace.

It is also observable that in today's world most conflicts take place within, rather than between, states. This emphasises the role of democracy in achieving peace because, it is argued, democracy assists both the avoidance and the resolution of internal conflicts and contradictions. It also makes clear that contemporary peacekeeping is concerned with internal political, legal, electoral, administrative, economic, developmental and reconstructive problems. This was demonstrated in the international community's involvement in Rhodesia/Zimbabwe (a particularly Commonwealth concern in its final phase), in Namibia, in Cambodia, and is likely to be important in the outstanding issues of Western Sahara, Liberia, Angola and the various other conflicts awaiting resolution. Peace is no longer a condition brought about by the force or threat of arms: 'Military force—especially when wielded by an outside power—cannot bring order in a country that cannot govern itself'. To those words of Robert McNamara [in his memoirs *In Retrospect* (1995)], based upon bitter experience, should one add, after the word 'govern', the word 'properly' or, even better, 'democratically'?

Preventive Peacekeeping

The need for managing transition within states while reducing the risk of conflict, rather than merely ending it, is another clear contemporary need involving peacemaking and peace-building. This has been the case in a range of situations, such as moving from minority government to majority rule in South Africa or from one party dictatorship to democracy in Malawi. It may be called for in other circumstances, including ending military or unrepresentative regimes resulting from *coups d'état*.

In addition there must be a readiness on the part of the international community to assist states in carrying out their responsibility for building and maintaining sustainable democratic institutions. This

means capacity-building in all areas of government and administration, reinforcing common political principles, supporting economic
development, including the softening of the social rigours of
economic structural adjustment programmes and, where necessary,
assistance in reconstruction to cure the ravages, not of war, but of
consistent under-development. For these preemptive tasks the UN
system is well equipped with specialised agencies from the Bretton
Woods institutions, through the UN Development Programme
(UNDP) to the UN High Commissioner for Refugees (UNHCR).
Other institutions such as the Commonwealth are similarly, if less
richly, endowed but enjoy alternative comparative advantages. It is
not clear, however, whether they are all sufficiently aware of their
potential for ensuring peace by acting before conflict or full-scale
war breaks out.

Whether peacekeeping operations are post-conflict, pre-conflict
or needed to manage transitional situations in order to avoid conflict,
they will almost inevitably be comprehensive. Thus they require a
capacity to provide a secure environment in which the ceasefire,
cantonment, disarmament and demobilisation can take place. They
may also need a capacity to manage the return and resettlement of
refugees, supervise or execute all phases of an election, establish a
minimum level of respect for human rights, ensure the existence of a
basic judicial and policing system subject to the rule of law, the
foundation of a civil administration which provides objective government and, probably, the essential elements for economic development
and reconstruction. There will be considerable variation in this menu,
so for example in Cambodia and other post-civil war situations, there
was a desperate need for mine clearance as a first step towards
reconstruction and development.

A Culture of Learning

This raises immediate questions regarding the most suitable
international organisation to carry out these tasks. Should the UN be
regarded as the sole body responsible for such activities? Should the
burden be shared, in which case with whom? One aspect of this
relates to evaluation of the activities undertaken thus far by the UN.
There has been a notable absence of rigorous post-mission analysis
and evaluation or, when this has happened, of readiness to publish
and learn from experience. The first attempt at a comprehensive
evaluation of UNTAC only took place as a combined initiative of

UNITAR (UN Institute for Training and Research) and the Singapore Institute of Strategic Studies over a year after the mission.

UNTAC has been the only comprehensive peacekeeping operation to date, which makes it imperative to learn from it. It is also an appropriate case for considering the issue of cooperation and 'load-sharing' with others. UNTAC has been described as a 'flawed success'. There is no doubt that UNTAC avoided the real possibility of a disaster of Titanic proportions. But it suffered, in both political and organisational terms, from a level of mistakes, miscalculations and managerial insensitivity comparable to those made on another, much later trans-Atlantic voyage—that of the *Queen Elizabeth II* around Christmas 1994, when passengers on a supposedly luxury cruise found themselves sharing their cabins with plumbers and other workmen. Those passengers, like the people of Cambodia, survived the experience, but their understanding of Cunard Luxury, like the Khmers' idea of UN democracy, must leave much to be desired. The services should have been better, even if they could not have been absolutely blue ribbon.

UN Capacity and Suitability for Comprehensive Peacekeeping

A first concern is the UN's ability to choose the tasks it undertakes and the mandate it is charged with. Cambodia is a good example of an operation which the UN could not refuse. It had been involved for years in the achievement of the Paris Agreements which sought to end a tragedy, UN inaction in respect of the early stages of which had been criticised by many. With the Cold War and the automatic veto gone and the New World Order at hand it was inevitable that the Security Council would accept. The same may be true of other situations such as Somalia, the Balkans and Rwanda. What may need further consideration is whether the UN should impose more realistic conditions upon its acceptance and, even more important, take steps to prepare and plan for such undertakings. The solution to the Cambodian problem took over a decade to finalise, and a contingency plan should have been considered well in advance of the final months of 1991.

The second concern relates once more to taking the comprehensiveness of peacemaking seriously. Peace must be sustainable, and this can only be achieved by a sustained and well thought out commitment to a long-term solution. Despite the fact that it was well recognised that there were many dimensions to the problem, reflected in the multiple component nature of UNTAC, the organisation was not able to resist the temptation to believe that peace and democracy could be achieved on the one-dimensional basis of successful election. One election doth not a democracy make.

The first need was time, a readiness to accept that peace cannot be achieved in a day. More specifically in the context of Cambodia: stable, sustainable government could not be achieved within fourteen months. Peace 'in a nutshell' or 'instant democracy' are not real but ersatz solutions. A peace operation which is more concerned with good photo-opportunities than serious, committed follow-up risks long-term disaster and the possibility of having to re-do the entire exercise.

The second need is the recognition that a greater degree of professionalism is required. The idea that a UN staffer is a master of all trades is wrong. Fortunately this idea was never applied in the first generation of UN peacekeeping to the military skills they needed. It was shown to be wrong in Cambodia, especially by the gross failures in the Civil Administration Component where recruitment of professionals was left until too late, and by the contrasting fortune of the Electoral Component where professional recruitment was insisted upon from the beginning and UN expertise was used selectively where it was really necessary, in dealing with the Byzantine peculiarities of the UN's administrative bureaucracy. Allied with this is the need for a more outcome-oriented rather than process-oriented approach to tasks. UNTAC was an early post-Cold War operation, and the crippling effects of decades of UN recruitment policy and practice based not on merit but on crude political bargaining were, hopefully, worse than they will be in the future as better management practices take hold. Professionalism must however be recognised as essential, especially in comprehensive operations.

There is at present a serious credibility gap between the awesome authority of the Security Council to make binding decisions and the will of its officers and member states to carry them out or provide the resources to do so. Essentially, the tendency to choose the cosmetic quick-fix rather than the more substantial long-term solution to problems needs to be examined. It would seem that the Council, and possibly the Secretariat which advises it, are too remote from the realities of the situation they are dealing with. The same remoteness and unreality has been true of the relationship between the decision-makers in the Secretariat in New York, and the functionaries in the field, whether the latter are UN staffers or specialists brought in to do the task. This gap is a problem at all stages of a mission, the planning being especially important. An example often referred to in the UNTAC context was the fact that component heads, such as those in the Military and Electoral operations, who would have to depend on one another and work closely together often in, quite literally, life and death situations, did not meet before they arrived in Phnom Penh. Delegation is another practice which needs development in the UN management culture, which is often characterised by mutual distrust and defensiveness, sometimes to the point of paralysis. In situations of great chaos and infrastructural inadequacy, of which Cambodia was a typical, if exaggerated example, practised delegation becomes an absolute necessity.

Electoral Problems

It is suggested that the electoral dimension of democracy is a fundamental building block in the edifice of democratisation and peace building. The qualities inherent in a credible election, conducted within a convincing electoral framework, are basic qualities for a working democracy. These include the acceptance and practice of: the rule of law (rather than influence and power), reconciliation and tolerance (accepting former enemies and their supporters as legitimate opponents), and competing within a predictable and even playing field where a fundamental assumption is that the other side is entitled to win power. It is also clear that an election, in a transitional process such as from war to peace, can also act as a catalyst for peace and even a motivation for compliance with a ceasefire. It can provide a window of democratic opportunity.

Security

The Cambodian exercise also demonstrated other typical aspects of a peace election. On the face of it an election is a preeminently open activity and demands a high level of security to be meaningful. In fact, once electors are convinced of an election's potential for achieving peace, they will brave considerable dangers to support the process by registering and voting. What is essential is to create sufficient confidence among voters to bolster their enthusiasm. To a degree the election is a 'Theatre of Safety' at the centre of which is the idea of the secret ballot. To achieve this in a transition between war and peace, where quite typically the promised ceasefire has not held, requires considerable confidence, discipline and skill of electoral and other officials.

This need was well served in UNTAC by a unique combination of professional electoral officers, many of them from Asian countries with experience of difficult elections, and volunteer development workers with high levels of motivation and dedication. These UNV officials, especially those operating in the districts of Cambodia, were the personification of the electoral system. They gave a living reality and a human structure to an alien and invisible ideal. In this they were significantly supported by the UNTAC military, who generally demonstrated an understanding of and support for the electoral 'presentation' which added significantly to its credibility. This combination achieved, at the earliest stage of the process, an important bridgehead for the electoral endeavour through the massive registration of Khmer voters. This was the first opportunity given to the people themselves to express a view on the idea of an election. It was their overwhelming endorsement which created a new level of obligation upon UNTAC which it was to find impossible to shirk, despite the erosion of support for the process among the Khmer political leadership.

Logistics

Timely and efficient delivery of electoral services are essential to a credible election. It was immediately clear that the UN's own logistical capacity was inadequate to serve the needs of the electoral operation in Cambodia. Fortunately the priorities of timely delivery and advance planning were well appreciated by the UNTAC Military Component, and a functional relationship was rapidly developed which enabled a convincing service to be planned for and provided. Electoral and military operations share a common need for advance planning, strict adherence to time-frames, and discipline, which made this cooperation relatively easy despite some basic differences as to other priorities. For example, in an insecure situation the natural desire for the military is to close up its lines of communication, whereas the electoral service, as long as the election is to be held, will expect to have the most extensive service and coverage and to put security second.

This tension existed in UNTAC, especially over the final

problem of the spread of polling stations. It was resolved by a reasonable compromise reached at the provincial level, where both sector commanders and electoral officers were aware of the realities on the ground. This was made possible by the components' managerial philosophy, necessitated in part by the realities of inadequate communications, which demanded decision-making delegated to the provincial level within the framework of a well established, centrally determined policy.

Legislation

The development of an electoral system and the recruitment and training of the staff needed to execute it must be done within the framework of a precise set of laws. Thus the starting point is the basic electoral law upon which are built more detailed regulations, instructions, manuals and training programmes. Since it was necessary to recruit and train a Khmer staff of 8000 for the registration exercise, due to commence in October 1992, and to ensure that the Cambodian political parties and people be able to discover and become familiar with the law, a massive translation operation was needed. All of this involves time which is, here as elsewhere in the electoral system, of the essence. The basis of the Cambodian electoral law was the Paris Agreements in which the parties established the fundamental rules by which the process would be governed. It is vital to the credibility of an electoral system that the agreed rules be maintained throughout the 'game'. Thus the electoral law was drafted in New York in January 1992. UNTAC was established with the arrival of the Special Representative of the Secretary-General (SRSG) on 15 March 1992. After consultation within the UN and with electoral specialists, the draft was finalised and presented to the Cambodian Supreme National Council (SNC) on 1 April. The power to make this law and to implement it was one of the essential qualities of UNTAC. Ultimately it was in fact passed by the SRSG.

This legislation and its enactment was to be the source of considerable delay and difficulty for the electoral preparations and implementation. It was not passed until August 1992. The justification for this delay was: consultation with the SNC and the need to ensure that it had a sense of 'owning' the law. In fact, after almost five months of argument and what was essentially an attempt (partly successful) to renegotiate the Paris Agreements, only one of the four factions approved of the law and the chairman found it impossible to enact it on his authority. Hence its enactment by the SRSG, using the legislative power he had been given by the Agreement. It was this attempt by the SRSG to employ and prefer political expediency to legal clarity and certainty which set the stage for further dangerous political compromises which progressively reduced the credibility of the UNTAC peace process as a serious attempt to bring democracy and the rule of law to Cambodia. Short-term political advantage was consistently to be preferred to the long-term benefits of actions based on the agreed law, rather than on political or power considerations.

The renegotiation of the Paris Agreements, sought primarily by the Khmer Rouge, seeking to make the most of the Khmers' long-standing chauvinism and anti-Vietnamese racism, was centred on the agreed franchise. This in essence gave the vote to all persons living in Cambodia and to returning Cambodian refugees, including those whose parents had fled the terror of the Khmer Rouge. The demand being made was that the vote be restricted to those who could be racially defined as Khmer. No rational definition of a 'khmer' could be provided, and in a country where all records had been deliberately destroyed, no sensible bureaucratic alternative screening method was feasible. It was also immediately clear that what was sought was fundamentally in contradiction of well established UN principles of non-discrimination. Yet the debate was allowed to continue for almost five months.

The outcome was an adjustment to the law and the Agreements which avoided importing a racial definition of a voter, but had the effect of stiffening the residential qualification, thus potentially excluding recent (Vietnamese) immigrants from the vote. Ironically there were very few sustainable objections to registered voters on this ground during the registration process, but one of the champions of the attempted racial exclusion, the BLDP leader Son Sann, was disqualified because he had been born, like many so-called Khmer Krom, in South Vietnam. A special amendment, passed in the final weeks of the election, excepting from this law the leaders of any of the competing political parties, but designed especially for him, was necessary to avoid his disenfranchisement.

Joined with this demand was a less objectionable attempt to amend the Paris Agreements by allowing the registration of Khmers outside of Cambodia, especially the considerable numbers in Australia, the US and France. This would have imposed additional costs on the UN and was refused. By way of a compromise, which undermined the logic if not the parsimony of the UN, it was accepted that polling stations would be set up in those countries. Not surprisingly, very few votes were cast at these polls, since very few had been able to go back to Cambodia to register.

More destabilising than either of the above, because the uncertainty this demand generated continued until well into January 1993, was the suggestion that the election should become two elections. In Paris it had been agreed that the UN would conduct an election for the members of a Constituent Assembly, to debate and design a new Cambodian constitution. In mid-1992 the idea began to be circulated that this election should coincide with an election for a new president of Cambodia. The obvious candidate for the post was Prince Sihanouk. The idea was said to be strongly supported by certain members of the UN Security Council as the only means of ensuring stability after the elections. The fact that it was totally unconstitutional and illegal, and would have amounted to a 'constitutional *coup d'état* ', did not prevent it being allowed to proceed as a serious proposition. It was only dropped by virtue of the fact that Prince Sihanouk himself declared that he would not wish to be a candidate. This was apparently because the Australian Foreign Minister had suggested that such an idea might be unconstitutional. By this time voter registration was virtually complete and it was only three months before the proposed election date. What this meant was that until then, regulations, instructions and training manuals for the 50,000 Khmer polling officers could not be finalised and translated, and planning had to proceed on the basis that two ballots, rather than one, would be needed.

This last complication is a good example of the contradiction between political expediency and legal consistency. The dalliance with the Presidential election idea arose from a conviction that *ad personam* stability—promoting the elevation of Sihanouk to power based on the political judgment of certain major players in the Security Council—was preferable to the stability achieved by adherence to the law and reliance upon a constitutionally elected assembly. It illustrates the inconsistency of the Security Council and its unreliable support for the democracy it was proclaiming it saw as the source of real peace. It was unfortunate that that same ambiguity was reflected in the actions and attitudes of senior UNTAC staff dealing with the situation. This attitude created other problems for the proper conduct of the election and the laying of a sound foundation for democracy in Cambodia.

Political Expediency and Electoral Impartiality

It is quite normal for political parties and politicians when they compete in an election the results of which they do not control, to be neurotic and to believe that whoever does manage the system is biased against them. This paranoia increases as polling approaches, and is especially intense in the case of a political party which has held arbitrary (frequently brutal) power for a long time and is faced with the prospect of defeat. Such a scenario is typical of any peace or transitional election and was true of the situation in Cambodia in 1993.

This paranoia is the reason for the absolute need for electoral commissions or their equivalent institutions to be, and be seen to be, scrupulously impartial. They must not only be able to prove their integrity during and after the election, they must be able to 'over-emphasise' their impartiality throughout the process so that, ideally, none of the parties become suspicious during the registration, campaigning, voting or counting stages. The best means of achieving this is to have well understood laws and regulations in place, communicate them to the parties clearly, and act scrupulously in accordance with those rules in all dealings with the parties. This is not an easy state to achieve, even in a well ordered, homogeneous, democratic society. Politicians will do virtually anything to win power. It is infinitely more difficult to achieve in a situation where a civil war is still raging, violence is endemic, none of the parties has any real experience of a democratic election, and the management of this entire intimate, dangerous process is in the hands of total strangers. This was the case with UNTAC.

Of course the granting to UNTAC of its unique power to legislate for and then implement the entire Cambodian election was the result of the fact that the UN was an 'outsider', an alien international organisation with no trace of Khmer identity. It was for this UN neutrality that it had been invited to do what the Khmer parties could not trust any one, or any combination, of themselves to do. There is however a distinction between the neutrality of an international civil servant and the impartiality of a professional electoral officer. This distinction was not understood and not respected by UNTAC's political masters and this caused significant problems, short-term and, I would suspect, long-term, for the cause of democracy and peace in Cambodia. In future similar missions this distinction should be understood well in advance. The attempt to explain and maintain the distinction by the Electoral Component was misinterpreted as an inexplicable desire to distance the Component from others for reasons of 'empire-building' or similar non-functional reasons.

This is the same tension that is often observable, in the context of a purely state-run election, between a governing party and its more political administrative arms, and its electoral commission. This tension will often lead to the Commission (if it is not strong and effectively independent) allowing the administration to impose 'political' decisions in place of electorally correct decisions, often discrediting the elections as a result. These political interventions will sometimes be clearly party-politically biased, but they may often be rationalised as being necessary for 'security' or the avoidance of a politically inconvenient or undesirable situation. Their essence is that they are imposed for political reasons, which are regarded as of superior importance to the electoral law, of which they are generally in breach.

It was fascinating, if somewhat surprising and disturbing, to discover that an almost exact parallel pattern of behaviour was exhibited by the international political leadership of UNTAC as is typical of the purely national administrations described above. The tension which resulted was explained within the Electoral Component as the consequence of two diametrically opposed concepts of impartiality: a rule of law impartiality, and an 'equal time' impartiality. The latter was characterised by the conviction that impartiality could be sufficiently demonstrated, not by subjecting all parties to equal treatment according to the rules, but by doing equal favours according to the 'political realities' at the time, and balancing them according to contemporary political judgments.

It is suggested that the importance of this concern goes beyond the immediate credibility of the election in a comprehensive peacekeeping operation. Consistency and compliance with the rule of law are certainly the foundations of electoral credibility, but they are equally the essence of true democracy, which abhors arbitrariness and the rule of power and violence.

There were several significant examples of the operation of this contradiction in UNTAC. One typical example concerned the freedom of movement. In any election it is essential that the political parties and candidates should have access to the electorate, and thus must be free to move wherever they wish. This freedom was guaranteed in the Paris Agreements and the Electoral Law in Cambodia. The reality was otherwise. The CPP incumbent, controlling 80 percent of the country and effectively uncontrolled and unrestrained by the UNTAC Civil Administration, made surface travel by FUNCINPEC and the BLDP candidates a lethal activity. In desperation FUNCINPEC, which could afford it, turned to aircraft. All the airstrips in the CPP areas, where most of the election was fought, were controlled by the CPP (State of Cambodia) Ministry of Aviation. Its head refused to allow FUNCINPEC aircraft to land or take off. Despite weeks of negotiation by UNTAC the ban remained, and aircraft attempting to ignore the ban were threatened with anti-aircraft fire.

A legal solution was available to the SRSG: his power to order the removal of any of the factions' officials obstructing the electoral process. This was not used because, it was argued, it would create a dangerous political conflict. Instead, as the crisis became more pressing and FUNCINPEC was refused permission to fly even in locally hired aircraft, weeks of the official campaign had been lost. One morning, at the daily meeting of heads of components with the SRSG, it was learned that the leader of FUNCINPEC, Prince Norodom Ranariddh, was due to fly to a rally in Kampong Cham, the home province of the CPP Prime Minister Hun Sen and the biggest electoral prize in the country. He was stuck at the airport by the CPP-imposed ban. The credibility of the freedom to campaign was severely in doubt. The solution was not to use UNTAC's legal powers, but to allow UNTAC to do the prince a favour. It so happened that the Chief Electoral Officer was due to visit the Kampong Cham provincial electoral office and the sector commander that morning. There would be room for the Prince's party on the helicopter so they would be air-lifted by UNTAC. The point that this action might be construed as showing bias by the Component was not accepted. Thus the CPP neurosis with UNTAC bias was given a significant boost.

A second example concerns provisions for curtaining electoral booths. Electoral regulations and rules tend to go into great detail to ensure that almost every eventuality is covered and the electoral official is relieved of having to rely on his or her discretion as much as possible. Some three weeks before polling the point was suddenly raised by FUNCINPEC in a meeting of the SNC, that the rules relating to the polling booths made no provision for them to be curtained 'as they were in France'. It was pointed out that the arrangement for booths would protect the voters' privacy and the secrecy of the ballot. FUNCINPEC, and in particular its very vocal chief electoral agent Sam Rainsy did not find this satisfactory. Because we were so near to the polls, and because the Khmer Rouge remained adamant in their rejection of the election, the FUNCINPEC threat to join the boycott and effectively destroy the election (after millions of dollars and many UN political reputations had been invested in the mission) a promise was made by the SRSG to provide curtains. This was done on the spur of the moment after the briefest, whispered 'consultation' with the Electoral Component. It was an impossible promise to fulfil—to find, order and deliver, to some 1600 polling stations throughout Cambodia, many thousands of metres of cloth, which would then have to be fitted by electoral officers already overwhelmed by basic tasks. In fact the cloth was procured and quite widely delivered, but in very few places was it fitted to the booths.

FUNCINPEC voters cast their ballots without the promised, curtained protection. Fortunately FUNCINPEC won the election. Had they lost, the broken promise would certainly have provided an excellent excuse for a complaint that UNTAC had been guilty of irregularities in the conduct of the election. Apart from that, the instant, unconditional accession to the demand was noted by the CPP as yet another example of bias in favour of its opponents, despite its own objection that curtains were not required according to the published rules.

A third example involves CPP access to safe havens. It had been decided, in the deteriorating security situation during the immediate lead-up to polling, that the ballot boxes could not be guarded at over 1600 stations. Security would be strengthened by consolidating their protection at selected UNTAC military installations. These would be the centres to which boxes would be brought at the end of each polling day, to be returned (if they were not filled) the following morning. These were termed safe havens. The change could not be avoided, but it created considerable difficulties for the electoral management. It meant that the military commander of the safe haven would be placed in the role of an electoral officer, having overall charge of the ballot boxes when they were in the havens. It also meant that the boxes would have to be moved much more than had been envisaged. This resulted in a strain on the box seals much greater than planned, and their failure in a number of cases, a problem which the losing party (CPP) was to exploit to the full.

This situation gave rise to a serious example of the preference of political over legal impartiality. This emerged some 36 hours before the polls opened. On the Friday evening prior to the early Sunday morning start of voting, the CPP leadership demanded an urgent meeting with the SRSG. They argued that their supporters were deeply concerned with the integrity of the election, especially because they had been denied the right to place their own party seals on the ballot boxes. (It would have been physically impossible to allow all parties this promised facility and the Electoral Law had been duly amended to this effect.) This concern, they claimed, was exacerbated by the news that all boxes were to be moved to UNTAC military safe havens, rather than being left at the polling stations where their party agents would be on guard. This hiatus in the parties' surveillance of the boxes would, they claimed, lead to the other parties impugning the results, which they confidently believed would be a CPP victory. When it was pointed out that no other party had opposed the safe haven plan, the CPP leaders made it clear that their real problem was that they did not trust the UN, including the UN military, who would be in sole control of the boxes in the safe havens. UN impartiality had been eroded, and in the circumstances the electoral impartiality of the Electoral Component had also been compromised in the eyes of the CPP.

It was now the CPP's turn to threaten to boycott the election and demand an 'instant' favour. This was the grant of the right to party election agents to follow the boxes to the safe havens, to enter the safe havens and inspect the facility in which they would be held, to wait outside the haven and to follow the boxes back to the polls. The SRSG had little option by now but to give the CPP 'equal time' to that granted to FUNCINPEC earlier. Again there was a consultation with the Electoral Component which was largely nominal. But it was pointed out that to change the ground rules at this late stage was to invite chaos and problems. Communications in Cambodia even at that late stage of the mission were unreliable, and to expect to get this message through to, and clearly understood by, UNTAC military and electoral officials was unrealistic. In addition the same message should be communicated equally effectively to all other political parties so that they would benefit equally from the new rule. This was an even more remote possibility. Had FUNCINPEC lost the election it would have provided yet another good ground for challenging the result.

The result of this eleventh-hour change of rules was that the first night of polling was a continual struggle between electoral officers, safe haven commanders and CPP agents to get the message clear and to provide the promised access to the havens. In many cases the soldiers, without clear orders, refused the agents entry into the military installations, as one might have expected. This merely served to confirm CPP's paranoia and belief that UNTAC had something to hide and was determined to defraud it of its rightful victory. Despite the clear evidence, carefully produced over the next week or more, to show that this was not the case, the doubt had been raised and full use was made of it by the CPP when it decided to challenge the integrity of the election with direct charges of irregularity and the 'theft' of CPP votes connected with the broken seals.

The fourth example comes from the 'auto-destabilisation' of the election. The ultimate proof of the destabilising effect of dealing politically rather than legally with the electoral issues outlined above, was the fact that UNTAC itself was unable to maintain a consistent position on the propriety and integrity of its election. Having lost the vote, the CPP arranged that its most militant and military leadership would stage a secession of the Eastern Provinces of Cambodia. It was in this context that those who had not joined the secession insisted that the result was fraudulent as a result of UNTAC irregularities, and demanded an 'independent' inquiry. They reduced this demand to an UNTAC inquiry, though the rationale of this was not clear. When Hun Sen and Chea Sim, the CPP leaders who claimed to wish to save the election rather than join the secession, admitted that the demand for an inquiry into the alleged electoral irregularities was essentially to enable them to save face and have a 'hook' upon which to hang their acceptance of the election (once the political deal to grant them an effective 'draw' had been sealed), UNTAC did not hesitate to grant an inquiry into the election which the Security Council had just endorsed as free and fair. This was the short-term, expedient solution.

It was assumed that such political sleight of hand would mean nothing to the future of elections and democracy in Cambodia. It appears now, at least to some observers, that the outcome of the election and the entire UN mission to bring a change from past practices, and to start democracy in that country, has resulted in the fact that it is not the electoral winner, but the loser, which has taken all. But part of the reason for that, as we know, is that the 'loser' never lost the essence of what remained the real source of power in Cambodia, even in the eyes of the SRSG namely, military, police and administrative power. Had UNTAC neutralised those, as its comprehensive peacekeeping mandate required it to, peace and democracy may have had a more realistic prospect. It is to these other elements of comprehensive peacekeeping in Cambodia that I will now briefly turn.

Other Neglected Comprehensive Foundations of Peace in Cambodia

The Khmer factions and states who negotiated for so many years leading to the Paris Agreements produced a unique institution to set Cambodia on a path to democratic government. They knew that this could not be done by a one-dimensional act of peacekeeping, but would need to address many different dimensions if a proper solution was to be found and 'to ensure that the policies and practices of the past shall never be allowed to return'. Thus the Agreements on a Comprehensive Political Settlement of the Cambodia Conflict sought, quite seriously, to be exactly that. The Security Council accepted responsibility for implementing the Agreements, it did not exclude or make any part of the mandate conditional. It had never undertaken such a responsibility before, and with the benefit of hindsight it may have been better had it thought more carefully before it made this awesome promise. In the event it did not provide the proper resources, time or personnel to fulfil its promise, and the foundations which could and should have been laid by the implementation of the Paris Agreements were not put in place.

Fostering an Environment of Respect for Human Rights

UNTAC was required by the Paris Agreements to make provision for:

a.   The development and implementation of a programme of human rights education to promote respect for and understanding of human rights;

b.   General human rights oversight during the transitional period;

c.   The investigation of human rights complaints and, where appropriate, the taking of corrective action.

To carry out these tasks a Human Rights Component was provided for in the Agreements, but it was clear from the start, in the Secretary-General's report which outlined for the Security Council how the work was to be achieved, that the commitment was largely symbolic. The report indicated, and the realities confirmed, that the human rights education and training, as well as investigation, monitoring, and appropriate corrective action, would be undertaken by a 'modest' human rights staff in Phnom Penh. The total staff was less than twenty, with the initial complement for the human rights education programme (despite it being foreseen by the Secretary-General 'as the cornerstone of UNTAC's activities in fostering respect for human rights') being four people. The convenient rationalisation for this bizarre plan to educate the 5,000,000 Khmer voter population which had survived over two decades of conflict, the rule of the Khmer Rouge, and over a decade of Vietnamese installed doctrinaire communist rule, was that the entire UNTAC staff (being UN experts in everything including human rights) would do the education in addition to the specialised tasks for which they had been appointed.

The history of the Human Rights Component was a sorry tale of a constant struggle by its head for resources, a consistent and principled use of the powers granted to UNTAC, and the timely establishment of a legal framework which would make his task possible. The result was considerable frustration and embarrassment as UNTAC myopia in relation to the comprehensive task increasingly marginalised and ignored this critical long-term responsibility for the future. As he observed in his paper for the Aspen Institute, 'The perceived political imperative of the mission increasingly became the holding of a UN-supervised election, although this was only one aspect of the original mandate'.[2]

Similar neglect was shown with regard to other aspects of the human rights tasks which might have had significant long-term benefits for Cambodia. The incumbent SoC police were not subjected to any serious large-scale attempt at retraining or reorientation, consequently the ethos of the police state was hardly diluted when UNTAC left. The same was true of the equally glaring lack of a judiciary with the slightest pretence of respect for, or understanding of, the idea of judicial independence and the rule of law. This not

2   Dennis McNamara, 'UN Human Rights Activities in Cambodia: An Evaluation', in *Honouring Human Rights and Keeping the Peace* (Washington, DC: The Aspen Institute, 1995), pp. 57–83.

only made human rights protection where it would involve arrest and trial impossible, it also led UNTAC itself in moments of extreme frustration to act in contradiction of these principles itself.

Yet another glaring neglect of the responsibility which the UN purported to undertake under the Paris Agreements was in relation to the constitution which was to be made by those elected to the Constituent Assembly. This was to be in accordance with certain principles set out in the Agreements (Annex 5). It noted that 'Cambodia's recent history requires special measures to assure protection of human rights. Therefore, the constitution will contain a declaration of fundamental rights...'. UNTAC's mandate was for the transitional period, from the entry into force of the Agreement to the making of the constitution, the conversion of the Constituent Assembly into a legislative assembly and thereafter the creation of a new government. It was clear from the realities of Cambodia that a great deal of assistance would be needed to build the capacity needed for the proper planning and development of the constitution. There was a small amount of time, money and effort devoted to this task by UNTAC. What was done was entirely the result of the SRSG's realisation in the midst of the mission that there was a yawning gap. These ad hoc measures, undertaken by a combination of the Electoral Component and the Office of the Legal Adviser to the SRSG, were combined with the Human Rights Component's attempt to inject some education on this into its very truncated operation. There was no budget for the constitutional task in the UN implementation plan, and quite clearly the problem had not been foreseen.

An even more embarrassing situation arose when the Constituent Assembly came together after the election. The national assembly building, dating from the days of Prince Sihanouk's rule in the 1960s, had served the SoC government after its installation following the Vietnamese expulsion of Pol Pot. Having been defeated in the election the CPP moved out, taking much of the furniture and facilities, including telephones and typewriters, with them. There was literally no place for the members to work, no library or trained staff to service a constitution making process that was required to be complete within three months. Once again, this problem had neither been foreseen and therefore not planned, nor budgeted for by the UN.

This coincided with the final, somewhat bitter, negotiations surrounding the creation of the Government of National Unity and the installation of the CPP as equal partners with FUNCINPEC.

Relations between the Khmer politicians and UNTAC were understandably at a low ebb. This anger manifested itself in, amongst other things, their refusal to discuss or take any advice from UNTAC on the constitution. This did not however preclude them, in their desperate need to obtain chairs, phones, computers and the other basics to run an assembly, from turning to UNTAC, by this stage in the process of extracting its vast impedimenta from the country. Thus UNTAC found itself scaping the bottom of a non-existent budget to help get the very basic elements of work started. The author, though *functus officio* with regard to the election, was still with UNTAC, and spent much of these weeks begging, borrowing and very nearly having to steal, UNTAC materials to ferry to the constitution makers. Apart from the interesting change in my own relationships with the erstwhile candidates which this produced, it turned out to be a useful 'ice-breaking' instrument for reopening, on a strictly informal basis, the opportunity to discuss aspects of the constitution with the legislators.

It is interesting to compare the serious gap in this dimension of the Cambodian operation with the UN role in Namibia. The organisation had been intimately involved, through the Council for Namibia, in many preliminary studies and discussions within the Southwest African People's Organisation (SWAPO) of the constitution. This may account for the very deep involvement and preparedness of the UN, through its Legal Division, in the drafting of the (rather impressive) Namibian constitution. But, as mentioned above, the UN had also been involved for many years with the preparations and negotiations leading to the Paris Agreements and the setting up of the Constituent Assembly. Why had there been no institutional memory to pick up the possible similarity and make plans for a comparable and equally impressive UN contribution? It seems that drawing lessons based on past experience—good, bad or indifferent—is not a strong point of the UN. It should not go on being the case.

Civil Administration

The failures of this component of the UNTAC mission have been well catalogued. The particular aspect I would wish to draw attention to is the contrasting success achieved by the UNTAC officials dealing with finance, customs and immigration aspects of control, despite the dreadful delays in getting properly chosen experts into place, and the generally sad failures of the UNTAC provincial administrators who were meant to control the SoC bureaucracy in the cities and towns.

It would seem there were two reasons for this. First, the former success was achieved by professionals, chosen from outside the UN system for their expertise and experience. The same good fortune was enjoyed by the Electoral Component. The latter were UN staffers with no particular experience or expertise in the work they were expected to do, and often with very limited motivation other than the various generous allowances such a posting bestowed upon some of them. There were fortunately some important exceptions. Second, and this was a major problem for the smooth operation of the electoral aspect of the mission, the deployment of the Civil Administration was not done with a resolve to ensure that UNTAC control was, or at least was seen to be, exercised with equal determination on all factions. Clearly the major attention would be upon the SoC existing administrative structures, if only because they controlled 80 percent of the country. But there were the structures of the other three factions, nominal though they may have been, and they should have been subjected to equal attention and the same rules and restrictions.

This failure also contributed to the CPP's sense that it was unfairly treated, adding to the resentment created by the 'favours' referred to above. It was another example of the UN officialdom believing a symbolic gesture or a superficial compliance would be enough. Peacemaking needs to be treated more seriously.

Rehabilitation and Reconstruction

Here again the Agreement provided a role and created expectations of the UN. The provisions of the treaty dealing with this were entitled a Declaration. In this sense it was more hortatory than substantive. But the importance of reconstruction for the restoration of stability and faith in government was obvious, hence its inclusion, and the UN's acceptance of the task. Unfortunately the provision in the declaration in which the UN Secretary-General was 'requested to help coordinate the programme guided by a person appointed for this purpose' seemed to have been taken too literally by the UN. The Director of the Component ostensibly set up for this task found that he had an establishment which consisted of himself.

There were serious political difficulties with the programme, since most reconstruction, of necessity, would be in the SoC areas and thus be automatically opposed by the Khmer Rouge and the other opposition parties. But with serious resources and careful deployment of projects much might have been done that would have contributed to stability and set a pattern for reconstruction in Cambodia. As it was the programme withered to virtually nothing, the director left the mission and the responsibility was incorporated into the Civil Administration brief.

Democracy has long been said to be interrelated to development. A good example of the reality of this can be observed today in South Africa where it is understood that the 'benefits' of democracy will lose their meaning unless some concrete progress is made in improving the material lives of the citizens. The people of Cambodia needed some assurance on this front in the context of the democracy they were being brought, and it was a mistake not to have taken this need seriously.

Burden Sharing

The difficulties and errors outlined above provide useful lessons for future UN operations. There is no viable alternative to the UN, and the need is to seek means which will enable the tasks which are being foisted upon the international community to be done effectively. Experience in such situations as Cambodia also raise more general questions. Briefly these include:

a. The task of achieving peace is not one capable of 'instant' solutions. To achieve the national capacity to sustain democracy and thus stability and peace, requires ongoing solidarity and support. This is not always measured in financial terms. The question this raises is one of the 'identity' of the UN. Is it a friend or merely a fire brigade? It is argued that fire brigades will not do much for the peace-building or peacemaking needs of societies seeking peace through democracy, and that a long-term friend is more appropriate.

b. It should be noted that in this regard the international community consists of other organisations which may have a comparative advantage with regard to these more long-term needs. Among these are the regional organisations, especially, from a New Zealand perspective, the Commonwealth. The latter consists now of 51 states, representing all regions of the world, a multitude of cultures and languages bound together entirely voluntarily by ties of a shared language, habits of administration and proclaimed commonly shared values. This familiarity is associated with qualities of patience, consensus and solidarity which may be particularly valuable in the process of assisting the evolution of democracy and thus the achievement of peace. Peace for such a 'family' is not an event but a process. It cannot be dealt with purely on the basis of emergency action, it requires long-term commitment. When looking at the role of the international community in these tasks the Commonwealth, in cooperation with the UN, should be remembered.

It should also be noted that the long-term achievement of peace through democracy, being as it is ultimately the product of national capacity, can be contributed to not only by inter-governmental organisations, but also by the activities of associations of people. There are other levels of activity which bring about change and capacity in a society. In this regard again, the Commonwealth has a special contribution to make, through its multitude of professional associations and non-government organisations (NGOs). Its character as a Commonwealth of people as well as of states is important. It is this which makes it an especially useful tool in capacity-building within small states which make up the majority of the Commonwealth.

Conclusion

As the UN reaches its fiftieth year, it is also facing its most testing times. Not only are the demands upon it increasing in volume, but also in comprehensiveness. It has had to move rapidly to adjust from a well tried and tested pattern of peacekeeping to tasks of peacebuilding and peacemaking which it has had to make up as it went along. Mistakes in such situations are inevitable. But they cannot and should not be hidden. They must be used constructively. It is becoming increasingly clear that the UN's enormous authority, characterised by the decision-making power of the Security Council, is not matched by the will of its members to back that authority with the appropriate resources and political will. Thus not only must the UN establishment make proper use of other institutional and human resources, the organisation must also share the burden of the expectations, and seek appropriate partnerships.

In the field of peace-building through democracy there are some obvious candidates for this. But equally such other international associations must be ready to respond to this need for cooperation. Fortunately this is already taking place on a variety of fronts. The UNOMSA (UN Observer Mission in South Africa) operation in South Africa is a case in point, where the UN, acting as coordinator, was involved in the most massive exercise of international solidarity in the birth of democracy in that country with the European Union (EU), the Organisation of African Unity (OAU) and the Commonwealth. It is important to note that that task only began with the election of President Nelson Mandela, and that the long process of building upon that foundations continues, with the cooperation of the United Nations and other dedicated organisations. That, it is argued, must be the way ahead.

Displaced persons camp, Kibeho, Rwanda, January 1993. (Photo: Australian Defence Force)

Jorge Heine

A UN Agenda for Development:
Reflections on the Social Question in the South

I have been asked to comment on the UN Secretary-General's *Agenda for Development* report, 50 single-spaced pages which make an eloquent case for the need to put the development question front and centre as we reach the end of the millennium. The report underscores the degree to which the end of the Cold War, 'donor fatigue' and other factors conspire to create a 'development crisis'. It goes on to identify five different dimensions of development—peace, the economy, the environment, social justice and democracy—as key factors for the sort of development we need.[1]

Rather than attempt to examine each and every one of them, an overly ambitious task, I have chosen one of them—the social dimension, which will also allow me to refer to my own country's experience and programmes in this matter.

These days, it has become fashionable in certain circles to argue that 'poverty will take care of itself' if economic systems 'get prices right' and there is growth. It is difficult to quarrel with the need for economic growth to have any significant policy options at all. But the point to be made is that the gap between the North and the South continues to widen and that extreme poverty remains a way of life for much of humanity. Unless a concerted effort is undertaken to deal with it, this condition is likely to get worse before it gets better.

The figures (provided by the United Nations) speak for themselves. One out of every five human beings—one billion people—lives under the poverty line today. One out of every ten members of the labour force cannot find a job at a reasonable wage. The effects of this on the social fabric are not difficult to fathom. In

1   UN General Assembly, *An Agenda for Development.* Report of the Secretary General, A/48/935, 6 May 1994. On the extensive consultations on the subject, see UNGA, *Agenda for Development.* Note by the President of the General Assembly, A /49/320, 22 August 1994.

South Africa, where unemployment hovers between 40 and 50 percent, every three minutes one person is murdered and six are assaulted. In 1994, more than 800,000 violent crimes were reported, including 18,000 murders. In the United States, 35 million crimes are committed every year; reported crime has been growing at 5 percent a year on a worldwide basis.[2]

Drug trafficking has become one of the most profitable ventures— up to US $500 billion in profits are made in it annually. Internal conflicts, which have claimed most of the 20 million victims of strife since 1945, are spreading, not only in Africa and Asia, but also now in Eastern and Southeastern Europe, in ways that would have been unimaginable only six years ago. These are not problems that will disappear simply because of an upturn in the world economy—far from it. They are the result of severe social dislocations that need to be addressed promptly.

The New Urgency of the Social Question

The fact that 20 percent of the world's population lives under the poverty line makes it imperative to confront the social question immediately. Many say: 'Poverty has always existed, and will always exist; it is part of the human condition. Do not worry unduly about it'. This, of course, comes very close to blaming the victim. Yet, quite apart from the classic ethical reasons impelling us at least to attempt to remove poverty from the face of the earth, as we approach the end of the twentieth century there are additional, perhaps even more compelling reasons for doing so. Why do countries have to act quickly on the matter?

As Ricardo Lagos has pointed out, a massive attack on poverty is needed because in today's world 'competitiveness depends heavily on the capacity to integrate a growing number of social actors into the processes of investment, production and technological change'. This necessarily implies leaving behind the traditional 'welfarist' approach to poverty alleviation, focusing instead on strategies designed to incorporate hitherto marginalised sectors into productive activities. This does not mean that the state can ignore traditional tasks designed to allow human development under conditions of dignity. But it does mean it has to integrate both the old and the new items on the social

2   See the leaflet, *Why a Social Summit?* (New York: UN Department of Public Information, 1994).

development agenda.[3]

To start with, it means that the state has to recuperate fully and rebuild its capacity to design and implement social policies, by recovering its fiscal and financial solvency. A bankrupt, heavily indebted public sector is hard pressed to meet its own needs, let alone those of civil society. That is why it is so important to do whatever is necessary to reconstruct a state that can stand on its own. We do not need a 'lean and mean' state—presumably we want a lean and good natured one—but reaching that point does entail some painful exercises to get rid of the accumulated fat that will stand in the way of the sort of performance needed in the struggle against poverty.

Second, it means careful targeting of existing social programmes. Given the scarcity of available resources, one has to ensure that they reach only those who truly need them and that the highest share of the resources assigned to these programmes actually reach the people they are supposed to reach, thus minimising overhead and administration costs. For all the glamour attached to financial managers in many Southern countries today, in many of our nations we sorely lack qualified, professional 'social managers', that is, people trained to deliver social programmes efficiently and effectively.

Third, for much the same reason, overcoming poverty cannot depend solely on the public sector budget. Only an association between the state and civil society will allow for a genuine breakthrough in this matter. Needless to say, this is a challenge confronting both would-be partners in such an endeavour.

In short, the integration of marginalised social sectors into the economy depends heavily on increased access by the former to productive employment. Given the dualism extant in many societies in the South, that is, the coexistence of a modern sector with an informal, more traditional one, this implies creating jobs in both. Nonetheless, the requirements of doing so in the modern sector are often extremely costly. The argument is often made that one potential area for job creation in South Africa would be that of a greater beneficiation of the many minerals the country exports. Yet some estimates indicate that creating a competitive position in this area entails a capital investment of R100,000. To provide jobs for the 800,000 people who join the

3   This and the following paragraphs draw on the arguments developed in Ricardo Lagos, *Después de la Transición* (Santiago, Chile: Ediciones B, Grupo Zeta, 1993), Chapter 4, 'El Requisito de la Integración Social', pp. 89–123.

labour force every year—without referring for the moment to those already out of work—one would need an investment of R80 billion: almost one fifth of GDP and, therefore, simply not practicable.

Given the significance of the informal sector, creating jobs means, above all, expanding the entrepreneurial base of society and thus reducing the gap between the modern and the informal sectors of the economy. But this will not happen simply through 'getting prices right' and the free hand of the market, but will need very deliberate public policies and programmes.

There are, then, significant economic reasons leading us to conclude that, in many cases, an important *sine qua non* for economic growth lies in the improvement of social conditions. This, in turn, is closely linked to the training of human resources, a prerequisite for people being able to join the modern sector of the economy. Job creation and the expansion of the society's entrepreneurial base, human resource development, and the selective but effective presence of the state in these endeavours are thus vital for eradicating poverty.

The UN Social Summit

It is for those reasons that Chile took the lead in proposing the World Summit for Social Development held in Copenhagen in March 1995. We believe that in the post-Cold War era, in the world emerging after the age of ideological confrontations, social problems not only have a major bearing on, but are an integral part of, the security of this planet. In that regard the conference was not simply another in the confrontational course of the twentieth century, but one of the first in building the world of the coming one.[4]

The Social Summit was convened to confront what Secretary-General Boutros Boutros-Ghali has called 'a social and moral crisis which, in many societies, is of immense proportions'.[5] In response, the idea was to set forth a new ideal of social progress, 'based on

---

4   See President Eduardo Frei's column, 'Una tarea de la democracia', *Cooperación* (Santiago) 3 (January–February 1995), p. 24. For a general discussion of the purpose of the Summit, see Josef Thiesing, ed., *For Democracy and Social Justice: Documents and Recommendations of the Konrad Adenauer Foundation to the World Summit for Social Development in Copenhagen, 1995* (Bonn: Konrad Adenauer Foundation, 1994), especially the chapter by Chile's former President Patricio Aylwin, 'Justice and Solidarity: A Challenge for the One World', pp. 17–25.

5   In *Why a Social Summit?*

responsibility, freedom and solidarity'.[6] The purpose of the meeting was to produce a new vision of human-centred growth, environmental protection, societal justice and democracy, without which peace may simply not be attainable.

Once again, as over one hundred heads of government gathered in Copenhagen, there were those who said if all the money spent on the meeting had been given to the poor instead, much more could have been accomplished. This is the same Dickensian approach that wants to substitute targeted social programmes for charity and supplementary income programmes for orphanages. The truth is, the globalisation of the economy and of culture has meant that this problem has to be faced on a planetary scale.

As we all know, the powers and resources of government in this day and age are limited. One of the things they can do, though, is give signals and set priorities. And that was what was done in Copenhagen: governments agreed that key problems such as poverty and unemployment 'are addressed through principles based on social justice and democracy and through actions built on respect for human dignity, individual freedom and equality of rights and responsibilities'.[7]

Needless to say, this renewed commitment of the international community to restart social development among the most disadvantaged of its members must pay special attention to sub-Saharan Africa, the most impoverished of all continents. The end of the Cold War has meant that the protracted conflicts that afflicted so much of southern Africa have been left behind, a conclusion ratified by the peace process in Angola, the successful outcome of the elections in Mozambique and, of course, the new South Africa.[8]

Chile's Program to Eradicate Poverty

Before the Copenhagen conference, one *Financial Times* columnist, Edward Mortimer, asked himself what social development meant, saying it could not be equated with economic progress.[9]

To answer that question, rather than move up the ladder of

6   Ibid.
7   Ibid.
8   On the conclusions of the Summit, see Juan Somavía (Chile's Ambassador to the UN and chair of the Preparatory Committee for the Summit), 'Towards a Political Economy for People', *Socialist Affairs*, 1 (1995), pp. 12–15.
9   Edward Mortimer, 'We all need to change', *Financial Times*, 2 November 1994.

abstraction as Professor Rosenau does so eloquently in his chapter in this book, I am going to do the opposite—that is, be very specific and set forth in summary fashion what one country in the southern hemisphere is doing to confront its own social problems. In Chile, one of the main tasks of our reborn democracy has been to reduce poverty. In fact, our aim is to eradicate poverty in ten years' time. We do think this is a critical element of any development agenda.

Although we still have a long way to go, we have been making some progress in this regard. From 50 per 1000 in 1977, our infant mortality rate had dropped to 14 per 1000 in 1991–92; during the same period, our life expectancy had risen from 68.7 years to 72. The 5 million people below the poverty line in 1989 have dropped to 4 million today—out of a population of 14 million.

As serious a challenge as these absolute levels of poverty is that of income disparity and inequality. The lowest income decile of the population gets only 1.9 percent of national income, whereas the top decile gets 42.3 percent. While this is down from 44.4 percent in 1990, it is still an enormous gap, in which the top ten percent of households make 22 times as much as the bottom decile.[10]

Our national development plan, therefore, aims at deepening and broadening the measures for achieving greater equity in the context of relatively high and sustained growth, while at the same time keeping up our competitiveness, increasing productivity and thus improving the quality of life of the population. This means paying attention simultaneously to economic development, social and territorial equity, environmental sustainability and political democracy. It also means that the state has to take on a vital role in the design and implementation of policies in those areas for which the market has no ready answers—of which there are quite a few.

To our mind, growth with equity is central for the sort of social integration we need and want, and to I which alluded before. The National Program to Eradicate Poverty, therefore, includes a number of targets. What we aim for is to keep the average growth rate of 6 percent per annum that we have had over the past ten years, which will require an investment rate of at least 28 percent of GDP.

An important part of this will have to go to infrastructure. But we are also aiming at reaching 7 percent of GDP in our education budget

10   See Government of Chile, *Informe Nacional, Cumbre Mundial Sobre Desarrollo Social* (Santiago: Ministerio de Planificación y Cooperación, 1995) pp. 20–21. The following paragraphs also draw on this report..

before too long—figures comparable with those of Germany or Britain. Social spending is now 70 percent of all public spending and 15 percent of GDP, but we must do better than that.

To eradicate extreme poverty from Chile by the year 2000, then, and mirroring my earlier references to the new urgency of the social question today, our priorities are:

a. *A better state apparatus*, and one in closer relationship with civil society. In addition to a leaner and better managed public sector, the idea here is to empower civil society as much possible—and this links up with the enormous proliferation of non-government organisations (NGOs) that Minister McKinnon alludes to in his chapter. Many tasks in this battle against poverty can be performed by NGOs, and there is no reason why they cannot be empowered to do so.

b. *An active human resources policy,* one that has been sorely lacking until now. One figure someone has produced is that the average worker in Latin America can count on a grand total of five weeks of training during the course of his working life. This is appalling, and must be rectified.

c. *Social integration in the full sense of the word*, one that avoids the corporatisation of social demands and that, in periods of change, avoids privileging the stronger and better organised social sectors, leaving behind the weak and the dispossessed. It is the demands of the former that often stand in the way of social policies aimed at the sort of development that is both more equitable and promotes social integration.

We have identified 71 localities, out of the more than three hundred existing in Chile, as those most in need. We are proceeding with targeted programmes and close collaboration and cooperation between the central government which provides the resources, and the regional and local authorities who are supposed to use them and implement the programmes.

A key notion has been that the labour market will play a critical role in any effort to eradicate poverty. A major effort has therefore been undertaken to modernise it, make it more transparent and flexible, stimulating participation by the more vulnerable groups like women and youth, improving the quality and the number of jobs, and providing the mechanisms that will open the gates for greater productivity and better salaries.

Three specific areas that have been identified as especially promising in this regard are the development of micro-enterprises, small farms and small-scale fishing.

Conclusion

From the very opening of this Foreign Policy School, we have heard much about the UN's peacekeeping and peacemaking operations. No doubt they have come to the fore as the most visible of the UN's activities in the course of this decade. Chile has also played a small part in them, with an Air Force helicopter unit in the post-Gulf War operations in Kuwait and with our Navy's participation in Cambodia. Many speakers have also underscored the significance of early warning systems and conflict prevention mechanisms. But in the end the best conflict prevention strategy is one that has nothing to do with the battlefield. Only if we remove the many sources of social dislocation that threaten our planet today will we be able to forge the sort of world we need and want.

Tom O'Reilly

Peacekeeping in Africa:
A New Zealand Defence Force Perspective

I have been asked to address the topic of peacekeeping in Africa from a New Zealand Defence Force (NZDF) perspective. By virtue of my most recent experiences, I intend to concentrate on the UN's peacekeeping operations in Angola.

With world attention focused on Bosnia and that country's sad problems, it is easy to forget that New Zealand has personnel deployed in other places around the world, operating in many cases in appallingly difficult conditions. For instance, since 1979 over 300 servicemen and service-women have served in various missions in Africa under the most demanding circumstances. I am grateful for this opportunity to write about their contribution and the significant role that the NZDF has played in Africa, and in particular in Angola. This chapter is based very much on my own experiences in Africa, and especially in Angola.

Angola has been ravaged by over thirty years of war, invariably referred to as the 'forgotten war'. The human and material costs have been staggering. The United Nations became involved in Angola for the first time in 1989. Since then it has completed two operations. While partially successful, these missions have failed to bring peace to this country.

The first UN operation, UNAVEM I,[1] which did not involve New Zealand personnel, was a success. Unfortunately the same cannot be said for the second operation. In this chapter I will explore some of the reasons for its lack of success. The United Nations is currently embarked on its third mission of peace in Angola. While this mission has a greater chance of achieving success, it also faces some major obstacles.

1. The first UN Mission in Angola was simply titled UNAVEM (UN Angola Verification Mission). Once UNAVEM II was established, the first mission was then commonly referred to as UNAVEM I.

In the first part of this chapter I intend to review briefly the NZDF's involvement in Africa. During my work in Angola I was able to draw not only on my own experiences, but also on the collective experiences of over 300 servicemen and women who had served with great credit in Africa over a long period of time. I reaped the benefits of the impressive reputation they had built up. I will also review briefly the root causes of the conflict which has all but destroyed a country which is potentially one of the richest in sub-Saharan Africa. I will also look at the UN's involvement and some of the problems which beset its second mission.

In the second part I will look at some of problems we faced in planning UNAVEM III. Most of my time was spent planning and preparing for the anticipated expansion of UNAVEM II to UNAVEM III. It was during this planning that I experienced some of the most interesting and rewarding moments and, I have to say, some of the most frustrating. Some of the problems we were able to resolve. Unfortunately the more significant issues were those which could only be solved by the UN where, I believe, there is a need for some radical rethinking in relation to the management of peacekeeping operations if the UN is to be more successful in its operations.

NZDF Involvement in Peacekeeping in Africa

Our first major involvement in Africa was in a non-UN operation. Seventy-four New Zealand Army officers and soldiers were part of a 1500-strong Commonwealth Monitoring Force sent to Rhodesia in December 1979. This force had been established to supervise the ceasefire between the warring factions and to monitor the elections which led to the transition of Rhodesia to democratic Zimbabwe. It was a successful operation lasting no more than four months. The force succeeded because it was virtually autonomous in terms of command and control; it had guaranteed funding; it enjoyed the full support of all major parties; and it had clearly defined tasks. In other words it met the basic criteria necessary for a successful peacekeeping operation.

From 1989 on New Zealand was involved in a number of operations, beginning with Namibia. We contributed engineers[2] as part of an ANZAC contingent to the UN Transitional Assistance Group (UNTAG) in Namibia. This mission had been set up to oversee

2   New Zealand also contributed a contingent of some 30 police to UNTAG.

the elections and the transition of the country from 74 years of South African rule to independence. It is worth noting that this operation was very closely linked to the one in Angola in that it was set up following the signing of an agreement between the South African, Cuban and Angolan governments which saw the withdrawal of the Cubans from Angola and of the South Africans from Southwest Africa (now Namibia). Our contingent served in Namibia from September 1989 to mid-1990. The mission in Namibia too was a success. It also had the necessary political and financial support from all parties and a clear mandate with relatively straight forward tasks.

In 1992 New Zealand was requested to provide support for the UN force which was established in Somalia primarily to assist with the delivery and distribution of humanitarian aid. Between November 1992 and late 1994 almost 150 NZDF personnel from the army and air force were involved in providing both logistic and air support. While the UN succeeded in achieving its limited objective of providing aid, it allowed its aim to become confused, and suffered what General John Sanderson referred to as 'mission creep'. As a result it lost its way and ended in failure.

In December 1993 we sent personnel to assist with the mine action programme in Mozambique. As an aside, this is an area in which our engineers have built up an impressive reputation, to the point where they are now in great demand to provide assistance in mine-clearing operations. We have retained a small group of two engineers in Mozambique to continue assisting with that programme.

The NZDF next provided an aircraft and support personnel for a short period to assist in the human tragedy which struck Rwanda in early 1994.

Angola

In 1991 we got involved again in Africa, this time in a country which few New Zealanders knew anything about: Angola. Over the next four years we were to get to know it well. It is a huge, fertile country of 1.2 million square km (the size of England, Spain and France combined) with a population of about 10.5 million. It is potentially one of the richest agricultural countries in sub-Saharan Africa with the ability to be self-sufficient in all cash crops. It has the richest fishing grounds in Southern Africa. It has no desert droughts and is free of the geographical calamities which affect countries like Somalia and Sudan. It also boasts significant reserves of oil and diamonds.

At the height of production in 1992, Angola produced more than 1.3 million carats (worth US $270 million) of mostly gemstone quality diamonds. Even in 1993, when *Uniao Nacional para a Independencia Total de Angola* (UNITA), the main faction opposing the government, occupied the principal mining areas in the northeast, it was estimated that UNITA was exporting up to $250 million worth of diamonds a year to finance its war efforts. Angola also produces some 600,000 barrels per day of oil, earning approximately $3 billion in revenue, 60 percent of which goes directly back into the defence budget. Unfortunately there is little evidence that any of the revenue is put back into rebuilding the country's infrastructure, destroyed by years of war. However, petrol is heavily subsidised. Those lucky enough to own a vehicle or a boat can get very cheap petrol. Petrol is cheaper than water. For instance a bottle of filtered water costs $1.50. For this one could fill an average sized vehicle and get change back (if change was available). Since most Angolans do not own anything with a motor, this measure does not provide much relief for them at all.

Unfortunately the flight of the Portuguese settlers, the collapse of the marketing and distribution organisations and a 20-year civil war has prevented the country from reaping the benefits of these boundless riches.

The Roots of the Conflict

Angola had been colonised by the Portuguese in the late sixteenth century. Following over 400 years of repressive rule, the 1950s and 1960s were marked by the emergence of a number of resistance movements. Many of these were brutally repressed. The three major nationalist movements—the *Movimento Popular de Libertacao de Angola* (MPLA), UNITA and the *Frente Nacional de Libertacao de Angola* (FNLA)—sought to remove the Portuguese colonial presence but were unable to unify their forces or achieve much success against the Portuguese army.

The turning point came in 1974 when the Portuguese government was overthrown and replaced by a military council keen to decolonise. In January 1975 an agreement was reached in which a transitional government of all three nationalist movements was established to prepare Angola for independence on 11 November 1975, on the withdrawal of the Portuguese. Portugal had failed as a colonial power. It did not prepare the Angolans for independence. While the nationalist movements were suppressed ruthlessly, little education was provided and very few Angolan administrators were trained. These factors, together with the ethnic and regional differences between the nationalist movements, contributed to the intensified conflict which followed Portugal's departure.

The transitional arrangement did not last and the parties split. The MPLA assumed the mantle of government while UNITA and the FNLA set up a separate coalition government in the central city of Huambo. Attempted reconciliation of the movements deteriorated into civil war and external involvement. Troops from South Africa and Cuba entered the fray with support from the Soviet Union, China and the United States. The South Africans withdrew in 1976 but the war continued unabated. The Cuban involvement continued to increase and the South Africans re-entered the war on several occasions until the late 1980s. In 1989, as the result of a regional peace plan which guaranteed Namibian independence, South Africa withdrew its forces from Namibia while Cuba also withdrew its forces from Angola under the supervision of the first UN mission in Angola, UNAVEM I.

The United Nations in Angola

Interestingly, the creation of UNAVEM I resulted not from a political settlement between the parties to Angola's long civil war, but as part of the political settlement that led to Namibia's independence. UNAVEM I was a small mission charged with verifying the withdrawal of the Cubans from Angola. It began its task in 1988 and successfully completed it in May 1991, two months ahead of schedule. Again, here was a mission which had the necessary political and financial support. It also had a clear mandate with clearly defined tasks and a realistic timeframe in which to complete them. It had all the necessary ingredients of a successful mission, which it was.

Unfortunately the withdrawal of the Cubans and South Africans from Angola did not bring immediate peace. UNITA and the MPLA felt that each had the ability to gain the upper hand and win a military solution. Very quickly a stalemate developed on the battlefield. This, together with the rising costs of the conflict for both sides, led them to search for a peaceful solution in earnest.

An agreement was finally reached in May 1991 in Portugal under the auspices of the United Nations. UNAVEM I's mandate was expanded to monitor the new accord. The new mission, UNAVEM II, was deployed in June 1991. The force comprised some 350 military observers and 126 police with a mandate to monitor the ceasefire, including the assembling and disarmament of both armies; monitor the integration of the two armies; and supervise parliamentary and presidential elections.

Initially the ceasefire held because both sides thought they had a good chance of winning the elections. Consequently, by late 1992 UNAVEM II had achieved some success in assembling the troops of both sides. It had also organised parliamentary elections, which the MPLA won. However, the presidential elections were not completed. Jose Eduardo dos Santos, the MPLA Leader, did not get the necessary votes and a second round was called for. Unfortunately, before this could take place, UNITA's leader Jonas Savimbi had declared the elections unfair and mobilised his forces.

The government was slow to react. However, by the end of October 1992 UNITA had been driven out of the capital Luanda, and its top leaders killed or imprisoned. By mid-1993 the government had captured most of the provincial capitals except Uige in the north and Huambo in the central region, while UNITA controlled 75 percent of the countryside. Because of the deteriorating situation, by late 1992 UNAVEM II had been reduced in size and withdrawn to the relative safety of the government-controlled areas. It was relegated primarily to a liaison and good offices role in anticipation of a new agreement being reached and the eventual re-establishment of the mission.

NZDF Involvement

With UNAVEM II came New Zealand's first involvement in Angola. While we had no defence interests in Angola, we took part for primarily humanitarian reasons. In addition, New Zealand was at that time campaigning for a seat on the Security Council. It was therefore doubly in our interest to be seen to be actively supporting the UN initiatives and operations. In order to enhance our credibility as a potential Security Council member we needed to participate.

In July 1991 we deployed twelve army officers to Angola as observers. They, together with some 450 other observers, were deployed throughout Angola to monitor the assembling of government and UNITA forces. Conditions were extremely difficult for this operation. Nonetheless, they did achieve a degree of success initially.

This group was replaced in March–April 1992. The second group arrived in time to witness the collapse of the ceasefire and the return to full-scale war in late 1992. By this stage UNITA had developed a tremendous mistrust of the United Nations, blaming it for the unfavourable election results. UN observers were being constantly harassed and were rapidly becoming an endangered species. Under these difficult conditions the New Zealand observers, along with the remainder of UNAVEM II, were forced to withdraw to the relative safety of government-controlled areas. We finally withdrew all our people from Angola in early 1993.

Lessons from UNAVEM II

UNAVEM II had been hamstrung from the beginning by a flawed agreement and an unclear and unrealistic mandate. It also lacked adequate financial support and commitment from all the parties involved.

The agreement reached in Portugal was flawed in that it gave UNAVEM little power in supervising, coordinating and controlling the implementation of the ceasefire. While the operation was overseen by a Joint Commission, the UN's status in this commission was little more than that of an observer.

Although the operation was supported politically by the superpowers, this did not translate into full financial support. Because of the lack of finance and resources, UNAVEM was forced to play a limited role only. The two parties to the conflict were therefore charged with the sole responsibility of implementing the ceasefire and ensuring its success with the assistance of the UN. The UN had little power to enforce or control the agreed implementation schedules. For instance, the UN did not have a direct role to play in the process of demobilising the assembled troops. It was therefore not able to coordinate this process with the completion of the elections.

For the peace to succeed it was essential to complete the process of assembling, disarming, integrating into the National Defence Force and demobilising of surplus troops before the elections. Unfortunately, the UN did not have the power to do this. Therefore, at the time of the elections three armies still existed; the government, UNITA and part of the newly formed integrated army. When the elections failed, the two leaders were able to continue the conflict with their forces largely intact. This was undoubtedly a major factor contributing to the lack of success of this operation.

The mission's timetable was also unrealistic. UNAVEM II was required to assemble all troops by August 1991, three months from the start of the operation. This timetable took no account of the actual situation on the ground. The road and rail systems had been badly damaged with most of the roads mined and the bridges destroyed. Most of the airfields were unusable. In addition, the country's administration was in disarray and unable to support the deployment of UNAVEM. For instance, in reading through the files on my arrival in Angola, I noted a message from the Chief Military Observer to the UN advising that the deployment of the observers into the field had been delayed because of disruptions in the scheduled commercial flights within Angola. This created significant difficulties for the deployment of the observers, their support and the movement of the troops of both parties to the assembly areas.

The approval of the mission budget had also been delayed, resulting in a shortage of critical items of supply, both for the mission itself and for the preparation of the assembly areas. In addition, the deep mistrust between the two parties resulted in serious delays in getting approval for observer teams to carry out their reconnaissances and deployments.

Lack of financial support was also reflected in the size of the mission. Three hundred and fifty Military and 126 Police Observers were expected to assemble, disarm and integrate some 150,000 fully armed, battle hardened soldiers who had been fighting for over twenty years. In fact most of these soldiers had known no other occupation but fighting since their early teens. While the UN observers did an admirable job, the task given to them was unrealistic and the resources to complete it were inadequate. Even in Zimbabwe, there were 1500 of us to carry out a similar task for a lot fewer soldiers. Similarly in Mozambique a force of over 7000, including over 1000 police, was needed to assemble forces a fraction of the size of those of UNITA and the government.

The net effect of these problems was that UNAVEM II was late in deploying, inadequately resourced and unable to carry out its tasks effectively. By the time that it had deployed fully the renewed war was almost upon it.

The Lusaka Accords

In 1993, intense pressure was put on the parties involved in the Angolan conflict to return to the negotiating table. The United Nations and the international community had had enough. In fact the Angolan people themselves had had enough; they had suffered terribly. The war had cost dearly in terms of human suffering. In 1993 alone it was estimated that 1000 people were dying each day as a direct or indirect result of the war. During the period of the conflict there were an estimated 500,000 casualties; one million displaced people; 100,000 orphaned children; over 100,000 amputees, many of them children; and over 3 million people (37 percent of the population) requiring humanitarian aid. There was little food and the state infrastructure had been largely destroyed. The country had become a monumental humanitarian problem which could not be sustained.

Both sides were also beginning to 'feel the pinch'. UNITA for instance had lost much of its traditional support. Discipline and morale within the party was low and it had suffered several major setbacks on the battlefield. The cost of the conflict to both sides in financial, materiel and human terms, together with international pressure, forced the parties to search for yet another solution. The end result was that by October–November 1993 a new round of talks commenced in Lusaka, the Zambian capital. These talks were conducted under UN auspices and were chaired by the UN.

It was at this point that we again became involved. In October we sent two observers to UNAVEM II and later that year in December, I went across as Chief of Staff and Deputy Chief Military Observer.

The talks made good progress until January–February 1994, by which time the police and military aspects of the accord had been agreed. However, for the next 10 months it was a frustratingly slow stop-start process with frequent delays over issues relating primarily to UNITA's role in the new administration. I was part of the UNAVEM delegation which negotiated the final military details. Even in the closing stages of the negotiations I recall moments when the talks were in jeopardy. For instance the first item on our military agenda was to negotiate an immediate truce. At this stage the government had ignored all overtures and was about to move against the last two provincial capitals held by UNITA. One of these, Huambo, was at that time the fighting headquarters of UNITA. One can imagine the effect that the loss of this city was likely to have had on the peace process. We were keen to prevent this by instituting an immediate truce.

The government wished otherwise and used delaying tactics. The principle of a truce had been agreed but we could not agree on the time it would come into effect. The issue was a relatively simple one. We wanted the truce in place within 12 hours; the government wanted 48, and we knew why. This time it was we who threatened to walk out. The government took notice but continued to delay, telling us that they would need to refer the matter back to their president for advice. As we expected, when we next convened they agreed to our proposal. But by then it was too late; they had already taken both Uige and Huambo. For a while it looked as though the peace process could be in jeopardy. Thankfully we convinced UNITA to remain at the table.

There were to be one or two other incidents of this nature but eventually we reached an agreement which was finally signed on 20 November 1993. UNAVEM II would be expanded to some 350 Military Observers and 260 Police Observers. In addition, this time it would also have about 6500 peacekeeping troops and 160 staff officers to monitor the new ceasefire.

UNAVEM III

The present agreement and mandate are based to a large degree on the 1991 agreement which resulted in the establishment of UNAVEM II. In essence UNAVEM III is required to complete the tasks started by UNAVEM II. The mission would verify the extension of state administration throughout the country and monitor the process of national reconciliation. UNITA will take up the seats it won in the 1992 elections as part of the process. UNITA would also take up the various positions allocated to it with the state administration structure. The UN's role will be to ensure that this process is completed and that the conditions are suitable for the holding of the second round of the presidential elections. The United Nations will then be responsible for supervising these.

UNAVEM III's role is stronger in comparison to that of its predecessor. The peace process is again supervised by a Joint Commission. However, this time it is chaired by the UN. Further, while the two parties are still primarily responsible for the success of the process, the United Nations now has greater power to ensure that they play their part.

On the military side, UNAVEM III is required to complete the tasks started by UNAVEM II. These include: supervising the disarming and quartering of all UNITA troops; supervising the movement of government troops into barracks; supervising the completion of the formation of the integrated Angolan Defence Forces; supervising the demobilisation of surplus UNITA and government soldiers; and assisting with humanitarian tasks, including demining.[3]

---

3.   The humanitarian responsibilities of UNAVEM III, particularly in relation to demining, are significant, but will not be addressed to any great degree in this

Given the size of the country; the state of the country's infrastructure; the mine situation and the number of troops involved from the two parties (approximately 150,000 in total), the tasks for the new mission are still monumental. In theory, with a stronger mandate and a larger force it should have a better chance of success than its predecessor. However, there are still some major concerns.

Planning and Implementation Issues

Let us now look at some of the major issues that plagued us as we planned this operation. There is no doubt that the present agreement and mandate give the UN more power to coordinate, control and supervise the operation. Unfortunately there are still a number of crucial areas in which they are flawed. These deficiencies could determine the success or failure of this mission.

The Agreement and Mandate

The mandate for the current force envisages only one side being disarmed and quartered, UNITA. This is in contrast to the mandate for UNAVEM II in which both sides were to be disarmed and quartered. The government forces are required only to return to barracks. In any operation involving two belligerents, it is imperative that both sides are treated equally; this is obviously not so in this case. The government had insisted on its right, as a sovereign government, to retain its armed forces. The UN acceded to this. UNITA had little choice but to accept it as well, although they were not happy for obvious reasons, not least their fear of being attacked. If they are attacked, UNAVEM III will not have sufficient force to protect them.

The plan for UNAVEM III provided for six infantry battalions to monitor and supervise 14 UNITA quartering areas and eight weapons storage sites. Each site will therefore have only a company of about 200 personnel to provide security. Each quartering area is likely to have some 4000 UNITA troops. It is not difficult, therefore, to see that it would be impossible to expect the company to provide the protection required by UNITA. Although we developed detailed plans for the disarming of UNITA, I fear that this will not be an easy task. The peace process could fail on this issue alone.

---

paper.

Finally, the mission has again being given an unrealistic time-frame in which to complete its tasks. For instance, within three months of the approval of the mandate, the quartering of UNITA was to have commenced. Some six months into the operation, this process was not even close to starting. The reconnaissance of the quartering area locations had not been completed. Significant delays had resulted from such 'minor' details as the lack of funding and resources; the delay in approving the budgets; and delays in confirming the availability of troops. The whole operation was to have been completed within 15 months; this will clearly not be achieved.

The consequence of these delays is that the troops from both sides have now been 'sitting' facing each other for over seven months with little or no food and little prospect of moving into quartering areas or back to barracks immediately. This situation has resulted in a rapid increase in dissatisfaction among the troops, desertion and banditry. The risks for the UN observers and troops have increased proportionately.

Command and Control

UN Headquarters (HQ) micromanages peacekeeping operations to an unacceptable degree. UNAVEM III was no exception. The implementation of the expansion plan for UNAVEM III was unnecessarily hampered by HQ's desire to be involved in the detailed management of the implementation. When Force HQ needed to have its attention focused on the implementation, it was too often distracted by UN HQ's preoccupation with minutiae and management at the micro level. This was exacerbated by its continual interference in operational command and control matters and its reluctance to fully devolve to the Force Commander the management of resources allocated to the mission.

There is a need for the United Nations to devolve greater responsibility for the detailed command and control of its operations, including the management of resources, to the mission staff. While it should certainly retain strategic oversight and provide political, operational and financial direction, it must devolve funding and authority to either the Special Representative of the Secretary-General or the Force Commander to get on with it. This would allow the Special Representative or Force Commander to tailor the needs of the operation to meet the situation. More importantly, the UN HQ can divest itself of much of the day-to-day minutiae. As we have witnessed in the New Zealand public sector, devolution and the provision of greater autonomy in running the operation leads to greater efficiency and effectiveness and a more responsive operation.

Resource and Financial Management

This issue is closely allied to the preceding one. The lack of control by the Force Commander over the resources available to him restricts his ability to act decisively when the operation faces difficult or changing circumstances. We suffered from this constraint many times during the operation of UNAVEM II and the implementation of UNAVEM. Many is the time we could not react to a particular situation because 'it had not been provided for in the budget'.

The problem begins at the top, at UN HQ in New York. The UN controls the resources and finances allocated to a mission through career civil staff. They do not come under the control of either the Force Commander or the Special Representative but report directly to New York. They do not even answer to the same department as the Force Commander. The Force Commander therefore has little control over the resources allocated for him to carry out his tasks. This lack of control places unnecessary limitations on the Force Commander. Logistics and finance are critical functions to a mission which most modern officers are trained to carry out effectively. There needs to be greater integration of the military and civilian functions within a mission. The United Nations will need to address this issue with the objective of providing commanders in the field greater control of their resources.

The UN and National Bureaucratic Constraints

We were further constrained in our planning by two major bureaucratic obstacles which the UN has not been able to overcome; the inability of the UN to approve provisional or advance funding; and its inability to confirm at an early stage those countries which will provide troops.

The lack of early provision of funds and resources has already resulted in a serious delay in the deployment of UNAVEM III. The original timetable envisaged the force being in place within six months. Unfortunately, lack of funds meant that we were barely able to cater for the observers, never mind the troops. We could not put in place the infrastructure and facilities necessary for the reception of the troops. In fact we could barely house and supply the observer teams who were deployed early into the field.

By mid-February we had deployed some 500 observers to almost 60 team sites throughout Angola. With few supply routes, they had to be supported by air. To do this we had one small transport aircraft initially which had to be used both to deploy and support the teams, an almost impossible task. It was not until much later that we received an additional aircraft. Some of the teams could only be supported by helicopter, which the UN would not provide. We were forced to rely on the Angolan Air Force to provide civilian helicopters, whose pilots more often than not refused to fly because of the security situation. On those days when they did fly, the aircraft invariably broke down. It was a nightmare which we had to work through slowly.

The provisional size of the expanded UNAVEM III force and its tasks were identified very early in the planning process. Preparation for the implementation of the operation would have been significantly assisted if the UN had been able to confirm early in the process what troops would be available and what equipment they would have. Although initial approaches had been made to potential troop providers, there were no commitments until after the agreement had been signed. By then it was too late. This created significant delays in the deployment of the force.

The UN's inability to confirm at an early stage the availability of troops is a significant problem. Unfortunately the solution to this problem would involve commitments from contributing nations and, as we know, such commitment is not easy to obtain. It is accepted that some of these issues can only be resolved with the cooperation of contributing nations. Nonetheless the UN must be more proactive and less reactive. While the current planning to establish standby forces may alleviate some of the problems, the need to provide early budget approval and seek early commitment from contributing nations is essential to the success of a mission.

Status of Forces Agreement

This is the contract between the United Nations and the host nation which sets out what support the host nation will provide to the mission. It is a crucial document. In our planning for UNAVEM III, we had great difficulty convincing the Angolan government of the need to provide facilities and resources for the mission. Many requests inevitably, and to some extent understandably, had a price tag attached. We spent many largely fruitless months negotiating such things as accommodation space, and airport and port facilities. An agreed status of forces agreement may not have resolved the problem, but it would certainly have provided us with a firmer base from which to negotiate.

Unfortunately even as I left Angola in April 1995, four months into the operation, a status of forces agreement had not been successfully negotiated with the Angolan government. The planning of UNAVEM III was severely hampered for the lack of an agreed document. Notwithstanding political and bureaucratic considerations, it is crucial that this document be agreed to before the operation is implemented.

Effective Information and Intelligence Gathering Systems

Effective planning and sound decision-making relies on the receipt of quality and timely intelligence. UNAVEM had no system to achieve this and neither was the UN able to provide. This is a critical capability deficiency which the UN must resolve. Since late 1992 we had lost contact with UNITA and had been restricted to operating within government controlled areas. We therefore had no access to sources which could provide reliable, up-to-date information about the state of the country's infrastructure or about UNITA strengths and dispositions. For that matter we had very little reliable information on the government. The problem with the UN operations is not a lack of information but the inability to collate and interpret this information effectively. We were invariably inundated with information from humanitarian agencies, locals and even our own observers. Unfortunately, we did not have the appropriate systems to process this information into useful intelligence.

Allied to this was our concern over the lack of information available from both sides concerning the mine problem. Mines have been laid continually over the past thirty years by the independence movements and the Portuguese, by UNITA, the government, the Cubans and the South Africans. It is estimated that as much as 70 percent of the country is mined with between 9 to 15 million mines and unexploded munitions. Neither side has been forthcoming with information which would allow us to plan for the eventual massive clearing operation which will be required. A more effective information or, dare I say it, engineering intelligence-gathering system, may have provided us with enough information to ensure that planning was more advanced than it is at present.

Political Will and Cooperation

The need to gain the trust of both sides and their cooperation is fundamental to the success of any peacekeeping operation. To a large extent we, the military, had achieved this in Angola because we ensured that our dealings with both sides were scrupulously fair. However we could never be absolutely certain of their sincerity.

Great mistrust still exists between the two parties. This, together with a lack of clear will for peace, will severely test the chances of achieving real peace. For instance, in private, senior UNITA officials made it quite clear to us that they did not trust the government and were 'too scared' to return to Luanda following the summary execution of senior UNITA members after the renewal of fighting in late 1992.

Of greater concern is that the parties have little reason to adhere to the accord. The government believes, incorrectly in my view, that it can still win a military solution. On the other hand UNITA continues to believe that it has nothing to gain from the peace process and that it can continue to make the country 'ungovernable' unless its demands are met.

Future of UNAVEM III

These are just a few of the issues which made life difficult in planning the expansion of UNAVEM. It would be easy to believe that, with all these problems, the mission has no chance of succeeding. This is not necessarily so. Within the constraints I have mentioned we developed a plan which can succeed. It will, however, require the will and the concerted efforts from, and support of, all parties to prevent its failure a second time. The recent meeting between dos Santos and Savimbi was a significant step towards ensuring the success of the process. We can but watch in hope and hope for a better result. Furthermore, New Zealand's confidence in the process is such that we have increased our commitment to five military observers. In addition we are in the process of sending a team of nine to assist with the mine action programme.

Conclusion

Angola is a country ravaged by war, whose people want nothing more than an end to the suffering and to be able to return to their land. In effect there are 10.5 million people being held to ransom by a mere handful of megalomaniacs. It is hoped that an end can soon be put to this suffering. I believe that at present the United Nations has a good chance of doing just that. It is almost Angola's last hope for peace and will need all the help it can get from all parties to ensure its success.

During my time in Angola I was able to witness the good and the not-so-good facets of the UN operations. For a professional soldier, the opportunity to participate in what could turn out to be a momentous occasion is a memorable one. It is a rare opportunity to be involved so intimately at such a high level in both the negotiation and implementation of a peace agreement which could see an end to years of misery.

My experience there was also enlightening. I had the opportunity to address directly the problems that affect UN mission planning. While there were some which we could resolve, unfortunately there are many which will only be resolved by a radical change of philosophy at higher levels within the UN. These are the problems which frustrated us in our planning and which could end up frustrating the efforts of UNAVEM III.

The UN has made significant progress in restructuring its peacekeeping organisation. It has effectively combined the operational and logistic support sides under one roof, and since 1992 it has employed more professional military planners within the peacekeeping organisation. However, if it is to improve the effectiveness of the operations themselves the UN will need to devolve greater responsibility, together with the necessary accountability, to the field commanders. Greater responsibility also needs to be given to the commanders for the management of the funds and resources available to them.

In addition, the United Nations needs to ensure that the mandates approved for missions are clear and unambiguous and contain realistic time-frames for the completion of the missions' tasks. These must have the necessary political and financial support of all parties involved. Budgets and funding must be provided early enough that the manpower and materiel resources can be identified and provided in a timely manner. For many of us here who have experienced financial management reform, these all make common sense. Unfortunately in a bureaucracy such as the UN they are anathema.

There remains a place for the UN as the world's peace-broker. The organisation has taken significant steps to improve its ability to manage peacekeeping operations. However, there are still many issues it must address. If it does not, it will lose what credibility it still has, and lose also the very support it must have from the rest of the world.

Secretary-General Dr Boutros Boutros-Ghali, Prince Norodom Sihanouk, Lt. Gen. John Sanderson and SRSG Mr Yasushi Akashi, Cambodia, April 1992. (Photo: Australian Defence Force)

John M. Sanderson

The Lessons Learnt from UNTAC: The Military Component View

The Peacekeeping Debate

I have made many presentations on the subject of peacekeeping in Cambodia since I left Phnom Penh at the end of September 1993. Much of the media attention there is on the difficulties faced by the United Nations in places such as Somalia and Bosnia. At the professional level, there is an increasing interest in peacekeeping generally, generated by Australia's involvement in a number of operations, and in Cambodia in particular, in view of Australia's major contribution to the diplomatic and operational aspects of the successful resolution of that conflict. The UN's fiftieth anniversary has also stimulated much debate over the organisation's effectiveness, and speculation about its ongoing relevance.

On a broader dimension, the book *Cooperating for Peace* by Australia's Foreign Minister, Senator Gareth Evans, has sought to put peacekeeping into the context of multinational conflict resolution and preventive diplomacy generally. The interest this has aroused has been encouraging.

During many of the presentations I have given, I have stressed the importance of developing skills in the planning and conduct of peacekeeping operations at the operational level, that is, the level between the strategic level, where higher political direction occurs, and the tactical operations in the field. As in war, it is at the operational level that peacekeeping operations are won or lost. I have become convinced that the problem with many other missions is due to something of a disconnect between the strategic and tactical levels, which is almost inevitable if the operational art, which brings the capabilities of diverse elements into harmony to work towards the common objective, is not exploited to its fullest extent. Despite enormous difficulties, in the UN Transitional Authority in Cambodia (UNTAC) we were able to establish this essential link and I hope that this will become clear from what follows.

UNTAC in Context

It is important to make the point early in any discussion about UNTAC that it was unequivocally a success. Even at the time, it was not the biggest United Nations operation—the UN Operation in the Congo (ONUC) was marginally larger; the UN Protection Force in former Yugoslavia (UNPROFOR) is much larger and, it seems, is still growing. But UNTAC was, and remains at the time of writing, the most complex to date. Despite the difficulties experienced, we were able to repatriate nearly 370,000 refugees, and we were able to allow the Cambodian people to have their voice heard in determining their future. The UNTAC-sponsored electoral process led to the formation of a constitutional authority, which could eventually be recognised by the international community as the legitimate Cambodian government—the fundamental purpose of the Paris Agreements of October 1991. Although attempts to obfuscate this outcome continue, any ambiguity over sovereign authority in Cambodia has been removed. While many problems remain, they are beyond the scope of a United Nations transitional authority, which terminated with the ascent of the Cambodian Government.

There remains a tendency to look at UNTAC in terms of Cambodia's tragic past. I would like to make the point that UNTAC was about the future of Cambodia, not the past. Through the process made possible by the Paris Agreements, UNTAC was able to act as a stabilising influence on the Cambodian parties. We were able to moderate the effects of almost thirty years of instability and war, to give Cambodia the opportunity to become a unified member-nation of the United Nations, rather than continue as a potential destabilising influence in the region as well as an international humanitarian concern.

Nevertheless, it is important that we ask ourselves if a better outcome might have been achieved:

- Could we have left Cambodia in better shape if we had done things differently?

- And, perhaps more importantly, could we have prevented some of the problems experienced and their enduring effects, if the mission had been approached differently?

From my perspective as Force Commander, UNTAC was an exciting and challenging experience of enormous significance to Cambodia, to the Asia–Pacific region, and to the world. There is inevitably considerable interest in the operations of the Military Component, which was by far the largest and most visible element of UNTAC. To a large degree, the significance was reflected in the diversity of the 34-nation force under my command. Many nations were participating in a UN peacekeeping mission for the first time. Both Germany and Japan deployed troops outside their sovereign territories for the first time since the end of the Second World War, against a background of intense domestic political scrutiny. It was also China's first such mission. A number of former Iron Curtain countries also participated. All three nations of the Indian sub-continent were represented together for the first time. Uruguay's involvement saw it deploy troops outside its borders for the first time in over one hundred years. Shortly before the elections, Namibia, at the time the most recent beneficiary of UN peacekeeping efforts, deployed a small contingent. The command was both joint and combined. Australia and New Zealand combined to provide the vital communications links which allowed the totality to be pulled together.

It was clear that the maintenance of the commitment of contributing countries and the readiness of many nations to contribute troops to future missions would be influenced by the outcomes. There was therefore a heavy responsibility on the Force Commander to ensure success. In many respects, UNTAC was as important to the future of United Nations peacekeeping as it was to Cambodia. Accordingly, I think that it would miss the point to focus on the Military Component alone and I therefore intend to focus on its activities in the context of UNTAC as a complete operation.

General UNTAC Framework

When I arrived with the Special Representative of the Secretary-General, Mr Yasushi Akashi, on 15 March 1992 to establish UNTAC, the political climate had deteriorated to one of extreme volatility. The Paris Agreements had been signed five months earlier. Their purpose was to enable the international community to sponsor a comprehensive settlement agreed by the Cambodian parties. UNTAC's role was to generate confidence through neutral oversight of agreed mechanisms. However, at the time of our arrival things were definitely not going according to plan. An examination of those Agreements helps to explain why the situation had deteriorated to the extent that it had.

The central pillars of the agreed process were the stabilisation of the security environment and the creation of a neutral political environment. These were not sequential, but parallel and interdependent military and civil actions designed to open the way for the repatriation of the refugees and the electoral process; followed by a constitutional process leading to a legitimate government. In essence, the difficulties resulted because the Khmer Rouge were unwilling to participate in the military actions on the basis that the civil actions had not been implemented.

The fragile climate of trust reflected in the Agreements was undermined from very early in the process. What does not seem to have been foreseen was the activities initiated by the Agreements themselves, as the Cambodian parties, and some nations, manoeuvred to gain advantage from the new political dynamics. These dynamics were manifested in November 1991 when attempts were made to form an alliance between the State of Cambodia (SoC) Prime Minister, Hun Sen, and the leader of the royalist party FUNCINPEC (the French acronym for the National United Front for an Independent, Neutral, Peaceful and Cooperative Cambodia), Prince Norodom Ranariddh; and when the Khmer Rouge were driven from Phnom Penh following orchestrated demonstrations. At about the same time, both the SoC and the Khmer Rouge launched military operations against each other in the countryside.

In this climate, the influence of the moderates, which had probably been instrumental in bringing the major parties to accept the Agreements, was weakened by the inability to deploy substantial UN resources at an early date. The planning and preparation for UNTAC had only been initiated by the signing of the Agreements and proceeded all too slowly. The UN Advance Mission in Cambodia (UNAMIC) proved powerless to influence events. Its presence was far too small even to attribute responsibility for disturbances in the countryside. As a consequence, the Khmer Rouge were blamed for everything, which led them in turn to question the neutrality of the United Nations. With the Agreements only a few months old, they already appeared to be stillborn.

The Phase Two Ceasefire

In essence, the functions of the Military Component were concerned with ceasefire supervision and other confidence-building measures.

Their centrepiece was the Phase Two ceasefire, involving regroup-
ment, cantonment and disarming of the armed forces of the Cambodian
parties, and eventual demobilisation of at least 70 percent of them.

Phase Two was only partially carried out because, as is generally
known, the Khmer Rouge refused to participate, for reasons which
still require a great deal of analysis. The right of self-defence meant
that substantial elements of the other armed forces had to remain in the
field. The continuing confrontation and the inherent security risks
impacted on the other UNTAC programmes.

However, the Phase Two ceasefire was not a stand-alone activity.
It was linked to other provisions for the control of the machinery of
government. In particular, the SoC police forces were a matter of
concern. With a strength of some 45,000, these were not community
police, but the politicised forces of a one-party state, designed to
protect the interests of the regime. Moreover, with the armed forces of
the parties cantoned, disarmed and largely demobilised as the Agreements required, the relative power of the police would have been
markedly increased. The Paris Agreements placed the police forces of
the parties under UNTAC supervision or control. However, the
Agreements did not specify any control measures similar, for example,
to those measures governing the disposal of the armed forces.

A Justice Package for Cambodia?

When the Paris Agreements are looked at even more broadly, it
becomes clear that one of the major omissions was the failure to
include provisions for the building of a justice system, in the form of
an impartial, non-political police force and judiciary, and provisions
ensuring due process. In theory, the administrative systems of the
Cambodian factions were to do this, but the absence of an effective
justice system was a major cause of the demands, throughout the
operation, for peacekeepers to move beyond self-defence to a form of
enforcement. But UNTAC was a peacekeeping mission under Chapter
VI of the UN Charter. Of necessity, respect for the Agreements was
assumed; therefore force (in a law-and-order context) could only be
exercised by the parties themselves.

The Paris Agreements did at least lay the foundations. They
obliged UNTAC to foster respect for human rights (Article 15).
UNTAC was granted supervisory or control powers over law-and-
order processes to ensure that they were maintained effectively and
impartially and to ensure that human rights and fundamental freedoms

were fully protected [Annex 1, Section B, paragraph 5(b)].

These provisions were built on during the life of the mission. On 20 April 1992, the Supreme National Council (SNC—the quadripartite body enshrining Cambodian sovereignty during the UNTAC mandate) acceded to the International Convention on Civil and Political Rights, and the International Convention on Economic, Social and Cultural Rights. Those instruments entered into force in Cambodia on 26 August 1992. In addition, on 10 September 1992, the SNC passed the Provisions Relating to the Judiciary and Criminal Law and Procedure. The preamble to the Criminal Law noted the deficiencies in the structures, laws and judicial institutions in Cambodia, as well as UNTAC's responsibilities in improving those which existed, and in assisting to establish them where they did not. Adequate foundations therefore existed for a proactive approach by UNTAC in the justice area.

In the event, the UNTAC Criminal Law itself contained many deficiencies. But in any case it was largely left to the parties to implement. By November 1992 it was clear that the main human rights breaches were murders being perpetrated by the police and military of the factions, and they were either unable or unwilling to enforce the law using their own processes. As a result, in January 1993 UNTAC gave the power of arrest to the UNTAC Military Component and the Civil Police Component (CIVPOL), and created the Office of Special Prosecutor with the authority to issue warrants and prosecute cases before the Cambodian courts.

This process degenerated into farce. Firstly, UNTAC had no access to the Party of Democratic Kampuchea (PDK) structures. The structures in FUNCINPEC and the Khmer People's National Liberation Front (KPNLF) areas relied on summary justice. Only the SoC had anything approaching a recognisable justice system and resented its being 'singled out'. In any case, the police and judiciary refused to implement the law without political direction. In the face of this obstacle, UNTAC Civil Administration and CIVPOL lacked the commitment to see the justice issue through.

It makes sense for peace-building missions such as UNTAC to focus on the longer term objective of establishing within that society a respect for human rights. The critical element is to understand that it is only through influencing the values of the society that a human rights culture of any substance will be inculcated. Along with issues of peace, reconciliation and sovereignty, those of human rights and justice form an important element in conflict resolution. Agreed and unambiguous provisions aimed at ensuring the creation of non-political police forces were also needed, for example through training schemes and the provision of funding, which would have removed their dependence on the parties and could have facilitated UNTAC control. In addition, a system of laws and an independent judiciary similarly held accountable to UNTAC would have enabled these police to prosecute offenders effectively. A comprehensive justice package would have balanced the UNTAC mandate and could have helped to strengthen the constitutional government when it assumed power.

The Khmer Rouge Dilemma

It can only be conjectured at this stage whether the Khmer Rouge seriously intended to participate in the process. Nevertheless, the lack of implementation of adequate control measures undermined the prospect for a quadripartite process. Looked at from the Khmer Rouge perspective, the National Army of Democratic Kampuchea (NADK) was their protective shield. In terms of the fanatical Khmer Rouge nationalist ideology, the SoC equated with the hated Vietnamese presence which forced them from power in 1979. With the SoC police intact and still under party control, the Khmer Rouge could not allow UNTAC to disarm the NADK without making themselves vulnerable. It is important to recall that the Khmer Rouge only accepted compromise in 1991 on the issue of quadripartite government (which would have given them a share in the government of all Cambodia) because of the inclusion of the control provisions in the Paris Agreements. But by themselves they were not enough.

Any expectation that they might have held about the collapse of SoC administration with the return of Sihanouk to Phnom Penh would have dissipated with his statements about forming a SoC–Royalist coalition, and the realisation that the majority of UN rehabilitation funds were to be spent in the SoC areas. Added to this was their clear concern that the electoral law was not going to exclude Khmers of Vietnamese ethnic origin—a difficult issue in view of what they had been telling their rank and file about the overwhelming Vietnamese presence in Cambodia.

By August 1992, the Khmer Rouge were calling for power to be given to SNC; for the SNC and UNTAC jointly to control the 'five fields' of SoC administration (finance, foreign affairs, information, defence and public security); and for the withdrawal of Vietnamese forces which, in effect, was aimed at sustaining their propaganda line amongst their own rank and file. The demands relating to the authority of the SNC and administrative control were beyond the scope of the Military Component. In accordance with its mandate to verify the withdrawal and non-return of foreign forces, the Military Component tried to find the Vietnamese forces which the Khmer Rouge said were in Cambodia, but they never helped in any way: no allegation was ever substantiated and no forces with any significance in the terms of the Agreements were ever found.

These conditions were all cited by the Khmer Rouge as prerequisites for their cooperation in the process. A little later, in early 1993, they called for quadripartite military and police forces. In essence, these were a return to the power-sharing proposals which had been rejected by the SoC at the first Paris Conference in 1989. They were still unacceptable and clearly beyond the Paris Agreements as they existed when they were signed. Perhaps the Khmer Rouge thought that they were achievable in the light of the new dynamics. But in any case, by 1993 they were the only conditions with which the Khmer Rouge could feel safe—they left the NADK intact until the SoC police could be somehow neutralised, either politically by UNTAC and a strengthened SNC, or by the SoC's ultimate collapse as the peace process lost direction.

The Khmer Rouge evidently reasoned that, threatened by a loss of power in the election, elements of the still well-armed SoC could be expected to resort to violence and intimidation. By not disarming, the Khmer Rouge sought to increase the SoC's unpopularity and made it easier to defeat politically, with the added potential of avoiding an election in which the Khmer Rouge could itself expect to be marginalised. Although it is noteworthy that all parties declared their full support for the Agreements, the delay in UNTAC deployment simply made it easier for elements within the parties to evade their responsibilities. Both the SoC and the Khmer Rouge stated that they could not implement the Agreements because of UNTAC's failure to control the other. These were continuing themes.

It is possible that the Khmer Rouge were not alone in their concerns over the SoC police. They would have almost certainly been shared by the smaller parties. Khmer Rouge intransigence also served the interests of the Cambodian People's Armed Forces (CPAF), the SoC army, which wanted to maintain their prerogatives into whatever new order emerged. On demobilisation, its members too would have been vulnerable to opponents in the SoC.

UNTAC's Troubled Beginnings

As Force Commander, in early 1992 I could feel the ground moving away from under myself and those moderates of all military factions who were committed to the process. I held numerous discussions with the Khmer Rouge military commander, General Son Sen, about this time, but it was clear that he could no longer deliver all Khmer Rouge forces in the countryside to the process. Perhaps this would never have been possible without the Agreements generating an irresistible momentum for peace. Nevertheless, this undermining of the moderates was partly due to a new-found assertiveness by reactionaries in the factions, and partly to a rapid decline in confidence in the UN.

The Military Component deployed in the period May–July 1992 in a climate of growing mistrust. The Civil Police Component deployed even later. The Civil Administration Component was not complete until nearly one year after the Agreements were signed, its staff of some 170 woefully inadequate for the task in any case. By then the repatriation programme was only proceeding with difficulty, into a countryside with the armed forces still holding the field and some areas heavily mined.

The point to be drawn from this is not whose fault it might have been, but simply that the signing of the Agreements should have been a 'trigger' for the execution of an integrated and comprehensive set of plans already in place—plans which gave the United Nations the means to exercise transitional authority in Cambodia from the outset. Regrettably, for almost everyone in UNTAC except the Military Component, the process was one of on-the-job training, while implementing plans prepared by someone else! Such arrangements are not conducive to success and should not be repeated. In my view, such plans need to be prepared by the people who will be responsible for their execution, people who are aware of the subtleties within the peace agreement, and the interrelation of its provisions. This is an important lesson for future peacekeeping missions and requires a clear break with the practices of the past.

Enforcement or Peacekeeping?

Although UNTAC had started badly, it still had a number of options available to it. These options did not include enforcement action by UN peacekeepers. To do so would have required a force several times larger than the one we had, one structured and equipped for a pro-tracted counter-insurgency war, and at a significantly greater cost.

I take the view that such a mission would have been doomed to disaster, even in the unlikely eventuality that it had been given wide international support. It would have required a United Nations force to take sides in an internal conflict. While the Khmer Rouge was usually seen as the disturbing party, there were nevertheless deep divisions internationally, within the Security Council and within UNTAC, about who really was at fault. Both UNTAC and the international unity which had been built up behind the Cambodian peace process would very likely have been torn apart on this issue.

Enforcement action requires much stronger consensus than peacekeeping, both internationally and within the contributing coun-tries. Regrettably, as Force Commander, from beginning to end I was plagued by suggestions that the UNTAC Military Component should become involved in internal security operations. Peacekeepers are part of an agreement between parties which have been in conflict and are protected by that agreement. They operate in the open as an expression of their international neutrality—this gives them acceptability and great strength. When used for enforcement, they lose their neutrality and are stripped of their political protection.

Much of the basis of criticism of the self-defence philosophy might be due to passion over events which blind the advocates of violence to the realities of the situation and the potential to unleash an uncontrollable dynamic of violence. Some might also be due to the remnants, in some armed forces, of an interventionist tradition developed in colonial times, which sees peacekeeping operations as a dilution of military potency. Such views, if allowed to prevail, could only bankrupt the moral authority of peacekeeping. In true peace-keeping, member states of the United Nations deploy an international force with the agreement of the parties to a conflict, to assist them in the resolution of a dispute between them. The parties want resolution of the conflict, or at least its suspension, while the diplomatic process works to find an agreed solution.

Even if the agreement is broken, or in the case of some humanitarian missions where peacekeepers might be deployed without a formal agreement being reached among the parties, it is difficult to argue that peacekeepers have the right to kill people in their own country. Everyone has the right of self-defence, and peacekeepers are lightly armed in view of the increased threats in world trouble spots. But it seems difficult to argue that a mandate which draws its authority from a Charter designed to defend the sovereignty of states can authorise hostile intervention against any party within a state.

Unity and Neutrality

A better option for Cambodia was the one we followed, namely, to preserve the unity and neutrality of the force through strict adherence to the peacekeeping ethos. Without unity of purpose, command and understanding, the force fractures very quickly and can no longer represent the will of the international community. From that point on, its ability to retain neutrality is also doubtful. Unity and neutrality represent the true strength of a peacekeeping force. Without unity and neutrality, you either go to war or go home! And in UNTAC, it would have been the civilian components which would have been the most exposed and vulnerable in such a climate. Other than in the climate of a peacekeeping mission, they could not have done their job in any way.

The good fortune in Cambodia was in having a clear objective— the election. No matter how circumstances changed, the conduct and verification of the election stood out as the focal point of the mission and it was critical not to be diverted from it. The problem was to convince everybody that the election could be held within the framework of the mandate. UNTAC's belief in its own ability to meet its obligations was subject to many assaults. It was imperative to overcome these if we were to claim any right to remain in Cambodia.

There were many distorted views among influential expatriates in Cambodia about why we were there, including from some UN personnel, members of non-government organisations (NGOs) and journalists. Some of these actually succumbed to factional propaganda and took partisan positions. The diversity of views served to confuse the international community and made our task among the Cambodian people even more difficult, since their confidence in the United Nations tended to be undermined.

The Khmer Rouge recognised the importance of these issues and there were definite attempts to break the unity of the force. Very early in the mission, the Khmer Rouge began classifying some units as 'good UNTAC', and others as 'bad UNTAC'. Some elements of UNTAC were acceptable in their areas and others were not. There is no doubt that some contingents were directed by national interests to take positions which were not in harmony with the overall directive of the Force Commander, and perhaps the Khmer Rouge were seeking to widen these divisions. This is a serious matter. A United Nations force cannot afford to be a collection of national contingents each pursuing its own agenda—it has to be seen to be unified in the pursuit of those objectives of the agreements which mandate its presence.

This has to be recognised by the parties also. The UN Force Commander cannot be seen to be discriminating between the members of his force. To have done so in UNTAC would almost certainly have led to further demands aimed at dividing the Force and weakening the Agreements. It is important to note that while some were urging us to meet the demands of the Khmer Rouge, the latter began firing on UNTAC helicopters.

Generating cohesion among 16,000 troops, representing 34 member states of the United Nations, was not an easy task. Despite this, in many respects the cultural diversity was an advantage—as a unified entity, we could claim that we truly represented the international community. Moreover, many troops came from countries with similar economic and social problems to Cambodia, or similar cultural backgrounds. As a result, they were often better attuned to Cambodian needs and sensitivities, strengthening our relationship with the people. However, a small number of contingents, one in particular, held very different attitudes about the relationship between the military and the population. These caused serious problems which also affected UN civilians and members of the NGO community.

Cohesion was generated by involving everyone in the planning process, by continuous briefings, and by clear directives and orders. In the end, the peacekeeping force was united by the desire of most soldiers to be seen as military professionals, the one thing we all had in common.

The UN Secretariat alone reserves the right, in the light of the views of the five permanent members of the Security Council (P5), to decide which troops come from which countries. This is done in accordance with the Secretariat's priorities, which in the case of UNTAC were not always consistent with the needs of the mission. The Force Commander is held accountable before the international community for the actions of the members of his force, but he has no say in the selection. There might be good reasons for this, but it is an important question to be addressed, if the risks of shattering unity and undermining command are to be avoided in future missions.

An Alliance with the People

What became clear was that the Cambodian people desperately wanted peace. The essential task was to forge an alliance between UNTAC and the people which would overcome the distortions created by the power struggles between and within the factional leaderships.

The first requirement was an information programme which was undistorted by factional propaganda. The difficulty in convincing the UN Secretariat that UNTAC needed its own radio station meant that 'Radio UNTAC' did not commence operation until more than one year after the signing of the Agreements. I do not believe that anyone could now deny the criticality of Radio UNTAC to the whole process. In my view, this was obvious from the start and only the United Nations bureaucracy delayed it.

When we started to develop a penetration into the countryside, the Khmer Rouge, realising that they had a highly plausible competitor for the hearts and minds of the people, staged a series of intimidatory hostage situations designed to establish control over the way UNTAC interfaced with the people in the countryside. Despite the widespread diplomatic concerns for their safety, UNTAC troops continued to push out into the villages and into remote corners, including along the fringes of the Khmer Rouge-controlled zones. Of greater concern was the SoC propaganda which sought to erode respect for UNTAC by asserting that it lacked the commitment to face up to the Khmer Rouge. But peacekeepers can only use their weapons for self-defence. So other, neutral ways of gaining respect among the people had to be found.

We all know that large groups of people who are disadvantaged by circumstances are in a highly exploitable state. Often they see no choice but to lend what weight they have to the support of a party to a conflict. Alleviating the cause of these grievances can often only be possible with the intervention of outside agencies. This is where the partnership between peacekeepers and humanitarian agencies comes into play. Civic action programmes which bring improvements to conditions of life are an obvious way. Unfortunately, there seemed to be a prevailing view that this sort of activity was the responsibility of other UN agencies and NGOs—not the business of the Military Component.

This misses the point—the military has a much deeper presence, and 'hearts and minds' activities always form an essential part of a military component's method of operation in these circumstances. In the event, we were able to establish a reasonable programme through the generosity of donations from individual countries, close co-operation with other UN agencies and NGOs, as well as effective use of the nation-building and other skills that many of the UN soldiers brought to Cambodia. The protection afforded by peacekeepers and the manpower they provided also enabled the humanitarian agencies to reach more members of the population.

I stress that humanitarian and peacekeeping objectives are not in opposition, but rather they are different instruments of the same purpose. The humanitarian effort must itself be the subject of properly constructed plans which themselves form part of an overall integrated plan working towards the common objective.

Civil–Military Integration

Although we continued to seek the parties' compliance with the ceasefire provisions of the Agreements, in September 1992 it became clear to me that the Khmer Rouge were unlikely to enter the Phase Two ceasefire and that consideration had to be given to the conduct of the election in an insecure environment. Initially, it had been planned to reduce the strength of the Military Component by more than one half after the demobilisation of the armed forces of the parties. But the changed circumstances now necessitated the maintenance of the Force at full strength. A plan was developed to redeploy the Force to dispositions based on foreseen threats to the electoral process and to align command responsibilities more clearly with both the administrative and electoral boundaries of Cambodia—rather than with military regions.

By this stage, UNTAC was receiving strong support from the Cambodian people. The voter registration process reflected the Cambodian people's strong desire for a chance to express their opinions on the question of Cambodia's future. From 5 October 1992, when the operation began, to 31 January 1993, some 4.6 million Cambodians registered to vote, representing about 97 percent of eligible voters.

The wishes of the Cambodian people had been made clear. Voter registration was a clear vote for the UNTAC-sponsored process. At a media conference in mid-January, I observed that these unprecedented electoral rolls represented 'a shift in the balance of power to the Cambodian people'. UNTAC now had the moral obligation to meet the people's expectations. Moreover, realising them was a means for generating both legitimacy and the international support necessary for resolution of the crisis. The legitimacy of the Cambodia operation was established in the Paris Agreements whereby the United Nations would act as the transitional authority in the country. The object of that authority was to enfranchise the people. If this could not be done UNTAC had no right to stay. As long as everybody, Cambodian and international alike, believed that it was possible to conduct the election, the mission retained its legitimacy.

But the mission came close to failure on this issue. It was clear that the elections would not be taking place in the neutral political environment envisaged under the Paris Agreements. The question of whether to proceed with the election still lingered, even on the eve of its conduct. Senior UN staff in Phnom Penh and New York questioned the legitimacy of the results of an election carried out in such an atmosphere. The fundamental importance of UNTAC's belief in its own authority and capacities was not comprehended. In fact there was no choice but to proceed.

The security situation had imposed the requirement for close collaboration between the civilian components and the Military Component. The Military Component had to provide not only security for civilians and military alike, but a logistic support structure which penetrated to district level. An integrated approach was adopted which established a planning and control alliance for the electoral process between the Electoral and Military Components, and Information and Education Division. Centred around military plans in Phnom Penh, and sector headquarters in the field, this also drew in the Civil Police Component. These arrangements were instrumental in the effective conduct of the election. Without them, UN civilian casualties would have resulted and there could not have been an election.

At a sector commanders' conference in January 1993, to which I had invited UNTAC provincial directors and electoral officers, the Head of the Civil Administration Component, Mr Gerard Porcell, observed that although the Paris Agreements did not rule out an election in the absence of disarmament, this reality nevertheless steered it towards a climate of violence. He went on:

> This situation, not envisaged by the Accords, has the effect of increasing the role of the Military Component in the pursuit of civilian objectives. Ensuring the security of the electoral process in its entirety is now, following the adoption of UN Security Resolution 792, the principal mission of the Military Component. In a country disarmed as it should be, Civil Administration and CIVPOL, which is not armed, could be sufficient to assure this security. But it is clear that, in a country where weapons are everywhere to be found, the Military Component becomes indispensable:

to protect our electoral teams;

to protect the officials and members of the political parties, or even, more generally, to act in such a manner that public order is ensured in the conditions suitable for the holding of elections;

to assist in the implementation of administrative control as envisaged by the Accords, especially with regard to customs and immigration, which materialises at the checkpoints;

to assist in the implementation of decisions taken by the Supreme National Council, for example, the establishment of a moratorium on the exportation of logs.

It follows that there is a need for more frequent contacts between the members of the Military Component and those of Civil Administration. Our respective activities, which were envisaged by the Accords before as being parallel and independent, are becoming complementary and profoundly linked.

From one viewpoint, this participation of military personnel in the realisation of civilian objectives is, for us civilians, a veritable godsend: free of the constraints of the task which they were originally assigned, the Military Component can utilise its technical competence (which is large), its important materiel and personnel capabilities as well as its remarkable faculty for organisation resulting from its own techniques of military command, which together act to enhance the control activities normally carried out by the Civil Administration Component.

We cannot but wish that the aid of the Military Component, however unexpected, will allow our civilian activities to be more effectively carried out.

As the election approached and concerns heightened, to many the solution appeared to be the infusion of more troops. Many diplomats urged me to seek additional contingents. However, I judged that the additional administrative and logistics burden they would impose would draw off scarce resources from priority work. The time lags involved suggested that they would not be available in time to be of any real use. I turned down any such offers, deciding instead to proceed with the now experienced force of 16,000 peacekeepers already in-country.

The assessment of the Military Component was that in global terms the Khmer Rouge could not physically prevent the poll. Khmer Rouge strength was limited and was only concentrated well away from population centres. Unfortunately, it was difficult to convince civilian components and the media of this, and the psychological effect of threats and small attacks had to be countered. Acknowledging that violence and attacks were possible in some (mainly remote) areas, UNTAC aimed to conduct the most impartial election possible under imperfect circumstances. The election was be held from 23 to 28 May 1993. During the first three days voting was held in the populated areas, almost without incident capturing nearly 80 percent of registered voters. In the remaining three days, an additional 10 percent of voters cast their ballots in remote areas, supported by the maximum effort of the Military Component, but already a clear mandate had been achieved.

The UNTAC security arrangements also drew in the armed forces of the Cambodian parties which participated in the elections. Agreement was reached in April 1993 for them to use minimum force and proportionate response to help protect the electoral process against any threats. Military operations which went beyond this were unacceptable. In effect, the Cambodian armed forces became an extension of the UNTAC peacekeeping force. A division of responsibility was also agreed in which the Cambodian armed forces secured the countryside to enable the people to vote, while UNTAC secured the electoral process itself and guaranteed its integrity. Consistent with neutrality, this was open to all parties. But the Khmer Rouge maintained their opposition to the elections.

An encouraging aspect to this was that by establishing our credentials as neutral peacekeepers who intended to implement the mandate, we had won the confidence of patriotic Cambodian military leaders, among them men of integrity, who were now willing to bind their forces to Cambodia's future. Shortly after the elections, we concluded negotiations in Phnom Penh which led to the unification of the three armed forces. We had been conducting negotiations to this end for many months, but without much progress. Now the shared experience of supporting this truly democratic process, in concert with the international community, had engendered great professional pride and had drawn former enemies together. This unification paid critical dividends in the politically ambiguous period immediately after the elections, when some of the losers tried to unravel the process. No political arrangements had been foreshadowed in the Agreements and nothing substantial had been prepared, but the united armed forces provided essential stability. No coup attempt could be sure of success without the support of an army. Up to the time of writing, the unified armed forces and general staff continue to provide the major stabilising influence in Cambodia.

This initiative was supported by a number of member states of the United Nations who offered to fund salaries of the armed forces, as well as of the police and bureaucracy, as long as they committed themselves to the constitutional government which was to emerge from the electoral process. Such proactive initiatives are an essential element in peace-building and can have enduring benefits long after the end of the mission.

Proactive Military Negotiations

Of particular importance in all this was the Mixed Military Working Group Secretariat. The forum of the Mixed Military Working Group was set up under the Paris Agreements to resolve problems relating to the ceasefire but, due to the difficulties confronted in the peace process, it became my main instrument for dealing with the military forces of the parties. The Mixed Military Working Group Secretariat was a grouping of officers from many nations which prepared agendum papers, maintained continuous liaison with military staff of all factions and acted as a coordination agency with the civil components and other UN agencies. The main work of the Secretariat was directed at supporting the meetings I held with the military liaison officers and leaders of the military of the Cambodian parties.

The Mixed Military Working Group Secretariat's work enabled me to seize the initiative in negotiations and was a valuable tool in establishing the correctness of the UNTAC position, especially to the diplomatic community. The effective liaison work made a strong contribution to the establishment of a climate of trust between the UNTAC Military Component and the military of all factions—even the Khmer Rouge. No other component had an effective secretariat and this area warrants very close study to determine its applicability to other peacekeeping missions.

Coalition Building

A crucial element was the maintenance of the international coalition behind the Paris Agreements. In Cambodia, the coalition was reflected in the expanded permanent five (EP5), which had been established soon after signing the Paris Agreements. This body grouped around the representatives of the Permanent Five Members of the Security Council, plus the representatives of Indonesia, Australia, Germany, Thailand and Japan; India and Malaysia eventually joined as well. My relationship with the EP5 was a corporate one, as was that of the

Special Representative of the Secretary-General. The EP5 received regular briefings to ensure it was fully and accurately informed of our activities.

The EP5 closely paralleled the grouping in New York known as the 'Core Group', and was instrumental in ensuring that the realities on the ground were communicated to the missions in New York and, through them to the Security Council. The Security Council was also in receipt of mission reports processed by our own military liaison officers deployed to New York for the purpose.

Through these mechanisms UNTAC was able to proceed towards the elections and the formation of a constitutional government, the goal of the Paris Agreements, despite the difficulties and confident of the legitimacy of its actions and of the support of the world community. Such a process became necessary for UNTAC because the UN Secretariat was constantly distracted by other missions, particularly in former Yugoslavia. In effect, we were able to overcome the difficulties experienced by the hard-pressed UN Secretariat in conducting a number of complex missions simultaneously. The Secretariat simply does not have enough qualified staff to act as a strategic headquarters. Accordingly, the issue of improving the effectiveness of the strategic planning direction and control of operations needs to be a priority area for the member states of the United Nations. In the interim, the Secretariat must be ready to be supplemented by skilled manpower from member states for this purpose.

It is regrettable that there was no strategic integration and planning for the UNTAC mission, nor was there broad consultation in the preparation of the Secretary-General's report which could have linked the programmes of the various components in an ordered way, or effective strategic integration once the mission started. This imposed penalties throughout the mission and was only overcome by component heads networking as problems arose, and by the Military Component becoming the focal point for the planning and conduct of the operations of UNTAC as a whole. I believe that the effectiveness of an integrated approach is an essential lesson for other peacekeeping missions to be drawn from the UNTAC experience.

Conclusion

Cambodia was an operation in which we were able to implement the mandate and withdraw in good order, under budget and on time. We had no authority to remain and, had we done so, it is likely that we would have been progressively drawn into the continuing internal strife. In any case, internal security had become a matter for the legitimate government, which we had helped to establish, and their armed forces, which we had helped to bring together. Internal conflict in a sovereign member state is not a matter for the United Nations, without authorisation from the legitimate authority and the support of the international community.

In the implementation of the mandate, strict adherence to the peacekeeping ethos was an essential ingredient of success. If unity and neutrality had not been scrupulously preserved on a multifaceted mission of such complexity, the prospects of an outcome which met the aspirations of both the Cambodian people and the international community would have been gravely prejudiced.

If it can be accepted that unity and neutrality extend beyond peacekeepers to all participants working towards the mission objective, then it becomes clear that the effectiveness of the United Nations can be markedly improved by cooperative arrangements which bring their operations into harmony. Specific opportunities exist in areas such as civic action programmes to raise the condition of the population, public information and education, logistics, electoral activities, and establishment of a system of justice to maintain law and order and to defend human rights. One can only imagine what might have eventuated if the integrated approach had been used from the outset and maintained throughout. If this central lesson can be learned, peacekeeping operations, rather than being the confused and directionless affairs they often are, can become an effective instrument for conflict resolution by the international community. The lesson from UNTAC is a lesson of unity.

My own conviction to emerge from the UNTAC operation is the need for a strategic alliance between peacekeepers, both military and civilian, humanitarian organisations, and those NGOs which feel that they have a role to play in pursuing common objectives. An integrated approach needs to be adopted all the way from the UN Secretariat to the forward area, across the components and interested agencies, for the duration of the mission. This means that both civilian and military personnel must be trained to operate in an integrated environment. This strategic alliance must be aimed at the development and execution of timely plans which include building structures which help sustain the outcomes of the mission after it has ended. The plans need to be dynamic, with clearly signposted exits for the various components and agencies once their programmes are completed. Moreover, operations of the complexity of UNTAC are major undertakings and have to be managed accordingly. At the strategic level, the full provisions of the UN Charter for strategic planning and direction of operations need to be implemented in such cases.

In the end UNTAC was a great success. But the greatest triumph of UNTAC has been essentially one for the Cambodia people. They had the courage to come forward and vote in overwhelming numbers, despite the efforts to thwart their will and the direst predictions. Convincing the people of our commitment by securing the mechanism in the countryside was the challenge UNTAC faced. It was through co-operation that we were able to fulfil our obligations to them.

I would like to conclude by stating that throughout the operation, the Force Communications Unit, an ANZAC grouping, was the glue that held it all together. Young Australian and New Zealand men and women, officers, non-commissioned officers and soldiers, were deployed to all parts of Cambodia. They went about their duties in the finest traditions established by their forebears over eighty years ago, often in the most difficult and dangerous of circumstances, setting an example for others to follow. Australian and New Zealand civilians in other components displayed similar resourcefulness and initiative. They were team players, rallying their international colleagues to the UNTAC cause, and tirelessly seeking new ways to make it all work.

New Zealand soldiers on peacekeeping patrol in Bosnia. (Photo: Ministry of Foreign Affairs and Trade, New Zealand)

Michael Rose

The Bosnia Experience

I am delighted to be invited to give the concluding address at this distinguished conference here in New Zealand, a country whose Armed Forces' high reputation on the battlefield remains undiminished even after 25 years of peace. New Zealand is a country that has made a very substantial contribution, small though it is, to the business of preserving peace, truth and freedom and democracy throughout the world in the last two major world wars and before that time. In addition, since 1945 it has also played a very significant part in peace-keeping operations around the world. I believe that as peacekeeping moves up the spectrum of conflict towards war-fighting, the best performers on the battlefield undoubtedly make the best peacekeepers, and the company of Kiwis who I was fortunate to command in Bosnia were no exception to this rule. I also believe that it is particularly appropriate that I should be talking here at a Foreign Policy School, for of course security is always a balance of diplomacy and force—and in peacekeeping this is particularly so.

When I started in the business some thirty years ago, peace-keeping was a relatively simple matter. We were issued with a tin helmet, a .303 Lee Enfield rifle, a pair of khaki drill shorts, and a banner which said 'Disperse or we fire'. And when we fired they always dispersed, and therefore things were very orderly and easy to cope with. Now of course we live in a very different world indeed. We drop bombs from F18 aircraft, we use the most sophisticated surveillance target-array-to-acquisition systems, tank main armament, rocket launchers, .20 machine guns: and all they do is take you hostage. So it has come to be a much more complex affair.

Sadly, in the 50th year of the United Nations, the views of the international community with regards to peacekeeping have been somewhat blighted by past experiences in Somalia and by the perceived failures and costs of the UN mission in former Yugoslavia and elsewhere. This had led to a fundamental questioning of the value of peacekeeping operations. Yet if the countries of the world, and in particular the United States, lose faith in peacekeeping operations, and the responses of the international community to the challenges of the new world disorder are to be limited to the extremes of non–involvement or armed intervention, then the world will undoubtedly become a more dangerous place than it is at present. Do we really want the terrible scenes that we see taking place currently in Chechnya being re-enacted over Sarajevo? Of course not. Therefore, rather than lose faith in the peace process, it may be more productive to analyse the changed operational circumstances which now face peacekeepers, and subsequently try and determine new doctrines and concepts of operation for peacekeeping which will allow the United Nations to perform these missions more effectively, and so prevent the world from becoming involved in wider conflict. I believe that over the past three years the UN mission in former Yugoslavia has provided the necessary environment and experience for this to be done, and that although the lessons that can be drawn are stark, they undoubtedly have great relevance for the future.

Bosnia remains a place where savage traditions and a bloody history are being acted out once more today. The scenes that we see on television of countrysides being laid waste, modern cities being destroyed and entire populations dispersed and slaughtered can only compare with what happened in Europe 600 years ago during the 100 Years' War. Only this time the horrors are being performed with all the destructive power of modern weapons. When I went to live just over a year ago in Sarajevo, a modern city but one existing in conditions of medieval siege, 1200 shells a day were falling in the city, and people were living like rats in their cellars—coming out only at night to scavenge. There was no electricity or piped water, and the only food that had been available for two years was provided by the United Nations. There was no transport, and for much of that winter the temperature remained well below zero. Life for the 350,000 people there really was, as Thomas Hobbes said, poor, nasty, brutish and, sadly, in at least 10,000 instances, short. Elsewhere this chilling situation was being repeated with ethnic cleansing, murder, extortion, theft and propaganda lies and distortion the common order of the day.

I would like to read a letter I received recently from someone who is no longer living in Bosnia:

> My friend. We hope that you will not be surprised that we call you a

friend since we hardly know each other. In spite of that, for everything you did for us we simply have to consider you a friend. You helped us to escape from the hell of Sarajevo thus saving our lives. And one can only consider as friends those who were prepared to sacrifice themselves to save others. We often remember bad moments from Sarajevo and that still gives us the creeps. However we have started living normally again, not being afraid of armed gangs, shells and snipers. We are slowly forgetting Sarajevo, although it is our native town. Insane nationalistic policies meant that we have lost our old state. We never agreed with those policies.

I believe that what we are seeing in former Yugoslavia concerns us all—for the horrors that are being perpetrated there, are daily being repeated elsewhere on this troubled planet. Dealing with such situations is surely the tough end of the spectrum of conflict. There are no quick decisive victories, nor clearly defined political end states. Sometimes there is no precisely defined national interest. Very often those who are voluntarily risking their lives so that others may live, end up being shot at by all sides. Yet it is our duty to persevere. In spite of all the horrors that befell them, I never once heard anyone involved in the delivery of aid or peacekeeping once decry the value of the mission. As General Gordon A. Sullivan, the recently retiring Chief of Staff of the US Army, said, 'We have no other choice but to be strong'.

If the civilised world is to survive then surely we must learn how to deal with such anarchy, chaos and savagery. Nor will the application of direct military force always provide the solutions. We can only succeed, if we continue to put faith in the basic principles of truth, freedom and democracy, and in those values and standards which have made this country great and still makes it one of the safest and most civilised places in which to live. We must strive to give everyone who is the victim of war, the oppressed and the poor, the same order, peace and civilised living standards that we all in the West take so much for granted. We cannot simply walk away from problems such as Bosnia, let the fires burn out and natural regeneration take place—for we are not talking about trees in a national park, we are talking about human lives.

Nor, on the other hand, can we reasonably expect anyone necessarily to fight an interventionist war in these sort of situations—even for a just peace in Bosnia—not when the North Atlantic Treaty Organisation (NATO), the most powerful military alliance in the world and one in whose backyard the conflict is taking place, is not itself prepared to fight. The wrongdoings of the Serbs may be judged to be morally reprehensible and politically unacceptable in the eyes of the world, but the UN Security Council cannot ignore the simple fact that no country is prepared to take up arms against them. When we criticise the United Nations for not doing something, we are of course criticising ourselves: for all of us are the United Nations. In short we need to understand not only the aspirations of the collective will of the world, but also its limitations. We need to understand the difference between goals of peacekeeping which are subscribed to and those of war-fighting which are not.

Nor does it make much sense to accuse the UN mission in Bosnia of complicity in genocide. This is to confuse a perfectly respectable moral position with political reality, and rhetoric with reason. Neither has any place in serious international policy making. Indeed it is my contention that it is the very presence of the United Nations in the former Republic of Yugoslavia which has prevented a far greater degree of slaughter and suffering from happening. It has also, in my estimation, preserved the very state of Bosnia itself from extinction and the conflict from spreading.

Amidst all the distortion and misunderstanding surrounding the UN mission in Bosnia, it is often forgotten that its mandate is simply to sustain the people of that country in the midst of civil war, and to try and bring about the conditions necessary for a peaceful resolution of that war. Through a heroic endeavour on the part of some 23,500 brave young men and women in the office of the UN High Commissioner for Refugees (UNHCR) and the United Nations, that mandate by the end of 1994 had, by and large, been fulfilled. Over 2.7 million people had been sustained through the daily delivery of 2000 tonnes of aid in the midst of bloody civil war, entire populations preserved from wholesale death and dispersion, and the war in Bosnia contained. The target figures for the delivery of that aid, which was set not by the UNHCR but by the World Health Organisation (WHO), were met. That is a simple statement of fact. The United Nations in the midst of this bloody civil war was asked to deliver so much tonnage of food and it did. That to me is a heroic achievement. There were two thousand metric tonnes of food delivered across the battle lines and in a three-sided civil war every single day in 1994.

This was not done without considerable cost. Over 300 peacekeepers have been killed in the course of their duty in the former Republic of Yugoslavia during the past three years, which is many more than the losses suffered in the Gulf War by the multinational coalition. It is also true to say that as a result of the Cessation of

Hostilities agreement signed between the parties to the conflict on 31 December 1994 the guns had largely fallen silent, thus creating the conditions for a peaceful end to the conflict. The failures of the Cessation of Hostilities agreement and the decline in the secure situations which have occurred since the end of 1994 cannot of course be attributed to the peacekeepers. The failures must be attributed to the political leaders of that country who were so quick to take their people to war, and who have now been so slow to take them back to peace. It is they who have not availed themselves of the opportunities for peace which have been so hard won. Peacekeeping cannot continue forever in a political vacuum, and it is my belief that because the momentum gained last year was not followed up by political action, we now see renewed conflict and suffering of the people today.

Use of Force

The central principle governing any peacekeeping mission is that force can only be used at a minimum level to achieve a specific aim. Force cannot be used to change force correlations, or adjust political positions. These are war-fighting aims. Nor should a peacekeeping mission allow itself to be hijacked by outside international powers or alliances who may wish to use the presence of peacekeeping forces in a country to change political states. This will result in mission creep. To use more force than that which is prescribed by the bounds of peacekeeping, especially in order to pursue war-fighting goals, is to cross the line which separates non-combatants from combatants. It is to cross what I call the Mogadishu line, because of course in Somalia another well constructed, well intentioned force went out to sustain the people of Somalia and changed its aims half way through, with the terrible consequences that then befell them. Crossing this line will spell disaster for the mission, as well as the country involved—for a peace-keeping force is neither mandated, deployed nor equipped to fight a war. Nor do the nations which have voluntarily contributed their troops to a peacekeeping mission deserve to see their brave young men and women return home in body bags.

Although the UN peacekeeping force in former Yugoslavia has adopted a very forceful approach to peacekeeping, and has certainly been obliged to resort to high levels of force on occasions in pursuit of its mandate, it has never allowed itself to be seen in the perceptions of those engaged in the conflict as being unduly partial. It has always attempted to remain neutral and impartial as a third party, one that is capable of providing the whole machinery of the humanitarian aid delivery programme and also the machinery for mediation. All parties to the conflict have until now generally been persuaded that the continuing presence of the United Nations has been ultimately in their own strategic interests. However, retaining a non-combatant status is no easy feat in the midst of civil war. Not only will each party try to draw the United Nations into taking sides, but inevitably all sides will use humanitarian aid itself for their own political and military ends. Even the delivery by the United Nations of basic food and fuel to a besieged population will be considered as a hostile act by those carrying out the siege. It must also be accepted that deployment on such a mission inevitably makes the force a hostage to the situation itself.

I think it was Dag Hammarskjöld who said this is not a job which soldiers should do; but only soldiers can do it. Notwithstanding the difficulties encountered in Bosnia, I believe that military force has a clear role to play in peacekeeping missions, and that the bringing in of NATO in support of a UN peacekeeping mission was a major achievement and indispensable to the continued exercise of the mandate. Without the support of NATO, it is quite clear to me that the UN mission in Bosnia would have failed. For it was the presence of NATO airplanes in the skies which gave me the confidence to deploy peacekeepers and those delivering aid in dispersed and remote places, and of course it was NATO that preserved the regimes of total exclusion zones for heavy weapons around Sarajevo and Gorazde. It was also the action, and threat of further action, of NATO aircraft which deterred attacks by the Bosnian Serbs against the safe areas. However NATO always remained within the limitations prescribed for the use of force in a peacekeeping mission. Its peacekeeping doctrine accords precisely with that of the United Nations and this is well demonstrated by the correspondence between the late NATO Secretary-General Manfred Woerner and UN Secretary-General Boutros Boutros-Ghali in the Spring of 1993.

I believe that the experience of Bosnia has served to widen the horizons of NATO in a way not foreseen by the New Strategic Concepts document of 1991 which lays down the basis for the future of strategic activity. Nowhere in that document is the word peacekeeping mentioned. So from a set of strategic concepts which were predicated on the continuation of some kind of ersatz Cold War possibly on the flank, NATO has had to reorient itself, restructure itself, to take on the role of peacekeeping. Where difficulties have occurred it is because the

UN and NATO political mandates have not been wholly aligned.

But that is something at the high strategic level. At the tactical and operational level, things worked extremely well. To give an example of how NATO and the United Nations used force (which doesn't necessarily mean the dropping of a bomb). Much force takes place in everyday ground-to-ground contexts. And of course the threatened deterrent value of the use of force is equally important.

One day I was telephoned by the chief of staff of the Bosnian Serb army General Manojlo Milovanovic who said, 'It is quarter to twelve. You have a convoy running north of Tuzla. We are going to shell it at twelve o'clock if it doesn't turn back'.

We asked him what he meant by this.

He said, 'That is an illegal run of weapons to the Muslims who we are pressing heavily in that area'.

We said, 'No it isn't, it is a white convoy, a UN convoy, UNHCR convoy, being driven by young civilians, escorted by the military, unarmed, delivering food for the people that you pushed out of some town just north of the contact line last week'.

He said, 'It is now five to twelve, I don't care what you say, we are going to now start shelling in five minutes'.

We said, 'If you do that, we will call down NATO air against you'.

In that particular place they were in a bowl. He had three artillery regiments around the area, and shelled from time to time. One thing the Bosnian Serb army is good at is shooting large pieces of artillery. He said, after we warned him that we would use NATO air against him, 'You don't frighten me with your NATO airplanes'.

We replied, 'You don't frighten us with your threats of artillery shoots either'.

We both slammed down our receivers in thoroughly ill humour with each other, and I gave the order for the convoy to run. The convoy did run. It was shelled. But it was only shelled in a face-saving way, a sort of one shot over there and one shot over there. One came a bit close, and I rang up General Milovanovic and said, 'What the hell are you doing'?

He said, 'Oh well, they don't always go precisely where you mean them to go'.

But what was certain was that he was not out to kill peacekeepers. Now that was a hell of a gamble to take, because these were not people under my command, these were civilian drivers—the voluntary drivers who go out there and drive these trucks, who are working for other organisations.

On the other hand there is a credibility line. I have mentioned that there could be the Mogadishu line at one end. There is also a credibility line at the other end, if you allow yourself to be manipulated away from your position. You do stand on a high moral ground as a peacekeeper. You are not out there killing anyone, you are there trying to create conditions of peace, order, civilisation. If you get manipulated off that, and can't fulfil your function, then of course the mission has no sense or purpose. And so these are the sorts of decisions that are being taken every day, not just by the commanders at the top, but by young men and women on the ground who are being continually confronted by questions of 'Should we use force?' 'Should we just stop, talk, or should we go back?'. It is an enormous testimony to these people that they daily feed 2.7 million people working through these very difficult circumstances indeed.

Notwithstanding everything that I have said, it must also be recognised that there exist obvious limitations on the use of air power in any confused civil war situation—especially when, as in Bosnia, aircraft cannot fly for much of the time because of poor weather. It simply is not militarily possible to secure safe areas or enforce the passage of convoys by the use of air power alone. For example, the route for UNPROFOR and UNHCR convoys from central Bosnia to Gorazde transits 55 miles of Bosnian Serb-held territory. It crosses two mountain ranges and passes through narrow defiles and over 44 bridges. It would be exceedingly simple, therefore, for a few determined men to deny that route to convoys either by direct fire, indirect fire, mining, destroying bridges or even getting the civilian population to block the road.

On one occasion in 1994, this did indeed happen when a handful of women held a French convoy hostage only a few miles from Sarajevo. It couldn't move, and we lost that convoy for five weeks. There was no way force could be used in that situation. We came to some agreement with the local Serb commander that we could change the hostages. So the French rotated their personnel: some did duty hostage one week and then had one week off. In the end by moral persuasion, by pressure, we got that convoy through and they never put another one there again. It wasted a lot of their time and it wasted a lot of our time, but for some reason they did it.

But strong robust enforcement action takes place daily. On

another occasion, a young French corporal had a convoy stopped near Tuzla by some Rambo-type kids, much bigger than him incidentally, with all the sort of machine guns and RPGs pointing at his convoy which happened to be a fuel run. He jumped out, reversed his rifle, laid out this Serb commander to the surprise of all the Serb commander's subordinates, jumped in the lorry and drove straight on. What made him do that I have no idea, but he got the convoy through. Maybe he had been one of the hostages who had been held for five weeks previously, and wasn't going to be held again. But that is the sort of tough action that is going on almost on a daily basis.

In spite of all the difficulties recently encountered regarding the taking of hostages and the enhancements to the Serb air defence systems, I still believe that NATO airpower has an important part to play in supporting the UN mission—if only in providing robustness to the self-defence capabilities of the ground forces. But airpower and military force have only a limited role to play. That is the point of telling you these stories in these circumstances. If food doesn't get through, people start to die. The 2.7 million people one is feeding there are the people most in need. They are the elderly, the displaced and the children. If the food and the fuel are not delivered, almost immediately people start dying. So if you do use undue force, or what in the opinion of one side or the other is undue force, then they will block your convoys and people will start dying, and you have to balance what you are trying to do against the risk of that outcome.

Role of the Media

The final lesson that I will draw from the past year in Bosnia concerns the influence of the media on the success or failure of peacekeeping. That the media is a powerful instrument for good or bad is obvious to all, as what is reported and seen on TV directly affects policies being developed abroad as well as attitudes within the country. If the media falsely shows images of war, exaggerates facts or distorts opinions, then there is of course a very real danger that international policy will become based on propaganda and rhetoric rather than on practicality and reality. It is of course quite understandable that a government struggling for survival should have a propaganda machine. It is not understandable that certain elements of the international media should become part of that machine. Mischievous distortion of reality can only undermine the work of those who are pursuing the path towards peace—especially when false images of war are created.

I can give you endless examples of it. I will give one. In late 1994 there were images shown by a major international satellite news gathering organisation, whose name I shall not mention because they might sue me for libel, showing harrowing scenes of shelling in Bihac after the Cessation of Hostilities agreement had been signed, and refugees fleeing on ox-drawn carts. Clearly, nothing breaks down in Bosnia–Herzegovina so quick as a ceasefire, or a cessation of hostilities agreement. When people up the line see that their colleagues and relations down the line are now being subject to some act, like shelling after a ceasefire agreement has been signed, they immediately pull the line ends. The whole thing unravels at the speed of a fire in a brush forest. We pointed out to this television channel that there was no snow in any of the images they had shown, and yet there had actually been snow on the ground in Bihac for two months. This gives us an example of the sort of level of distortion and lies which people are knowingly indulging in, in order to support a position which may be quite justifiable morally, but cannot be justified in terms of the means which they use to sustain that particular position. And in the end they are causing more deaths and more suffering amongst the people of that country through their insane actions and their poor reporting than if they took a more objective line, whether they agree with it or not. That is just one example. I could go on at inordinate length on this subject.

How the United Nations deals with this centrally important problem is currently under active consideration in New York—for it is widely recognised that in the high intensity conflict end of the spectrum of peacekeeping, a more dynamic and effective approach to information policy is required. I think it is becoming accepted that the sort of public information organisation machine that was needed for the old traditional forms of peacekeeping, when we were there with the consent of all parties of the conflict and trying to create with this consent the mechanics for a peaceful resolution to the problem, is no longer appropriate. The sort of people we need in that environment is very different from the sort of people we need in the public information machine. In a very fast moving, very distorted, highly propagandised context, well, we need people of enormous clarity of thought, with great confidence in their own judgment. We need people, most of all, who are able to explain and justify the long term policies that are being pursued against the short term tactical horrors, the situations that may be unfolding on the ground. Because they often will be being deliberately developed by the elements working against the long-term strategic interests.

The political will of the United Nations is never going to be particularly clear. It is a consensus amongst people who do not always have the same point of view about the way the world should be. So we are never going to get the clear political mission statement from the political level. Therefore, we are very often going to have to write our own. Not only are we going to have to write our own, we are going to have to be able to persuade other people, because we have people working in the aid delivery organisation, people working in the political field, and so on. All have to agree with our particular mission statement. And, of course, we are going to have to apply it and stick with it in the face of the distortion and manipulation that goes on.

The final point I would make is the enormous pressures that are placed on junior officers who are engaged in wider peacekeeping. Not only do they have to have a clear understanding of the political elements of the mission, but they have to have the experience to know when to use force and when to back off. They have to learn to speak softly but carry a big stick. This experience is not something that can be obtained easily by people used to applying the algorithms of war-fighting, but who now have to write their own mission statement and deal for much of the time in fuzzy logic. What the military mind likes is a very clear mission statement, with the end state established, and the resources given to him to achieve that goal. However the rewards of success are as satisfying as winning a battle.

Conclusion

I will conclude by saying that in these times of uncertainty, whilst we should remain eternally vigilant and militarily prepared for war at the high intensity end of the spectrum of conflict, we must not lose faith in the peace process. Moral posturing and political correctness will not provide the necessary inspiration or political formula for success in the resolution and prevention of conflict. The standards, ethics and belief in the indomitable spirit of mankind which have been defined throughout our long history will provide far better guidance. Although we are unlikely to get a clear mission statement from the Security Council because of the realities of international politics, we can at least have unity of purpose at the operational and tactical level amongst those involved in political action, humanitarian aid delivery and peace-keeping. We must continue the process of developing new doctrines, new concepts of operation, and we must design new equipment and procedures in order to improve our wider peacekeeping capabilities. Most important of all, we need to develop a robust information policy strategy to ensure that a clear picture emerges from the confusions and chaos of civil war.

We who represent the wealthy nations of the world need to set a moral lead and take care of our global village. We need above all to keep faith in the process of peace for in the words of John Donne:

> Any Man's death diminishes me, because I am involved in Mankind.
> And therefore never send to know for whom the bell tolls.
> It tolls for thee.

As an operational soldier who has spent much of his professional life at war, I have come to believe passionately in the cause of peace and in the need for an effective United Nations. I urge all of you, whose countries have contributed so much in their history to the preservation of human rights and to the fundamental tenets of truth, freedom and democracy, to give the necessary lead to the United Nations.

John M. Sanderson

Peacekeeping or Peace Enforcement?
Global Flux and the Dilemmas of UN Intervention

The resolution of conflict is one of the most pressing international issues of our time. We are living in a period of great change. Powers decline while others emerge as the world moves to a new strategic accommodation. During this century, the strategic shifts have been marked by the two World Wars and the Cold War. Each unleashed its own set of dynamics which led to the confrontation that followed.

While the current strategic shift has seen the threat of global nuclear war recede, the end of the Cold War has also weakened the influence of the superpowers on their client states and proxies which, for most of the fifty years since the end of the Second World War, seemed to contain many of the deep ethnic, religious and cultural tensions which have plagued modern history.

The collapse of the Soviet Union's capacity to pursue a global strategy led to the disintegration of the Soviet bloc and the fragmentation of the Soviet Union itself. The world's remaining superpower, relieved of the security burdens imposed by its former adversary and denied the crystalline certainty of its role as the defender of freedom, is itself divided. It moves towards a new role only with uncertainty, while burgeoning domestic problems cast a shadow over its ability to sustain a coherent international commitment.

In this global flux, concerns about national and cultural survival, often manipulated by emerging power elites, have led to extreme responses. Brutality and suffering on a scale unprecedented since the major conflicts of this century deaden the senses, despite a universal awareness of events made possible by new information technologies. The cost in lives and infrastructure, along with the diversion of finances to arms and military capabilities, continue to detract from prosperity and the social progress needed to alleviate the causes of conflict. The common humanity of peoples demands that an escape is found from this vicious cycle of violence before the nations are drawn into a widespread maelstrom of war.

In many respects, the post-Cold War world is an extension of the post-colonial world. The problems of divided ethnic, cultural, religious and economic groups are now emerging anew. These conflicts often occur within imposed boundaries which have never really encompassed sovereign states. Allegiances are frequently astride rather than within frontiers and, as in centuries past, the conflicts risk drawing in other powers whose political interests are seen to lie with peoples of shared identity in other countries. The enormous advances in information transfer across international boundaries compound these problems of transnational identity.

The internal nature of these conflicts challenges the international conflict resolution machinery designed for the essential purpose of preventing conflict between states. With its emphasis on sovereignty within recognised boundaries, the UN Charter has deliberately denied the reality that most international conflicts have occurred as a result of internal conflicts over economic or cultural prerogatives. The challenge facing the emerging order is whether a new strategic accommodation can be arrived at without major conflict. The massive power of modern weapons and the fragility of much of the environment makes the acceptance of this challenge an imperative.

The spectre of war is the major challenge to our capacity for collective action. Despite the advances in cooperation, the very nature of conflict makes it inherently difficult to resolve. While the international community gives preference to conflict resolution by peaceful means, such as negotiation and mediation, peaceful approaches often seem a weak weapon against the political forces which have led to the conflict. The effectiveness of our international efforts largely depends on the leadership of the combatant parties and of those nations which sense real or potential prejudice to their interests. The ability to generate confidence in and commitment to international conflict resolution processes depends on their willingness to compromise entrenched positions in the interests of the greater good.

We are also dependent on the extent of the control they exercise over their followers. In some circumstances (such as in many guerila or terrorist organisations), control is loose. Much of the decision-making is left to commanders or individuals who are not ready to accept constraints on their operations. Problems also arise with armed groups of civilians who operate outside an identifiable command framework. In Rwanda in 1994, for example, the worst excesses of the conflict were not perpetrated by professional soldiers, but by machete and club-wielding civilians, drafted into militias and driven by the ethnic passions of generations.

In an international system based on sovereign states, how does an organisation made up of those states intervene in a way which is consistent with its collective interest? How does it do so in situations where this fundamental concept has been cast into question?

The need for responsible international leadership is clear. Unfortunately, the United Nations, itself still in the process of emerging from its Cold War torpor, has been found wanting in its capacity to assume the full moral authority established in its origins.

The UN Charter

Fifty years ago, at the end of the most disastrous war the world has known, the representatives of fifty sovereign states signed the Charter of the United Nations. Those representatives were also able to recall the devastating effects of the earlier Great War. They were resolved that the United Nations would transcend the incapacity of the League of Nations to prevent conflict during the interwar years.

The UN Charter is a mighty document which does great credit to those who drafted it. Its spirit is reflected in its opening statement that:

We the peoples of the United Nations determined:
To save succeeding generations from the scourge of war which twice in our lifetime has brought untold sorrow to mankind, and
To reaffirm faith in fundamental human rights, in the dignity and worth of the human person, in the equal rights of men and women and of nations large and small, and
To establish conditions under which justice and respect for the obligations arising from treaties and other sources of international law can be maintained, and
To promote social progress and better standards of life in larger freedom....

The Charter is a framework for reconciliation. Its drafters sought to use the wartime cooperation to build confidence between nations. Through the united strength of member states, they hoped to provide defence against threats to the concepts of sovereignty within recognised frontiers, as well as advancing those rights and benefits, the deprivation of which was seen to be the cause of wars.

But in many parts of the globe, these concepts are not well understood. Or, if understood, they are an incitement to action to gain, for particular groups, the benefits which accrue to nation-state status. What is certain is that the massive human rights violations, hunger, disease and refugee flows caused by conflicts and friction cannot be ignored. The central issue is how to intervene in a way which holds the prospect of resolution of a crisis, while remaining within the framework of the UN Charter.

If there is to be any chance of arriving at comprehensive solutions, it is essential to view the world in the light of the emerging global flux, rather than simply of the past. Importantly, the approaches taken to resolve these crises must hold out the potential to set in train dynamics which could establish a pattern for enduring international conflict resolution, and cooperation generally, in the next century and perhaps even the centuries to follow.

One means of directing these dynamics towards a civilised course is through the Charter itself. Its strength comes from its moral authority, the source of which lies in the obligation of its signatories to serve the peoples of the United Nations.

Strategic Objectivity and UN Intervention

In the contemporary world, the deployment of peacekeeping forces has become the most visible face of the United Nations and is among its most important conflict resolution tools. Although never envisaged in the UN Charter, peacekeeping operations are an appropriate mechanism within the framework of Chapter VI (The Pacific Settlement of Disputes). Specifically, they come under Article 33 which provides for 'other peaceful means' among a range of peaceful options. Consent of the parties in conflict is the key issue here.

Operations which come under Article 42 in Chapter VII of the Charter (Threats to the Peace, Breaches of the Peace and Acts of Aggression), are not peacekeeping. The purpose of Chapter VII is, in essence, collective defence against an expansionist military power, such as the Axis forces of the Second World War. Article 42 legitimises international violence against offending parties to this end (which is otherwise proscribed by Article 2). The Korean War (1950–53) and the Gulf War (1991) provide the only clear examples of Article 42 action. These were conducted by war-fighting multinational coalitions led by the US and sanctioned by the Security Council.

Although Chapter VI and Chapter VII operations are both political acts, they are dependent on the moral authority of the Charter, to which all member states have indicated their consent. As with any binding document, the application of the Charter must remain objective and independent of specific national interests in order to sustain the collective consent of the nations. In this process it must be recognised that the generation of political consensus in support of any international resolution will normally involve compromise to accommodate diverse political goals. But if the political purpose is allowed to become ambiguous, is subject to frequent change or is of questionable morality, then consent is likely to prove illusory and the capacity for success gravely prejudiced.

By way of example, the US-led intervention in Somalia in 1992 and the French intervention in southern Rwanda in 1994 are both ostensibly Chapter VII actions sanctioned by Security Council resolutions. Both however, entailed the contradiction which plagues modern international policy-making of having Chapter VI and Chapter VII actions in parallel in an internal conflict. This fails to recognise that while some actions under Chapter VII can resemble those normally associated with peacekeeping, their jurisdictional base is quite different, and the implied capacity for violence is contrary to the pacific nature of Chapter VI. The confusion which surrounds these issues has had a corrosive effect on the moral authority of the United Nations. While not unfamiliar to former colonial powers, this contradiction is at odds with the spirit of the Charter.

The Dynamics of Force

In an environment of excesses and obstacles, the use of force as a preventive measure, to impose a settlement on recalcitrant parties or establish order over lawless groups, emerges as an apparent necessity. Experiences in the United Nations Transitional Authority in Cambodia (UNTAC) from 1992 to 1993, and more recent public commentary, suggest that, to many, enforcement by peacekeepers is seen as an option. The issues involved are not well understood and, in many peacekeeping operations, this confusion over the necessary constraints on the use of force can make effective command impossible.

From the perspective of a military commander, the use of force is essentially a command and control problem. Unlike the laws of physics, in which every action has an equal and opposite reaction, actions in war are likely to be magnified several-fold as passions are compounded by the fatal consequences of conflict. In these circumstances, an escape from the vicious cycle of violence is likely to remain distant until one or more sides bleed themselves to exhaustion.

This terrible reality seems to be little understood in many quarters.

This is why a successful conflict resolution strategy includes, at its core, absolute discrimination in the use of force. It should not occur haphazardly in a climate of passion and raw politics. Nor should it occur as a result of decisions made purely in the glow of television screens. It needs to be borne in mind that enforcement implies that someone does not agree to the role of the enforcer and is therefore likely to resist in a way which quickly moves affairs into a state of reciprocating violence. Force has to be directed only towards the achievement of the legitimate political objective. Where the control is loose, it is free to generate its own dynamic. The requirement for discrimination is even stronger in the case of enforcement action.

Anyone who thinks they can bluff their way through these things with a mandate and troops designed for peacekeeping has little understanding of the nature of conflict and the consequences of the use of force. They are also likely to compromise the neutrality of the United Nations and with it, its credibility and capacity to act as an honest broker in other conflicts. There are significant lessons to be learned from United Nations experiences in the former Yugoslavia in this respect.

This is not to suggest that there are no enforcement options. But force has to be lawful. It is difficult to argue that anyone has the right to kill or injure people in their own country without proper sanction under either international or domestic law. How can a mandate which draws its authority from a Charter designed to defend the sovereignty of states, and to promote and encourage respect for human rights, authorise hostile intervention against any party or individual within a state? And if responses are not firmly based within the framework of the Charter, how can the UN Commander issue lawful and sustainable orders to soldiers of another member state, or indeed, of his own country? Where does that leave the soldier who might have to make the choice between obeying or disobeying those orders, and bearing the consequences?

In Cambodia, there was no legitimate authority to engage in offensive operations, since all the parties to the Paris Agreements had not acceded to it. The enforcement of law and order was their responsibility, consistent with the human rights provisions to which Cambodia had agreed. The appropriate response was the one taken, namely, in the context of a peacekeeping operation to fulfil the mandated responsibility of establishing a recognisable legitimate authority which was capable of exercising sovereign jurisdiction.

Moreover, offensive operations impose significantly greater demands than peacekeeping. Enforcement is, after all, war by another name. It is only if there is almost universal consent that a particular party is in the wrong that international support for enforcement will follow. Universal consent does not simply mean the views of some journalists or commentators. Often these are encumbered by baggage from the past or are obscured by the horror and passion of more immediate events. There have to be interests of severe magnitude at stake before the consensus within the contributing countries will reach the necessary fervour to provide the forces and funds for war-fighting, and possibly to accept casualties on a significant scale.

A critical issue in such considerations is that of sustainment. Can a coalition response be sustained once it comes under stress? There are those of course who are prepared to make bold suggestions about enforcement, but often there is not even domestic consensus for it in their own nation, let alone in the multinational array of countries which contribute to a modern-day peacekeeping force.

Anyone who joins a conflict without the means or the intention of winning is betraying those who will be called on to make the sacrifices. A force commander in an environment where there is active debate about transition from Chapter VI peacekeeping to Chapter VII enforcement operations very quickly reaches the conclusions that most of the force is ill-prepared for such a transition, and that the wavering international support for whatever new objectives are chosen will make the command weak and vulnerable. It is no way to go to war!

Nothing could spell out this essential fact more clearly than the results of selective NATO offensive action in Bosnia. Successive commanders, aware of the vulnerability of those under their command, have been reluctant to authorise any form of enforcement action, despite the urging of those who, more secure and less responsible, have been extravagant in their judgment of the deficiencies of UN command.

Peacekeeping

Objective judgement will determine whether Chapter VI or VII action is warranted, what form it should take and the resources required. While consensus can be more readily generated in support of peacekeeping, if Chapter VII action is required, peacekeeping cannot be used as a substitute. Peacekeeping is based on international consent and that of all the parties involved, including that of the peacekeepers. This requires, for their own protection, an overt display of impartiality on the part of peacekeepers to establish their credentials as 'honest brokers' in the process. This display is totally different from the display required for enforcement, which is warlike and concentrated to establish seriousness of intent.

Peacekeeping operations seek to resolve disputes on the basis of an agreement between the parties to a conflict while impartially seeking to generate the climate for compliance with that agreement. The fundamental building block for diplomatic responses (outlined under Article 33) which can be most readily agreed is the peaceful intent of the operation. Article 2 obliges this and Chapter VI provides the legitimate framework for UN action.

Member states deploy an international peacekeeping force to facilitate a settlement, or to inhibit escalation of a conflict. It matters little whether the agreement of the parties in conflict is due to diplomatic pressure, economic sanctions or exhaustion. The opposing factions want either resolution of the conflict, or at least its suspension while diplomacy proceeds. The peacekeepers are legally protected by the agreement; their legitimate purpose is confidence-building and there are clear limits to what they can do while retaining consent.

A peacekeeping force gains and retains its acceptability because it is impartial. The peacekeepers' impartiality gives them their unity and their strength. They are constrained to limit the use of force to self-defence. If peacekeepers exceed their jurisdiction and move beyond their inherent right of self-defence, experience shows that they will almost inevitably compromise their neutrality and become another party to the conflict. When this occurs, their unity is shattered, they are stripped of their strength and, because of their nature, are without the protection of the array of combat and support systems that any able commander will seek to support his forces in the achievement of their assigned military objectives. Peacekeepers are instruments of diplomacy, not of war.

Defending a Peacekeeping Mandate

With the extension of UN intervention into the area of peace-building, peacekeeping operations have become finely balanced affairs, involving the need for harmonisation of widely diverse activities and interests, in environments of an increasingly dynamic nature. It is now more than ever essential that UN forces maintain their peacekeeping bona fides throughout. If this is to be the case, then force can only be used in self-defence.

Regrettably, the confusion over these issues is exacerbated by a wide interpretation of the meaning of self-defence among contributing countries and analysts. In UNTAC, for example, interpretations covered the full spectrum, despite clear definitions in standing operating procedures and continuous briefings. Initially, responses among UNTAC contingents ranged from some troops allowing themselves to be disarmed when threatened, to others opening fire with all available weapons at the slightest provocation.

The Cambodian operation was conducted in a country which had suffered a quarter of a century of civil war, genocide and more civil war. Despite the pledges of the parties to the Paris Agreements, UNTAC peacekeepers and civilian components eventually deployed into a climate of escalating violence, demanding 'go' or 'no go' decisions, with the ability to defend the various components of the mission being a prime consideration.

The key element in UNTAC's success was the readiness of the people to vote. This depended in a large part on the perceived commitment of the United Nations to that end, and the Cambodian conviction of that commitment. At the outset, the delayed start by UNTAC eroded much of the hard-won opportunity provided by the Paris Agreements, opening a new set of conflicting dynamics.

The Khmer Rouge claimed that UNTAC was not implementing the Agreements fairly and that the people would reject the UNTAC process. They said that the violence in the countryside, including the massacres of innocent civilians, was a manifestation of the people's anger. On the other hand, the Phnom Penh faction claimed that UNTAC lacked the will to prevent the Khmer Rouge from subverting the peace process. How to respond was the dilemma the United Nations faced.

On a number of occasions, in response to atrocities, the Force Commander was called on by people, both within and outside the United Nations, to use the peacekeeping force for the conduct of operations against the Khmer Rouge. These would have been offensive operations—no one could draw any other interpretation. But what was most astonishing was the passion with which the use of force was espoused. Often, the most fervent advocates of violence were those who would otherwise declare their total opposition to war.

It is easy to understand the frustration of people when they cannot achieve the results they aspire to, or when they see atrocities committed within their reach and vision. But it is also deeply disturbing when they are moved to exhort publicly the transition to enforcement by peacekeepers in the face of this. Such exhortations are not only very dangerous, but are often counter-productive to the outcome of the mission. The difficulty here lies in ensuring that everyone understands the purpose of peacekeeping operations: why they are deployed to these volatile areas in the first place; their objectives; and what they are legally entitled to do. The issues of consent and jurisdiction are the key themes here. The only way to avoid the need to consider peace-enforcement, with all its consequences, is to generate and maintain consensus on the steps for peaceful resolution of the conflict.

To do this, everyone has to have something at stake, and the benefit of complying with an agreement has to exceed the consequences of not complying. In this process, leaders have to be forced into considering the needs of their followers. Their actual leadership may have to be put at stake. There has to be an element of coercion in this, but there sometimes seems to be an almost compete comprehension gap about the difference between political coercion and the dynamic nature and the effect of the use of force at the international level. Closely related to this is the need to understand the effects of the use of force by peacekeepers on the activities of all UN personnel and non-government organisations (NGOs) in the mission area.

In Cambodia, the civilian components had their mandated responsibilities, and humanitarian agencies and NGOs had their programmes aimed at alleviating the suffering of the people. For most, this included extensive field work. In their interests, UNTAC had to avoid conflict as much as was reasonably possible. The command assessment had to be that, although there was a climate of violence, it was manageable, provided UNTAC did nothing to contribute to it, while containing it to the extent possible through negotiations and moderating its effects through diplomatic efforts. The long-term objective of the mandate had to be the focus.

But at a critical point, UNTAC had to stay and defend the mandated political objective—the conduct of an election for a constituent assembly in as neutral an environment as could be created by these means. The Cambodian people expected this of UNTAC and only the Military Component could provide it for them. It was a case of bluff in which the risks could only be taken where UNTAC could be relatively sure of its support and the commitment of its own people.

Self-defence

From the point of view of the UNTAC Force Commander, self-defence meant defence of anyone going about their legitimate business under the Paris Agreements. This was intended to include defence of any Cambodian who, disarmed, placed trust in the United Nations by remaining in the mandated cantonment process. In the light of changed circumstances, self-defence was extended to the use of minimum force and proportionate response in defence of the electoral process.

Self-defence not only meant an individual's defence of himself alone—it meant collective action. In some instances, company-level defensive battles had to be fought, but it is important to understand that in these engagements, the use of force by peacekeepers was never offensive—only those actually using force against mandated activities were engaged, and then only engaged to the extent necessary to provide protection. In this context, self-defence was passive—it did not actively seek combat. While the majority of the military units were eventually mentally and physically prepared to do this, it was important that their operations were seen to be conducted strictly within these constraints. It was only in the context of self-defence that this outcome could be reasonably certain.

Contributing to the confusion on these issues is an apparent unwillingness or inability on the part of the United Nations to define clearly the fact that armed and active military forces cannot be embraced by these defence mechanisms. Refugee camps such as in Rwanda, or protected zones such as in Bosnia, cannot be defended by the international community unless they are demilitarised. If they are not, the authority of the United Nations to secure them will be violently contested.

The UN operation in Cambodia was brought about by unprecedented international consensus made possible by the end of the Cold War. When the Paris Agreements were signed in October 1991 by the four Cambodian parties and eighteen interested countries, they established the status of the parties and of UNTAC, and the legal obligations and relationships between the signatories, and between the signatories and the United Nations. The UNTAC operation was a continuation of the dynamic of diplomacy that the Agreements reflected. It was a step in an ongoing process.

If the mission in Cambodia was to succeed, it was critical for UNTAC to retain the peacekeeping ethos under the prevailing political circumstances. In addition to the practical and ethical issues, there were strong strategic reasons, as discussed in my chapter above, why enforcement was never an option. Any force, even self-defence in support of the mandate, was only possible with cohesion in the Security Council and consensus in the countries contributing troops to the peacekeeping mission. The two issues are synergistic; each depends on the other. When they are drawn together, diplomacy is concentrated to support action. This emphasises the need for absolute discrimination in the use of force.

Strengthening UN Intervention

Regardless of whether the United Nations intervenes under Chapter VI or VII, the nature and timing of that intervention needs to be such that it can achieve the identified political purpose. Various options have been suggested over the years to strengthen the UN's capacities, including standing armed forces in order to allow a rapid response to emerging crises. Against the background of the tragedies we have witnessed in Bosnia and Rwanda, and the difficulties in obtaining sufficient forces for the tasks envisaged, this proposal has recently received support from some quarters. But the major difficulty lies in generating support among member states generally for the creation of such a force, and agreement on the framework for its employment.

It is important to maintain a strategic view on this issue. Any military response by the United Nations can only ever be part of the solution in a range of civil–military options. Moreover, effective operations require clearly defined and achievable objectives, which are properly planned for and resourced. Decisions on any use of military forces must be made in the light of detailed and carefully considered military advice which enables the full implications and risks to be assessed. Military operations also need to be commanded effectively by trained professionals, conscious of the strategic context of their operations, their integrated civil–military nature and the implications of their directions on broader international political goals.

There is general international agreement on the need for improved UN crisis response. But any arrangements for rapid provision of military forces may be counter-productive if the necessary command and control arrangements are not in place to allow these forces to contribute to more effective conflict prevention and resolution.

The capacity of peacekeepers to effect their mandate impartially is sometimes constrained from the outset. This is often the result of a fundamental contradiction between the diplomatic compromises needed to gain a mandate, and the essential requirement for objectivity in the development of effective military operations.

In all of this, it must be recognised that military operations cannot be an end in themselves. Commanders will always be confronted with circumstances which require action, which will in turn generate a reaction. Without objective direction, there is a strong probability that those actions will disconnect from diplomatic action, thereby corrupting the mission and causing its failure. The resulting tendency of the involved actors then to blame each other will affect the credibility of the structures provided by the United Nations, causing an erosion of confidence in the organisation. Money and troops will be difficult to find.

The critical issue here is not who might be to blame, but that peacekeepers need to be actively supported by diplomacy. That diplomatic support is likely to be gravely weakened if strategic objectivity is lacking in the initial resolution.

Command Structure

It is also critical that objective decisions are passed to those charged with their implementation in a way which focuses their actions. This requires an effective command structure. The military doctrine of most countries identifies three levels of command; strategic, operational and tactical. These have different functions and nature, but all three have the common purpose of passing objective directions to their subordinates, and ensuring that they are empowered and resourced to do the tasks. If one of these levels is deficient, or their roles become merged, the capacity of the others to function effectively is severely limited. If the strategic level becomes involved with tactics, it is likely to lose its broad perspective and diminish the power of commanders on the ground. At one and the same time, tactical actions which are not focused can impact adversely on the strategic plan. The operational level both separates and binds the strategic and tactical levels, ensuring that tactical actions are coordinated to achieve strategic objectives.

For example, the levels of command were represented in UNTAC as follow:

- The strategic level was the UN Security Council in New York, supported by the United Nations Secretariat and the state structures of Security Council members, with their links to the national capitals of interested states and the highest level headquarters of involved agencies of the United Nations or NGOs.

* The operational level was the UN Headquarters in Phnom Penh, with its links to the leadership of the Cambodian parties, the diplomatic community and the most senior authorities of the various agencies in-country.

* The tactical level was the military units, civilian groups and elements in the field, coordinated by regional headquarters, normally located in provincial capitals.

The key issue is that the three levels are mutually supporting and are complementary elements which form an effective whole. Each functions in the light of the realities of the others. Much of the success achieved in Cambodia was due to the operational level, despite all sorts of interventions, being able to achieve an effective harmony between all levels and to maintain it up to the end of the mandate.

Strategic Level

Within a nation-state, the strategic level is where decisions are made about enduring relationships between elements of society; between the people and the state; and between the state, other nations and international organisations, multinationals and the like. The central issues involve adjustment of national priorities in response to changing circumstances. It is a continuum in peace and war. However, in war, the military dimension assumes higher prominence.

Because of the essentially political nature of this activity, the processes are more dialectic and less direct than those normally associated with the exercise of military command. For this reason, it is at the strategic level that the ambiguities of the political nuances have to be absorbed and focused into directives to the next level, which are at once designed to provide clarity, flexibility and inspiration to action. This is a hugely demanding task.

In the case of the UN, the strategic focus must be even broader, involving issues of ongoing harmony between member states, groupings and international bodies. Decisions made by member states are collective, but the purposes of pursuing and balancing the objectives of the Charter must be paramount.

The central task would seem to lie in determining the international will on issues which are raised within the context of the Charter. While the Security Council is in a position to provide a lead, its capacity for action will be limited without broad international commitment. This is especially so in peacekeeping which requires substantial international representation. Achieving a consensus which is at the same time objective is clearly very difficult—more so, because objectivity has many dimensions.

A central issue is the ongoing viability and credibility of the organisation itself. It is critical that the interests of individual states, or even groups of states, do not subvert the Charter if the existence of the Organisation is not to be brought into question. This can occur both in the formulation of resolutions, and in the conduct of operations on the ground, if those resolutions are not sufficiently objective and binding.

Operational Level

The operational level of command is that level at which field elements are orchestrated to achieve the objectives of strategy. In military terminology, the operational level is sometimes referred to as campaign strategy, identifying the distinction between the tactical and operational levels as the responsibility of the operational level commander for the overall outcome of the military campaign.

The key determinant of success at this level of command is the military principle of the selection and maintenance of the aim. This is the principle that connects the strategic level to the operational level of command and should therefore emerge from strategic level analysis to which the operational level commander must be a contributor. Key to the derivation of, and successful conclusion to, a campaign strategy is timely and accurate intelligence in all its forms. A combination of insight and superior knowledge is most conducive to the achievement of the desired psychological effects.

At the operational level, it is unity of command which provides strength and cohesion. While the complexity of many post Cold-War peacekeeping operations usually means that they are civil–military affairs, it nevertheless remains critical that all elements engaged come under one common authority. Somebody has to be responsible for issuing clear, unambiguous directives, and looking the commanders, troops and civilian field staff in the eye before, during and after they have committed themselves to their assigned objectives. Leadership of missions must reflect this essential requirement.

Tactical Level

The tactical level is more finite, with objectives being defined in the more material terms of boundaries, time, numbers and resources. This is not to say that leaders at this level do not have to contend in a dynamic environment which will test their powers to bring complex factors into harmony. It is simply that they are responsible for specified outcomes in a given area rather than the overall outcome of the campaign.

In peacekeeping operations, the tactical level involves much more than military units and, in some circumstances, such as humanitarian relief which is not subject to dispute or exploitation, military forces might only be in a supporting role. It could, for example, involve electoral teams, human rights monitors, police and monitors of the parties' administrations, as it did in Cambodia. Each had to be harmonised with the others, across the chains of command reaching up to the operational level in Phnom Penh.

No tactical level leader can change his objectives without referral to the next higher level. In the ultimate, to do so would be to unravel the overall strategy, risking a significant shift in the relative strength of the contending factions and prejudicing the entire mission.

For this reason, it is of particular importance that tactical units do not respond to national or other chains of command on operational matters. Nor can they be allowed to develop their own interpretations, outside the operational level commander's intent, especially on critical issues such as the use of force.

Cooperating for Peace in Cambodia

The earliest forms of UN peacekeeping were observer missions. Begun by the United Nations shortly after the Second World War, these were relatively simple affairs. At the other end of the peacekeeping spectrum, complex post-Cold War operations, like UNTAC, have to be approached and managed like major operations, with the levels of command functioning in the relationship described here.

Although the Cambodian operation is acknowledged as a UN success, it was clear that all three levels were deficient in some way. From the outset, there was no strategic coordination in UNTAC. Each component survey team developed its own plan in isolation, lacking the benefit of even a coordinating conference beforehand to determine the strategic direction. The bringing together of these plans only occurred when the Secretary-General's report was prepared for the Security Council in January–February 1992. Few component leaders participated in this process.

The first coordination at the operational level, between those component heads who were available, occurred en route to Phnom Penh from Bangkok on the day that UNTAC was established. Some component heads were not available to the mission until five months later. Among them all, only the Force Commander had participated in the preparation of his component's plan. None of them had participated in the negotiations which had preceded the Paris Agreements on which the strategy for the UN mission in Cambodia was based. The initial strategic disconnect was severe.

Within the mission, harmonising the activities of the various elements of UNTAC was always problematic. Senior staff meetings were held regularly, chaired by the Special Representative of the Secretary-General (SRSG) or his deputy, and attended by component heads and other key senior staff. But there was a tendency for meetings to become bogged down in matters of detail which were more appropriately the concern of the tactical level. This was almost certainly contributed to by the lack of formalised coordinating structures at lower levels. Rather than being solved where they belonged, problems were often simply passed upwards, where the operational level was already too busy to perform its own role effectively. In many cases, the problems were not solved at all.

In the execution, coordination was achieved through component heads networking as problems arose. There was no UNTAC-wide operations centre. To some extent, the civilian logistics organisation assumed a directing role in the early period of the UN presence. But the logistics staff, being constrained by UN procedural considerations, were, for the most part, deterred from focusing on outcomes. By the end of 1992, the Military Component's Plans Branch became the focal point for a planning and control alliance between the Military and Electoral Components, and Information and Education Division, for the critical voter registration and electoral phases.

At the same time, at the tactical level, the Military Component's ten Sector Headquarters, spread throughout Cambodia, adopted the coordinating role. This eventually drew in the liaison mechanism put in place to work with the Cambodian military and police of the parties supporting the UNTAC-sponsored elections, as well as the UNTAC Civilian Police and the other civilian components. These cooperative arrangements were sufficient to see the UNTAC-sponsored elections of May 1993 through to their successful conclusion.

These observations are not intended to denigrate the UN effort in

Cambodia, nor to suggest that such shortfalls are not being addressed. Rather, they are intended to highlight the systemic problems of command and control, which continue to plague all UN missions.

In fact, success in UNTAC could not have been achieved if there had not been unity at and with the strategic level. The Paris Agreements had been long in gestation and formed an objective document. Among the signatories were the main strategic supporters of the four Cambodian parties. Their legal relationships were thus redefined by this act.

Obstacles were overcome politically by the operational level generating new dynamics both at the diplomatic level and in the field. This allowed the Cambodian people to be made sovereign by the electoral process, despite the conflicts between and within the Cambodian factions. This cohesion weakened after the election, but adhered for long enough to conclude the UNTAC mandate. With the UN's moral authority progressively diminishing as the mandate reached its culminating point, it was a race against time.

The strategic level grouping was essential to unify and focus the diplomatic support. At the same time the operational level needed structures to concentrate its efforts on its important task of defining and refining a policy framework for the implementation of the mandate laid down by the Security Council and adjusted by subsequent resolutions according to emerging circumstances. But rather than the ad hoc arrangements in UNTAC, it would have been better if structures had been planned for and put in place at the outset.

Command and Control and the UN Charter

In multinational operations of the complexity of the one in Cambodia, nothing is a set piece. International sentiment, generated by media coverage, will ensure that those responsible cannot wait for everything to be put in place. The situation will always be reactive and dynamic. Decision-makers must be able and prepared to act in pursuit of the defined objectives and to account for their actions.

To discriminate in this requires a highly responsive command and control system. Responsiveness at the highest level requires a strategic headquarters which is purpose designed to be responsive. Among other things, it requires a deep intelligence process in order to be able to make valid judgments in the light of all the issues involved. Unbiased and independent analysis is the key here. Dependence on any individual national intelligence system is likely to involve some bias which will confuse the response.

And there is the dilemma for the United Nations. It does not have a responsive command and control system. It is a simple fact that deployed operational level commanders do not have a superior head-quarters. To have one, the structure and workings of the organisation have to be addressed in a fundamental way.

The problem experienced by the United Nations in Rwanda in 1994 is a case in point. Setting aside the issues of legitimacy and preventive action, the response to events lacked strategic objectivity. Enforcement action on a large scale was required to stop the genocide. Enforcement was still required to stop the consequences of the genocide. But the force was capped at 5500 and given a peacekeeping mandate in response to expectations which were well beyond it as a result. A brief foray into enforcement was endorsed by the Security Council to stabilise the mass movement of refugees into Zaire, but even this action contributed to an impression of crisis decision-making rather than strategic objectivity. While a glowing example of humani-tarian mobilisation, Rwanda has done nothing to contribute to the credibility of UN peacekeeping.

Significantly, the command and control systems for UNPROFOR operations have been a Gordian Knot of European and UN pre-rogatives, with strategic policy-making not matching the dangerous realities on the ground. Anticipation of and preparation for what seem to have been predictable responses (the primary role of a strategic level headquarters) appear to have been a responsibility not accepted.

No one should be surprised when contributing countries find difficulty reconciling contributions to such missions with their existing policy. Placed on the horns of a dilemma, they are called on to accept the consequences without being able to effect a solution. Responsible national political authorities cannot function in this way. They are unlikely to commit forces in the face of such decision-making.

Under Article 43, all member states undertake to make armed forces available to the Security Council for operations within the framework of the Charter. In recent times, governments of many member states have issued policy directives or guidance defining the circumstances under which they will commit forces to UN operations. In essence, the purpose of these has been twofold:

- to reassure their own people that any national commitment will be justified by the realistic prospects of the potential ends justifying the risks; and

• to signal to the United Nations that it must get its house in order if it expects governments to be able to generate support from their domestic constituencies.

Apart from protecting the interests of the states concerned, the definition of a framework for involvement reflects a demand for strategic objectivity on the part of the United Nations which includes a requirement for morally sustainable responses.

Mandates which are framed with objectivity and aimed at the accomplishment of realistic goals are more likely to generate sustained consensus, confidence, and commitment to provide resources, including forces. The settlement of the dispute, in a way consistent with the objectives of the Charter, must be the aim. To do this, the structures supporting complex operations need to be at least the equivalent of those of a relatively advanced member state, or alternatively, allow formalised access to the structures of member states in a way which does not compromise the essential need for objectivity in UN decision-making.

The best starting point for reforming these processes is the Charter itself, which has already been agreed to by the member states. The Security Council has specific responsibilities under both Chapters VI and VII, and its central role as the strategic authority designated by the Charter must not be eroded. In this regard, it is critical that risks of perceived bias in Security Council decisions are avoided. The Secretariat has the essential role of ensuring that the deliberations of the Security Council members maintain their objectivity. Often it is only the Secretariat which can gain the necessary access to trouble spots to determine the viability of strategic options. This places the Secretary-General and his staff in an onerous position of responsibility.

Regardless of this essential role for the UN Secretariat, it has always been recognised that it would not be capable of providing comprehensive military advice, nor of controlling complex military operations. Many of the difficulties experienced in places such as Somalia and Rwanda can be attributed to this fact.

It is only under Chapter VII, in response to 'threats to the peace, breaches of the peace and acts of aggression', that the Charter provides for the strategic direction of response forces to be exercised by the Military Staff Committee, made up of the Chiefs of Staff (or their representatives) of the armed forces of the P5. While it is envisaged that the chiefs or their representatives would cooperate together, they would still be answerable to their own governments, which themselves would have agreed to cooperate.

The Cold War made almost any form of military cooperation between the P5 impossible, including the empowerment of the Military Staff Committee. But we should be very clear in our minds that the UN Secretariat cannot act as a substitute. It is neither structured nor equipped to act as a strategic headquarters. This is why the original role of the Military Staff Committee for advice to the Security Council was established.

Moreover, the fact that military advice to the Security Council should be provided by the structures responsible for the implementation of those operations mandated by that advice is also acknowledged in the Charter. Clearly, the Military Staff Committee needs to be empowered to perform these responsibilities for complex Chapter VI operations as well as those mandated under Chapter VII. Undoubtedly, it would require discrete secretariat services to enable it to coordinate separate national military advice to form agreed collective advice, plans and directions. Broader representation would probably be needed to generate the necessary climate of trust in these extended activities if the Military Staff Committee were to be acceptable in this role, and this is also provided for in the Charter.

Conclusion

Reconciliation is the basis of all successful strategies. This is the underlying theme of the UN Charter. The United Nations brings together most of the sovereign states on earth which, by their ratification of the Charter, establish the moral authority of the organisation. When a UN mission is mandated, it thereby assumes a measure of the moral authority from the Charter, the extent depending on the purpose of the mission, the objectivity with which the mandate is framed and the consensus upon which it is based. Throughout the mission, successes consistent with the mandate can contribute to that moral authority, while failures will erode it. If the initial mandate is flawed, the erosion can be rapid.

In a media environment, where the membrane between the past and the future becomes thin, and the passion of the moment becomes a marketable product to be flashed around the world as events unfold, successes are likely to be less obvious than failures. Sustaining an international commitment in the light of this reality requires a comprehensive public relations strategy based on a firm understanding of the central place of the moral authority of the United Nations in international peace initiatives.

Moral authority resides in the great ideals of the Charter, and is generated through the belief which the peoples of the United Nations have in it. That belief is variable and is the sum total of the perception of successes and failures of the United Nations at any point in time. Where the perception of success is high, so is the faith in the organisation. The commitment to both its principles and activities is therefore likely to be strengthened. The future of the United Nations depends on its capacity to seize the full weight of the moral authority enshrined in its own Charter, and to bring it to bear in the interests of its peoples. The processes for mandating and directing operations must be reinforced to this end.

Over 170 years ago, Carl von Clausewitz, the renowned Prussian military theorist, in his treatise on *Absolute War and Real War,* stated that:

> No one starts a war—or rather, no one in his senses ought to do so—without first being clear in his mind what he intends to achieve by that war and how he intends to conduct it. The former is its political purpose; the latter its operational objective. This is the governing principle which will set its course, prescribe the scale of means and effort which is required, and make its influence felt throughout, down to the smallest operational detail.

This principle applies equally to peacekeeping under the auspices of the United Nations. Proposals to support conflict resolution, including those for standby forces for UN intervention, must be cognisant of this fundamental fact. For the United Nations to lose a war—which would surely be the case if, once committed to enforcement, its member states were unable to sustain that commitment, or if its command and control systems were ineffective—would spell doom for the organisation for many years to come. Its moral authority might be destroyed forever.

Takahiro Shinyo

Reforming The Security Council: A Japanese Perspective

More than five years have passed since the demise of the Cold War. The world's political developments are moving so fast that the expression 'post-Cold War era' seems somewhat obsolete. The world is clearly moving from a hegemonic bipolar world to a multipolar system. Though it is not easy to say whether a multipolar system is politically less stable than a bipolar world, one might be able to assume that international disorder is a temporary phenomenon at least for the moment.

Under such circumstances the UN celebrates its fiftieth anniversary this year. The role of the United Nations in resolving regional and ethnic conflicts has been dramatically increased in the post-Cold War period; at the same time, however, we are aware of the limitations of its capability.

A tacit agreement among the five permanent members of the Security Council (P5) seems to prevail in the present United Nations. We need to consider carefully whether this 'concert of powers' is a temporary phenomenon as a reaction against the hectic confrontations among P5 nations during the Cold War, or an indication of the opening of an era of so called 'pax consortis' (peace with concert) which will extend over a longer period of time.

During its two years as a non-permanent member of the Security Council, a term that expired at the end of 1993, Japan played a part in addressing the issues involved in creating peace under the UN's aegis. This included participation in peacekeeping operations for the first time ever. Nevertheless, my first-hand experience with Japan's UN diplomacy at the time left me with three strong impressions: that the UN may have overstepped the bounds of its competence, that over-emphasis on humanitarian concerns drives the Security Council to make decisions based on sentiment, and that perception of the propriety or impropriety of using force has been dulled. It is time for the international community to stop a moment and take a good steady look at these considerations, which tend to be swept from view by the tide of events.

Times have changed. Put simply, the post-Cold War era is one of collective responsibility; no country seeks to take sole responsibility for running the world. This being the case, as a universal organisation, the UN is attracting attention again as a forum for achieving international coordination. Recognising how anachronistic this mechanism—unchanged since the UN's founding in 1945—has now become, Japan should press for Security Council reform with clearly articulated will and firm conviction. It is also essential that powerful nations like Japan and Germany be brought into the Council and participate in its reform.

What is important for Japan is to determine how it will participate in the Security Council, the decision-making body for the UN's key function of collective security and peacekeeping, and how it will bring its influence to bear upon the consensus-building process that takes place there. These are the considerations that should be at the heart of our UN-centred diplomacy in this new age.

In Japan, arguments concerning the United Nations have focused too much on issues of organisational matters, including the reform of the Security Council and the right of veto, as well as legal aspects of the possibility and limitation of Japan's military contribution as a permanent member of the Security Council.

What we need to do at this moment, however, is to have a clear understanding of the meaning of the present era which necessitates a reform of the United Nations. In other words, we must understand the importance of the post-Cold War era in the history of humankind. The Cold War is over and the 'Cold Peace' is casting its shadow over the world's political constellation, the world in which there is as yet no chart drawn for the new order. There seems to exist among the countries of the world a rather optimistic view that a war among major powers is not likely to occur in the current post-Cold War era. It is rather difficult to judge whether that will remain the case in the years to come.

Although there may be an assumption that a nuclear war between the two major nuclear-weapons states, the United States and Russia, has become unlikely, the proliferation of nuclear weapons in the developing world is of growing concern. The imminent or latent threat of nuclear-weapons proliferation, when coupled with the spread of regional conflicts, poses a greater concern to every nation of the world even after the recent decision to extend indefinitely the Nuclear Non-Proliferation Treaty (NPT).

Regional conflicts involving conventional weapons are fought nowadays among ethnic groups within a nation-state rather than between states. This calls for an urgent need to develop new strategies and concepts of conflict management for the United Nations as well as for individual countries to cope with such new situations. Nevertheless, the permanent members of the Security Council and the major countries in the world began to look more inwardly to restore their national economies exhausted during the Cold War, and to give first priority to preserving their national interests. This has made it more difficult for them to pay attention to the international public interest or to the maintenance of world order. It is therefore imperative for all the countries in the world to strengthen the United Nations, which is the sole universal system in the post-Cold War era, to maintain balance between the national interest of each member state and the international public interest. If this fails, it may be impossible to preclude international conflicts involving major powers.

To maintain international order in a multipolar world is not an easy job at all. The modern history of the world shows, however, that the 'Concert of Europe', a multipolar system created at the Congress of Vienna in 1815 after the Napoleonic Wars, more or less preserved peace which lasted nearly 100 years in Europe. The question can be addressed to the United Nations as to whether it can maintain a stable global order for another fifty years, as the Concert of Europe did, by preventing and deterring conflicts which might endanger international peace and security. This, I believe, is the task entrusted to the United Nations in the 21st century.

Overcoming UN Pessimism

It has long been said that the era of the United Nations has come. Yet the peacekeeping activities which have become the core function of the United Nations in the post-Cold War era are now facing great difficulties, such as failure and withdrawal in the case of Somalia and meandering and confusion in the case of former Yugoslavia. The lack of financial resources and the reluctance of member states to provide personnel to the UN are impeding the effectiveness of the peacekeeping operations. Thus the gap between reality and the ideal to maintain and restore peace through the UN is widening.

We have recently witnessed an increase in pessimistic observation with regard to the role of the United Nations. Such pessimism may be conducive to moderating the excessive expectations of the United Nations which have been the case in the immediate post-Cold War era and to look more objectively at the UN at the time of its fiftieth anniversary. We should prevent the further spread of pessimism, however, in order to stop major powers from disengaging from the work of the United Nations. We cannot afford to miss this chance to revitalise the United Nations. The history of the League of Nations after the First World War, in which major powers stayed outside the system (by their own will or because they were compelled to do so), must not be repeated.

Selective Engagement

To avoid rash action, and also to keep from damaging its authority and credibility, the UN needs to distinguish carefully between problems that warrant a concerted response and those that do not. This is far from easy for an international organisation whose guiding principles are neutrality and universality. Nevertheless, the limits to the human, material and financial resources that nations can provide to the UN, and limits to the UN's own responsiveness, make it important to distinguish between ideals and reality and to adopt the approach of 'selective engagement'.

Generally speaking, the approach known as 'legalism' narrowly defines an organisation's actions; anything not expressly permitted is forbidden. 'Politicism', by contrast, represents a more flexible approach, emphasising the judgment made by the organisation's decision-making apparatus. The United Nations is considered to be an organisation based on politicism because although it stipulates security-related procedures, it gives the Security Council broad dis-cretionary powers in determining specific actions. Therefore, actions authorised by Security Council resolutions, even if not expressly stipulated in the Charter, are not perforce illegal. Even with this as the basic premise, UN-controlled actions, precisely because they are carried out directly in the organisation's name, will naturally be scrutinised very closely for consistency with their political objectives, compatibility with international law, and legitimacy and credibility.

The Charter invests the Security Council with leadership in accordance with the concept of politicism. At present, however, the Security Council's efficacy and legitimacy are being severely questioned. Therefore, even if the Council were equipped with both nominal and actual authority and capability, it still lacks sufficient grounds to insist on the correctness of its decisions and actions. Two things are thus necessary in regard to future enforcement actions under the direct UN command. One is political efforts to rebuild the Security Council's authority. The other, based on a legalistic viewpoint, is the concrete provision of grounds for the Council's authority to enable such enforcement action on the basis of the Charter. Those grounds must be recognised as representing the consensus of the UN member states following full debate in the General Assembly.

Previous Japanese Proposals

Japan's proposal to reform the Security Council goes back to the early 1970s. In 1971, in his speech at the 26th Session of the General Assembly of the United Nations, Foreign Minister Kiichi Aichi voiced the need to review the composition and function of the Security Council. In 1979, Foreign Minister Zentaro Kosaka also proposed in the General Debate of the General Assembly to review the composition of the Security Council's membership. Those proposals were received positively and supported by the United States in the General Assembly, as demonstrated in the speeches by Secretaries of State William Rogers in 1972 and Henry Kissinger in 1973. However, Japan's proposals were not regarded as realistic at the time of the Cold War, in which the United Nations and the world were divided by an East–West confrontation.

The ending of the Cold War presented an entirely different picture with respect to the argument for reform of the Security Council. Three main reasons can be considered for Japan's initiative to put forward new proposals for Security Council reform. First, in the General Assembly in 1991 eight countries including India and Brazil began substantial debate over Agenda Item 40, the 'Question of Equitable Representation on and Increase in the Membership of the Security Council'.

Second, in the case of the succession to the permanent seat of the former Soviet Union in the Security Council by the Russian Federation, there seemed to exist a tacit agreement among the permanent members not to open the discussion on the amendment of the Charter; the attitude of the P5 was very conservative in order to ensure that a Pandora's box was not opened by this issue.

Finally, Japan felt very much depressed by its defeat in the diplomacy during the Gulf War. Although Japan extended huge financial cooperation totalling US $13 billion to the coalition forces and to the countries in the Gulf region, it received little attention and appreciation from Kuwait and coalition forces. This caused a very embarrassed feeling and frustration on the side of Japan, which could not participate in the important decision-making in the Security Council but was expected to shoulder the heavy financial burden to implement the resolutions. This last point has reminded the Japanese Government of the notion 'no taxation without representation'.

These three elements have been the incentives and motivations for the Japanese government to initiate the process of restructuring the Security Council.

Present Japanese Views

Pursuant to the Resolution of the General Assembly (A/47/L.26. Rev.1 and Add.1), the Government of Japan submitted its written comment on a possible review of the membership of the Security Council in July 1993. The gist of the comment is as follows. In order to enhance the legitimacy and credibility of the Security Council it is necessary to increase the number of the Council from 15 at present to around 20. The criteria for permanent membership are primarily the will and capability to bear responsibility for international peace and security, while taking into consideration the growing recognition among countries in the world that the concept of security has been changing from purely military security to a comprehensive one to include non-military aspects in the post-Cold War era. A permanent member of the Security Council is a country whose influence is of global nature in political, economic and other aspects. Japan is prepared to do all it can to discharge these responsibilities on the Security Council.

In this comment the intention of the Japanese government regarding Japan's potential permanent membership on the Security Council was blurred rather intentionally. The government wished to avoid giving an impression that Japan wanted to become a permanent member at any cost. This attitude could be attributed to two things: the cultural behaviour of the Japanese people which tends to avoid taking a definite stance and calls for a modest attitude, and the uncertainty about strong political back-up for this issue by the people of Japan. As a matter of fact, the Japanese government's comment raised pros and cons in the public opinion at home.

Permanent Membership and Military Contribution

The greatest concern of those among the Japanese who oppose or have reservations about Japan's permanent membership on the Security Council is that it may entail a commitment to military contribution. They believe Japan would be obliged to make military contributions which far exceed the parameters of the present constitution. Those who oppose Japan's positive involvement in international security affairs, including military contribution for peaceful purposes which have no mandate to use force, are called 'one-country-peace' lovers. They are sometimes reluctant to make even a positive non-military contribution to preserve peace and to maintain international order due to their reliance on a very narrow interpretation of Article 9 of the Constitution of Japan which renounces war and the threat or use of force. Those opposed to Japan's greater political and security role, and therefore the enlargement of the Security Council to include Japan as a permanent member, insist that there exits a linkage between Japan becoming a permanent member and the intensified efforts by the government to engage in UN peacekeeping operations, such as in Cambodia, Mozambique and Zaire.

Actually, commitment to a military contribution, including peacekeeping, is not a condition of permanent membership either in the Charter or politically. The criteria are the will and ability to play a long-term, global role for international peace and security to the extent that national conditions permit, and the establishment of the necessary domestic apparatus. When Boutros Boutros-Ghali visited Japan for the second time as UN Secretary-General in December 1993, he repeatedly expressed the opinion to both the prime minister and the media that a military contribution is not a condition of permanent membership. His statements are a clear indication that this is the perception of the United Nations itself. According to him, there is no obligation even to participate in peacekeeping. Japan itself, he said, should determine its contribution to world peace and stability within the framework of its constitution.

Though the United States and other countries have expressed the hope that Japan will participate in peacekeeping, there have been no demands for any greater military contribution than that. Our participation in peacekeeping on the basis of the five principles[1] as set out in

---

1 The five principles are (1) the existence of a ceasefire agreement, (2) consent by the countries or parties in conflict to the deployment of the UN

the International Peace Cooperation Law (known as the peacekeeping operations or PKO law in Japan) quite adequately fulfils our responsibilities, whether as a permanent member of the Security Council or as an ordinary member of the United Nations.

In order to prevent such misunderstanding among people both at home and abroad, the Government of Japan deemed it necessary to separate the two different policy priorities: namely permanent membership and participation in peacekeeping.

The new coalition government composed of Liberal Democrats, Socialists and the Sakigake Party tried to make this point clear to establish a common position in their policy platform. This attitude culminated in the speech of Foreign Minister Yohei Kono at the 49th session of the General Assembly in September 1994. He emphasised as part of Japan's basic philosophy of extending its international contribution that 'Japan does not, nor will it, resort to the use of force prohibited by its Constitution'. Having said this, the Foreign Minister finally noted that 'Japan is prepared, with the endorsement of many countries, to discharge its responsibilities as a permanent member of the Security Council'.

In order to avoid possible misunderstanding in regard to the scope of the prohibition of the use of force under the Constitution of Japan, it is necessary that the following points should be made clear. There is a wide range of opinions with respect to the interpretation of Article 9 of the Constitution. An extreme interpretation is that not only the right of collective self-defence but also that of individual self-defence is prohibited. This is a far too extreme interpretation of the Article 9. The government's interpretation is that under the constitution individual self-defence is permissible as an inherent right of a sovereign state, but the right to collective self-defence exceeds the territorial defence needs of Japan and is thus prohibited. Japan is not able to participate in multinational force-type operations because it exceeds the territorial defence needs of Japan. Nor is it possible for Japan to participate in peace-enforcement units or expanded peacekeeping under Chapter VII of the Charter.

The question, pertaining to the possibility of Japan's future

---

peacekeeping mission and the Japanese participation in it, (3) the impartiality of the mission, (4) withdrawal of Japanese units if any of these conditions are not met, and (5) limitation of the use of weapons to the minimum required to protect the lives and persons of the mission members.

participation in the United Nations Force to be established according to the provisions of Article 42 and 43 of the Charter, has not been cleared yet as a matter of interpretation of the constitution. Thus, at present the participation of the Japanese Self Defense Forces in the UN collective security system is limited to a considerable extent.

Whereas peacekeeping does not fall under the measure of the collective security paradigm under Chapter VII of the Charter, it is conducted as a measure lying somewhere between Chapter VI and VII, namely 'Chapter VI and half'. The participation of the Self Defense Forces in peacekeeping forces is 100 percent permissible under the constitution. The activities usually conducted by the infantry battalions, however, are frozen in the International Peace Cooperation Law for the moment, for the sake of cautious conduct in the operations.

The Problem of the Veto

The question of the veto is a highly sensitive issue. The problem is twofold: one question is whether the new permanent members should possess the veto or not; the other is the possibility of limiting the scope of the existing veto right possessed by the P5 or even abolishing it. The latter possibility is very unlikely though not impossible, because ratification of any amendment to the Charter provision needs the unanimous approval of the P5.

With respect to the problem of possession or non-possession of the veto by new permanent members, there still seems to exist no consensus among the member countries of the UN. The US has not made its position clear. Only the governments of France and the UK see it necessary to give the veto right to the new permanent members including Germany, Japan, and a few regional powers if the last were nominated as candidates for permanent membership. France, in particular, explains that there should not exist differences in status among the permanent members of the Security Council in respect to their rights and obligations. This connotes that the present status and privileges bestowed upon the UK and France shall not be affected in any manner by the expansion of the number of permanent members.

As for Japan's stance on this issue, it has not made its position clear. Although Japan does not insist upon the veto right, it is not rejecting it in a positive manner either. 'Neither confirm nor deny' has been the policy up until now. The government might be of the view that this issue should be solved in the context of overall reform of the

Security Council in which all aspects of its expansion are addressed while taking into consideration the treatment of the other related issues.

Differences between Japan and Germany

Germany sees itself qualified as a full-fledged permanent member of the Security Council once the Council's restructuring becomes a reality, though the country is not going to take the initiative in reforming the Council. This position was reinforced in July 1994 by the newly authorised interpretation of the Constitution of Germany [Article 24 (2)] by the Federal Constitution Court. According to this new interpretation, German forces are able to join fully in peacekeeping operations of the United Nations. Included are participation in enforcement actions (the use of force) by expanded peacekeeping operations under Chapter VII of the Charter, as well as in future peace-enforcement units and even multinational forces authorised by the Security Council. The Government of Germany is required to obtain the Bundestag's explicit approval for each deployment of German armed forces. Thus the limitation of German military contribution was substantially alleviated not through parliamentary debate, but by a judicial decision on the interpretation of Article 24(2) of the Constitution.

Japan cannot and will not follow Germany's example, in order to clear the obstacles to become a permanent member of the Security Council. Because of the stringent restrictions in the Japanese constitution to contain Japanese military activity, because of people's aspiration to act as a civilian power, and because of the extreme sensitivity against Japan's military role harboured by neighbouring countries in Asia–Pacific, Japan's approach to the permanent membership must be different from that of Germany. Japan will seek new and different approaches to the permanent membership, relying strongly on its non-military principles to neither possess nor produce nuclear weapons, and to renounce arms exports to all regions of the world. As a permanent member of the Security Council Japan would thus represent the non-nuclear and civilian nations around the world. It would not represent any particular region, including Asia–Pacific, since permanent members of the Security Council are not regarded as regional representatives.

Future Perspectives of the Reform of the Security Council

There seems to be a general understanding in the discussions in the open-ended Working Group that the membership of the Security Council should be increased to a certain extent to reflect the reality of the post-Cold War era. The problem, however, is the extent of the expansion of both permanent and non-permanent seats as well as the distribution of the new permanent seats to possible candidates.

According to the various proposals put forward by the member countries to the Working Group, the total size of the expanded Security Council will range from 20 to 29, and that of the permanent membership in particular will be between 7 and 10. With regard to the non-permanent members the number is fluctuating between 13 to 21 or more. The creation of new categories of Council membership has also been proposed, including quasi-permanent membership (either on a rotation or fixed basis). The removal of the existing ban on immediate re-election [Article 23 (2)] is also another proposed pattern of de facto quasi-permanent membership.

It would be difficult to have only Germany and Japan as new permanent members, since it would contradict the nonaligned countries' position to democratise the decision-making process in the Security Council. There are three options for accommodating the political stance of the nonaligned countries which constitute the majority of the member countries in the UN: designating additional permanent seats to some of the regional powers; creating new categories of Council membership (such as quasi-permanent member); and increasing the number of the non-permanent members and enabling immediate re-election of those increased non-permanent members. It may be very difficult to reach an agreement among members of the UN regarding options 1 and 2, because compromise might not be easily attained, even among the members of the nonaligned countries, as to who should be nominated as candidates for permanent or quasi-permanent membership. The option proposed by the nonaligned countries, however, of temporarily increasing only non-permanent membership if there is no agreement on the increase of the permanent members, is very inappropriate and should be avoided.

In any case the negotiation will be very complicated and difficult, particularly because such issues as the treatment of the regional powers, the method for selecting permanent members, and the handling of the veto prerogative, are all highly political and sensitive for all the members of the UN. It is rather unlikely that we will see any concrete results of the examination of this issue being handled in the Working Group before the autumn 1995 General Assembly which will commemorate the 50th anniversary of the establishment of the United Nations.

The momentum to reform the Security Council should be maintained, however, in order to reinforce its credibility, legitimacy and effectiveness as a centre for common efforts by the world community to maintain international peace and security in a multipolar world in the 21st century. However, the discussions in the open-ended Working Group, in which every member country is able to participate, are wide-ranging and rambling. Therefore the working method of the Working Group should also be changed so that issues are examined by a core group which would consist of a small number of countries that represent member countries in every aspect and promote acceleration of the examination of the issues with a view to reaching a compromise.

Japan's Future Stance

Japan's foreign policy is often described as consisting of nothing but ad hoc responses to situations, as being bereft of ideals and principles. Recently the government has taken a more principled stance in regard to foreign policy involving economic issues, as seen in the recent trade disputes with the United States, but this stance does not extend to international politics and security. The legislative branch of the government has a mandate to debate the nation's basic course and underlying principles and to present its conclusions to the executive branch for implementation, but at present it is barely functional in this regard.

The international climate surrounding Japan is harsh. North Korea has been suspected of developing nuclear weapons. China has territorial disputes over the Spratly Islands with its Southeast Asian neighbours, the Philippines and Vietnam in particular. Also, China's military build-up with its increase in arms imports from Russia and the resumption of nuclear testing immediately after the indefinite extension of the NPT pose additional concerns to its neighbours in Asia–Pacific. Further, the crisis in former Yugoslavia has become more than a purely Western concern; it now threatens to affect global security. It is both misleading and dangerous to let the fact that Japan–US trade problems are now the dominant bilateral issue lead us to think of foreign policy *vis-à-vis* the United States in exclusively economic terms, or to let economic considerations govern our approach to domestic issues. What the international community as a whole wants most from Japan is not continuous expansion as a global economic power but clarification of the role our nation is prepared to play in non-economic areas. It wants a clearly articulated vision of the goals of our prosperity, the global objectives that can be attained through active contributions of our economic strength. The way in which we approach the restructuring of the Security Council and future participation in peacekeeping operations will be the touchstones of our non-economic foreign policy. Japan's stance *vis-à-vis* the United Nations in general, and UN peacekeeping in particular, as well as its overall posture as a member of the international community, should be the subject of vigorous national debate.

The 'Normal Country' Thesis

Recently there has been much talk within Japan about the so-called 'normal country' thesis. Its gist is that Japan, fully cognisant of its responsibilities as a member of the international community, should stop being a 'wait-and-see country' preoccupied with the economy and become a 'self-reliant country'. Furthermore, Japan should not exempt security from its sphere of international contributions but should think and behave like a 'normal country' in this area as well.

This thesis clearly indicates the desirable future course for Japan in the international community. The most problematic aspect of this argument, however, has to do with the extent of Japan's military. If Japan wishes to bear part of the responsibility for global security as an autonomous country, it must make clear to the rest of the world the possibilities and limitations of its military role.

The 'normal country' thesis has been advanced in one way or another to sweep away Japan's military constraints. What worries me most is that if this argument is presented too impetuously, unrealistic debate could create a climate of opinion that would make it difficult to participate even in peacekeeping activities as permitted by the Japanese constitution.

Quite apart from Japan's own intentions, the United States is worried about the possibility of Japan becoming a military power. There is a danger that other countries will conflate this anxiety over Japan developing into a 'normal great power' with the 'normal country' debate within Japan. Careful and precise discussion is necessary for the sake of relations not only with neighbouring countries but also with the United States.

This is not to say that Japan's international cooperation can be limited to the parameters of a non-military 'global civilian power'. While devoting even more social resources, in the form of personnel and funds, to cooperation with humanitarian and environmental causes, Japan should seek to become a self-reliant country playing an active political role in conflict resolution with both a military and a civilian role in traditional peacekeeping operations.

That does not call for jumping to the conclusion that Japan's constitution must be amended, but it does call for wisdom and action to utilise to the fullest extent the latent potential of the constitution as it stands. It also calls for the courage to rid ourselves of the lazy attitude that the constitution is an excuse for doing nothing and thus avoiding involvement. As long as we take a passive approach of waiting to be called on to act, we cannot choose our own timing for advancing our point of view or leading international opinion in the direction we would like.

With peacekeeping now at a turning point, the time has come for Japan to speak out, both at the UN and in bilateral talks with other major powers, on the fundamental problems regarding the United Nations. These problems include the limits to engagement, military action, humanitarian intervention, and so on. This, I believe, is one way in which we can contribute in a concrete manner to strengthening the UN's credibility and can encourage constructive debate as a post-economic power.

Meanwhile it is time to think calmly about our future involvement in peacekeeping operations, taking into consideration Japan's own experiences in Cambodia and Mozambique, and in the humanitarian relief operation in Zaire; as well as other countries' reaction to our participation. In connection with this, I would like to set forth three points for consideration.

First, in light of the Somalia experience, the trend towards reversion to traditional peacekeeping has been strengthened. In this case, Japan should be responsive to traditional peacekeeping operations that meet the criteria of the 'five principles' as set out in the above-mentioned law [such being the case with the UN Disengagement Observer Force (UNDOF) in the Golan Heights, the Japanese participation in which is now seriously discussed]. Japan should also be fully aware that no 'moratorium' on participation will be allowed. It is necessary for both political responsibility and public acceptance to be strengthened.

Second, Japan's approach to peacekeeping operations should emphasise conflict prevention. Participation in preventive deployment is legally feasible as long as the host country agrees, and Japan should be responsive when conditions permit. For example, serious consideration should be given to contributing military observers or logistic support to the preventive-deployment units in Macedonia. Japanese involvement in this peacekeeping mission is important not for the sake of cooperation with Japan's own Yasushi Akashi, who is serving as Special Representative of the Secretary-General in former Yugoslavia, but for the sake of playing a global security role. Preventing the conflict in Bosnia from spreading to the entire Balkan Peninsula is an important mission for world peace and is also an effective way of strengthening UN credibility and efficacy.

Third, one of the two pillars of the International Peace Cooperation Law, 'humanitarian international relief operations' (contribution of personnel to the international organisations' humanitarian activities other than peacekeeping), has been utilised for the first time for the sake of the Rwandan refugees in Goma, Zaire. A problem remains even in the case of this kind of assistance. Because such cooperation is subject to the same 'five principles' as are peacekeeping operations, including the existence of a ceasefire agreement, we cannot even send civilian personnel to places like Bosnia, where ceasefire agreements are shaky. When the law is reviewed, thought should be given to finding a way around this problem.

*Mr S K Singh addressing the Otago Foreign Policy School, Dunedin,
1995. (Photo: Ian McGibbon)*

S. K. Singh

An Asian Perspective on the United Nations System

Fifty years ago the Second World War ended. The UN Charter was born. It was a multilateral treaty asserting the principle of equality of all sovereignties; at the same time negating this principle, by naming five major powers permanent as veto-wielding members of the Security Council. Three developments followed.

First, the United States and the USSR, wartime allies, became uninhibited and implacable foes. However, the Mutually Assured Destruction (MAD) factor alone prevented the Cold War from becoming a hot one. The sophistication and deadliness of nuclear weapons and their missile delivery systems rendered them unusable. Second, China's UN membership, including its permanent seat on the Security Council, was denied to Mao Ze Dong's communists who controlled all China. It was assigned instead to Chiang Kai Shek's Kuomintang (KMT) group who controlled the off-shore island of Taiwan. Third, Japan and Germany, the World War II enemy states that were precluded from joining the UN, were assisted economically, provided with the American security umbrella, and gradually brought into the Western alliance system as de facto friends. Soon these two former enemy states were friends of the West on the same level as France and UK, the two principal wartime allies and buddies.

From the 1960s onwards, the economic productivity and technological superiority of Japan and Germany translated into ever increasing political clout for them. During the same period the economic and political reach of the UK and France declined, and they came to be perceived as two civilised, tired, has-beens.

The powers of the Organisation for Economic Cooperation and Development (OECD), until the mid-1970s, managed to deny the communist powers (the USSR, its Warsaw Pact and Comecon allies and China) any significant interaction with the General Agreement on Tariffs and Trade (GATT), the International Monetary Fund (IMF) and the World Bank. The principal ingredients in the calculus of world power, by now, were not just brute military force, but technology, global communications, and economic reach and success. The years 1989–92 saw cataclysmic changes in the power structure of the world, shaking it all up, and transforming our world comprehensively.

The Soviet state abolished itself. Its successor was a feebler state, the Russian Federation. Internal ethnic and sub-ethnic tensions in this state are currently working themselves out. Fourteen constituent units of the former Soviet state chose to become separately sovereign, with separate UN memberships. Through the birth in Central Asia of five sovereign states (Turkmenistan, Uzbekistan, Tajikistan, Kazakhstan and Kyrghizstan) a new Asian regional balance has emerged. Asia now comprises: West Asia and the Gulf region; South Asia; Southeast Asia; East Asia and the Pacific; and the new Central Asia.

Soon the old Yugoslav and Czechoslovak states too splintered; changing the territorial, geographical, military and economic picture of the eastern wing of Europe.

While Europe's eastern wing was splintering, the European Community (EC) as a whole moved a considerable distance towards total integration and the European Union (EU) was born. By now it has expanded into a larger union. Separately Germany re-united itself, and became the largest state in Europe west of Russia. The Warsaw Pact evaporated wordlessly, while the North Atlantic Treaty Organisation (NATO) persisted in growing and prospering, thus ensuring that the USA and Canada continue to be engaged and involved with the military security of Europe. Meanwhile Russia has been engaged in restructuring its economic and industrial systems. It is attempting to deregulate and globalise its economy, and develop an infrastructure for industrial revival and its society's non-ideological economic development. In this process, it is facing problems and dilemmas normally associated with Third World economies. Economically, politically and in security terms several East Europeans are aspiring to be integrated into Europe. The Russians are uncomfortable about this, but seem to have little leverage to veto such a development.

This then is today's wider world as seen by Asians; and into which Asia's present and future have to be interwoven. And now let us examine where Asia itself stands today.

Asia

Japan has become an acknowledged giant amongst the world's major economies. Many recognise it as the sole economic superpower. The US has been declining economically, even though its economic size still remains larger than that of the EU. Japan's disagreements and differences with the United States and its competitive edge are no longer mentioned in whispers. It recognises that its economic and technological preponderance must make it try to be more autonomous in future in managing its security. The new equation between a rampant yen and an emaciated dollar may, for a while, hurt Japanese exports but in the long run a sinking dollar psychologically erodes US leadership of the world.

The political facade of China remains Marxist–Leninist–Maoist, even though for the last two decades its economy has been based on free market systems and practices. Its productivity and prosperity have expanded. What direction these contradictions in China will take once Deng Xiaoping has departed is a big question mark.

Societies in Asia's Southeast and Pacific regions [South Korea, Taiwan, Hong Kong and the Association of Southeast Asian Nations (ASEAN)] have shown a prodigious capacity and proclivity for growth these last two decades and more. India too has abandoned its earlier policies of rigid bureaucratic controls for ensuring greater economic self-reliance and self-sufficiency. It has liberalised and deregulated its economy, with success and enthusiasm.

The five permanent members of the UN Security Council have remained the five monopolistic possessors of nuclear weapons, and also of their own comprehensive missile delivery systems. The recent unlimited and perpetual extension of the NPT despite its discriminatory character, and ignoring the demands for general and complete disarmament, seems to freeze forever the current nuclear and missile status quo. It is not clear what impact this will have on future power generation and electricity systems, especially in the developing world. The complexity of this seems even greater when we recognise how successfully the major economic powers have managed to keep world oil prices depressed. The economic leverage and might of oil producers has been greatly eroded.

The hitherto popular concepts of North–North and South–South economic cooperation are no longer even mentioned now. All aspirations and dreams of building a New International Economic Order have vanished.

During the last decade and more, certain new transnational structural fault lines have appeared. These cannot be wished away. By now these fault lines have also become major transnational issues: narcotics smuggling; cross-border terrorism; migration; human rights violations; ethnic and sub-ethnic secessionist trends; global warming and other environmental concerns; AIDS; and technology-related offences. Even major powers have recognised their incapacity to solve unilaterally any of these issues and problems. No dictats from on high are relevant or effective in tackling these.

The dichotomy between the Bretton Woods institutions on the one hand, and the Dumbarton Oaks concepts on the other, has prevented the UN and its agencies from taking effective or firm action to build serious and continuing international cooperation. And, unless such co-operation is built, it is well-nigh impossible to tackle the global fault lines listed above. Clearly, these issues can be handled either collaboratively, on a global basis, or not at all.

The end of World War II and the birth of the UN coincided with the end of Asia's European Age. The end of the Cold War coincided with the birth of awareness in Asia that Asians are capable of competing successfully with Europeans, Russians and Americans in most areas, including the fields of technology, industry and economic growth. Also, that without the collaboration of Asians, problems of the environment, narcotics, arms control, terrorism, migration and so on will not be amenable to solution.

This raises another question: to what extent has the United Nations, in the first half century of its existence, equipped itself to understand and assist Asia? How much or how little attention has the UN given to Asian problems and peoples?

The United Nations and Asia

The process of history does not pause for the historian's analysis. The process of history also refuses to be interrupted. All historical delineations and divisions made by historians, howsoever logical these may appear, tend to be arbitrary. Subsequent events inevitably colour the historian's appreciation of preceding events. This then is my present dilemma. I am asked during this fiftieth anniversary of the UN to give an Asian perspective, for scholars, academics and decision-makers of a Pacific Ocean nation which is both close to us in Asia, but also in many ways enormously distant.

Conflicts and Crises

While the UN was still young and innocent, came the Korean War which should have indicated to the world that the Soviet Union and China did not share the same ideology, except in name; had vast differences in their cultural, geographical and nationalistic perceptions. Also both were aware of not sharing strategic objectives. Each was indeed distrustful of the other, and cynical enough to pursue its own specific agenda. Neither was squeamish about allowing the Korean people, both of the North and the South, to incur the costs of this crisis. Since each had its own objectives to achieve, the body bag count did not overly upset them.

This crisis demonstrated too that the major powers were not punctilious about following the letter and spirit of the UN Charter. With the votes then available in the General Assembly the US quite cheerfully got the Uniting for Peace Resolution adopted, shifting to the General Assembly certain elements of the authority normally vested in the Security Council. This first sizeable UN peacekeeping operation was thus mounted by the UN General Assembly, with one superpower providing both the resources and guidance. In the name of the UN, the undertaking became basically an American one. While the Soviet Union made loud condemnatory noises, it was not too unhappy accepting whatever the US was doing. The international community turned to India to provide military leadership in this, as in many subsequent UN operations. General K. S. Thimayya and his custodian force of officers and men was in charge, with 434 officers and 5696 other ranks.

In the Indochina crisis of 1953–54 the UN was not permitted any role. Nor was it in the negotiations leading to the Geneva Accords, which established the International Control Commissions for Vietnam, Cambodia and Laos, with India, Poland and Canada as members. In all this the UN was not involved. Later, France withdrew from the strife and the US took over and got sucked into the war in Vietnam. Even then the UN was kept out of it. Later, after President John F. Kennedy's death, UN Secretary-General U Thant wanted to appeal to all parties to agree to a ceasefire and resume negotiations. US President Lyndon Johnson snubbed him, rather brusquely. On a later occasion it was he who wanted to use Thant's good offices. By then Thant had become indifferent.

The UN was able, in certain crisis situations in Asia, to apply a healing touch. When the Soviets tried in 1946 to muscle into Iran's Azerbaijan province, the crisis was quietly defused through UN intervention. China's resumption of participation in the work of the

UN in October 1971 was managed with grace and without unseemly discord, through moves in the UN General Assembly and, later, the UN Security Council deciding to 'restore' China's rights.

The UN played no role in finalising the Japanese peace settlement. The German peace treaty, however, was managed quietly through the UN Security Council, with the concurrence of all concerned European powers. The Japanese peace treaty required US pressure to be applied on several Southeast Asian countries which had been ravaged by Japan during the Second World War, and were therefore chary of some of the clauses. Apparently Australia and New Zealand too were a little reluctant.

India had taken the Kashmir issue to the UN Security Council in 1947. And there it has remained ever since. In the 1950s, some effort was made to solve the Kashmir problem through UN negotiations. Some Australian personalities were involved in certain aspects of this effort. The political calculations of the former colonial power Great Britain, and the new superpower the United States, resulted in the ignoring of objective ground realities. For their prime objective then was to support and reward the new-found loyalty of Pakistan, which had joined them quickly and cheerfully as their CENTO (Central Treaty Organisation) and SEATO (Southeast Asia Treaty Organisation) partner. The UN thus was led into a series of misjudgments and the Security Council debates and UN negotiations took an unrealistic attitude and direction. Pakistan, encouraged and misguided by the US–UK–Western backing, plunged into the 1965 and 1971 wars. Indeed the 1971 war began as a bitter civil war between the Western and Eastern wings of Pakistan itself and resulted in the birth of a new country, Bangladesh.

In West Asia, in 1967 the UN agreed somewhat helplessly to terminate the mission of the UN Emergency Force (UNEF) in Sinai just before the outbreak of Israeli–Arab hostilities. Once again the UN remained paralysed for four years between 1974 and 1978, when Israeli troops were repeatedly entering Lebanese territory, before the UN Security Council, somewhat reluctantly, was forced to create the UN Interim Force in Lebanon (UNIFIL) to observe the withdrawal of Israeli forces from Lebanese soil. Even in the current, on-going Middle East peace process the UN's role is and has been minimal.

During the entire long and tragic Afghan crisis from 1979 to 1992 when the Soviet Union violated Afghan territory by sending its army into that country, and the US and Pakistani intelligence services built up a guerilla force of Islamic fundamentalists, the UN's role was reduced to managing the flow and feeding of refugees; and at a later stage providing backing to the negotiations and photo opportunities for the US, Russian, Pakistani and Afghan guerilla diplomats who met a few times in Geneva. The Security Council's role remained somewhat ambiguous in these negotiations. It made no move to create a peace-keeping force to calm the situation. As a result the Afghan civil war goes on merrily and destructively, even now, several years after the Russian forces went home, and the covert US personnel bade adieu to both Pakistan and Afghanistan. The Afghan crisis and war are real but they are no longer on the world's list of crises, as nobody is watching this war daily on TV. For the Afghans there is no peace. For the world there is no longer any anxiety.

In the case of the Cambodian crisis too, the first years of efforts to settle it peacefully, were strictly outside the purview and involvement of the United Nations. When the UN was inducted during the final stages, for conducting elections, the entire Asian continent applauded.

During China's attack in the Indian Himalayas in 1962, and her brief, sharp war with Vietnam in 1979, and also during the Sino–Soviet border clashes in the early 1980s, the UN maintained silence and took no action, or even note. During the eight long years of the Iran–Iraq war too the UN remained largely uninvolved. There were no significant moves for either the resolution of these disputes, or a return to peaceful conditions.

It is true that the UN's capability is the sum total of the capabilities, aspirations and initiatives of its members, especially its more significant members, the permanent five and the other global and regional players. For whatever reasons, the UN has chosen to be the least active in Asia.

During the Iraq–Kuwait war, also called the Second Gulf War, there were numerous American initiatives to mobilise the UN Security Council, and to use its instrumentality in a speedy and firm fashion, for a well orchestrated opposition to Iraq's cynical aggression. The motivating force was the preponderant American interest and the US ability to initiate action and follow their moves through, as well as the inability or disinclination of the others, including at least two permanent members and several non-permanent ones, to oppose US moves. Neither the global nor the regional powers could afford to be seen as condoning the cynical and unethical actions of the aggressor.

Economic and Social Affairs

Similarly in the Economic and Social Affairs field too, the UN role in Asia has never been of adequate activism. Asian countries have not appreciated the withdrawal, from time to time, of various major powers from UN bodies like UNESCO and ILO. Such withdrawals always dislocate the internal and financial working of these bodies. We must recall that for many years Burma showed an ostentatious indifference to the UN. Also for two years in the 1960s Indonesia chose to withdraw from active participation in the UN's functioning.

From the mid-1950s until the end of the 1960s the Economic Commission for Asia and the Far East (ECAFE) did try to draw up worthwhile plans for developing, integrating and uniting Asia. The Mekong Valley Development Plan, the Asian highway scheme and the completion of the Asian railroad system were all ideas that sparked enthusiasm in Asia, but the major powers who were also the major source of international financing prevented their implementation through abstaining from discussing provision of resources and a general air of indifference. They encouraged the world to forget about these ideas and plans. One wonders whether it is now too late to revive these ideas. Could they be part of the building up of overall infrastructure in Asia? ECAFE's present incarnation, the Economic and Social Commission for Asia and the Pacific (ESCAP), needs to think in broader and more comprehensive terms.

Asia has long waited to see some dynamism and activity in the UN in the pursuit and fulfilment of its own Charter principles and purposes that may touch our continent. Neither in the peace, security or disarmament area, nor indeed in the economic and social development field, has there been much appreciation in the UN of Asia's aspirations and interests, despite Asia having one-third the world's land and one-half its population.

All these last fifty years, somehow non-Asian world powers have been, in several different contexts, indifferent or careless about Asian interests and feelings. Did this begin in Hiroshima and Nagasaki? Is that why Asia has been so quietly but deeply appreciative of New Zealand's nuclear sensitivities? Even as we discuss these matters here today, all this may be undergoing change due to market forces and pressures, the same forces and factors that impel the North American Free Trade Agreement (NAFTA) now to seek to build closer links with the Asia–Pacific Economic Cooperation (APEC) forum.

Resurgence of Asia

The economic, industrial and technological success and resurgence of Japan, followed by the rapid progress of South Korea, Taiwan, Hong Kong, and thereafter the entire ASEAN group of countries, has been remarkable. China's recent economic performance too has been a success story. India appears determined to follow the same path to progress and economic resurgence.

India and China together make one huge economic and demographic presence. Their rapid economic and technological restructuring and progress are bound to have repercussions, one hopes of a positive nature, for the world. Both countries are conscious of the urgency of abolishing poverty amongst those segments of their societies that have long functioned below subsistence levels. Some initial thinking is now going on about these two countries evolving into a free trade grouping of their own.

When we discuss how economic factors are transforming our landscape, it is salutary to recall that as recently as in the early 1960s, Japan and South Asia together used to account for just 4 percent of the world GNP, while the USA, Canada and Mexico (the three countries of today's NAFTA) represented 37 percent. Today both groups have about the same share of the world's GNP, some 24 percent each. During the 1990s, more than half the world's economic growth has taken place in Asia. The economies of North America and Europe are progressing, but in relative terms are smaller than they used to be. The average rate of economic growth in East Asia has been around 5.8 percent per annum during this decade while in Europe and the NAFTA region the average has hovered around 2 percent.

This has been made possible by the faster spread of ideas, technology, capital, communications and services across national, regional and intercontinental borders. The fact remains that the real world is changing, and in real terms.

It needs to be noted that the pace of growth today is much faster. In the late 18th–early 19th century Britain took almost sixty years to double its economic output per capita. And this despite all the capital transfer to Britain from its colonies and the empire. The US took almost fifty years to achieve the same, doubling of its per capita economic output, during the second half of the 19th century; Japan took thirty years towards the end of the 19th century. Indonesia has taken seventeen years, South Korea eleven years, and China ten years during the last quarter century.

Asia in general is moving away from the earlier automatic acceptance or emulation of the European and North American concepts of growth. It is clear that they have to work out their own philosophical, conceptual, political and social norms and principles of application, especially in respect of democratic disciplines, human rights, and freedom of the press and media. There are military rivalries. These have to be subsumed and phased out or abandoned. There are applications of our own traditional values to our own concepts of good governance, discipline and democracy. Asia must build in its own specific manner, keeping in mind its own requirements, traditions and needs. On this point, Jawaharlal Nehru earlier, and Mahathir Mohamad and Lee Kuan Yew more recently, have expressed themselves clearly and authoritatively. They have underlined that our modernisation cannot comprise some sort of aping the West. It has to be according to Asian concepts, philosophies and traditions.

The UN Role in Asia Today

Can the UN help in this effort? What has been UN's track record in such matters in Africa, or the Pacific, or Latin America? During the first 25 years of the coming century what kind of Asian development and growth may be expected or anticipated? What direction is the thinking of the UN or the world community taking in these matters? These are profound and troubling questions, with few answers.

What is being done about our dream of abolishing and banning all weapons systems of mass destruction? Has humanity evolved adequately to be able to ensure universal, non-discriminatory disarmament? What can we do in the nuclear arena? What has been done in respect of chemical weapons? Is the world ready to implement the universal Law of the Sea legislated some years ago? It is clear that a resurgent Asia, which is involved both with the Pacific and the Indian Oceans, will seek answers in this regard.

Will there be a voluntary, realistic initiative within the UN, for a serious Charter review taking into account all aspects of the interests of humanity, including global ecology and economy and all important items of physical and mineral resources like crude oil, iron ore, coal and rare stones? Will the UN's vision be broad enough to be able to encompass together population growth, human rights, availability of land and water, and the broad pattern of political and international law, in a meaningful way for the future of humanity? Must the world community's thinking about vetos in the Security Council remain frozen at the level of how things were in 1945 or 1975? Must countries like India and Brazil be kept out of the charmed circle of authority and influence while the global purveyors of established power insist on maintaining an essentially European stranglehold on veto-wielding in the Security Council?

In land area, Asia is one-third of the planet. In population, it is half of the world. More than 2.5 billion people of diverse ethnic origins, cultures, religious persuasions live here. They are at different stages of political, economic, technological and social development. Should there be no thinking by the world about all this?

The continent today accounts for 25 percent of global exports, 22 percent of global imports, and 33 percent of global international resources. In economic terms it is the fastest growing area on earth. The total GDP of Asia in 2020 AD, according to current estimates, will be between US $21 trillion and 28 trillion.

During the 21st century, Asia is likely to be the economic nerve centre of the world. The Asians are beginning to recognise that there is much that is wrong with Asia that has to be put right. We may have been too much on the defensive, for too long, apologising and apologetic. This has changed. We are ourselves continuing to change.

The wisdom of the old Asian concept of the golden mean is again accepted. Asia must work within the parameters of peace and security, of law and order, and the old-fashioned notion of decency. All this must be based on justice, morality and ethics. Neither extreme individualism nor extreme communitarianism is to be accepted.

Against this background what do we need or expect from the United Nations, the political global society of nations and communities in which some powers have a greater role than the others? Clearly there are challenges we have to meet in coordination with the UN. We in Asia have our own list, which at another level can be considered our charter of objectives, of challenges:

- The challenge of cooperative peace and security;
- The challenge of human rights and responsibilities;
- The challenge of democracy and the rule of law;
- The challenge of productivity and competitiveness;
- The challenge of dynamic, robust, and sustainable growth, with social justice; and

• The challenge of social and psychological transformation.

Much that Asians were thought incapable of achieving is already being achieved. The following two examples will show what has happened. A blue ribbon economic review commission in Japan concluded in July 1947 that the productivity of Japanese labour had fallen. Wages were too high. Enterprises had become heavily subsidised and inefficient. The country had virtually priced itself out of international markets. Its products were getting shoddy. It was grossly overpopulated, and in danger of becoming grievously more so. Prime Minister Katayama Sen decided to reform, so as to inject dynamism in their economic functioning. Japan pulled itself out of the trough.

The second example concerns South Korea and Taiwan. In September 1954 the World Bank, after a most rigorous analytical study of the economies of Asia, concluded that the two Asian economies with the least hope of any sort were: South Korea and Taiwan. They too have made themselves powerhouses of productivity and export.

In the last several decades several American observers like President Lyndon Johnson, Walt Rostow and President Richard Nixon were quick to pronounce India as the world's 'basket case' unlikely ever to be capable of feeding its ever-growing population. Gunnar Myrdal of Sweden did not, in his writings, mince words about all that was wrong with Asia. Nevertheless, he was one of the few economists who believed, even in the early 1960s, that there was a future of hope for Asia in general and for India a little more specifically. One of the lesser known facts of Asian growth is that India has raised its food grain production from 50 million tonnes in 1950, to very nearly two hundred million tonnes this year. And all this through indigenous effort and research and ingenuity.

Is the rest of the world ready to take Asia into greater account, or would it like to treat this continent as a huge growing market, meant for absorbing the goods and services from other areas and countries? Will the major powers wish the United Nations to provide the world, during this post-Cold War era, direction towards real peace, or will they remain wedded to the status quo? The Big Five must change their attitude and work for real non-discriminatory disarmament, and for trade and aid policies that assist the development of the least advantaged countries. For the realisation of all of these goals, the claims of Asia, as also of Africa and Latin America, must be heard.

James N. Rosenau

The Adaptation of the United Nations to a Turbulent World

While I am the only American participating in this symposium, you are not about to read either an apology for or a critique of what is surely a recent negative turn in US conduct towards the United Nations. I have strong views on this topic, but I am going to base my presentation on my strengths which are not so much those of an American as of a social scientist, an analyst who is interested in tracing multiple causes and nuanced relationships.

As my students would readily report, I get into my social science mode by asking a six-word question. It is the most powerful question I think anybody can ask. The question is, 'Of what is this an instance,' in which the word 'this' refers to anything you observe, whether it be in personal life, professional life, world affairs, national affairs, or community affairs. 'Of what is this an instance' is a powerful question because it drives you up the ladder of abstraction and compels you to find a larger category into which to put that which you observe.

So I want to address the question of what is the United Nations an instance today. Earlier I wrote a paper seeking to respond to the question and I came up with 23 answers,[1] which is to say there is no one final answer. One's answers to such a question depend on the perspective one brings to bear at the rung on the ladder of abstraction of greatest interest. Here I want to go high on the ladder and ask about the context within which the United Nations is presently ensconced and besieged.

Assessing of what the United Nations is an instance today is a difficult task. On the one hand, the world is undergoing enormous

1   James N. Rosenau, 'Powerful Tendencies, Enduring Tensions, and Glaring Contradictions: The Challenge of Studying the United Nations in a Turbulent Era', a paper prepared for the conference on 'The United Nations: Between Sovereignty and Global Governance?' organised by the School of Politics, La Trobe University, Melbourne, 2–6 July 1995.

transformations that have encouraged the international community to turn increasingly to the United Nations in a variety of ways. On the other hand, much remains the same in spite of the changes. Thus there is the challenge of how we proceed to analyse the UN in systematic ways; how do we avoid both starry-eyed optimism and paralysing pessimism? My way of doing this is to schematise the problem, to set forth in diagrammatic form the context in which the UN presently persists and then to elaborate on the main categories in the scheme.

As can be seen in Figure 14.1, the scheme places the United Nations in the centre confronted by a huge question mark. On the left-hand side are entries that attempt to summarise the transformations and continuities at work in the world that I developed in a recent book.[2] On the right-hand side are listed some of the UN's prime characteristics as the 20th century ends. Figure 14.1 also highlights the thought that present-day turbulence adds up to an increasingly less stable environment for the UN, while the characteristics of the UN add up to an increasingly vulnerable international organisation. In the middle of the diagram the two listings come together to face the question, 'How will the United Nations adapt in the future, readily or resistantly'? Towards the bottom of the middle of the diagram a series of possible ways in which adaptation might occur are noted.

Present-Day Turbulence

Deepening Interdependence

Let us look first at the left-hand side of this formulation and examine some of the dynamics of the environment within which the United Nations currently has to function. The first main category embraces the central tendencies in world affairs whereby peoples, societies and individuals are becoming ever more interdependent. A number of sources of this interdependence are cited, starting with the ways in which national economies are now globalising, with facilities for producing goods and services moving readily across boundaries, corporations decentralising their production facilities, currencies moving in milliseconds across national boundaries. Governments have lost, in some important ways, control over their own economies because of the processes of globalisation.

2   James N. Rosenau, *Turbulence in World Politics: A Theory of Change and Continuity* (Princeton, NJ: Princeton University Press, 1990).

FIGURE 14.1: THE UNITED NATIONS IN A TURBULENT WORLD

PRESENT-DAY TURBULENCE

Deepening Interdependence
- globalising economies
- communications revolution
- spreading consumer culture
- global repercussions of events, crises
- convergence around human rights norms
- trends towards democracy, open markets
- growth of micro and macro regions

Socioeconomic Dynamics
- growing gap between rich and poor
- continued population explosion
- family decay on global scale
- vast movements of people

Growing Subgroupism
- ethnic, linguistic, religious nationalism
- social movements
- decentralisation of political systems
- militia, voluntarism

Lessening Capacity of Governments
- stalemated executives, divided legislatures, minority governments
- budget deficits, foreign debts
- diminished authority, contested legitimacy
- defiant citizenries
- weakened militaries
- collapse of ideologies

New Interdependence Issues
- fragmegration
- environmental threats, AIDS
- currency crises
- drug trade, crime syndicates

an increasingly less stable environment for the UN

HOW WILL THE UN ADAPT?

Readily
or
Resistantly?

?

What would effective adaptation require?

* * *

- prolonged prosperity?
- global catastrophes?
- weakened states?
- more active NGOs?
- organisational reform?
- powerful leadership?

an increasingly vulnerable international organisation

THE UNITED NATIONS TODAY

The Sovereignty Principle
- still powerful, but not absolute
- shifting normative foundations: from the-convenience-of-states to states-are-sometimes-obliged-to-go-along
- not operative with respect to human rights, elections, other domestic issues

System Overload
- involvement in proliferating internal wars
- insufficient trained personnel

Antiquated Structure
- designed in 1940s for immediate post-war world
- permanent members of Security Council no longer reflect power distribution
- swollen bureaucracy

Resources
- acute funding shortages
- no independent armed forces
- prestige and legitimacy in decline
- most NGOs supportive
- path dependence

The second dimension of interdependence is the communications or microelectronic revolution: the advent of global television, the fax machine, the Internet, the videocassette recorder, and all the other gadgetry through which ideas, pictures, formulations and ideologies readily move across national boundaries today. This movement has also diminished the control of governments and is part of the shrinking of the world, part of the greater interdependence within which the UN must operate.

A third dimension concerns the spreading consumer culture. Representative in this regard is the fact that there are now some 12,000 McDonald's in the world, surely a figure expressive of the globalisation of consumer tastes.

A fourth dimension involves the global repercussions of events and crises. Tiananmen Square, for example, was an experience for people everywhere, as have been the horrendous scenes from Rwanda. Some of the critiques we have heard of the United Nations are experienced everywhere as scenes from Bosnia clog our television screens.

Fifth, the emergence of global norms around human rights is certainly a big dimension of the world's greater interdependence. There are still places in the world where human rights are not adequately respected, but if you want to feel good about things late in the 20th century, focus on the fact that there is more attention to, more sensitivity to, and more work on, advancing human rights than ever before in history. Similarly, global norms and practices are emerging with respect to the environment.

Sixth, and related, since the end of the Cold War there has been a trend towards various forms and norms of democracy, with the managed economy having been replaced by open markets in most countries, a pattern that is also part of the greater interdependence.

A seventh dimension has to do with regionalisation, a trend which is unfolding both across countries and within countries.

Lastly, a category not indicated in Figure 14.1 needs to be noted, as it reflects all the other dimensions, namely the increasing porosity of the boundary between foreign and domestic affairs. This is becoming a very difficult boundary to trace even though a geographer can do it; even though public officials refer to the identity and borders of their country; and even though you have to get a visa and passport to cross the boundary, it still is the case that these boundaries are increasingly porous.

Socioeconomic Dynamics

Turning to the second major category of Figure 14.1, what I call socio-economic dynamics, the world is marked by a growing gap between the rich and the poor, not only within countries, but also among countries, and surely the UN will continually have to confront the problems that this gap poses.

A second dimension, well known and widely researched, is the continuing population explosion and all that means for any organisation that seeks to promote global stability and peace. Closely related, and extremely important to the work of the UN, is the organisational explosion. There has been an *enormous* proliferation of all kinds of organisations, at the local, provincial, country and international levels. This explosion is so great that nobody has really been able to trace it, even though no one denies its continuing vitality. There is, moreover, a direct link between the population and organisational explosions: the much greater number of people represented by the population explosion has given rise to the need for more organisations.

Third, a recently published report of the Population Council in the US stresses that families are in decay throughout the world. With both parents having to work out of the home, family ties are being eroded and undermined. The consequences of this dynamic are complex, but it is surely part of the present-day turbulence. Much the same can readily be said about the last socioeconomic dynamic listed in Figure 14.1: that vast, restless movement of peoples—political and economic refugees—looking for a better life by moving elsewhere.

Next is a category based on a word I made up, 'subgroupism'. I use the term instead of nationalism because there is a more generic phenomenon of which nationalism is but one form. I refer to the tendency of people faced with so much interdependence, with so much globalisation, to want to retreat to close-at-hand and like-minded forms of support. In the former Soviet Union and Yugoslavia, this phenomenon has taken the form of nationalism. But it is also evident in other kinds of organisations and so the more generic term 'subgroupism' seems appropriate. Subgroupism, for example, is now unfolding in the Mafia. One thinks of the Mafia as perhaps the most hierarchical type of organisation. Hence, if it is recognised that some of the Mafia's sub-units are protesting and going their own way, one gets a sense of how pervasive subgroupism is beyond the familiar ethnic, linguistic and religious nationalisms.

Just as the world is globalising, in short, so is it localising.

Indeed, I would argue, from high on the ladder of abstraction, that the main tensions confronting world affairs today are those between globalising and localising dynamics, between integration and fragmentation. As Figure 14.1 implies, new social movements in the environment, human rights, and women's rights fields are very much part of these tensions, especially as they are not linked to governments. But even as they are quite independent of governments, so do they span national boundaries and thus have important consequences for the conduct of world affairs.

Lessening Capacity of Governments

The next major category on the left of Figure 14.1 suggests that, partly due to subgroupism, political systems are decentralising in important ways, thus resulting in a weakening of governments at the national level. For reasons having to do with interdependence, globalisation of economies, the spread of ideas, the advent of worldwide norms, and many other boundary-spanning dynamics, it seems clear that states and their governments are less and less capable of achieving their goals than they were in the past. Put more succinctly, the trendline depicting the competence of states involves a downward slope. Yes, it is true, governments can point guns and get people to comply through the use of force; but if you ask the question, 'How well are governments doing' in solving their social, economic, and cultural problems, I think the trendline is down, with the result that stalemate and paralysis tends to prevail at national levels in most parts of the world.

Another way to think of the tendencies towards stalemate is in terms of authority and legitimacy. Historically the world was founded on 'traditional' legitimacy: the king says do it, and you do it. It is a habit. Compliance is a habit. Law-abidingness is a habit. But as a consequence of the turbulence of our time, traditional legitimacy has undergone transformation to 'performance' legitimacy: you perform well as a leader and I will support you and comply with your requests; but you lose my support if your performances are inadequate. Ferdinand Marcos came down in the Philippines due to a lack of performance legitimacy, and one can talk about many other governments and organisations that have since gone through upheaval because performance legitimacy has replaced traditional legitimacy.

Related here is the defiance of citizenries. That, in my view, derives from healthy adults in all countries and corners of the world being more analytically skillful than their predecessors—more able to construct scenarios that trace the course of events back to their pocket-books and living rooms. I call this development 'the skill revolution,' which I see as underlying the changes in legitimacy and authority crises that are at work within governments, major political parties and other organisations. The major parties of Japan and Mexico offer good illustrations of authority crises outside of governments.

As indicated in Figure 14.1, militaries around the world have also been weakened, for a variety of reasons. Perhaps a classic example is the Russian military, which has experienced numerous desertions, an inability to draft soldiers, and a high degree of incompetence in battle (e.g., in Chechnya). This may be an extreme case, but it does seem reflective of morale problems in militaries around the world, including my own country. And it is further intensified by the reluctance of publics to risk the lives of their sons and daughters in distant wars.

New Interdependence Issues

The last major subcategory on the left-hand side of Figure 14.1 is 'interdependence issues,' the first of which is another word I made up. It is a word that represents what I said above about the tensions between integration and fragmentation at all levels of community and in all parts of the world. The word is 'fragmegration,' which seeks to capture the simultaneity of these contrary tensions.

You could almost say—I would say, just to emphasise a point—that every increment of integration gives rise to an increment of fragmentation, and vice versa. I think that the driving dynamic of world affairs is the globalisation, and that much of the localisation is a reaction against the globalising processes. The surge of religious fundamentalism today is not just confined to Iran; it is occurring in many parts of the world. I see it as a reaction against globalisation; people fear that their close-at-hand lives are threatened by these large forces. I like to quote Paul Friggerio. He is an Italian who was a politician in the Northern League, when the League first came on the political scene and won some by votes. And Paul Friggerio was recorded in the *San Francisco Chronicle* as saying, 'We are Lombards first, Europeans second; Italy means nothing to us'. That I see as the integration inherent in fragmentation.

So it could well be that the localising reactions against the globalising processes will in some ways, in some parts of the world, focus on the UN and undermine support for it. On the other hand, I see the United Nations as not lacking in strength. I think the world needs the UN. As an American, I think the US needs the UN, so much so that the present politics of Washington is probably temporary because the need of the US for the UN will eventually reassert itself.

The other new interdependence issues—such as environmental threats, currency crises, AIDS, the drug trade and crime syndicates—are high on the global agenda precisely because they are rooted in the dynamics of globalisation. Unlike traditional issues on the agenda, these new ones cannot be addressed unless governments and non-government organisations (NGOs) cooperate across national boundaries. Rivers and winds carry pollution across boundaries, just as huge amounts of money pass through borders in milliseconds every day, and just as AIDS, the drug trade and crime syndicates have learned how to avoid being caught by border guards. It is hardly surprising, therefore, that we have had to construct international institutions to cope with all these new interdependence issue-areas.

I am not saying that the state is on its way out of existence. Whatever one might wish for, I think that is not the case. There are still collective needs that are served at society-wide levels. The state is that institution. I do not see it as withering away; rather I see its capacity as eroding. And I see the erosion as a continuing process, but I see no logic in the idea that the erosion will reach the point where states will go out of business. Some will. Some have. And in Europe, the process has led to an international union, which has some clout over its members, and it may well be that in the future there will be comparable developments in other regions. But I do not see a world government. If that is dismaying for those who are active and activists in world affairs, let me suggest that instead of working for world governments, they might be better served by working for social movements that are effective in issue-areas, not to mention working towards making their own states more responsive to global needs.

The United Nations Today

In sum, a wide range of factors add up to an increasingly less stable environment for the United Nations. The conditions that gave rise to turbulence in the 1950s still persist. And as far as one can see into the future, they are conditions with which the UN must contend.

The Sovereignty Principle

With this in mind, let me turn now to the right side of Figure 14.1, to

the United Nations today. Here I have identified four main sub-
categories that seem worthy of attention. The first concerns the sovereignty principle, which I view in a somewhat different way than is
usually the case. While there is no doubt that the principle of
sovereignty continues to have a powerful hold over publics and their
governments, there has been a subtle transformation of the norms on
which sovereignty rests. It has undergone a transformation from an
attitude that sees action occurring at the-convenience-of-states to one
that asserts states-are-sometimes-obliged-to-go-along. This shift does
not negate the sovereignty principle, but it does alter it. It suggests
why the veto has not been exercised very often in recent years. It can
even be said that the use of the veto is in acute decline—that is, states-
are-sometimes-obliged-to-go-along. China is a case in point. It
consistently abstained from the votes through which the UN conducted
the Gulf War. China is probably the country that values the
sovereignty principle more than any other, and yet when push came to
shove—and there was lots of push and lots of shove—it abstained on
the Security Council. So I would like to suggest to those that feel
things are bleak and that the sovereignty principle is undermining the
UN, you might take heart at the thought that whatever may be the
expression of the principle, action based on it may be shifting.
Sovereignty is not a constant, it is a variable. It does not, for example,
apply fully in the realm of human rights.

Indeed, with respect to the monitoring of domestic elections the
sovereignty principle has proven equally elastic. It has become
commonplace, where major factions fear that elections might be stolen
from them by internal machinations, to appeal to the 'international
community' for monitors to come in and cross their national
boundaries to supervise their elections. It happened in South Africa; it
happened in Mexico; it has happened all around the former Soviet
Union. And it happens often in Latin America.

Let me illustrate with a personal anecdote. I had the privilege of
being on Jimmy Carter's team of 30 people from 15 countries who
went to Paraguay in May 1993 to monitor that country's election.
Incidentally, we were just one of many teams on the scene. Another
was a UN team and indeed, the UN has become the major force in this
regard and usually sends the largest delegation of monitors. When I
got to Paraguay I was given a badge that had my photograph. It said in
Spanish that I was an 'observador'. Our assignment was to visit
polling booths to watch the voting process and to check whether

parties checked on each other. Our final assignment was to be present at a pre-assigned polling place to watch the counting of the ballots. But our driver got lost, and we were 20 minutes late at the school where we were to watch them count the ballots. When we finally arrived at the school, the gate was closed and in front of it was a large marine with a menacing gun on his hip. All I had was my badge attached to my lapel. But herewith testimony based on my own personal experience: it is possible to walk from the international community through a boundary into a domestic setting, because that marine swung open the gate when he saw my badge. Perhaps this one encounter did not make the world a better place, but it is part of the process wherein the sovereignty principle is being altered. So, if you want to get an uplift as you think about the United Nations, you can surely get it by thinking about its role in domestic elections.

System Overload

The next category has to do with system overload, which is the focus of other chapters in this symposium. Many of them stress how the end of the Cold War and the outbreak of innumerable internal civil wars has led governments and others to turn to the United Nations for assistance. Others note the need for better trained personnel to cope with the new expanding burdens.

Antiquated Structures

Then there are the antiquated structures of the UN, an organisation that was designed for the immediate post-war world. But we are no longer in the immediate post-war world; we are no longer in the Cold War; we are in something called 'post,' with the result that the permanent members of the UN Security Council are no longer a reflection of the distribution of power in the world today. Then there are numerous problems associated with the UN's swollen bureaucracy.

Resources

The last major subcategory of Figure 14.1 highlights the resource problems of the UN. Most notable in this regard is the acute funding shortage. This is a topic which makes me greatly embarrassed about my US citizenship, since my country has long been in arrears in paying its dues. And matters are likely to get worse since the turn in American politics away from the UN. Or at least there has been a leadership turn, although polls still show the American public in support of international institutions by substantial majorities. To be sure, those figures change depending upon how the question is asked. If respondents are asked whether they would like their son to go to Bosnia, then the figures collapse. But generally, there is an underlying public support for the UN even though the Congress is ready to reduce further the US contributions.

Another resource shortage is the absence of an independent armed force controlled by the UN. Still another is the decline in the UN's prestige and legitimacy. However, the decline may not be as great as it sometimes appears. Or at least it can be argued that the decline is more a loss of respect for states and their insufficient support for the United Nations. If you want to blame the UN, the argument would be, then blame the states since they are the actors that run it.

On the more positive side is the organisational revolution that has led to lots of support for the UN. I have in mind the interaction between the UN and NGOs. The turbulence model posits the world as having undergone a bifurcation in which states in the state-centric world compete or cooperate with diverse actors in the multi-centric world. The latter consists of NGOs, ethnic minorities, multinational corporations, professional societies and many other kinds of actors. In 1992, on the issue of the environment, the UN held its conference in Rio de Janeiro at one end of the avenue, and at the other end of the avenue the multi-centric world convened an equally large conference called the Earth Forum. I still kick myself for not having gone to Rio, because I would have liked to watch the traffic back and forth along that avenue. A year later it all happened again in Vienna. But this time the issue was human rights and the two meetings were held in the same building: the state-centric world met on the first floor and the multi-centric world was on the third floor. And it happened still another time recently in Beijing on the issue of women's rights, although in this instance the Chinese insisted on a 30-mile separation between the two worlds.

My final entry, at the bottom of the right-hand side of Figure 14.1, involves a social science concept which I use to describe a little-recognised but important UN resource. The concept is that of 'path dependence,' which posits all social systems, all families, all countries, etc., as being on a path, a path on which previous choices excluded future alternatives, thus propelling the system down a path which narrows its choices in the future. Viewed in this way, it is important to emphasise, when we think about how to reform the UN, that the world has long since chosen a path that includes the UN as a major institution and, in so doing, the world is deprived of the choice of starting over. It seems clear to me that the UN is going to be part of the global scene for centuries, that its path dependence is such that there are limits to reversing its course, that it has to be seen as on a path that has a course which is the result of earlier decisions, crises and patterns.

How Will the UN Adapt?

So I return to a view of the United Nations as an increasingly vulnerable international organisation and to the question of how it will adapt: readily or resistantly? I think it remains to be seen. As the questions towards the bottom of the middle of Figure 14.1 indicate, there are several possibilities. Will it take prolonged prosperity? Certainly prolonged prosperity would do the UN no harm. Will it take global catastrophes? The question puts one in the awkward situation of saying, in effect, 'I wish there was a global catastrophe so that the UN and other institutions would work better.' I can't say that, but it may well be that catastrophes will have beneficial consequences. Will it take a weakening of states; more active NGOs; organisational reform?

Let me echo the theme in other chapters, that tinkering with machinery does not change the turbulence in which the organisation functions. So the clear-cut answer to this question is that organisational reform will help, but surely it will not solve everything. As for powerful leadership, the world does not have many heroes. Indeed, it is lacking in heroes. I do not know where powerful leadership is going to come from. Leaders of states are constrained by their states and by their desire to be re-elected. I am a fan of Jimmy Carter's, but he had to leave office and get beaten in order to rise to the status he has now achieved in world affairs.

Conclusion

Summing up, if one asks of what is the UN an instance, the answer seems to be that it is presently an instance of an international institution that is in place and will remain in place even though it is not likely to lessen the turbulent conditions that underlie the structures of the global system. We ought not exaggerate our hopes for it, but neither should we dismiss it as irrelevant.

Keith Suter

Reforming the United Nations

This chapter examines some of the ideas currently in circulation for reforming the United Nations. It begins with a basic question: is UN reform really the issue? The UN's problems are partly due to the unwillingness of many governments to honour their current commitments. Creating a new document may be time-consuming and ultimately of little value if governments still remain unwilling to honour their commitments under the new document. Amending the Charter is a very difficult process. There has not been any substantive amendment to the document since it was created in 1945. Therefore I distinguish between 'micro-amendments' (which could be implemented today if there were the political will) and 'macro-amendments' (which require an amendment to the Charter). The extent of the micro-amendments shows how far governments could go in making greater use of the UN Charter without having to amend it—and, by implication, how reluctant they are to make full use of the current document.

The chapter then looks at the spectrum of options for UN reform, beginning with 'micro-reforms' and then 'macro-reforms'.

The third part of the UN reform spectrum is based on the decline of the nation-state as the basic unit in global politics. The UN is a club of nation-states. In 1945, nation-states ran the world; they do not have that same monopoly in 1995. The UN and national governments need to examine ways of involving transnational corporations in the UN's work because ultimately global governance requires also giving recognition to the role of transnational corporations in the world's affairs.

The chapter concludes with some speculations on how the push for UN reform may gather momentum.

Is UN Reform Really the Issue

The assumption that underpins some of the UN reform debate is that the UN Charter is inadequate and so needs updating. But it could also be said that the UN Charter itself is a great deal better than may be implied from the current debate, and that the real issue is that governments should do more to honour their existing obligations under the current document rather than speculate on the need for amending it.

As a corollary, since many governments have such a poor record for honouring their current UN Charter commitments, would a revised UN Charter have any better rate of implementation? In other words, there is the usual issue of political will: getting governments to honour their international commitments.

These questions cannot be answered in this chapter. But they are worth asking as a warning that we need to note that however fine a document may sound, there has to be a governmental commitment to honour its obligations. The current UN Charter was not created to fail: a great deal of thought went into it. The problem is that the enthusiasm which existed for the UN fifty years ago, evaporated fairly quickly in the Cold War and so governments acquired other priorities. The same problem could happen with any new UN Charter.

The Difficulty of Amending the UN Charter

It is very difficult to amend the UN Charter. According to Article 108, amendments have to be adopted by a vote of two-thirds of the General Assembly and ratified in accordance with constitutional processes—including the five permanent members of the Security Council (P5) (US, Russia, UK, France and China). This latter provision provides a blocking veto—including a possible veto on any proposal to change the veto.

There are also political problems. According to Article 109, there was to be a review conference of the UN Charter no later than 1955, but this could not be held because of the Cold War. It has never taken place, and there is at present no governmental support for it to do so. Since 1945, the only changes have been to the number of member-nations on UN bodies; these changes have arisen because of the increase in the UN's overall membership. For example, the UN Security Council's membership was increased in 1965 from 11 to 15.

The Cold War is over but other problems remain—and may even be worse. At least in the Cold War, life was simpler: countries either supported the US (First World) or the USSR (Second World) or disliked both and so tried to be neutral (Third World). But now with the Second World trying to join the First World, and the Third World unsure how it is to be neutral, life is much more complicated.

For example, Japan and Germany are trying to become permanent members of the Security Council and like to give the impression that their inclusion would represent only a minor change to the UN Charter. However, James Jonah (then a UN Under Secretary-General, writing in his personal capacity) has set out some problems in their campaign. His assessment is an indication of just how difficult it will be to achieve what might be seen as an obvious UN reform:

> In this context, both Germany and Japan have received widespread attention, especially now that the United States has indicated it would support granting them permanent seats on the Council. There are valid reasons for this change, but many observers fear that such action may open a Pandora's Box, with other states from different regions requesting similar status. It is difficult to envisage that the alteration of the Council's membership could be restricted only to allow Japan and Germany to become permanent members. It is also difficult to logically identify which other countries should be considered for equal treatment. In Asia, should it be India, Pakistan, or Indonesia? In Latin America, Brazil, Mexico, and perhaps Argentina would be contenders. Among African countries, reference is made most often to Nigeria, but other countries may have strong claims, including perhaps a democratic and non-racial South Africa. It is this jumble of possibilities that frightens some Council members into concluding that no action should be taken at this time.[1]

The UK could, for example, go to Pakistan and draw to its attention that India would like to get on the Security Council. Pakistan would prefer the status quo rather than have India on the Security Council. The UK could do the same with Argentina *vis-à-vis* Brazil. The net effect would be countries preferring to stick 'with the devil they know rather than the devil they do not know'. Coincidentally, this would ensure that the UK would remain on the Security Council.

Thus, I think that it is important to distinguish between reforms to the UN that do require an amendment to the Charter and those which do not and so could be introduced immediately.

Micro-reforms

UN Finances

The UN has a severe financial crisis. But, then, such a crisis suits its

1 James Jonah, *Differing State Perspectives on the United Nations in the Post-Cold War World* (Providence, RI: Academic Council on the United Nations System, Brown University, 1993), p. 25.

members. Ed Luck of the United Nations Association (USA) has claimed, in the UN television programme *World Chronicle,* that governments like having the UN with a financial problem:

> The UN has always been in financial trouble. And I think that the Member States, in a way, like to keep it in financial trouble. It's [on] a shorter leash; it can't go very far because it doesn't have the finances. It can't print money, it can't borrow money, so it really is up to the Member States to give their money, and the US in particular uses its contributions for leverage. 'If you do what we want, we'll give you a little more'; we'll withhold some if you don't do what we want'.[2]

It is worth emphasising that the UN has a small budget. No governor of any US state has a smaller budget than that of the UN Secretary-General. Even the budget of the City Council of New York is larger than the UN's. The advantage that the New York City Council has over the UN is that it can obtain revenue more easily than the UN. About two-thirds of the UN's membership at any one time are in arrears. The US and Russia are the main debtors.

The current phase in the financial crisis has been brought about by the US. The Reagan Administration (1981–89) was the most anti-UN administration in US history. It withdrew from the UN Educational, Scientific and Cultural Organisation (UNESCO), cut back its contributions to other specialised agencies, and was slow in its paying its contributions to the central UN budget. The crisis was eased, ironically, in the mid-1980s, when Mikhail Gorbachev came to power in Moscow. He paid the USSR's back debts and so there was an influx of Soviet money to ease the lack of US money. At present, the US still remains slow in paying its contributions—and Russia has its own financial crisis and so it is also in debt once again.

The US and Russia have set a poor example: if they can get away with paying their subscriptions late, so other countries can do the same. In mid-1994, the UN was at a particularly low point, with only seven countries up to date with their subscriptions: Australia, the UK, Ghana, Kuwait, Micronesia, Namibia and New Zealand.

A variation on the proposal that all members should pay their subscriptions on time is that all aspiring members of the Security Council should have paid their contributions to the UN budget (this would knock out most of the current membership). More generally, there

2   Quoted in: *World Chronicle*, recorded 14 October 1994, p. 7 (transcript available from the Media Division, Department of Public Information, UN, New York).

should be more money for the UN system. For example, many people die from diseases that could be prevented—if there were more money for health care services. In May 1995, the World Health Organisation (WHO), in its first annual survey of global health, said that more than two billion people (about 40 percent of the world's population) suffered from varying degrees of sickness at any one time. Much of this disease and illness was preventable and tied to the widening gaps in health, education and access to care between rich and poor.

> Officials said poverty was the greatest underlying cause of disease, suffering and death, with more than one-fifth of the world's 5.6 billion people living under conditions that provide little or no resources for preventing or treating their illnesses. More than half of the world's people cannot get the most essential drugs and about a third of the world's children are undernourished, the organization said.[3]

Ironically, developed countries are now providing—as a percentage of their GNP—less foreign aid than they were two decades ago. As countries have become richer, so they have become meaner.

More Women at Senior Levels

More women should be appointed to senior positions. The senior level of the UN has traditionally had none or only a few women. This was similar to the lack of women as heads of national delegations to the UN. However, just as some countries are now making more of an effort to ensure equal opportunity at the head of delegation level, so the UN's own employment practices could reflect that same determination. The UN Secretary-General has little leverage over countries (such as in the slow payment of their dues) but he does have much greater scope for action in employing women in the Secretariat's senior level.

Peacekeeping Operations

'Peacekeeping' is not referred to in the UN Charter. It has been an ad hoc measure which the UN devised to cope with the Cold War's freezing of the procedure which is laid down in the Charter.

Generals always prepare to fight the last war; diplomats design methods to avoid having to fight the last war. The ghost of Hitler (who had died only two months before the San Francisco conference

3   'Billions Suffering Needlessly, Study Says', *New York Times*, 2 May 1995, p. C3.

which finalised the UN Charter) underpins the original vision for the Security Council. If, the reasoning went, enough countries had worked together in the League of Nations, then Hitler would have been deterred from his aggressive foreign policy. Consequently, the League's successor, the UN, was given—on paper—immense power.

All UN member-nations agree to be bound by Security Council resolutions (the only part of the UN system with such power) and all member-nations 'shall hold immediately available' defence forces to be deployed as required by the Security Council (Article 45). A Military Staff Committee was created, drawn from the representatives of the Chiefs of Staff of the P5, to coordinate the military operations.

Because of the Cold War, this elaborate system was never used. Instead, there evolved an ad hoc system of peacekeeping for intervention in disputes where the two superpowers agreed not to intervene if the other also agreed not to intervene. Instead of the P5 controlling the UN's military work, peacekeeping almost always avoided any involvement of the P5 (the British Army has been involved in the UN force in Cyprus because it was already stationed there when the communal fighting broke out). The bulk of the peacekeeping operations was, until recently, also financed by non-P5 nations.

The ending of the Cold War has seen a great increase in the UN's peacekeeping work. The UN is now mounting more peacekeeping operations than at any other time in its history. But the UN Charter's elaborate Military Staff Committee system is still not being used. The US, for example, has gone from the Cold War to cold feet. It is highly selective as to where it commits its troops. It has consistently refused to commit soldiers to the UN's current biggest operation (where half of the UN's total peacekeepers are deployed) in former Yugoslavia.

In October 1994, Razali Ismail, the Malaysian delegate to the UN, complained about the way in which the Security Council adopts resolutions but leaves the implementation to other countries:

> The major powers are not prepared to put out the adequate number of soldiers for peacekeeping, for example, so they count on us. Malaysia has 2,700 soldiers on various fronts. We are in Somalia, in Angola, in Bosnia. Politically, it is no longer tenable for all of us to supply troops—to pull the trigger, as it were, for the UN—without having the right to say something about the process of decision making and what peacekeeping is all about.[4]

4   Quoted in: 'At the UN, a Drive for Diversity', *New York Times,* 24 October 1994, p. A6.

The UN Secretary-General has made some suggestions for improving the UN's role in the maintenance of international peace and security.[5] He has proposed the creation of a standing force to be drawn from the defence forces of nations around the world, to be ready for instant deployment. The perpetual problem of financing operations could be addressed by governments paying for UN operations out of their defence budget rather than their foreign affairs one (since the former are always much larger than the latter). The report also mentioned—but did not endorse—a tax on arms sales, a levy on international air travel (which is dependent on the maintenance of peace), and tax exemptions for private donations made to the UN. It also pointed out that military force will always be of limited use and that there should be greater recourse to arbitration and mediation. Also, greater resources devoted to human development could reduce some of the causes of conflict: prevention is better than peacekeeping.

The Military Staff Committee and the UN system for maintaining international peace and security—as set out in the UN Charter and as dealt with in the Secretary-General's *Agenda for Peace*—could be implemented fully. This could also include the creation of a training centre for senior military officers who are on standby for UN operations; the centre would help standardise procedures and equipment, and provide training in conflict resolution techniques.

Jurisdiction of the International Court of Justice

The International Court of Justice (ICJ) is the world's main legal body. But attendance at it is not compulsory. Only about a third of the UN's membership accept its jurisdiction. For example, Portugal took Australia to the ICJ because Indonesia does not accept the ICJ's jurisdiction. In 1975 Indonesia invaded the Portuguese colony of East Timor; the UN and Portugal have never recognised Indonesian control over East Timor; in the early 1990s, Australia and Indonesia divided up East Timor's marine area. Portugal regarded this as a division of its own marine area but it could not take Indonesia to the ICJ and so it could only complain about Australia. In June 1995, the ICJ decided that it could not adjudicate on the Portugal v. Australia dispute because Indonesia was not a party to the case. The obvious reform is that all

---

5   Boutros Boutros-Ghali, *An Agenda for Peace: Preventive Diplomacy, Peacemaking and Peace-keeping* (New York: United Nations, 1992). The second edition, with additional material, was published in 1995.

countries should accept the ICJ's jurisdiction and make greater use of it in the settlement of their inter-national disputes.

More Specialised Agencies

Proposals for international action on a particular topic often include recommendations that there be a new international body to implement the ideas. For example, former Sydney lawyer Peter Clyne, writing in the 1970s in response to the aerial hijackings, proposed that there be an Air Crimes Commission (ACC), which would run its own International Court (the ICJ does not deal with individuals) and its own International Prison. Member-countries in which hijackers landed would undertake to arrest them and hand them over for trial by the court, regardless of their country of origin. If found guilty, they would be imprisoned beyond the control of any member state. If any member state failed to comply, all other members would be obliged to boycott it, by denying landing facilities to any of its aircraft and by refusing to fly their own aircraft to its airports.[6]

The principle of there being such a court could have been useful to New Zealand in dealing with the two French agents responsible for the destruction of the *Rainbow Warrior* in 1985. Only since the early 1990s has there been any progress on the creation of an international war crimes court to deal with former Yugoslavia and Rwanda.

Benjamin Ferencz, a former US prosecutor at the Nuremberg War Crimes trials, has provided a series of ambitious proposals to augment the Security Council's work in maintaining international peace and security. He has called for the creation of UN Disarmament, Sanctions, Police, and Social Justice agencies.[7]

UN Secretariat

The Secretary-General could be appointed for only one, seven-year term.[8] The present arrangement is for the person to have five-year terms, with the understanding that only two terms will be served.

---

6   Peter Clyne, *An Anatomy of Skyjacking* (London: Abelard–Schuman, 1973), p. 166.

7   Benjamin Ferencz, *New Legal Foundations for Global Survival: Security Through the Security Council* (New York: Oceana, 1994).

8   See Brian Urquhart and Erskine Childers, *A World in Need of Leadership: Tomorrow's United Nations* (Uppsala: Dag Hammarskjöld Foundation, 1990).

There is a temptation to use the end of the first term as an election campaign to get reappointed. One term in office would remove that need and perhaps make the office-holder a little more independent.

The UN Secretariat could be a truly international civil service. UN staff promise not to take instructions from their national governments but there is a temptation to maintain close links with their governments. The USSR and the former Eastern European bloc staff were the worst examples of how UN staff were controlled by their governments.[9] Similarly, national governments ought not to use the UN as a dumping ground to reward retired politicians or relatives of ruling households who need a job—or whom the government would prefer to have out of the country. Recruitment should be on merit; it generally is at the lower levels but not necessarily at the senior level.

To sum up, all these micro-reforms could be implemented this day if there were the political will. The list indicates that—contrary to some of the assumptions of the UN reform debate—the problems with the UN lie less in the Charter itself, and more with national governments not being willing to honour their current obligations.

Macro-amendments

Macro-amendments require a change to the UN Charter. This list is not in any order of priority; it is simply based on the UN's 'principal organs'.

The Security Council

The UN Security Council is designed to meet day or night to handle threats to international peace and security. Its core consists of the P5, which were the Allied leaders in World War II. The other ten countries serve two-year terms and are elected via the UN's quota system to maintain a representative balance of the world.

Ideas for reforming the Security Council focus on its composition and the veto power. The P5 are no longer necessarily the world's main countries as they were in 1945. The UK and France are the most obvious members to be dropped. Germany and Japan (ironically the two big losers of World War II) are the obvious candidates to join the Security Council. Germany would like permanent membership on the Security Council since this would reflect its economic strength. It was

9   See Arkady Shevchenko, *Breaking with Moscow* (New York: Ballantine, 1985).

said of the UK in the early 1960s that it had lost an empire but not yet found a new role. It can be said of Germany that it has regained its unity but it has yet to find a new role. Being on the Security Council would give (Germany evidently hopes) a clear sense of direction. Japan has given the UN similar signals. Japan is increasing its financial contributions to UN operations. There is an element now of taxation without (permanent) representation.

An alternative approach to reforming the Security Council would be to break the nexus between the P5 and the veto power. The P5 would remain permanently on the Security Council but the veto power would be abolished entirely. The P5 would not have to worry about an election every two years—and the cost of retaining their permanent membership would be the surrender of the veto.

Another proposal is to increase the Security Council's overall size. A common suggestion is 24 (since it would give each country the chance to chair the Council for one month during the two-year cycle of Security Council membership).

The chances of any immediate major Security Council reform are slim, if only because the P5 states could use their veto power to block reform.

The General Assembly

The General Assembly is the world's main political forum. It meets for about the last four months of each year, with all UN member-nations (now 185) present. It adopts non-binding resolutions which indicate how the world's governments think on particular issues.

The main debate on reforming the General Assembly has been generated among non-government organisations (NGOs), especially the Campaign for a More Democratic United Nations (CAMDUN).[10] The UK Medical Association for the Prevention of War (now part of UK MEDACT) first proposed in 1982 that Article 22 of the UN Charter be amended to create a subsidiary body for the General Assembly. The new body would have an advisory status and would represent the views of NGOs. Representation would be based on the size of national population.[11]

---

10   See Frank Barnaby, ed., *Building a More Democratic United Nations* (London: Frank Cass, 1991).
11   'Submission of MEDACT Evidence to the Commission on Global Governance', *Medicine and War* (London), October 1993, pp. 352–53.

Another NGO urging UN reform is the New York-based Center for War/Peace Studies, headed by Richard Hudson. Hudson has pioneered the 'Binding Triad' proposal. The General Assembly each year adopts hundreds of non-binding resolutions. Hudson has proposed a shift in power, so that the General Assembly could adopt binding resolutions (thereby absorbing some of the Security Council's power). This would require a change to the present one state–one vote system to a system reflecting global population and economic realities. For a resolution to be binding, it would need to get two-thirds of the votes in three tiers of voting: of all the members present (a continuation of the present system), of the world's most populated states (thereby favouring the Third World and reflecting the majority of the world's people), and of the world's richest states (which would favour the developed countries and reflect today's economic reality).[12] Far fewer resolutions would be adopted under this system but any resolution that did make it would obviously reflect today's global realities.

The Trusteeship Council

The Allied and Associated Powers at the end of World War I decided that they would not—as was usual for military victors—divide up the territory of the vanquished between themselves as a reward for winning the war. Instead, it was agreed that the colonies would become Mandates, to be put on the road to independence. The policy was continued after World War II, with the Mandates becoming Trust Territories. Each territory was looked after by a country which was a member of the League/ UN, and that country reported to the League/ UN on the progress made in preparing the territory for independence.

As all of the Trust Territories are now independent, the Trusteeship Council has effectively worked itself out of a job. But it cannot be abolished because that would require an amendment to the UN Charter. The Council structure could be retained, with its focus now as either an Environmental Council or as a Council for the World's approximately 300 million indigenous peoples.

The Economic and Social Council (ECOSOC)

ECOSOC has 54 member-countries elected for three-year terms.

---

12   Richard Hudson's ideas are presented quarterly in the newsletter *Global Report* (New York: Centre for War/Peace Studies).

ECOSOC initiates reports and makes recommendations to the General Assembly, UN member-nations and specialised agencies on economic, social and cultural matters. There are 16 autonomous specialised agencies, such as the UN Development Programme (UNDP) and WHO. There are also the big financial agencies of the World Bank and the International Monetary Fund (IMF). Additionally, there are subsidiary bodies such as the UN Fund for Children (UNICEF) and the UN Environment Programme (UNEP).

Klaus Hufner, of the Free University, Berlin, has set out some of ECOSOC's problems:

> Unfortunately, ECOSOC has never been able to serve effectively as a world policy forum for economic, social, and related questions. The criticism is harsh: for the time being, ECOSOC is nothing but an organisational accumulation of institutional bodies which do not and cannot comply with a minimum of political rationality, organisational efficiency and implementation strength. Although coordination issues have from the outset been a permanent and central preoccupation of ECOSOC, the members have never been satisfied with its performance.
>
> Over the years, the ECOSOC machinery became extremely complicated. Today, about 40 bodies are reporting directly to the Council. Since many of these bodies have their own subsidiaries, the total number of experts and inter-governmental committees in the economic and social field is close to 200.[13]

There is also need to bring the UN's big financial institutions (the World Bank group and the IMF) into line with the rest of what the UN is doing to help Third World countries. A Third World economist working in the UN Secretariat ('who preferred to remain anonymous') has set out his/ her concerns about the way in which these agencies are 'tightly controlled by a handful of Western treasuries' and so are not working directly for the Third World or in coordination with other agencies such as the UNDP:

> Their secretariat staffs, technically highly competent, are picked for their clear conservative ideological bias, mostly from industrialised countries.
>
> These institutions are highly monolithic, dedicated above all, to the soundness of their balance sheets, to collecting Third World debt, to facilitating Western exports to their borrowing countries, and in the process, maybe to doing some good in the development area.
>
> The highly conservative Western treasuries that dominate these institutions possess no vision of long-term global growth and equity. They

---

13   Klaus Hufner, 'Challenges and New Tasks for the United Nations', *Peace and the Sciences* (Vienna), December 1992, p. 35.

have, above all, no understanding whatsoever of the social and economic basis of peace and security.[14]

This is part of the larger problem of how the Specialised Agencies and functional commissions can be more tightly controlled by ECOSOC or the Secretary-General. Specialised agencies have their own agendas. The UN is a decentralised organisation. The General Assembly, Security Council and Secretary-General may attract the daily media coverage but—until the recent increase in peacekeeping operations—at least 80 percent of the UN's work is conducted through specialised agencies.

Each agency has its own governing board. The governing boards are then linked back to different government departments at the national level. Each agency has its own membership. Thus each country may choose which specialised agencies to join. The US, for example, resigned from UNESCO in the early 1980s and took the UK with it. The US has grudgingly remained in the other specialised agencies. By contrast, Switzerland, whose voters have consistently opposed in referenda joining the UN as such, is joining specialised agencies because the Swiss Federal Council thinks that Switzerland would lose out from not doing so.

Each agency has its own method of operating and its own objectives. This means that some agencies overlap in the field, with resulting confusion. In 1992, the UN took over much of the running of a member-nation: Somalia. The obvious way to have done this would have been for the Secretary-General to appoint some form of 'commissioner' or 'administrator' to govern all UN activities (peace-keeping, relief and reconstruction) and to requisition money and personnel from member-nations to be deployed for this task. The political reality is that such a centralised approach is impossible.

System Transformation[15]

The proposals for micro-and macro-reform are both based on retaining the UN's basic structure: an organisation of nation-states. However, a third part of the UN reform spectrum consists of ideas based on recognising the power of transnational corporations (TNCs) and so

---

14 'Development is Getting Lost in the Shuffle', *Just News: Bulletin of the Independent Commission on Global Governance* (Geneva), May 1993, p. 3.

15 See Keith Suter, *Global Change: Armageddon and the New World Order* (Sydney: Albatross, 1992).

ensuring that they get a formal role with in the UN. Additionally non-government organisations (NGOs) are also becoming increasingly important and so should enjoy greater status at the UN.

The Decline of the Nation-State

The present world order is called the Westphalian system. It began in 1648, at the end of Europe's Thirty Years War and the destruction of the Holy Roman Empire. It is based on nation-states. The previous international order was based on tribes and city-states and the imperial ambitions of some tribes and city-states (such as Athens and Rome).

One characteristic of the present nation-state system is the centralisation of power in some form of ruler. Because of improvements in technology such a person can govern large areas of land. Clear boundaries are very important for the Westphalian system because the globe is divided up into a neat patchwork of nation-states. A second characteristic is uniformity. Nation-states have many similarities in, for example, their political institutions (even though they may operate differently) and this similarity enables governments to cooperate with one another.

But the Westphalian system cannot cope with many of today's problems. National governments are too small for some problems and too large for others. For example, pollution is not a new problem but its global character certainly is. Acid rain is generated in one country and falls in another; and a nuclear disaster in the USSR resulted in radioactive contamination going across Europe. Additionally, diseases such as AIDS, can now sweep more easily from one country to another because of improvements in transport which permit people (and diseases) to travel from one continent to another.

Governmental authority is being eroded. The Westphalian system is being undermined. On the one hand, some national governments have difficulty in keeping their states in one piece. Seventy percent of national borders were established by Europeans. In Africa, for example, the Westphalian system was imposed on a network of over two hundred major tribes. As the European colonial era ended, so the colonial boundaries became national boundaries. But most national boundaries do not accord with the local tribes. On the other hand, national governments cannot always deal with global problems. Pollution, for example, does not recognise national boundaries.

The nation-state will not disappear entirely. National governments will remain but will not be as important as the mass media like to imply (especially at election time). Instead, a new global order is evolving in which national governments are having to share their authority with international organisations (especially the UN), TNCs and NGOs.

Transnational Corporations

TNCs are the major global economic actors. They have greater liquid assets than all the major central reserve banks combined. With the deregulation of the international financial system in the 1980s, TNCs can move money around the globe even more easily. As Crough and Wheelwright observed in the context of the 'free trade' debate:

> There is little possibility of free trade emerging if protection is removed: rather there is a high probability that a pattern of trade will be imposed to suit the global corporations. Increasingly *trade is between corporations and not nations,* and is being conducted on the basis of comparative advantage created and manipulated by the very corporations that reap the benefits. The flows of trade, their direction, volume and pricing, are more and more at the discretion of global corporations, which make these administrative decisions internally for the purpose of maximising global profit, with little regard for their effects on particular countries.[16]

Meanwhile, national politics has become part of the television entertainment industry. Media attention is focused on comparatively small events (such as the private lives of government leaders). Television coverage is based on immediate events, rather than explaining the background to what is happening. British television producer John Birt recognised this problem almost two decades ago:

> Present television news programmes cover a large number of stories, often more than 20 items in a span of about half an hour. As a result, the focus in any one story is extremely narrow. But unfortunately, the most important stories of the moment—for example, stories about the economy, Northern Ireland or the European Economic Community or the Middle East or oil—suffer from such a narrow treatment.
> The news, devoting two minutes on successive nights to the latest unemployment figures or the state of the stock market, with no time to put the story into context, gives the viewers no sense of how any of these problems relate to each other. It is more likely to leave them confused and uneasy.[17]

16   Greg Crough and Ted Wheelwright, *Australia: A Client State* (Melbourne: Penguin, 1982), p. 14. Emphasis in original.
17   John Birt, 'Can Television News Break the Understanding Barrier?', *Times*

Since big stories are so complex, it is often easier to focus on small ones and—by saturation coverage—make them into big issues. In Australia, the big issues are economic decline, unemployment and environmental pollution (all partly related to the erosion of the West-phalian system), and family breakdown. But these are very complicated and are partly related to each other. It is much easier to discuss whether or not the country should become a republic or have a new flag. Everyone has an opinion on these issues.

The American writer Gore Vidal, in the 1992 presidential election, noticed a similar process: 'You know, there are only two great issues—converting from war to peace and managing the economy. Instead, we're talking about abortion and the [American] flag'.[18]

Therefore, with the politicians entertaining the population, TNCs are running the economy. In the Australian economy, for example, TNCs have a major role in mining, oil, finance, motor car manu-facturing, chemicals and tourism. In terms of TNC penetration, Australia is virtually a Third World country. But little attention is paid to this role by the mass media (many of which, incidentally, are themselves TNCs).

A recent survey of the size of transnational corporations is the *1993 World Investment Report* issued by the United Nations Conference on Trade and Development (UNCTAD).[19] According to the Report, as of the early 1990s, there were 37,000 TNCs (with 170,000 affiliates), up from 7000 TNCs only two decades earlier. These corporations control a stock of foreign direct investment (FDI) that has reached US $2 trillion, one-third of which is controlled by the largest 100 TNCs. All TNCs account for foreign sales worth some US $5.5 trillion. The sheer magnitude of this figure may be gauged by a comparison with the total value of world exports in goods and services which amounts to US $4 trillion. The largest foreign investor is Royal Dutch Shell (UK and the Netherlands), with US $69 billion in assets in foreign countries, followed by Ford, General Motors, Exxon and IBM (all US). The top 10 also include British Petroleum (UK), ASEA/Brown Boveri (Sweden and Switzerland), Nestle (Switzer-land), Philips (the Netherlands) and Mobil (US).

Incidentally, I think that UNCTAD's use of nationality to identify

(London), 2 February 1975.

18   'A Gadfly in Glorious, Angry Exile', *Time,* 28 September 1992, p. 22.

19   UNCTAD, *1993 World Investment Report: Transnational Corporations and Integrated International Production* (New York: United Nations, July 1993).

the TNCs is unhelpful. As this chapter has already indicated, TNCs are being 'de-nationalised' so that national labelling is misleading. As Osbaldeston and Barham have explained:

The larger companies recognise that they cannot thrive on domestic markets alone.... Their national loyalties are diminishing as they coordinate business assets in multiple countries. For example, the Swiss firm Nestle has only 4 percent of its employees based in Switzerland and generates only 2 percent of its sales there. The Swiss/Swedish company ASEA/Brown Boveri (ABB) has no more than 15 percent of its employees in any one country. Unilever employs 350,000 spread across 78 countries.[20]

Indeed, the UN Report goes on to note that TNCs are increasingly organising themselves into multi-tier networks including parent firms, foreign affiliates, firms linked through subcontracting, licensing and similar contractual arrangements, and firms tied together through alliances. These networks include all the major corporate functions—research and development, procurement, manufacturing, marketing, finance, accounting, and human resource development—and occur in both developed and developing countries. These developments are therefore fostering worldwide economic integration.

The Report says that the telecommunications revolution means that workers can be employed in cheap labour areas to do data processing for an entire TNC. For example, Swissair (Switzerland) has created an affiliate in Bombay, India, to handle revenue accounting functions for the corporation as a whole. Another TNC has located all the data processing for its insurance clients in Ireland, while a US airline company has located its booking system in Jamaica.

To conclude, transnational corporations are themselves becoming global entities. As Raymond Vernon, one of the pioneers of research into these corporations, noted in 1992:

Four decades ago, the transnational corporation (TNC) was widely regarded as a peculiarly United States form of business organisation, a manifestation of the existence of a pax Americana. Today, every industrialised country provides a base for a considerable number of TNCs which, collectively, are becoming the dominant form of organisation responsible for the international exchange of goods and services. Indeed, by the end of the 1980s, even the larger firms in some of the rapidly industrialising countries

20   Michael Osbaldeston and Kevin Barham, 'Using Management Development for Competitive Advantage', *Long Range Planning* (London), (December 1992), p. 19.

of Asia and Latin America had joined the trend.[21]

Ironically, although TNCs receive mentions in UN economic surveys, very little attention is given to them otherwise. For example, TNCs could easily help the UN's financial crisis by giving the UN some money. TNCs benefit from the UN's work, such as in Namibia and Cambodia, which resulted in an outbreak of peace—why not charge TNCs for services rendered?

Non-Government Organisations (NGOs)

There has been a dramatic growth in NGOs. People prefer to work for a specific campaign (such as saving the whale) rather than join a political party. NGOs are the most important way of mobilising public opinion and in focusing attention on a problem. They are adept at attracting media coverage, they appeal to people who are disenchanted with the usual party-political process, and they provide a sense of vision and continuity which outlasts the short-term perspective of governments.

NGOs have been involved in the UN's work from the outset. They were present at the 1945 San Francisco Conference which finalised the UN Charter. Partly as a result of lobbying, they were able to get official recognition for NGOs in the UN Charter in Article 71:

> The Economic and Social Council may make suitable arrangements for consultation with non-governmental organisations which are concerned with matters within its competence. Such arrangements may be made with international organisations and, where appropriate, with national organisations after consultation with the Member of the United Nations concerned.

A great deal has flowed from that one paragraph. NGOs have been very adept at using the paragraph to expand their role in the UN. NGO 'consultation' at the UN takes various forms. NGOs attend many of the UN's meetings of bodies under ECOSOC's jurisdiction, such as the Commission on Human Rights, Commission on the Status of Women, and the specialised agencies. Their material is distributed at such meetings. They also have the right to request permission to speak. Whether this is granted depends on the amount of time available. All of these procedures represent incursions on what is supposed to be a government monopoly.

21   Raymond Vernon, 'Transnational Corporations: Where Are They Coming From, Where Are They Headed?', *Transnational Corporations* (New York), (August 1992), p. 7.

NGOs not only provide information and ideas to UN bodies, they also help keep governments honest. In this era of greater complexity, NGOs monitor government behaviour. They can report to their members back home how their governments are speaking and voting at UN bodies. They can also scrutinise government reports to UN bodies and look for inconsistencies and errors.

NGOs have often been helped by UN staff. They see NGOs as a vehicle for transmitting UN material into nation-states. Much UN material is in dull, bland bureaucratic prose. It is often dealing with important issues but the style is that of avoiding offending particular governments. NGOs, being outside the UN, can take UN material and give it life and colour, and so get the public's attention.

Involving TNCs and NGOs in the UN

The post-Westphalian global order will need to find formal ways of drawing TNCs and NGOs into global decision-making and international law.[22] There has to be dialogue and cooperation—rather than confrontation. TNCs have no formal status at all the UN, while NGOs have only a consultative status. The third part of the spectrum for UN reform is, then, to alter the Westphalian system to give recognition within the UN to TNCs and NGOs.

The idea of TNCs being involved in the UN's work is not entirely without precedent. The International Labour Organisation (ILO), one of the oldest specialised agencies, has a unique tripartite system of representation within each national delegation. Each delegation to the ILO contains representatives of government, employers and trades unions. Philip Noel Baker, then a professor of international relations at the University of London, explained in 1926 that the ILO went for such a novel system so as to increase its level of expertise. The ILO

> ...can avoid the technical mistakes which it would make if it had not the help of experts personally engaged in each trade or industry which is discussed. Moreover, by their share in preparing the treaties which the [ILO] adopts, the goodwill of the leaders of both workers and employers is usually assured, and the chances are thereby increased that the undertakings of the treaties will be faithfully carried out.[23]

22　For example, see Australian Branch, International Law Association, *The International Status of Human Rights Non-Governmental Organizations* (Sydney: Butterworths, 1978).

23　Philip Noel Baker, *The League of Nations at Work* (London: Nisbet, 1926),

Additionally, some national delegations at UN conferences have contained representatives of TNCs and NGOs.

However, it is necessary to give a greater formal recognition to TNCs and NGOs. One way this could be done is to create two committees of the General Assembly, to work alongside it, in which representatives of TNCs and NGOs could provide their views (with no blocking veto) on proposed resolutions. This would be a minor step but it would help get governments accustomed to the fact that they will have to share their power with TNCs and NGOs.

Where to Now?[24]

The primary task is to make UN reform an issue in itself. The UN is taken for granted. It is older than most of the world's population; it has somehow always existed (like national departments of health or education—and no one makes a fuss about them). The UN is like wallpaper in a house: everyone knows that it is there but most people are unaware of the pattern or colour. NGOs have focused on issues and have viewed the UN though a disarmament prism or an environment one. The UN itself has not been an issue. It is only when an event such as the US use of the UN in the Gulf conflict comes along that suddenly there is popular interest in how the UN operates. UN reform is now on the international political agenda (if only because some governments are keen to reduce their already minute contributions to it). There is a foundation for an NGO campaign.

The task, then, is to publicise UN reform as an issue and to generate ideas. Some NGOs already have specific ideas (such as Dick Hudson's long-time campaign for changing the voting system to a Binding Triad). The role for other NGOs is, at present, 'to talk up the issue' and to generate ideas. For example, environment NGOs could look at ways of reforming the UN to enhance the UN's role in protecting the environment.

The cause of UN reform may seem impossible—especially given the dismal analysis here. There is a bureaucratic bias within all governments to do nothing on anything. They often prefer to stick with the devil they know rather than gamble on a devil they do not know.

However, there is a lesson here from Senator Evans's chapter.

---

p. 80.
24   See Keith Suter, *Global Agenda: Economics, the Environment and the Nation-State* (Sydney: Albatross, 1995).

He spoke well on the need for alternative ways to settle disputes. It is a pleasure to welcome him as a convert to the cause. Politicians are often slow to give acknowledgment of the campaign by NGOs to change government policy. Senator Evans's chapter is similar to the points made in his very good book *Cooperating for Peace.*[25] But that book fails to recognise fully the role of peace movement NGOs in shaping the national debate over peacekeeping. Page 34 of that book refers to some NGOs, such as those in the development field. But no mention is made of the peace movement NGOs that have kept up a steady flow of correspondence with the Foreign Minister over the years, such as the UN Association, Women's International League for Peace and Freedom, Medical Association for the Prevention of War, Greenpeace, and the Australian Peace Committee.

Another lesson comes from the current controversy within Australia over the proposed resumption of French nuclear testing. A major politician leading this cause is John Howard, the leader of the conservative Liberal Party. He had nothing to do with the Australian peace movement in the 1980s. But the values of the peace movement have been lodged in the hearts of Australians and so, even without an active peace movement, Australians have reacted spontaneously with anger at the French decision. Now John Howard has found it politically opportune to come out against the nuclear tests.

When the followers lead, the leaders will follow. The same could be said about the issue of UN reform. If the NGOs can create a climate of concern then there is hope for the cause of UN reform.

Edvard Hambro, Norway's delegate to the UN General Assembly, in 1971 spoke, as President of the UN General Assembly, to the American Society of International Law on the UN: 'We ought not to be satisfied when people tell us that politics is the art of the possible. Politics should be the art to make possible tomorrow what seems impossible today'.[26]

25 Gareth Evans, *Cooperating for Peace: The Global Agenda for the 1990s and Beyond* (Sydney: Allen & Unwin, 1993).
26 Quoted in Alan Geyer, *The Idea of Disarmament: Rethinking the Unthinkable* (Washington DC: Churches' Centre for Theology and Public Policy, 1982), p. 165.

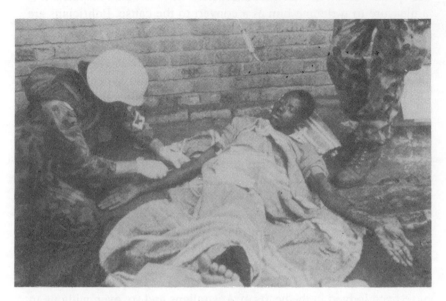

*UN peacekeepers struggle to cope with the humanitarian tragedy
in Rwanda, 1994*

Olara A. Otunnu

Promoting Peacemaking and Peacekeeping: The Role and Perspective of the International Peace Academy

I am delighted and honoured to be part of this symposium. It is especially appropriate that one should be commemorating the fiftieth anniversary of the United Nations in New Zealand which has provided a very important example. It is an example of what commitment, the force of ideas and participation can do within the UN. Even a country which may be relatively small can make a big difference to the work of the UN. The participation of New Zealand in peacekeeping activities, especially this last several years, and its very active role in the Security Council during its two-year tenure, have been much appreciated.

The Role of the International Peace Academy

The International Peace Academy (IPA) has played a pioneering role as an independent institution in promoting peacemaking and peacekeeping for 25 years. The IPA was founded in 1970 as an independent international institution devoted to the promotion of peacemaking and peacekeeping. Many international citizens contributed to the founding of the IPA. On this occasion, I wish to pay a special tribute to three of them in particular.

The principal inspiration for the creation of the IPA came from UN Secretary-General U Thant. He was animated by the conviction that, in view of some of the official constraints under which the UN and national governments often operate, an independent institution, working within a framework of cooperation with the UN, could make a special contribution to peacemaking and peacekeeping activities through practical and policy-oriented intellectual initiatives. The vision of U Thant was matched by the commitment of a truly remarkable woman of our times, Ruth Forbes Young of Philadelphia. Her staunch support and indomitable spirit were crucial in launching and sustaining the new organisation. The third person was Indar Jit Rikhye, the distinguished Indian general and peacekeeping veteran, who brought his considerable experience to bear on this enterprise. As the first President of the IPA, he translated the collective vision of U Thant and Ruth Forbes Young into an organisation with a significant role.

Over the years, the IPA has developed many areas of programme activities. Today our core activities fall into several areas of concentration, namely policy training seminars; policy symposia; research programme; facilitation of conflict resolution; Africa programme; and outreach activities.

Policy Training Seminars

The IPA organises and conducts a number of policy training seminars on peacekeeping and conflict resolution. The sessions are generally of one to two weeks' duration. Participants in these seminars are drawn from the senior ranks of diplomats, military officers, members of the UN Secretariat as well as the secretariats of regional organisations, and officials of humanitarian organisations. The seminar programme is designed to fulfil three inter-related objectives: first, to deepen the knowledge and expertise of participants on critical policy issues relating to peacekeeping and peacemaking; second, to provide opportunities for comparing various national and regional experiences; and third, to provide a setting for networking amongst participants coming from different parts of the world.

This year marks the 25th anniversary of the Vienna Seminar, the flagship of our seminar programme. We are proud to count many distinguished representatives around the world today amongst the alumni of the Vienna Seminar. The Paris Seminar has a particular importance for us as one of the few French-language international seminars of its kind. Plans are now under way to launch two new training seminars. We plan to organise in New York an annual seminar primarily for the benefit of members of the Permanent Missions and the staff of the UN Secretariat; the inaugural session for this seminar is scheduled for early next year. In addition, at the request of the eleven states of Central Africa and pursuant to UN General Assembly Resolution A.49/76C of last year, the IPA has agreed to organise a special French-language seminar programme focusing on trainers and on peacekeeping preparedness for the states of the sub-region.

Policy Symposia

Over the years, the IPA has developed a tradition of organising policy symposia of two or three days' duration, which bring together high-level policy-makers from governments and international organisations, scholars and independent opinion-makers for in-depth policy discussions on an important topical theme (e.g. 'Humanitarian Action in Conflict Situations', Princeton, October 1993; 'The Role and Composition of the Security Council', February 1994) or a cluster of cutting-edge issues (e.g. 'New Dimensions of United Nations Peacekeeping Operations', Tokyo, January 1995) relating to peacekeeping and conflict resolution. The policy symposia have two objectives: on the one hand, to provide an occasion for a deeper reflection on the issues in question and, on the other, to come up with specific insights and recommendations that can be of practical use to policy-makers.

We have organised two important policy symposia since the beginning of this year. In mid-January, we organised in Tokyo, in collaboration with the United Nations University and with the support of the Government of Japan, a symposium on the theme 'New Dimensions of United Nations Peacekeeping Operations'. In early March in Vienna, the IPA and the Government of Austria jointly sponsored a special high-level symposium on the theme 'Peacemaking and Peacekeeping for the Next Century'. That symposium was especially organised to commemorate the 25th anniversary of the annual Vienna Seminar and the 50th anniversary of the United Nations. The discussions in Tokyo and Vienna and their outcomes represent part of the IPA's intellectual contribution to the commemoration of the fiftieth anniversary of the United Nations.

Research Programme

The purpose of the IPA's research programme has been to monitor and assess UN and other multilateral peace operations with a view to drawing lessons from those experiences for the future. In this connection, we have just completed case studies of the peace processes in Cambodia and El Salvador. An IPA Occasional Paper on Cambodia (*UN Peacekeeping in Cambodia: UNTAC's Civil Mandate*, by Michael Doyle) was published in early 1995. A similar occasional paper on El Salvador (*Rights and Reconciliation: UN Strategies in El Salvador*, by Ian Johnstone) was published in mid-1995. An edited volume containing a comprehensive coverage of both the Cambodia and El Salvador cases will be published in early 1996.

In the next phase of its research programme, the IPA is proposing a two-year research project that explores post-conflict peace-building.

Building upon the IPA's established strengths in policy analysis and UN peacekeeping, the programme will be composed of two sets of research activities:

- Evaluating the legacy of multi-dimensional UN peace operations. A direct outgrowth of the IPA's previous research on Cambodia and El Salvador, this aspect of the programme will also examine Somalia, Haiti, Guatemala, and the Former Yugoslav Republic of Macedonia—in all cases seeking to learn about UN operations and, in particular, what difference they made in the countries in which they operated.

- Assessing the effectiveness of the strategies employed in peace-building, with a view to recommending improvements in how the UN and other international organisations conduct peace-building activities. We will seek to extract lessons about the causes of success and failure.

Facilitation of Conflict Resolution

The IPA plays a facilitating role in efforts to settle conflicts by bringing together parties in conflict to explore—informally and often off-the-record—ways to promote political settlements in particular conflict situations. In the past we have played this role in relation to conflicts in Central America, southern Africa and Cambodia. We are now engaged in extending this facilitating role into a an important programme on preventive action.

Africa Programme

We at the IPA recognise the important role that regional organisations must necessarily come to play in the field of peacemaking and peace-keeping. But for this to come to pass, no effort should be spared to assist them to develop their capacities for action more fully. It is in this context that, over the last four years, the IPA has worked closely with the Organisation of African Unity (OAU) to explore ways in which the pan-African organisation can respond more effectively to the drama of conflict on the African continent. These efforts have already borne fruit in the adoption, in July 1993, of the new OAU Mechanism for Conflict Prevention, Management and Resolution.

The tasks ahead, in many ways more formidable than the formulation of the Mechanism itself, are two-fold. The first task is to translate the OAU's intent, embodied in the Mechanism, into an instrument that can make a difference on the ground. The second challenge, equally important, is to build a broad constituency of support within Africa for the OAU Mechanism in particular, and more generally for all efforts aimed at managing conflicts more peacefully on the continent.

With these objectives in mind, the IPA is currently undertaking three projects in collaboration with the OAU:

- **The IPA/OAU Task Force on Peacemaking and Peacekeeping in Africa.** The mission of the Task Force is to formulate a graduated programme of practical step-by-step measures for the operationalisation of the OAU Mechanism. This exercise will have to take into account several factors and developments, including recent OAU experience; what the 'political traffic' in Africa can bear at any given moment; the role of the UN; the potential role of sub-regional arrangements in different parts of Africa; and the availability of resources, short and long term, within and outside Africa, for this purpose.

- **The IPA/OAU Consultation on Civil Society and Conflict Management in Africa.** This consultation, which will be the fourth in our series of consultations on conflict management in Africa, is scheduled for early next year. It will focus on the role of civil society and other non-official actors in conflict management and peace initiatives in Africa, and on how to link these activities to the OAU Mechanism. The consultation is also designed to facilitate networking amongst non-official actors in the field of conflict management in Africa.

- **The OAU Training Seminar.** At the request of the Secretary-General of the OAU, the IPA will soon launch a training seminar on peacekeeping for the staff of the OAU Secretariat in Addis Ababa.

Outreach Activities

The IPA directs a wide-ranging programme of outreach activities, designed to build public awareness and understanding of peacemaking and peacekeeping trends and issues within the international community at large. These activities include:

- **The IPA Roundtable**. The flagship event of the IPA's

outreach activities is the IPA Roundtable in New York. The Roundtable brings together a select, diverse group of leading members of the US and international community in New York, to exchange views on topical issues relating to peace and conflict in the world; the speaker is usually a prominent leader in a given field. Although relatively new, the IPA Roundtable series has rapidly become an important presence in New York's international calendar—a popular forum for informal policy discussion as well as a testing ground for new ideas. After each Roundtable, a summary report is prepared and distributed.

* **The Global Forum**. The IPA organises an annual Global Forum, a public lecture at which a distinguished world statesman with unique expertise and experience offers a personal interpretation of some aspects of the major developments unfolding on the world scene. Past speakers have included the Rt Hon. Lord Jenkins of Hillhead (Chancellor of Oxford University and former President of the Commission of the European Communities) and HRH Crown Prince Hassan bin Talal of Jordan.

* **The Internship Programme**. The IPA seeks to promote a wider understanding of peacekeeping and conflict resolution amongst a new generation of young people through an extensive Internship Programme, which provides students at the graduate and undergraduate levels with a broad practical and intellectual exposure to peacekeeping and peacemaking activities and to the work of the United Nations in general.

Some Observations and Perspective

A Sense of Perspective

In the second part of my paper, I should like to share some observations and perspective arising from our experience at the IPA. My first comment is about the need to restore a sense of perspective in the whole sphere of peace and security activities. Peace operations, including humanitarian relief, have increased by leaps and bounds in recent years. This dramatic development is leading to an increasing loss of perspective. Significant areas of imbalance are beginning to emerge in the overall vision and conduct of the UN peace and security agenda. Three such areas need to be examined with a view to restoring a sense of perspective.

The first area of imbalance has to do with the growing tension between peacekeeping operations and development activities. A serious disequilibrium is beginning to emerge between resource allocations for peacekeeping and relief operations, on the one hand, and resources available for long-term peace-building on the other. The resources devoted by the UN, other international organisations and by donor governments to peacekeeping and emergency humanitarian activities are beginning to outstrip the resources for long-term peace-building, in other words resources for development. In fact a number of governments and other donor institutions have started to divert resources from their development budgets to peacekeeping operations and humanitarian relief.

This trend needs to be re-examined. Investing in social and economic development is one of the surest ways to build a solid foundation for long-term peace within and between societies. This in turn means that development strategies must seek to address the roots of conflict, as for example, in a situation where a pattern of gross imbalance in the allocation of development resources is bound to provide a fertile ground for conflict. There is therefore a need to consciously build a conflict response component into the design of development projects, especially in countries where the potential for conflict or its escalation is high.

The second area of imbalance concerns the imperative for preventive action. The UN and other international actors need to invest a great deal more in preventive measures. Successful preventive action can be highly cost-effective, saving lives and sparing general destruction. In addition, it is considerably cheaper than an operation to restore a broken peace.

It is critical that a body of both serious knowledge and serious practice be built in the area of preventive action, through systematic preventive engagement in specific situations of actual or potential conflict. This will require innovation and long-term commitment. The ambition must be to develop in the area of preventive action something akin to what has been built over the last fifty years in the peacekeeping sector. Unless this is done, I fear that preventive action will remain an easy but largely empty slogan.

While we must probe the boundaries of preventive possibilities to the utmost, we should not lose sight of some serious constraints inherent in this enterprise. How, for example, shall we overcome the shield of national sovereignty, or, quite simply, a country's sense of national pride, the temptation for brinkmanship, asymmetry of response amongst parties in conflict, the tendency to misread a developing situation until it is too late, or the lack of interest or will on the part of international actors at critical moments? Indeed, efforts to intervene at the earlier stages of a conflict situation are likely to prove particularly frustrating for outside actors. For it is during this phase in particular that they are likely to come up immediately against the wall of national sovereignty. This is especially so when dealing with a strong state, a state which is itself the instrument of repression or is a major party to the conflict in question. In such cases, the challenge is how to induce the 'opening of the door' sufficiently ajar to allow for preventive initiatives.

The third area of imbalance is about the preoccupation with humanitarian action in a conflict situation *vis-à-vis* the need for a political process. It is important that humanitarian action be located within an overall vision of a society in conflict. This means, in particular, that humanitarian action should move in parallel with a political process aimed at addressing the underlying causes of a conflict and achieving a political settlement. Otherwise I fear that the tremendous efforts being deployed on the humanitarian front will inevitably count for very little. The experiences of Cambodia, El Salvador and Mozambique represent examples where a combined strategy of humanitarian and political actions was successfully employed. In sharp contrast to this stands the current situation in and around Rwanda where a major humanitarian operation is in place but no comparable concerted efforts are under way to find a political settlement to the conflict itself.

Division of Labour between the UN and Regional Organisations

My second comment concerns the need for a division of labour between the UN and other actors, especially regional organisations. It is apparent that the UN presently lacks the capacity and resources to perform well all the peace and security tasks that it has come to assume in recent years. An appropriate division of responsibilities between the UN and other international actors in the spheres of preventive action, peacemaking, peacekeeping, enforcement action and peace-building must therefore be developed to enable a more effective and comprehensive international response to conflict situations around the world. Such a division of labour could take advantage of the different capabilities and interests of regional organisations, national governments and non-government organisations (NGOs). The idea should be to identify areas of comparative advantage and build around that a system of complimentarity. A possible division of labour between the UN and regional organisations (including, for this purpose, such bodies as the Commonwealth which played an important role in Zimbabwe) may be developed along the following areas of comparative advantage.

In the light of recent experience, it would seem most effective for the UN to concentrate its efforts on preventive action, traditional peacekeeping, humanitarian missions, mediation, and peace-building activities through its various agencies.

In time, regional organisations must come to assume greater responsibility for peace and security. But for the time being, the areas of comparative advantage for regional organisations would seem to be preventive action, peacemaking, and confidence-building at the regional and sub-regional levels, while allowing for a more gradual development of peacekeeping capabilities.

But the emphasis on the role of regional organisations must not lead to a tribalisation of peacekeeping activities, whereby, for example, conflicts in Europe are viewed as the responsibility of the Europeans, or African conflicts as the domain of the Africans. This notion goes against the grain of the UN—its universality and its worldwide responsibility for maintaining peace and security. Moreover, the problem is compounded by the uneven spread and varying capacities of regional organisations in different parts of the globe. Clearly, member states from a particular region should be encouraged to spearhead an international response to a conflict situation within their region, but this must not detract from the importance of wider international participation in these efforts. This is necessary for reasons of broader legitimacy and solidarity, as well as for practical reasons of capacity.

Role of NGOs

My third concern is to do with the role of NGOs in this field. We are witnessing the emergence of independent actors in the field of peacemaking and peacekeeping. Drawn from the ranks of international civil society, these actors are increasingly making direct contributions to peace processes. On account of its informal and flexible character, this sector can often complement official efforts, particularly in the areas of early warning, preventive activities, peacemaking, humanitarian action and peace-building. Different independent organisations tend to specialise in various aspects of these activities.

In this respect it should be noted that the Security Council remains the only major decision-making body of the UN which does not have a channel of communication for receiving information, ideas and proposals from independent non-official sources. In other sectors of the activities of the UN, notably in the humanitarian, economic, environmental, social and cultural spheres, the input of NGOs is now well developed and accepted. There is no reason why the peace and security sector should remain an exception. The presidency of the Council could be the initial focal point of communication. The president could receive information from and hold informal audience with representatives of civil society and independent public figures. To avoid opening a floodgate, the interaction would have to be selective, restricted initially to organisations and public figures with known 'track records' and credibility, and who have specific contributions to make to issues under consideration by the Council. This arrangement could be extended gradually, by invitation, to include informal audiences with the Council as a whole, whenever this is judged to be useful.

The Challenge of the 'Grey Zone'

The fourth observation concerns what might be called the challenge of the 'grey zone'. Traditional peacekeeping remains the most developed of all UN response mechanisms to conflict situations. In general, peacekeeping works best when there is an agreed peace to keep and when an operation is based on the consent of the parties in conflict, while observing the principles of cooperation, impartiality and non-use of force except in self-defence.

At the other end of the spectrum, a more radical mode of response is available to the UN in the form of collective enforcement action. Enforcement action is a forcible collective military operation authorised by the Security Council under Chapter VII of the Charter, for the purpose of restoring compliance with international norms, following a major breach of the peace or an act of aggression. Although it involves war-fighting, enforcement action should be viewed and conducted in a different way from a war waged primarily to achieve national objectives. In its fifty-year history, the United Nations has so far sanctioned the prosecution of two full-fledged enforcement operations, namely in Korea in 1950 and against Iraq in 1991.

Recent experience, especially in Liberia, Somalia, Rwanda and the former Yugoslavia, has demonstrated that on the ground there is a growing 'grey zone' between these two well-defined modes of response. The grey zone is in effect the thin end of the enforcement wedge—it is the space between traditional peacekeeping (including an appropriate application of force for self-defence) and all-out war-fighting. Situations encountered in the grey zone often require responses that are neither traditional peacekeeping nor full-blown enforcement action, but something in between.

The following scenarios are examples of the contingencies that may arise in the grey zone:

- When an armed faction in a conflict unilaterally blocks the way, preventing a relief convoy from gaining access to a population in distress;

- When a 'safe area' under the protection of the UN is attacked and overrun by a party in conflict;

- When a peacekeeping contingent comes under a massive attack from a faction with superior firepower;

- When peacekeepers are taken hostage;

- When a no-fly zone is violated;

- The situation in Rwanda in April 1994, following the presidential plane crash, when the massacres started but before they swelled into a genocidal tide.

There is need for a less ad hoc and more systematic response to contingencies arising in the grey zone. But this will require that at least two projects be explored more fully. In the immediate term, the UN should develop clear guidelines regarding the conditions for a more forceful response, whenever necessary, including a determination of decision-making responsibilities between the contingent commander on the scene, the overall mission commander, and UN headquarters in New York.

More fundamentally, this may require the development of a third mechanism, separate from both traditional peacekeeping arrangements and massive enforcement action. In particular, the UN should examine more seriously the various ideas that have been put forward for creating some form of a rapid response capability. A rapid response force could be dispatched immediately to a conflict theatre in order to avert or minimise the deterioration of the situation to crisis proportions. Intervention of this kind would go beyond traditional peacekeeping, but still fall short (by its scope and duration) of a full-scale enforcement action. And being the thin end of the enforcement wedge, actions in the grey zone should necessarily be mandated by the Security Council under Chapter VII of the Charter.

Domestic Constituencies for Collective International Action

A critical challenge faces the international community as a whole today. In the face of pressing domestic preoccupations, budgetary constraints, low tolerance for risks of casualties and a creeping sense of crisis fatigue, how can we build domestic political constituencies in support of collective international action? In part this is the challenge of relating what has hitherto been a narrow concept of national interest to the broader imperatives of an increasingly interdependent world. Traditionally, national security was organised to respond to a particular conception of threats, usually military and territorial in nature or relating to strategic and geopolitical interests. These threats emanated from particular sources, with country-specific targets. This vision of national security may have worked well in the past, especially during the Cold War era, but is today rendered too narrow and inadequate against emerging global realities.

Leadership

The sixth concern is related to the need for leadership. To provide adequate multilateral response to the growing peace and security agenda will require political imagination and leadership at the national as well as international levels. At the domestic level, leadership is needed to articulate the nexus between national interest, broadly conceived, and international responsibility, by explaining to domestic constituents the ways in which national well-being can ultimately be affected by seemingly far-away dangers. This is a new reality being driven by the fact of growing interdependence. There exists a largely untapped reservoir of humanitarian concern in many societies. The question is whether national leaders are prepared to galvanise this resource and channel it in support of international action.

Conclusion

It is difficult to build an effective and sustainable framework for preserving peace and security without some kind of a normative underpinning. In the past this seemed less apparent because everything was subordinated to the logic of the Cold War. Today the task of constructing appropriate peace and security mechanisms needs to be related to the challenge of building a community of values at various levels of the international system.

At the global level, the UN has been instrumental in the development and dissemination of a core of normative standards, covering such areas as human rights, environmental ethics, peaceful settlement of disputes, women's rights, and minority rights. These universal principles can best be taken seriously when translated into a context of application at lower levels of the international system. A regional organisation or a sub-regional arrangement can provide a more concrete and local framework for the application of universally accepted principles of governance. The core principles might comprise the following: the general observance of universal human rights standards; the promotion of democracy; the peaceful settlement of internal and interstate conflicts; and the protection of minorities and other disadvantaged groups.

A formal and common commitment to these principles would then become the basis for assessing good citizenship within a particular region or sub-region, as well as the criteria for participation in the regional association. The idea here is to create a form of regional political 'code of conduct', by which the actions and policies of member governments can be judged. Unless translated into regional commitments of this kind that can give rise to regional discipline and peer pressure, universal norms can seem remote and abstract and, at times, compromised by overtones of big-power hegemony.

(Left to right): Professor A J R Groom, Mr Carrick Lewis and Dr Keith Suter, Otago Foreign Policy School, 1995. (Photo: Ian McGibbon)

A. J. R. Groom

Global Governance
and the United Nations

'Global Governance' is a term which has been given sufficient currency to warrant its use as a title of a new academic journal. However, it is a term which is used in many different ways. Anyone with a serious interest in international relations and international organisation knows what it means, yet it does not have a scientific meaning. What then are its component parts? First, global governance is multipolar in nature. It encompasses a wide range of differing actors, such as states, international organisations (government and non-government) and a plethora of transnational actors such as multinational corporations and think tanks. These actors contribute to the essential multidimensionality of the notion, for they broach questions of a political, economic, social or cultural nature. Their interactions have given rise to what is in effect a decentralised public process which is related to the governance of global civil society. The outcome of this process is a set of norms, rules and decisions which are directed towards the management of global issues. These public and private bodies interact in both a formal and informal manner to create procedures which focus on a range of issues that necessarily concern everyone. Global governance is necessary because there are global issues from which no one can escape, although the incidence may be different for each. For example, the rich may be able to protect themselves against the worst ravages of environmental degradation, but only at a price, so they too are necessarily involved in what is a truly global issue.

Global governance therefore is the decision-making process and the institutions whereby issues, which by their very nature are global, are broached and to a certain extent managed. Its multipolar, multidimensional and complex nature and its decentralised procedures make it totally different from previous notions of world government. Within this complex framework the UN system has a role to play and it is to the interaction of the United Nations in the framework for global governance, that this paper addresses itself.

The Present Context

Hedley Bull encapsulated neatly the *problematique* with which we are dealing in the title of his well-known book *The Anarchical Society*.[1] There are at the global level strong elements of anarchy, but there is equally a nascent societal framework. While the global system in political, cultural and social matters is weak, at the same time there has emerged, with the spread of capitalism, what is tantamount to a single world economy, and this system has existed in recognisable form for the last five hundred years. What is particularly striking at our present time is the growing acknowledgment that the anarchical political system needs to be put into a stronger societal framework if it is to broach the global issues that have come increasingly to the fore in our day. But for a society to exist, even an anarchical society, there must be some level of shared values which can form the basis for sets of rules and procedures for the translation of those values into agreements. The latter in turn will enable us to live better together and to take advantage of opportunities and manage problems as they emerge at the global level.

Historians may like dates, but the processes which give rise to the events that provide the historians with dates are often long. Perhaps, therefore, we should look for benchmarks in this long process. One such benchmark became evident around 1960 when, in a number of different dimensions, it became possible, with hindsight, to judge that we have moved from a situation of world politics to global politics. By world politics I mean that where an event, such as the Second World War, may have touched all continents of the world, it did not necessarily do so.

By 1960 the last round of decolonisation was under way.

Likewise, by 1960 the major developed economies had recovered from the worst ravages of the Second World War. This change was signalled when the Organisation for European Economic Cooperation (OEEC), which was the principal European agency for the Marshall Plan, was transformed into the Organisation for Economic Co-operation and Development (OECD). Apart from the socialist countries, which have since joined it, a world economy was in the making.

---

1   Hedley Bull, *The Anarchical Society: A Study of Order in World Politics* (London: Macmillan, 1977).

Nuclear weapons in considerable numbers were already in the hands of several states and the age of plenitude of intercontinental delivery systems was upon us following the successful launch of Sputnik. Thus a situation arose where an intercontinental missile could be targeted with great accuracy from any quarter of the globe towards any other quarter of the globe. The prospect of nuclear war was a global phenomenon from which no one could escape. If they were not affected by the immediate destruction, they would be affected by fallout, and the prospect of phenomena such as nuclear winter.

At about the same time the Club of Rome was publishing its well-known study *The Limits of Growth*[2] in which they predicted that if resource depletion and pollution was continued at the prevailing rates, in one hundred years there would be a catastrophic fall in industrial production and in population. Whatever the inaccuracies of their computer model, the question of the environment was firmly on the global agenda. It was something that would affect us all radically.

Major changes too were taking place in communications. Mass intercontinental travel was now possible—1960 was the first year in which more people crossed the Atlantic Ocean by air than by sea, and it was not just the rich who were on the move. Tamils were turning up at Heathrow Airport, Turks were providing additional labour for the German economic miracle, and soon millions of the poor were leaving the countryside to swell the great cities of the Third World, not to mention the refugees who, for political and economic reasons, were fleeing across state boundaries, particularly in Africa and Asia. Widespread access to radio and television, and later to the fax and e-mail, meant that information could be sent all over the world virtually instantaneously. This has had a significant impact on global politics, but even more so on the global economy. Financial transactions now amount to something like US $1 trillion per day. Everyone is affected by these new global phenomena that have been with us for the last third of a century in a new and potent form.

Disturbing Trends

It is now possible to identify a number of disturbing trends at the global level, that is, trends which for good or ill, are going to throw

2   D. H. Meadows, D. L. Meadows, et al., *The Limits of Growth: A Report for the Club of Rome's Project on the Predicament of Mankind* (New York: Universe Books, 1972).

issues on to the desks of decision-makers in the next quarter of a century, which will require management in the context of global governance. One such trend is the continuing importance of the arms race whether in vertical form, through the development of new weapons systems, or whether horizontally through the spread of existing weapons systems at either the nuclear or conventional level. The continuing importance of the arms race is derived from the perceived need of major powers to have the capacity to make their own military capital equipment. But since such weapons systems are horrendously expensive, there is also a strong compulsion to sell weapons in order to reduce the unit cost for their taxpayers at home. The spread of sophisticated weaponry is likely to alter substantially the hierarchy of military power, and has therefore considerable political implications. Already, the North Atlantic Treaty Organisation (NATO) feels constrained in the context of Bosnia in the use of its airpower because the Bosnian Serbs have at their disposal sophisticated electronic equipment enabling them to shoot down NATO aircraft. Each of these planes is itself a repository of highly expensive technological equipment and therefore the loss of such a plane with its equally highly trained and expensive pilot, is not a mere bagatelle.

At the other end of the scale of violence there appears to be a growing democratisation in the access to effective means of coercion. Small groups, if they feel that they have nothing to lose, have the physical means to wreak havoc in highly complex, interdependent and open societies. Developed countries are rich because they are open, and this very openness and pluralism renders them vulnerable. Small groups of determined and desperate people, who feel that they have been cut out from decision-making processes, therefore have powerful weapons at their behest. They cannot be ignored because they have the capacity to pull the house down. This has clear implications for the processes of decision-making. It means that no longer can the majority exercise its tyranny or its benevolence—decision-making has to be on the basis of some form of consensus.

If we turn to the sociological level, there is a growing awareness of structural violence, that is the existence of structures which deprive individuals or groups from what they might otherwise expect to be the normal development of their capacities. There is, for example, no reason why a black female should not be president of the United States, but there is a highly effective structural–psychosocial impediment which prevents this happening.

At the global level the processes of the world economy seem to transfer resources from the poor to the rich, not as a matter of deliberate policy, but through the development of the global market as a structure of capitalism. In order to change such processes, there is a demand for participation, not necessarily in the sense of controlling outcomes, but in the subjective sense of individuals and groups playing the role which they consider to be important in the decision-making processes of their choice. The other side of that particular coin is that authority must be earned. It is not derived through ascription or through a bureaucratic hierarchy, but through the acceptance of the constituency where a role is being enacted.

We live in an age of identity politics. We have been long familiar with questions of identity linked with nationalism and ethnicity but new aspects of identity are now playing a more important role, such as gender, race and professional identity. There is a clear need to fashion institutional frameworks whereby one dimension of identity is not denied by the flowering of another. This is an important aspect of the growing concern about human rights which need themselves to be conceived in the context of development. Development is not only an economic question directed towards the fulfilment of basic needs for food, shelter and the like, but also the provision of a context in which an individual or group can develop innate capacities to the highest level given the technical and institutional possibilities of the day. Structural violence often prevents development in this sense and it leads to challenges to the existing structures. If such challenges do not meet with a comprehending response then the means are abundantly available for small, determined, but deprived groups to make their presence felt.

All of this is part of a context of ever-increasing rates of change. In the past, technological innovation was relatively slow. For example, it took one hundred years from the first military use of gunpowder in Europe to its general use throughout Europe. However, it took a mere half century from the first instances of powered flight by human beings to the placing of a man on the moon. In the past, political, economic and social processes had time to adjust themselves to the phenomenon of technological change. Now, that time period is breathtakingly short. We have, in fact, fallen behind. We are broaching many of the problems of the late 20th century, and indeed the 21st century, with the social, intellectual, political and economic tools of the 19th century. Our great and guiding ideas, whether those of capitalism, conservatism, socialism, liberalism and the like, are not ideas of our century, but of previous centuries. Yet our problems are those of the 21st century. We are, therefore, attempting to grapple with the issues of the 21st century with the intellectual tools of the 19th century.

These trends have given rise to a number of issues which collectively form the agenda of global riot control. This agenda includes the arms race, environmental questions, drugs, terrorism, migration, refugees, famine, development, failed or failing states and human rights. It is an agenda largely formulated by the rich and developed, but it is also one that in its effects touches upon the interests of everybody, for we live in a global society. There is therefore a pressing need to formulate the agenda of global riot control on a consensual basis that involves everyone, not just the rich, and to ensure that the concerns of the poor are given appropriate priority in the context of the whole, concerns for economic development, for dealing with the ravages of famine, for the creation of an effective civil society in all parts of the globe.

Leadership

Although the phenomena that have been described are those of our present world, the dilemma is not new. The question of global governance has arisen in the past, as we can see in Michael Mann's stimulating analysis of the bases of social power,[3] not just in our own civilisation but in all civilisations of recorded history. Throughout history Mann finds that societies have been built upon the overlapping interaction of four sources of social power: ideological, economic, military and political. Each is a means to attain human goals and each is a form of social control. Each, from time to time, may dominate and dictate the form of society at large, but they overlap and they are not organic parts of a single social totality. Indeed the interaction and the cohesion of these four dimensions of social power is very loose-fitting. Each has the capacity to give rise to a spurt in global civilisation and they are most likely to do so when they rub up against each other like continental plates, often far from the centre of a dominant civilisation. This analysis suggests that global governance is likely to be highly decentralised. Whether that governance is predominantly economic, as in our own case, or ideological, political or military, as in past cases, it

3   Michael Mann, *The Sources of Social Power* (New York: Cambridge University Press, 1986).

will require leadership.

In another seminal work George Modelski[4] has tried to identify the requirements for leadership of the contemporary world system which has lasted for the last five hundred years. Modelski identifies a number of attributes that a leading power is likely to have if it is to exert leadership successfully, in the context of global governance. It must, for example, have global reach militarily. It is likely to be a stable society which is both open and pluralistic, out of which there is a clear political will to act in a leadership role. Economically a leading power is likely to be significant in terms of world trade, but it is more important that it be at the cutting edge of technological innovation than that it be the largest global economy. Of vital importance is the leading power's capacity to innovate and to respond to world problems. Indeed, the essence is the leading power's ability to exert functional network control, that is to act as the brain controlling the nervous system of global society. Based on such attributes a leading power can ensure, so far as is possible, that the requirements for global governance are met. It plays a major role in forming the global agenda. It mobilises others to act upon that agenda and to arrive at decisions. Those decisions must be implemented and a leading power ensures that this happens, and it must fulfil all of these functions in an innovative manner.

Over the last five hundred years a number of countries have played this leading role in global governance, often in a cycle which lasts for approximately a century which has stages of growth and expansion on the part of the leading power, consolidation and the exercise of the full plenitude of its leadership, followed by a period of decline. The century-long secular framework for political leadership is associated with shorter economic cycles of some thirty years, one such cycle for each major stage of political leadership, that is the growth period, the period of full exercise of leadership and the period of decline. Modelski identifies the countries that have exercised these roles over the last five centuries as Portugal, the Netherlands, Britain which went through two cycles, and now the United States which is in the third stage of its leadership role.

At the present time it is clear that the United States still has global military reach. But so does Russia, and others have the potential for it, such as Japan, China, India and, not least, the European Union. The

4   George Modelski, *Long Cycles in World Politics* (Seattle: University of Washington Press, 1987).

United States is clearly a mainstay of the global economy, but the same could be said for the European Union and Japan, but not of China, India or Russia. It is more difficult to analyse, in other than an impressionistic manner, the factor of cultural leadership, since it is often formed by an amalgam of language, religion, political institutions, consumer tastes and the like. Clearly the United States and the European Union both exert cultural leadership, and in significant portions of the world this is also true of China and India. Russia, on the other hand, has fallen from such leadership with the decline in esteem for communism, and Japan has, as yet, demonstrated scant capacity for cultural leadership on a global scale. The fourth criterion for leadership is the political will to act in such a role. At the present time the United States appears to be flirting again with the idea of isolation. The European Union, too, is intensely preoccupied with its own internal questions, as are Russia and China. The aspirations of Japan and India appear, for the time being, to be regional rather than global. Thus as the United States appears to be in the declining sector of its period of political leadership, there is countervailing power in all the main dimensions even though the United States is clearly the sole superpower in contemporary global politics.

Modelski has pointed out that in such a situation in the past there has usually been a rising power which has challenged for the leadership, often in the form of a general war. However, Modelski also points out that such a war is not inevitable and it is possible to see why it is unlikely in the present context. The ubiquitousness of nuclear weapons is clearly one such reason, but, more positively, there is a realisation that the global problems which give rise to the need for global governance can only be met globally and that we live in a world, not of separate competing powers, but of complex interdependence which is characterised by nodal points in a complicated network of transaction systems in a wide range of functional dimen-sions. These nodal points may be located in North America, in the European Union, and in East Asia, but they are not separate from each other. Indeed they are highly sensitive to each other and interactive. We live in a situation in which there is a realisation that we must hang together or we shall surely hang separately.

This complex interdependence also fortifies the notion that the self-interest of actors includes a strong acknowledgment of community interest. All powers, great and small, benefit significantly from the international community, the more so as the global issues are broached. Large societies may be able to survive better than small societies should the global community collapse, but they will not survive as well as they would within a strong global community. It is therefore in their interests to preserve that community and to look for the rules for good global governance. Small societies that are not willing to pay their community dues will find themselves excluded from the benefits of global governance. We all, therefore, have a self-interest in community interest. But what is, or should be, the institutional framework through which this interest can be expressed in such a way that we might be able to deal with problems, and more positively to take advantage of opportunities?

I would like to suggest that there are three major areas of global governance, that of peace and security (not *international* peace and security), the economic dimension, and the cultural and social dimension. The UN system plays an often important but varying role in each of these three major areas of governance and it is to the analysis of this that we now turn.

Peace and Security

The United Nations, like the League of Nations before it, is based upon the idea of collective security. Collective security is derived from the notion that all the major actors in the system, in this case states in the international political system, will agree upon a set of norms and rules to govern their behaviour, including rules with regard to change. They undertake to follow such rules and apply sanctions against any one of their company which fails to do so in the future. This is not an alliance against a third party, but a collective, that is, a universal security mechanism.

The first attempt to deal with this through an international organisation in the shape of the League of Nations failed because of a lack of universality which was itself an expression of disagreement about basic norms. Germany and the Soviet Union were not allowed initially to join the League and the United States refused to do so. After 1945 a similar failure to agree between the victorious United Nations was quickly evident when the Big Three fell out. Collective security, therefore, was written into the Charter, but the UN, as an institution, did not act upon its implementation. Matters, however, began to change a decade ago when the UN started to behave in peace and security questions along the lines that its founding fathers had intended with a dominant role being acted by the Security Council and, in particular, by its five permanent members (P5).

This change was due to the beginning of the end of the Cold War. Mikhail Gorbachev had come to power in the Soviet Union and he realised that communism was under threat within the Soviet Union. To meet such a threat it was necessary for that country to reduce its global vision and bring back its resources from the other continents of the globe and to use them to reinvigorate Soviet society politically, economically, culturally and socially. Gorbachev saw the UN as a way of effecting, in a relatively smooth manner, his reordering of global priorities for the Soviet Union. Indeed, he was very explicit about his intentions and they were not unnoticed. Sir John Thomson, the British Ambassador to the UN, together with his French colleague, seized upon the opportunity that the time might be right for the P5 to come together to act in concert in the context of the bloody war between Iran and Iraq which was then in stalemate. Eventually the P5 arrived at agreement and were able to sponsor a resolution which brought an end to the fighting between Iran and Iraq. Under British chairmanship the P5 learned new habits of cooperation which led to positive decisions to work together on a number of problems which for long had troubled international peace and security, such as Namibia, Afghanistan, Cambodia and El Salvador to mention but a few.

The Security Council proved to be a congenial environment for this new-found cooperation in matters of peace and security. Clearly it was not perfect, but it was a workable framework. It contained in its permanent members the two military super-powers and two other powers, France and Britain, which had a marginal capacity to exercise military power in a global manner. There were no other powers which were capable of accepting the awesome responsibilities of Chapter VII of the Charter for military enforcement measures, save perhaps India. Neither China, Japan, Germany, Indonesia, Brazil nor Nigeria had either the capacity or in some cases, the political will, to project miliary power globally in a somewhat independent manner. If the Security Council was to be what its name suggested, that is a *Security* Council and not a general political organ, which is the role of the General Assembly, then the most important and relevant powers for this purpose who were able and willing to accept the responsibilities of Chapter VII for enforcement purposes, were present and working in close harmony. Furthermore, the other permanent member of the Council, China, acted as a legitimising agent and the nonaligned members of the Council together held a collective veto. Moreover, the geographical distribution of non-member states in the Council ensured some degree of regional representation. The P5 had developed a new capacity to work together but under the watchful eye of other members of the Council and through them the membership of the organisation in general.

In his first annual report, UN Secretary-General Javier Pérez de Cuéllar had called upon the members of the Security Council to act in a cohesive and responsible manner if the organisation was to survive as a worthwhile agency for the promotion of international peace and security. By the end of the 1980s the Council was functioning in this manner largely along lines that had been intended by its founding fathers. It had built up a degree of legitimacy for its actions, although, as it became more effective in its behaviour, some non-permanent members, and indeed the membership of the UN at large, began to be watchful that there was no abuse of power. Nevertheless they were able to see the advantages of using the UN Security Council as a forum for action in peace and security questions since the role of China, the collective veto of the non-permanent members, and the general ethos of the UN acted as a restraining factor on any tendency of the permanent members, either individually or collectively, to act in an independent manner. Such differences are evident, for example, in the contrast between the unrestrained intervention of the United States in Panama and the degree of restraint and legitimacy that the UN Security Council was able to confer upon the US intervention, most recently, in Haiti.

The greatest test of the Security Council, and with it the P5, to implement collective security arose when Iraq first invaded and then annexed Kuwait. Here, clearly, was an instance when a member state of the UN had violated not only the rules but also the norms of international behaviour on which collective security had been based. While the motives of the P5 may have been mixed, nevertheless they were able, by using the legitimised processes of the UN, to create a coalition of the willing, but hitherto unthinkable, to attempt to bring Iraq back into the fold. The coalition included at its heart a relationship between the United States, United Kingdom and France with strong support from the Soviet Union and tacit support from China, together with substantial political and some military contributions from Syria, Egypt, Saudi Arabia and the Gulf states. In addition, Japan and Germany as well as the Gulf States made a considerable economic contribution. In the Council itself, only Yemen and Cuba expressed any considerable reluctance or opposition. This was therefore a grand attempt at the implementation of collective security through the institutional mechanisms of the UN in order to further the aims of global governance in the area of peace and security.

It is not yet clear whether it has succeeded. To be sure, Kuwait is now fully independent within secure and recognised international borders. There has been a sort of functional occupation of Iraq, not only in the north and south for humanitarian purposes, but also throughout its territory to ensure, through adequate inspection and verification procedures, that Iraq will continue *ad infinitum* to implement the clauses of Security Council Resolution 687—'the mother of all resolutions'—in regard to its nuclear capacity, its missiles with a range greater than 150km, and other weapons of mass destruction. To enforce these highly intrusive derogations of its sovereignty the UN has imposed, and continues to impose, draconian economic sanctions, backed with the threat and occasional implementation of further military sanctions. But has collective security been seen finally to work as an instrument of global governance?

To a significant extent the UN has failed. Although Iraq was defeated its government remains in office and, despite compliance with virtually all the provisions of Resolution 687, there is no guarantee that once sanctions have been lifted, Iraq will continue to honour these obligations. The government of Saddam Hussein may have seen the error of its tactics but it has certainly not seen the error of its ways. This faces those who have prosecuted a policy of collective security with an awesome dilemma. Should they maintain existing sanctions despite Iraq having fulfilled the letter of the law, in which case the coalition is likely to split? Should they lift the sanctions, and then be faced with the dilemma of what to do if Iraq no longer complies with its undertakings under Resolution 687? The United States and Britain therefore face the dilemma on how to lift sanctions without putting Saddam Hussein in a position whereby he can revert to the *status quo ante*. Coercion in the pursuit of collective security, if it is to be effective, must be continuous, and if it continuous it is costly.

By being inflexible Saddam Hussein has nothing to lose that he has not lost already. He can doubtless afford to wait for the resolve of others to weaken. In this sense for the coalition the price of victory and the implementation of collective security was merely a down payment. The leading powers of the coalition are weary of paying the subsequent instalments, an end to which is nowhere in sight as long as the Saddam Hussein regime stays in power. The present Iraqi government does not share the norms of collective security as set out by the international community in a number of important aspects. Saddam Hussein has withstood, at terrible cost to his people, the military and economic sanctions of collective security. He has been bent to the will of the UN in withdrawing from and acknowledging the sovereignty and the boundaries of Kuwait. He has bent to the will of the UN in implementing the provisions of Security Council Resolution 687 in their virtual entirety, but his will has not been broken and he is now in a position to test the will of the coalition. Collective security has worked, but it may yet fail because, ultimately, it cannot be based on coercion but only on the willing acceptance of basic norms by all actors in the system. If those who do not share such norms are able to survive in the manner that Saddam Hussein has done, then any victory secured in the name of collective security is likely to be both pyrrhic and burdensome.

Thus, even in the dramatic and clearcut case of Iraq, the principle of collective security as the main foundation stone of peace and security at the international level has not been vindicated. The P5 have played a useful role in the last decade in the global governance of international peace and security. Their approach from the top down has had a substantial degree of legitimacy from their constituency. However, their successes have also revealed that, while they can lead and cajole, they cannot in the long term command. In the long term global governance can only be brought about through consent.

Peacekeeping

The implementation of the full plenitude of enforcement action under Chapter VII of the Charter, as in the Iraq–Kuwait affair, has not been the normal way of dealing with questions of international peace and security. Although there is no mention of peacekeeping in the UN Charter the exigency of the Cold War meant that the UN could only act during much of the half century of its existence in questions of international peace and security through the development of the concept of peacekeeping. Peacekeeping is based on the three fundamental principles of consent by the parties in dispute, be they states or non-state actors; impartiality on the part of the UN, in the sense of no obvious bias towards any of the parties in dispute; and restraint from using enforcement measures Peacekeeping fell under a notional Chapter VI and a half, between the provisions of the Charter dealing with the pacific settlement of disputes and those dealing with threats to peace, breaches of the peace, and acts of aggression.

The new climate engendered by the end of the Cold War and the initial success of enforcement measures against Iraq gave rise to a notion there might be a possibility to go beyond traditional peacekeeping to peace-enforcement. This idea was enshrined in a paper prepared by the Secretary-General of the behest of the Security Council entitled *An Agenda for Peace*.[5] However, it has since become evident that the principles first laid down by Secretary-General Dag Hammarskjöld for peacekeeping were correctly based on the notion that there is a clear gap between action based on the consent of the parties and enforcement. What is sometimes called the grey area between the two is in fact a skid zone, which if ventured upon will quickly lead from peacekeeping by consent to enforcement action. The debate is still open since UN officials continue to embrace the idea of what they call 'strategic consent' in which there will be tactical enforcement in particular circumstances. But the division between strategic and tactical is not clear. What may be tactical for one may be seen as strategic by another; it all depends at which end of the barrel of the gun one is placed.

What is clear from these examples of collective security and peacekeeping is that there is no easy answer. Yet our views for the global governance of questions of peace and security through the UN institutions have advanced. Freelance intervention is now less likely and the legitimising approval of the Security Council, including its non-permanent members, is a growing necessity for any action which smacks of military intervention. But what of humanitarian intervention?

Humanitarian Intervention

The Security Council has encouraged humanitarian intervention, initially through Resolution 688 which has led to continuing military activity in support of humanitarian intervention in northern Iraq. But such muscled humanitarian intervention has also destroyed, or at least besmirched, the growing acceptance of UN humanitarian agencies, so that in some instances they are now seen as the more acceptable face of

---

5   Boutros Boutros-Ghali, *An Agenda for Peace: Preventive Diplomacy, Peacemaking, and Peace-keeping* (New York: United Nations, 1992).

the P5 and the Security Council, for example, the UN High Commissioner for Refugees (UNHCR) in Iraq. As humanitarian non-government organisations (NGOs) also often work within the protection of the P5 and the Security Council, they too take on a political colouration. Only the International Committee of the Red Cross (ICRC) appears to have maintained a pristine purity of neutrality. UN action for humanitarian purposes in Somalia demonstrated clearly the limits for humanitarian intervention and the dangers of moving towards war for humanitarian purposes. There have been similar instances in the former Yugoslavia. Nevertheless, from a humanitarian point of view, the UN Protection Force in former Yugoslavia (UN-PROFOR) has been a success. Politically there has been no extension of the conflict, although that may yet occur. The death rate has declined as the effectiveness of UNPROFOR has increased. In 1992 100,000 people died; in 1993, 3000; and in 1994, 1500. Some 2.7 million people have been fed including 600,000 Bosnian Serbs that their leaders would not otherwise have been able to feed. But in all of this peacekeeping is a palliative; it is not peacemaking.

Peacekeeping operations, humanitarian intervention and enforcement activity brings into question Article 2(7) of the UN Charter which protects the domestic jurisdiction of states. However, while the interpretation of Article 2(7) is changing, no member state of the UN is likely to call for its abolition. But the change is real, if subtle. Article 2(7) is no longer an absolute but it competes as one guiding principle among several. It may be the principle on which an approach to an issue turns, but unlike hitherto, it is not necessarily so. Other principles such as human rights, humanitarian intervention and the like, may gain precedence over the principle of domestic jurisdiction. This is particularly likely to be the case in the situation of failed or failing states, such as Yugoslavia, Somalia, Afghanistan or Haiti, examples which indicate that the phenomenon is not restricted to any one continent. Faced with the failure of a state, actual or potential, the UN is confronted by an agonising dilemma, should it and can it intervene?

It has become evident that the UN cannot act as an collective colonial power and it can only rarely use enforcement measures. However, the United Nations can take guidance, and perhaps comfort, from a central notion in the Charter, that of the self-determination of peoples. This, after all, is not only written into the Charter but has been part of the practice of the UN throughout the era of decolonisation. Thus, in the context of global governance, the UN may be empowered to help people in the exercise of their self-determination through the modalities of peacekeeping, humanitarian intervention, and technical assistance through the specialised agencies and programmes. The UN programme in Cambodia was a relatively successful attempt to give the people of Cambodia the possibility once again of exercising their right of self-determination. Given the magnitude of the exercise and the difficulty of the circumstances, the UN programme, in its totality, must be seen as a success. But such programmes are dependent on the availability of significant resources and they must be undertaken on the basis of a broad consensus led by the Security Council and endorsed by the local parties. The success of the UN operation in Cambodia has not created a panacea, but merely contributed experience to a difficult learning process.

The Economic Dimension

There has been a learning process in the management of the global economy when the 1930s is compared with the post-Second World War and contemporary practices and institutions for global economic management. In the 1930s it was a matter of pursuing 'beggar-my-neighbour' policies which ultimately led to the consequences being fed back on to those who had perpetuated such policies, often with interest added. This is no longer the case, and the institutional framework for the management of the global economy is partially within and partially without the UN system. Three key institutions are not in the United Nations, namely the OECD, the group of seven industrialised states (G7) and, by unanimous recent decision, the World Trade Organisation (WTO). The OECD was established in 1960, after the recovery from the Second World War, as a rich country club. The G7 is an even richer country club. It is hard to avoid the conclusion that the management processes are by the few and in the interests of the few. Even the WTO, which has a much broader membership, is in essence a most-favoured-nation treaty negotiated by the big three—the North American Free Trade Agreement (NAFTA) powers, the European Union (EU), and Japan. This is not to say that there is no recognition by the rich countries, that they, too, have a stake in the common interest which embraces the rest of the world but, nevertheless, their intellectual prisms start from the needs of the world's economy as conceived by those who are the chief beneficiaries of that economy.

It is important to note, too, that global governance in the economic dimension is severely hampered by the absence from the institutional framework of many important economic actors, such as transnational corporations (TNCs), banks and the like. For instance, if we compare the gross domestic product of states with the turnover of transnational corporations, then in terms of size TNCs would occupy 41 of the top 100 places. Such actors have no place in the UN institutions either—the principal two of which are the IMF and the World Bank. The IMF is a reflection of the economic power of its members, and the World Bank must reflect market conditions if it is to function effectively. Both therefore are top-down organisations which have made extensive use of conditionality before being willing to accede to the requests of their clients. To this extent they are quasi-enforcement agencies in the economic sphere, just as the P5 acts in the peace and security sphere. Those agencies within the UN system which are more geared to the interests and philosophy of its economically weaker states, such as UNCTAD (UN Conference on Trade and Development) and UNIDO (UN Industrial Development Organisation), are themselves under threat as institutions.

The UN system therefore is dominated by the structural adjustment programmes of the international financial institutions which have in effect destroyed the welfare states in the Third World. They have influenced policy on a wide range of issues such as state ownership, the role of the private sector, the expenditures to be made on development programmes and the external value of currency. The question must therefore be raised, to what purpose has this been done and in whose interests?

The Specialised Agencies and the UN System

The Economic and Social Council (ECOSOC) was conceived by the founding fathers of the Charter as the major forum for global governance in a wide range of economic, social, cultural and technical matters. It is universally held that ECOSOC has failed to achieve this goal and is unlikely to do so in the future. There are a number of reasons why this should be so. The first is that the UN specialist agencies themselves are separate institutions with their own constitution, membership, budget and secretariat, and while the membership of the agencies is largely the same as the membership of the General Assembly, states act in one forum to guard its privileged position against the exigencies of another, and against the establishment of a central system of control for the UN system as a whole. In short, the specialised agencies act in most cases as independent fiefdoms.

There has been some discussion in recent months of the possibility of establishing an Economic Security Council to match that which is concerned with Chapters VI and VII of the Charter in peace and security questions. However attractive in some ways the idea is, it would imply a dismantling of the agencies as independent entities which will be no mean task in itself, and also the willingness of the major economic powers to forgo their frameworks beyond the UN system, such as the OECD and G7, in favour of a UN entity. This they are unlikely to do, since they favour acting through limited membership organisations which reflect their particular values and interests rather than through the UN, which is, in the last resort, a universal organisation. As for the notion that any Economic Security Council might be matched by a Social Security Council, there is no market for this idea whatsoever.

The UN system has evolved from a concentration on the sectoral approach represented by the specialised agencies to a framework which embraces not only the sectoral approach but also a country focus, and has recently developed an important and new contribution to global governance in the shape of special conferences.

The establishment of a range of specialised agencies represented an institutionalisation of the theory of functionalism, that is, the notion that if particular functions, such as health or food and agriculture, could be kept separate from the political work of the UN system, then issues in these dimensions would be tackled in a less politicised manner with a greater scope for decision-making on the basis of technical knowledge. Thus health issues would not be negotiated from a power-political point of view, but managed on a basis of expert opinion. Unfortunately this institutional device has not depoliticised the issues in the specialised agencies to the extent that the US and the UK have felt constrained to leave the UN Educational, Scientific and Cultural Organisation (UNESCO). The United States also withdrew from the International Labour Organisation (ILO) for a short period.

The specialised agencies as a group are dominated by the big four—the World Health Organisation (WHO), ILO, the Food and Agriculture Organisation (FAO) and UNESCO. All of these have substantial successes to their credit, but they also have had difficulties. The political response by the US and the UK has already been mentioned and it is widely acknowledged that there are grounds for reform, not only of the system overall, in the context of ECOSOC, but also of the individual institutions. It is important, however, to note the

ILO has a unique tripartite structure in which governments, labour and management from each of the member states of the organisation act in an independent manner.

The more technical agencies, such as the World Meteorological Organisation (WMO), the International Telecommunications Union (ITU), the Universal Postal Union (UPU) and the like, are both less politicised and more successful. Moreover, it should not be forgotten that there is virtually no aspect of our lives which is not touched by the work of one or several of the UN specialised agencies. The number of international treaties and negotiated norms and standards that are required for an simple act like having breakfast, is a salutary reminder of the way in which the work of UN infiltrates into daily life. The controversy regarding these organisations, besides the question of politicisation, revolves around the extent to which the agencies should have active programmes with the consequent growth of budgets and secretariats, or should confine themselves essentially to norm evolution and standard setting. There is no controversy that a major function of the agencies is norm evolution and standard setting, and this they do well. Consider, for example, the ILO, which over the years has evolved several hundred standards concerning such basic questions of human rights as equal pay for women and the conditions of child labour.

But the world is organised not only on sectoral lines, and the work by UN agencies needs to be fashioned into a coherent whole in the context of a particular country. Thus, the UN Development Programme (UNDP) has brought together the work of the agencies, often on a subcontractual basis, to form a policy to meet the needs of particular countries, and it is the principal agency of the UN for the undertaking of programmes. It therefore plays, particularly in the Third World, a vital role in making the UN system as a whole effective in the field. It is at this level, too, that the UN system can work in harness with a wide range of NGOs. As general rule the further UN activities take place away from headquarters the easier it is to achieve coordination and complementarity in the setting of goals in a specific context, and the achievement of tasks derived therefrom.

It has been widely acknowledged that peacekeeping is a major UN activity that was not foreseen by the Charter, but it is not the only one. A feature of the last fifty years has been the growing number of NGOs established and an expansion in their expertise, resources and range of activities. It is clear, as we have seen in consideration of

UNDP above, that the UN system needs to collaborate with, indeed to incorporate, a wide range of NGOs if it is to be effective in its pursuance of its role in global governance. The founders of the UN recognised this in making provision for some incorporation of NGOs within the work of ECOSOC, but ECOSCO has not fulfilled the role in the system which the founders intended. Nevertheless, NGOs have been incorporated in the system through the development of special conferences of which several hundred have been held over the last thirty years.[6] These conferences take a single issue and attempt to establish norms and frameworks from which programmes can be derived in a coherent framework. A typical example of such a conference was the environment conference in Stockholm in 1972, and its recent successor-conference held in Rio de Janeiro.

At such conferences, besides the delegates, who spend many months preparing the conference, there is a parallel and interacting NGO forum whether in the preparatory conferences, the actual conference itself, or in the follow-up programmes. Indeed, there is a symbiotic relationship between the government delegations and the NGO presence at such conferences. NGOs bring knowledge and resources and therefore play a vital role in the establishment of standards. They are also an important vehicle for their implementation. To a significant extent they have been incorporated into the system in this manner and it is perhaps appropriate to see special conferences as a major new form of decision-making for global governance. They also constitute a significant development in the UN system which is complementary to the existing frameworks for the sectoral agencies and the UNDP with its country focus. However, this is not to suggest that all NGOs have these desirable characteristics. Some are no more than interest groups involved in special pleading and may be undemocratic in their structure and lack transparency. They can be inefficient and represent no one but themselves. But at their best they are a vital component in global governance and they have now been incorporated to some degree within the UN system. This therefore constitutes a significant new element in global governance.

As we have seen in both special conferences and in the agencies, a major activity of the UN system is the setting of norms. Nowhere is this more important than in the field of human rights. Early in its existence the UN, besides setting out human rights in the Charter, also

6   See Paul Taylor and A. J. R. Groom, eds, *Global Issues in the United Nations Framework* (Basingstoke: Macmillan, 1989).

negotiated the Universal Declaration of Human Rights of 1948. The value system which underlies this declaration has in recent years been under some challenge as reflecting Western values rather than universal values. It would, of course, be difficult to deny that there are cultural relativities. But there are also shared notions of right and wrong by which standards can be set in the UN framework. These notions of right and wrong are shared because they are often related to social assets that we all seem to need, such as personal and group security, a sense of personal and group identity, notions of development in the sense of self-actualisation for individuals and groups, and an ubiquitous demand for participation. There is, therefore, a shared starting point, but it has to be admitted that many of the ways in which these needs are manifested is through a cultural screen which gives them, in practice, a wide range of practical expression. Nevertheless, there is a substantial area of agreement not only in the formulation of the Universal Declaration of Human Rights, but also in support for the General Assembly resolutions on economic and social rights and other questions such as the rights of the child.

Norm setting by the agencies is also a method of expressing and implementing human rights and these are further buttressed by other UN institutions such as the Commission on Human Rights. Moreover, of late, Article 2(7) has lost a little of its potency in impeding the universal expression and implementation of human rights. For example, the campaigns against apartheid and humanitarian intervention in the face of gross human rights abuses in various countries are firm indications that Article 2(7) has lost its full rigour. However, this is merely an occasional example of a trend away from a restrictive interpretation of Article 2(7).

Towards Global Governance in the UN System

In its quest to be an instrument for the furtherance of global governance, the UN system faces many problems, three of which are of particular significance. The first concerns the incorporation of a wide range of actors into effective participation in decision-making processes; the second relates to the tension that the system often manifests between human and institutional values; and the third relates to the aspiration for a greater degree of democracy in the system.

The UN Charter opens with the words 'We the peoples of the United Nations', a phrase which, to say the least, is economical with the truth. The United Nations is an organisation of member governments. Some non-state actors have an acknowledged place in the system either through observer status with ECOSOC or through participation in special conferences. Yet the demands of global governance require that all major actors who have a role to play in the issues which are on the global agenda ought to be incorporated, within the UN framework, in a organic manner. Transnational corporations for example, have virtually no place in the system, yet it would be foolish to ignore them since they can command great resources, both material and psychological; they can act in a political manner; and they are an important conduit for the movement of ideas, goods, services and people all over the world. The problems of governance are not only of an interstate nature or of inter-governmental nature, but they also have an important and increasing intra-state and transnational aspect which demands that all manner of actors be incorporated into the decision-making process for their management. In short, the UN does not reflect global civil society and it cannot play its role in an effective manner in search for global governance until it does so reflect global civil society.

Fifty years ago the founders of the UN system were fully aware of the need to provide and safeguard human needs. They had just lived through the tumultuous experiences of two world wars and a great depression. They sought to fashion institutions which would reflect such human needs. But organisations over time develop their own institutional needs which may in fact frustrate human needs. Those governments and peoples which have greatest need of the services that the UN system can provide may be excluded from those services because of their incapacity to meet the institutional demands which are a prelude to the provision of services. The UN as a system is tied to the idea of sovereignty and to states and governments as members, and its institutional needs are based on this. They therefore need to be broadened to reflect the changing human needs of global civil society. Only fitful progress has been made in this direction, but without it the United Nations as a system will be inadequate, inept and plainly inappropriate.

Global governance does not equate with the United Nations. Rather, the UN is a part of the institutional framework for global governance. In the face of the demands for global governance, the UN has adapted, but not enough. This is typical of an anarchical global society. In order to overcome the worst aspects of the anarchical nature of global society, leadership is required. Can the leading powers and other leading actors of civil society provide it? Do they have the will to do so? Moreover, can they create conditions in which there are willing followers?

The need to satisfy followers as well as leaders has not been a prime concern of the UN system, as we have seen when examining the P5, the Security Council and the international financial institutions, not to mention some of the agencies. The UN system is a top-down institution which has a substantial democratic deficit. Democracy in this sense suggests a greater need for representation of global society, a responsiveness to its needs, the enhancement of means of participation in decision-making, and transparency in such processes, whether in that of establishing standards or of implementing them. The UN system is not good in any of these four functions, but it has improved. It also has to be acknowledged that there is a long way to go.

Perhaps now, after five hundred years, we are moving towards a clearer, more conscious system of global governance to match the global economic framework of capitalism which is the motor of the contemporary world system. We do indeed live in interesting times, which the Chinese wish upon people as a curse. For us it is a challenge to design a system of global governance which will be adequate for the growing integrated nature of global civil society. It is a challenge that must be met.

(Left to right): Lt. Gen. Sir Michael Rose, Ambassador Bruce Brown and Dr Roberto Rabel, Otago Foreign Policy School, 1995. (Photo: Ian McGibbon)

Bruce Brown

Summary:
A Mid-Life Crisis for the UN at Fifty

We have had a rich feast at the School with fourteen speakers producing a profusion of facts and ideas. I was reminded of a comment about the complexities of Sukarno's Indonesia, made by Marshall Green, then US Ambassador, in the 1950s: 'Anybody who is not thoroughly confused is just not well informed'. I will seek to dispel any confusion by dealing with key issues which arose during the conference and refer to speakers, directly and indirectly, in this process.

Trends in the World

Professor James Rosenau set the intellectual stage with his thoughtful analysis of trends, changes and tensions in the world. I found myself in agreement with most of his conclusions and share some of his pessimism although—not having his erudition, and not having to prove every statement to academic critics—I reached similar conclusions by a more direct route.

I was struck by his description of conflicting tensions between a state-centred world and a multi-centred world. I had thought of this as two conflicting tides, an economic tide flowing towards greater interdependence in the world, and a political tide flowing in the contrary direction, producing outbursts of nationalism, celebrations of local identity and self-realisation, and at times a rabid nationalism. I wonder now whether they are necessarily always conflicting. One may in fact create the other. Are we moving back towards a world of relationships more akin to the city-states and principalities which existed in the 18th and into the early 19th century, before the tide of nationalism, governmentalism and welfare of the later 19th and the 20th century overtook us? Perhaps the 21st century will become more like the 18th, plus mechanisation and electronics.

It was the ideal world of Ernest Bevin, British Labour Foreign Secretary at the end of the Second World War, that he should be able to go to Victoria Station and take a train to anywhere without a passport or visa. I doubt very much whether that world will come to pass. Today is the age of information and mobility of peoples. It is estimated that there are anywhere between 80 million and 100 million people in the world actively looking to shift to another country. I suspect that passports and visas will be with us for a long time yet. But certainly we are heading towards a much more complicated, decentralised and multi-headed world. Professor John Groom dated a marked acceleration in this respect from about 1960, an interesting conclusion.

Evaluating the United Nations

Successes

Malcolm Templeton gave us as an excellent account of the origins of the United Nations and New Zealand's role in it over 50 years. He listed its achievements and its failings. First, among its achievements, he cited its longevity—the very fact that it has already outlasted the League of Nations by 25 years.

Second was its universality—this is in contrast to the conception of 1945 which stressed that membership was open to 'peaceloving states'. In fact the United Nations represented the victorious wartime coalition. I can well remember as a schoolboy the tide of declarations of war on Germany and Japan by numerous Latin American states in early 1945, timed to permit them to attend the founding conference of the United Nations in San Francisco—although none of their citizens had fired a shot in anger during the war except perhaps at each other.

Third in Templeton's reckoning was human rights. The UN has put human rights into international law, despite some conflict between Article 2(7) which provides that nothing in the Charter should permit the UN to interfere in matters within the domestic jurisdiction of states, and Article 55 which deals with international economic and social cooperation and provides the basis for the UN to set economic and social standards. There is talk from time to time of some further clarification of the Charter provisions being necessary in this field. I would strongly support the view of Senator Gareth Evans, in his forceful opening speech, that this question should be treated like the development of common law, and made the subject of political decisions on a case-by-case basis rather than by legal definitions.

When in fact does a human rights situation justify UN intervention? My answer is—when the Security Council or a General Assembly majority says it does. I do have a caveat, however, about the preparation and adoption of international legal instruments. Templeton referred to the fact that many New Zealand critics of some of our recent social legislation failed to realise they were merely putting into our domestic law what we had accepted in international instruments at least twelve years previously. The point is, however, that very few people including parliamentarians realise this. One of New Zealand's leading constitutional lawyers, Sir Kenneth Keith, has urged that there should be a greater opportunity for parliamentary scrutiny of these international instruments before New Zealand signs or ratifies them.

Fourth, Templeton ranked the UN's achievements in improving the welfare of colonial peoples, particularly the ending of colonialism. This was achieved substantially after the influx of new African members post-1960 when the remaining colonial situations came under increasingly critical scrutiny from an anti-colonial majority in the General Assembly and its various organs, notably the Fourth Committee. The new member states—and over thirty African states were admitted between 1960 and 1963—were proud of their independence and jealous of their sovereignty. Something of the emotional atmosphere of that time is illustrated by the story of an ambassador from a northern African state, who looked and sounded like an elegant Frenchman, who attended a welcoming reception given by the delegation of a newly-admitted black African state. At it he met a black African woman delegate who was plainly surprised to see him. 'What African country do you represent?' she asked. He told her. She asked, 'How long have you been independent?' 'Seven years' he replied. 'Fancy that', she said, 'independent only seven years, and white already'!

Fifth, Templeton ranked economic and social work without, however, developing this theme, which indeed was not fully examined at the School itself.

Sixth—I would add—the development and codification of the Law of the Sea, in which Malcolm Templeton himself played an important role as New Zealand's chief representative in the negotiations for some eight years.

Failures

As to the failures, Templeton listed first the reluctance of member states to give up their sovereignty to the extent that the Charter might have envisaged.

Second, Templeton found the UN to have been wanting in keeping the peace, the heart of the organisation, although he conceded that it had had some successes notably in Korea (1950–53), Suez (1956), South Africa (its contribution towards the end of apartheid) and Kuwait (the defeat of Iraq in 1991). Bosnia he thought a failure. Is it? The Minister, the Rt Hon. Don McKinnon, delivered a corrective to this viewpoint in his opening speech when he listed the achievements of the UN Protection Force (UNPROFOR) in Bosnia even with the stalemate in the situation which then pertained, stressing that the UN was feeding a population of almost three million people and that it had led to a dramatic reduction since its intervention in the rate of deaths from the conflict, sadly though that continued.

Thirdly, Templeton ranked civil wars—the outbreak with increasing frequency of intra-state conflicts.

Fourthly, he listed disarmament in which the UN achievements were slight, in that the principal negotiations had taken place among the great powers outside its framework. I would raise a question here. The United Nations certainly has exercised an overview but if bilateral or multilateral negotiations outside it result in significant agreements, as they have, it seems to me that this itself is highly worthwhile. (Incidentally, New Zealand was the first to criticise the French decision to test nuclear weapons in the South Pacific—in the 1963 General Debate in the General Assembly—and the first to actually pronounce the six letter word 'France' in this respect. Other delegations which mentioned it—few—generally referred opaquely to 'that European power for whose long traditions of civilisation and culture we have profound respect' or some such circumlocution.)

The final two areas of UN failure, Templeton thought, were its continuing financial crisis and its excessive bureaucracy; and the failure of the Economic and Social Council (ECOSOC), which had defied many efforts at reform, to play the role envisaged for it in the Charter. To sum up, a mixed record over the years but some solid achievements too.

Reform of the United Nations

At the heart of our discussions and well analysed by many speakers, notably Senator Evans, Mr McKinnon, Ambassador Otunnu, Dr Bercovitch, Professor Shinyo, Professor Groom and Dr Suter, were the various problems of UN reform. I was reminded of their complexity and the barriers against them by the very title of a paper to be given by Professor Richard Falk at the forthcoming conference at La Trobe University, Melbourne, 'The necessity of reforming the United Nations and the impossibility of doing it'.

The Charter

I agree with Malcolm Templeton that 1945 represented a high point in international cooperation from which member states have since retreated. Frank Corner, New Zealand's Permanent Representative to the UN in the 1960s, remarked at that time that were we to put the Charter on the table for renegotiation we should be likely to lose large parts of it which were important to the Western world. I suspect that might well be true today, especially in areas related to human rights.

Olara Otunnu commented that the Charter was still surprisingly up-to-date in many respects but he noted two particular omissions: first, environmental questions; and second, transnational corporations. To these I would add a third, non-government organisations (NGOs) more generally. As Otunnu said, the UN represents an existing power structure. If it did not, he said, it would be utopian; but if it was only that, it would represent *realpolitik*. The United Nations, he concluded, must remain a place where ideas matter.

In my view, reform of the Charter should be approached with caution. I would judge it a better tactic to press for changes which can be made without a Charter amendment, 'micro-changes' as Keith Suter described them, rather than 'macro-changes', a subject to which I shall return.

The Security Council

There are two basic questions concerning possible reform of the Security Council. First, its composition which would, of course, require an amendment to the Charter, and therefore ratification by all five permanent members. Second, its modes of working which, however, could be altered by agreement among member states as to administrative practice.

But membership is a problem, especially that of the permanent members. Who will give up the right of veto? Would France? The addition of new permanent members is equally difficult. Should one add Germany and Japan? Who else? Where do you stop? There are no lack of suggestions but to obtain agreement would, I suspect, be very difficult and certainly too hard at present.

An increase in non-permanent members is likely to be easier. There are various suggestions—an increase of six, or eight, or ten. Don McKinnon, quoting New Zealand permanent representative Colin Keating, suggested there might be an increase of nine to give a total of 24 which would permit each non-permanent member to hold the presidency of the Council in the course of their two-year term. (The presidency of the Council rotates amongst the delegations each month, in alphabetical sequence.) It is the fashion, incidentally, for the incoming president to praise the outgoing president for his or her contribution to international peace and security in the preceding month. On one occasion, during my time in the New Zealand delegation to the UN, an incoming president praised the outgoing president, Adlai Stevenson, the US Ambassador, excessively since there had been no meeting of the Council in the preceding month and the world scene had been unusually quiet. This was a bit too much for Stevenson who, with his usual eloquence, replied along the following lines: 'Mr President, I thank you for your most generous remarks. Assuredly you will go to heaven for the virtue of charity if you do not first go another place for the sin of exaggeration'.

If a consensus could be developed it might well be that an increase of non-permanent members could be approved by the necessary amendment to the Charter. There is a precedent from 1963 when an Afro–Asian–Latin American majority (with New Zealand support) co-sponsored a resolution in the General Assembly which provided for an increase of four non-permanent members to the Council as well as an increase of nine members to ECOSOC. The permanent members were most unenthusiastic about this initiative. The United States and Britain abstained on the resolution, being prepared to support an increase of only two non-permanent members to the Security Council. The Soviet Union and France took the view that no increase at all was necessary and voted against the resolution. However, by the time of the 1965 General Assembly session, sufficient momentum had developed for the increase as to induce both the Soviet Union (the Beijing government having agreed, despite the presence in the UN of the Nationalist Chinese) and France, along with Nationalist China, Britain, and the United States, to ratify the necessary amendments to the Charter, and the increase was thus effected. It was in consequence of this that New Zealand stood for and was elected to the Security

Council at the 1965 Assembly for the 1966 year. The New Zealand role in the 1963 initiative had been a prominent one and the personal links Frank Corner had with members of the Latin American group (notably the Mexicans) played a part in bringing the Latins on board to an increase of four and their readiness therefore to co-sponsor the resolution with the Africans and Asians, which gave it its overwhelming character.

There was some discussion amongst speakers, notably the two Ministers, in response to questions, as to whether we might not need some major failure on the part of the UN in the peace and security field to provide a sufficient impetus to push for a reform of the composition of the Security Council. But it was widely felt, including by them, that such a price might well prove too high.

The question of the veto arises both in connection with the functioning of the present Council and more acutely with the question of whether any new permanent members might be given the same privileges. The veto was inserted in the Charter at the insistence of all five permanent members who would not have accepted the United Nations without it. There was a certain logic in this. The beginnings of great-power divisions were already apparent and none of the permanent members was ready to have a collective security organisation which could legalise coercion against them. In following years, however, there is no question but that the veto was greatly abused, particularly at first by the Soviet Union which exercised more than 80 vetoes when Britain and France had each used only one and the United States none. A change in the composition of the enlarged Council, however, later meant that the United States and the other Western powers were obliged to use the veto more often to protect what they judged to be their interests. In many cases they too used vetoes for what could not be rated as vital interests. The most recent example is the United States veto of a resolution supported by all the other 14 members of the Council which would have condemned Israel for its plans to extend settlements in Jerusalem on land disputed by the Palestinians. No doubt this veto was cast because of US domestic political pressures. It must be said, however, that even the vetoed resolution had some impact. The Israeli government suspended its proposed action, no doubt in large part as a result of bilateral pressure from the United States but also, one may suppose, taking cognisance of the clearly expressed opinion of the vast majority of the Council. In this sense the Council can act as a court of international opinion with some effectiveness, even where a resolution is blocked.

An interesting proposal has been made by Professor Lincoln Bloomfield, formerly of the Massachusetts Institute of Technology, and earlier an American diplomat, that the veto might be confined, by a convention in practice, to Chapter VII issues, which might be deemed by their nature to involve important interests. This, he has said, was discussed at the Yalta Conference of the Big Three in 1945, although it did not find its way into the Charter. It is possible that this change in practice could be effected without a Charter amendment in much the same way as there has been in effect an amendment to the Charter in the voting requirements of the permanent members. Article 27(3) requires that for a resolution to carry in the Council—other than on procedural questions—it must have the concurring votes of all five permanent members. For many years, however, since 1950 or before, it has been accepted practice that the permanent members do not need to vote in favour of a resolution. They may abstain and yet the resolution will still carry. This has often been the case and was recently so in a number of the resolutions directed against Iraq, on which China abstained without the resolutions thereby failing.

One further thought on the veto—if there are to be additional non-permanent members then the number of votes necessary in the Council to represent a majority sufficient to carry a resolution—at present 9 out of 15—would also need to be increased. This would mean that the five permanent members could more easily be outvoted by the non-permanent members. That in turn might put pressure on the permanent members to exercise the veto more often. We might therefore find that an increase of non-permanent members to the Council could result in a revival of the veto. Currently it has been used only twice in the last three years, once by Russia over the financing of the Cyprus Force (scarcely a vital interest) and once by the United States, as mentioned, on the question of Israeli proposals in Jerusalem.

Professor Shinyo set out very clearly the views of Japan on the reform of the Council and Japan's aspirations to permanent membership. On the question of the veto—whether Japan would accept permanent membership without that privilege—he responded that the position of the Japanese government was one of 'neither confirm nor deny'.

The central part of his paper dealt with the restrictions arising from the Japanese constitution on the use of Japanese armed forces and the differences on interpretation of Article 9 between the strict constructionists, who believed that it would allow only for self defence, and the more liberal constructionists, who believed that it could permit Japanese participation in UN peacekeeping forces. But both schools of thought were of the view that Japan could not participate, because of its constitutional restrictions, in UN enforcement actions under Chapter VII of the Charter. Professor Shinyo quoted Secretary-General Boutros Boutros-Ghali as saying that this should not inhibit Japan's aspirations for permanent membership and that there were neither legal nor political requirements for a permanent member to participate in enforcement actions. It may well be true that there are no such legal requirements but I would question whether there would not be some political expectations. It seems to me that it would be very difficult for a permanent member of the Council to authorise an enforcement action, join with the Council in appealing to member states to offer forces, but then to say that it could not itself participate.

Other Issues

There were, of course, many other questions of UN reform which were canvassed in the course of the School. One example was the possibility of a change in electoral groups for Australia and New Zealand, that they might look to join an Asia–Pacific grouping and leave the Western European and Other (WEO) group in which they were placed by the Afro–Asian–Latin American resolution for the expansion of the Council in 1963—with minimal consultation, incidentally. Along with Canada, we were simply informed that this was the majority's intention and had no real option but to go along with it. The possibility of our joining an Asia–Pacific group was then looked at but the numbers were not right (even if a change could then have been agreed) which conclusion has been reached on several occasions since. Perhaps it is time for another look at that prospect.

Other problems, such as the UN's continuing financial crisis, and the question of the excessive bureaucracy of the Secretariat—even although it is not a large one by comparison with the national bureaucracies of most member states—can all be tackled by means other than Charter amendment. It is essentially a matter of political will.

Peacekeeping, Peace-enforcement, and All That

There was some highly pertinent analysis of the problems of peacekeeping and the possibility of reforms, notably by Senator Evans on a macro-scale, and in greater detail by General Sanderson, General Rose, Colonel O'Reilly and Professor Austin. Some of their conclusions may be summarised as follows.

First, peacekeeping is fundamentally different from peace-enforcement and should be kept separate. If the circumstances of an operation change and a new mandate for it is needed it is better to have 'new faces', that is a new force, rather than simply an 'add-on force'. General Sanderson contended that the self-defence authority of a peacekeeping force might be stretched to include not simply self-defence but the defence of the mission's objectives. Obviously this is a delicate matter and Otunnu identified it as a difficult 'grey area'.

Secondly, command and control problems bulk large in the thinking of the military contributors. The UN Secretariat, General Sanderson observed, was just that—it did not have and was not likely to have the capacity to run a major military operation. From the discussions it did not seem that there was any real prospect of a revival of the Military Staff Committee but it may be that an advisory commit-tee to the Security Council, consisting of all members of the Council plus troop-contributing member states, might be a possible body which would not require Charter amendment. It was a view of military participants that the United Nations needed first, military command headquarters; secondly, clearer mandates from the Security Council (easier said than done, of course, in awkward political situations); and thirdly, that political and military action in a peacekeeping operation must be taken in tandem rather than in sequence.

In terms of practical problems there was much criticism of the tardiness of UN responses because of its bureaucratic procedures, observations which reminded me of the Australian comedian Clive James's comment 'We'll fall off that bridge when we come to it'. The practical problems were identified as lack of money; delays in obtain-ing and fielding the necessary armed forces; a lack of common military operating doctrine; differences of language among the differing contin-gents; and a lack of an intelligence analysis capacity. It was com-mented that it was not so much a lack of information as a lack of analysis which was the biggest problem in this field for peacekeeping force commanders.

The provision of forces by member states, in response to requests from the Secretary-General, remains a serious problem. Member states were often most reluctant to participate—for example, none of the participants in the Rwanda operation was prepared to increase the size of its contingent as requested by the Secretary-General. Senator Evans commented that if member states had more confidence in the United Nations in the peacekeeping field they might respond better, but he later observed that perhaps the current peacekeeping operational level of some 70,000 odd troops was about the most that member states would now be prepared to agree to.

There was some discussion of the prospect of a ready reaction force or a standing force for the UN. Canada is looking at the prospects for the first, with designated forces, common doctrines, and some stockpiling of equipment, which would however remain within the territories of the member states. The Netherlands, and also Denmark, were exploring the prospect of a standing force being put together for the United Nations—perhaps by secondments from the forces of member states—a force which might be located in a member state and trained and held there ready for urgent response. In my view the prospect for a ready reaction force rather than a standing force is the more realistic possibility. In any case, however, as Don McKinnon stressed, no member states would now be likely to agree to provide the United Nations with forces under Article 43, which would involve their automatic commitment to any operation on which the UN might decide. Member governments, he said, would continue to retain the right to agree or not to agree to the involvement of their forces. Their public opinions would insist on it.

Finally, in the field of peacekeeping, there was some discussion of new developments which arose from the plethora of intra-state conflicts, that of the UN providing a transitional government. This was the case in Cambodia with UNTAC (the United Nations Transitional Authority in Cambodia) which had provided the government of Cambodia prior to a general election, which UNTAC organised and supervised, and which then enabled a new government to be formed. There is incidentally some precedent for this under the League of Nations—admittedly politically less complex—in which the Saar, disputed between France and Germany, was administered by a League of Nations multinational force provided by Britain, the Netherlands, Italy and Sweden from 1920–34, when by plebiscite the Saar voted to return to Germany.

Some of the conclusions reached from all of these discussions were that first, time was of the essence. The Cambodian operation, for example, had suffered greatly because of delays in getting it established. Second, it was important for a peacekeeping operation to avoid alliance with local political factions (although, as General Sanderson commented, this was thought to be a good tactic by some in the UN Secretariat) but instead to seek to ally itself with the aspirations of the bulk of the people. In this way the force could avoid commitment to any faction. The role of the media, for good or ill, was highlighted by General Rose who remarked from his experience in Bosnia that the media often exacerbated the situation by tendentious reporting and in many cases allowed themselves to be used by the various factions involved in the disputes because, substantially, of their own ignorance of the subtleties of the situation. He stressed that one should not lose faith in peacekeeping operations in principle. It was not the UN so much which should be criticised as the member states. It was what they were prepared to contribute, and when, that was the determinant. He added, however, that in the case of Bosnia, no member state was (then) ready to risk enforcement intervention.

Preventive Diplomacy

The importance of preventive diplomacy was strongly emphasised by several speakers, notably Senator Evans, Mr McKinnon, Ambassador Otunnu, Professor Austin and Dr Bercovitch—almost an embarrassment of riches. I was struck particularly by the emphasis given to it by Senator Evans. Preventive diplomacy was the central theme of his speech. He elaborated the possibility of the establishment of central and regional preventive diplomacy functions and noted that a number of regional institutions might provide a focus for them—for example the Association of Southeast Asian Nations (ASEAN), the ASEAN Regional Forum (ARF), the Asia–Pacific Economic Cooperation (APEC), etc. He indicated clearly that he thought that the United Nations should be doing more in this respect, an implicit criticism of the Secretary-General.

Of particular note in his speech was the stress that he laid on the levers of influence which the international community could exert and his endorsement of the use of 'conditionality' by the Bretton Woods institutions, the World Bank and the International Monetary Fund (IMF), to encourage good governance among states. He believed that preventive diplomacy should be deployed not only between states but for intra-state disputes also, but he ruefully concluded that it was a thankless task in political terms. If it worked, nobody noticed; if it failed, there was blame. But it was worth trying anyway.

I fully accept that greater efforts at preventive diplomacy are well worth pursuing, but as a retired practitioner in diplomacy I must inject a word of caution. Preventive diplomacy and mediation is the stuff of both politics and diplomacy but there are limits to it, as the case of Bosnia has shown. Bosnia has not lacked for skilled negotiators of standing, in the persons of David Owen of Britain and Cyrus Vance of the United States, and now Carl Bildt of Sweden. But crises can have their season. In many cases the factions concerned will not make peace so long as they remain convinced that they can win more at acceptable cost by fighting on—as been the case in both Bosnia and Angola. Sometimes, however, they may be stuck in a groove and want an opportunity or an excuse to get out of it. There have been some surprising and welcome successes in this circumstance, notably by former President Jimmy Carter in both North Korea and Haiti. One must simply take these issues case by case. The essential basis for settlement, as General Sanderson stressed in the case of Cambodia and Colonel O'Reilly in the case of Angola, is reconciliation. Without it there can be no lasting peaceful settlement as the history of those two sad countries shows.

Mediation

Dr Jacob Bercovitch produced an interesting paper with some stark statistics on the role of mediation, which is a part of preventive diplomacy if tackled early or of peacemaking if not. He estimated that since the Second World War there had been between 1500–2000 efforts at international mediations. The UN itself had been involved in 355 such efforts of which 127 (some 35 percent) had been successful. These cases were mainly those concerned with the decolonisation process.

The fact that the UN ratio of success was relatively low was in part because—as former Secretary-General U Thant once complained—member states dumped disputes onto the UN when they could no longer think of anything else to do with them, and in part because member states in dispute were reluctant to accept UN assistance until they felt there was no recourse. The rate of success, Dr Bercovitch stressed, was closely linked to timing. More than two-thirds of the disputes referred to the United Nations were over three years old and over two-thirds had already seen more than 10,000 victims killed. That delay hardened disputes and made them very difficult to settle. What was important was to get the mediation process involved at the earliest possible stage.

In some cases, as with New Zealand and France over the

Rainbow Warrior issue, the United Nations provided a convenient stamp of approval for an agreement which was negotiated with the aid of a third party—in this case the Netherlands—and substantially by the two principal parties themselves.

There was some discussion as to how one moved from Chapter VI (peaceful settlement) in the Charter to Chapter VII (peace enforcement). S. K. Singh thought that might need a thorough Charter revision but Dr Bercovitch believed that ad hoc political decisions in each case was the better way to proceed, a view I share.

Development

Ambassador Jorge Heine raised a series of questions about currently prevailing policy assumptions underlying economic development, more particularly in developing countries—that if markets get prices right, poverty will take care of itself. He commented that from his own experience, in both Chile, and currently South Africa, this was not necessarily the case. While it was important that markets got prices right, he said, there was a role for government intervention in the alleviation of policy impacts.

He asserted that economic development was itself the best preventive strategy for the avoidance of conflict. That may generally be true—I hope it is—but I doubt that it is so always. For realists, yes; for romantic revolutionaries, no. Ambassador Heine noted also that the trend towards democratisation currently in vogue, and 'conditionality' which went with it, looked distinctly political. He thought that the opposition of Third World countries to such a politicisation was growing.

Concerning the role of the UN economic machinery, he thought the role of the Economic Commission for Latin America (ECLA) had been important in laying the foundations for the burgeoning economic growth that was now being seen in Latin America. This view was in contrast to the widespread criticism now current about the performance of the UN's regional economic commissions and even the passing suggestion—for example, in *Our Global Neighbourhood,* the report of the Commission on Global Governance—that they might well be abolished.

An Asian Perspective

S. K. Singh gave a fascinating historical sketch of developments in

Asia in its relations with the UN over the years. His theme was that the UN had in fact done very little for Asia and had enjoyed few, if any, successes there, political or economic.

He noted India's impressive record in peacekeeping operations—which indeed dated from the Korean War of 1950–53, despite Indian doubts about the UN's role there once it became clear that the operation was essentially US-directed. The value of Indian contributions to UN peacekeeping certainly accords with my own experience where the UN Secretariat, it was clear, welcomed Indian contributions for their high military qualities and their relative economy compared to the expensive forces of some others, notably the Nordic states.

S. K. Singh's valid criticisms of many of the UN's failings in Asia may perhaps be linked to some degree to the extreme divisions in that continent, by contrast with those of black Africa. For example, India–China relations post-1962, the continuing tensions between India and Pakistan, and the Japan–China–Russia nexus all were delicate if not at times dangerous relationships. There was little, if any, unanimity among the major states of Asia about their multilateral political goals. I used to wonder during my time in the New Zealand delegation in New York in the 1960s why the Asian member states, including as they did powerful and populous countries, far greater than those of Africa, allowed the African members to run the Afro–Asian majority in the General Assembly. It was the Africans who set the agenda—which included apartheid, Namibia, Rhodesia–Zimbabwe, and the Portuguese colonies of Angola and Mozambique. Asian issues were, by contrast, significantly neglected. The reason, I conclude, must be seen in these sharp political divisions in Asia by contrast with the black African member states whose agenda, after their mass entry into the Assembly in the 1960s, was virtually unanimous in seeking the end of colonialism in their continent.

S. K. Singh was critical, in particular, of the UN's failure to follow up early economic development programmes in Asia. Significant developments in the Mekong Valley, for the Asian highway and for regional railway development were all planned for the region, many under the aegis of the Economic Commission for Asian and the Far East, now the Economic and Social Commission for Asia and the Pacific (ESCAP). These had not been pursued however—one might note that in the case of the Mekong the war in Indochina interfered with that economic development—and the region had been deprived accordingly. There appear to be prospects now, notably in the case of the Mekong river development, that these plans are being revived.

Global Governance

I return now to the wider view and some of the questions with which we began. Professor John Groom, haling from that 'tired, civilised has-been', as one speaker described Britain these days, developed the question of the changes in the world and the pace of change which had been laid out earlier in our discussions by Rosenau. Groom thought that there had been such an acceleration of economic and technical developments that they had outpaced political and social changes. Too many of our political and social institutions were basically those first fashioned in the 19th century. Yet we were entering a completely new technological age. He discerned a dividing line, with an acceleration of trends towards globalisation and decentralisation, from about 1960.

These changes, he believed, posed particular problems for the United Nations and its organisations because it was essentially a top-down institution whereas the new world was being built from the bottom-up. He noted, for example, the immense importance in the international economy of trans-national corporations, 41 of which had total annual incomes which would have to be ranked within the first 100 of member states' GNPs. Further the number of NGOs active in the international field were now to be counted in their thousands.

He offered two particularly interesting insights. First, the phenomenon of *special conferences,* which had flourished in their hundreds. The most notable, beginning with the Stockholm environmental conference, might be listed as Rio (environment), Vienna (human rights), Copenhagen (social questions), Cairo (population) and Beijing (women's rights). He concluded that the influence of the deliberations and decisions of these conferences played such an important role that their existence amounted in practice to an amendment to the UN Charter.

Secondly, he suggested that there was a new political phenomenon which might be described as *'pooled' sovereignty.* This was not a federal system as commonly understood but was really based on the example of the European Union (EU), in which the sovereignties of its individual member states were managed by the EU Commission and EU Ministerial Councils—in effect sovereignty managed by committee.

Non-Government Organisations (NGOs)

Both John Groom and Keith Suter dwelt on the burgeoning of NGOs, a phenomenon of the late 20th century in a Western world much influenced by increasing affluence, greater education, and more leisure. This linked with Rosenau's point that the present generation was more socially skilled than their elders.

The question of the relationship of NGOs to the UN was explored by Keith Suter. He noted that once it was the practice that observer status was granted by the UN, after some scrutiny, to various NGOs which were then subject to a process of accountability. More recently, however, because of the increasing numbers, the gates had been thrown open and these rules were lifted. That had produced such a flood of numbers that there was now a UN review to see how NGOs might be assessed and made accountable. He commented that not all NGOs were necessarily 'good guys'—his example to the contrary was the National Rifle Association (NRA) in the United States. Many NGOs, it seems to me, may be single-issue pressure groups that do not necessarily have any great degree of mass support but which are expert at capturing media attention. It may well be that 'they represent nobody but themselves', in the language which the Soviet delegation used to use about the Nationalist Chinese in the UN.

As to institutional suggestions, I share the doubts expressed by Olara Otunnu about a parallel NGO assembly. That, it seems to me, would confer too formal a status upon them. Their parallel conferences with official UN conferences, of the type described by John Groom, seem to me to provide ample area for an NGO input.

There was no specific examination at the School of greater national parliamentary links with the UN. I would favour that— certainly the greater use of the accreditation of parliamentarians in national delegations—because I believe that it would do much to strengthen an understanding in national parliaments of the strengths and weaknesses of the UN, as well as giving the UN deliberations perhaps a keener political input. An assembly of parliamentarians of UN members has been mooted in various publications. If that were to be pursued I would think it important that they should be nominated by their national parliaments, to establish liaison between those parliaments and the UN system, rather than being directly elected, as has also been suggested, for example by Erskine Childers and Sir Brian Urquhart.

Conclusions

I come now to draw together some concluding thoughts. I do so with some caution, bearing in mind the unwitting aphorism of the late movie mogul Sam Goldwyn: 'Never prophesy—especially about the future'.

We have learned that:

1. Our world is changing fast but that some things stubbornly remain the same, like ethnic conflicts.

2. The nation-state is under challenge: it has lost control in some areas (e.g. in currency transfers), and by agreement in others, whether through a 'pooled' or conceded sovereignty, as in such institutions as the European Union, the General Agreement on Tariffs and Trade (GATT), and its successor the World Trade Organisation (WTO). These in turn have at times stimulated some nationalistic backlash.

3. The United Nations is preeminently an organisation of nation-states. 'We the people' at the beginning of the Charter, according to Harland Cleveland, was a public relations introduction by friends of Mrs Eleanor Roosevelt to replace 'the high contracting parties' in the original draft in the hope that in 1945 it would make a greater appeal to an American public which had spurned the League. In fact, however, it means 'we the member states' and is likely to continue to do so. But they are not immune from growing trends which are towards decentralisation and the increasing role of non-government actors. They will give ground in some areas and fight back in others. In my view the nation-state is tougher than some may think. Third World nations particularly are concerned to protect their sovereignty. So is the United States.

4. The United Nations itself, as Boutros Boutros-Ghali has said, is essentially dependent on its member states. They can have a strong United Nations or a weak United Nations, as they wish. Political will is the key—to resources both of finance, and military and other personnel. By the standards of the great powers these demands remain small. The UN will be pressed to respond to changes. Micro-changes, which do not require an amendment to the Charter, could be attained if members agree. Macro-

changes, which would require Charter amendment, might also be possible but such a majority or consensus seems less likely. One possibility is an increase of non-permanent members to the Security Council, to relieve pressure for better representation from the General Assembly.

5. Peace machinery, which involves preventive diplomacy, mediation, peacemaking and peacekeeping, can all be strengthened by greater political will and more money. There is no need for Charter amendments to achieve that.

6. The UN role will remain one of continuing importance. In my view it is worthwhile even as static conference machinery, which enables disputing parties to talk under the cover of a General Assembly session. One has only to imagine what the world would be like without the UN system to conclude that if it did not exist we would have to reinvent it. There may scope for trimming, yes—the UN Conference on Trade and Development (UNCTAD), the UN Industrial Development Organisation (UNIDO), and the regional economic commissions have all been suggested as likely subjects, but the core UN system should remain.

To sum up, the United Nations now represents the 'international community', itself a new and important concept. Universality of membership now prevails and is more important as a consideration for membership than the Charter's 'peaceloving' requirement. Second, it follows that the United Nations confers legitimacy on the actions of member states, for example enforcement actions under Chapter VII, authorised by the Security Council, and carried out by national coalitions. An example of the importance of this legitimacy may be seen in the actions of President George Bush once the Iraqi forces had been defeated in the Gulf War. Why did he not press on to Baghdad and overthrow Saddam Hussein? Probably for two reasons: first, had he done so it is likely that he would have lost the support of the Security Council. China may well have exercised a veto and Russia too might well have parted company. Second, of course, he was doubtless concerned not to allow American forces to enter into a political quagmire redolent of Vietnam, from which it might have proved difficult to extricate them.

Finally, we may reflect on other conclusions—that the success of peacekeeping, peace-enforcement, and peacemaking lies in an alliance of the peacekeeping efforts with the people of the country concerned and the readiness of the contending factions to accept reconciliation. That is the key to a lasting peace. To achieve it, leadership is required at the highest level. If we were to index it we might do so under the heading, *Leadership, lack thereof.* Linking these two conclusions one would say that the greatest qualities of leadership are shown in the readiness of the major political actors to accept reconciliation. By that test the outstanding leader in today's world, without doubt, is Nelson Mandela.

Index

Absolute War and Real War, 200
Adams, John Quincy, 57
Addis Ababa, 20
Afghanistan, 31, 38, 73, 222, 223, 286, 291
Africa, 47, 123, 128, 254, 303
Agenda for Development, 119
Agenda for Peace, 9–10, 70, 76, 78, 247 290
Aichi, Kiichi, 205
Aikman, Colin, 33
Air Crimes Commission, 248
air power, use in Bosnia, 174
Akashi, Yasushi, 147, 215
Albania, 65
Albright, Madeleine, 18
American Society of International Law, 261
Amici, 35
Amnesty International, 16
Anarchical Society, 278
Angola, 6, 95, 123, 127, 129, 130, 131, 133, 136, 246, 313, 315
  ceasefire, 132, 135
  landmines, 31, 141
  Lusaka Accords, 134, 135
  New Zealand and, 132, 133
  Status of Forces agreement, 140–41
  UNAVEM II, 132–34
Angolan Air Force, 140
APEC, *see* Asia–Pacific Economic Cooperation
Arab–Israeli conflict, 81, 82, 222
Argentina, 59, 67, 243
Arms Control and Regional Security (ACRS), 67
ASEA/Brown Boveri, 256, 257
ASEAN Regional Forum (ARF), 63, 67, 312
Asian highway scheme, 224

Asia–Pacific Economic Cooperation (APEC), 224, 312
Aspen Institute, 111
Association of South East Asian Nations (ASEAN), 219, 225, 312
Association of Southern African States (ASAS), 67
Austin, Reginald, 13, 21, 310, 312
Australia, 31, 44, 52, 55, 145, 156, 162, 222, 244, 247, 309
Australian Defence Force, 68
Australian Peace Committee, 261
Azerbaijan, 221

Baker, Philip Noel, 259
Balkans, 97
Bangkok, 195
Bangladesh, 222
Barham, Kevin, 257
Beagle, Jan, 38
Beagle Channel dispute, 67
Bercovitch, Jacob, 4, 304, 312–14
Bernadotte, Count Folk, 82
Bevin, Ernest, 302
Bihac, 176
Bildt, Carl, 36, 313
Bilkey, Caroline, 38
'Binding Triad' proposal, 251, 260
Birt, John, 255
Bismarck, 42
Bloomfield, Lincoln, 308
Bombay, 257
Bosnia, 2, 12, 13, 14, 15, 25, 35, 71, 74, 145, 167, 168, 172, 174, 190, 232, 246, 280, 304, 312, 313, 313
  Cessation of Hostilities agreement, 170–71, 176
  human rights abuses by UN troops, 17

Bosnia (cont'd)
war crimes tribunal, 24
Boutros-Ghali, Boutros, 9, 14, 17,
28, 57, 122, 172, 207, 309,
318
Brazil, 23, 227 243, 286
UN Security Council and, 55, 205
Bretton Woods institutions, 220
Britain, 49, 51, 217, 222, 225, 242,
244, 249, 283, 286, 287, 294,
306, 311
Security Council and, 21, 55,
209, 307
British Petroleum, 256
Buddhist Liberal Democratic Party
(BLDP), 90, 102, 106
Bull, Hedley, 278
Burma, 224
Bush, George, 73, 319

Cambodia, 2, 6, 7, 13–15, 30–31,
38, 93, 95, 126, 145, 153, 161,
162, 214, 223, 265, 266, 286,
292, 313
anti-Vietnamese feeling, 102, 151
comprehensive peacemaking, 93
Constituent Assembly, 112, 113
constitution, 103, 112–13
election, 90, 92, 93, 99–100, 101,
155, 158, 159–61
Electoral Law, 106
force, use of, 184
Government of National Unity,
91, 112
human rights abuses by UN
troops, 16–17
humanitarian action, 270
International Control
Commission, 221
landmines, 31, 96
legal system, 101, 102, 111
police, 111, 195
political expediency, 103–110
president, election of, 103
Secretary-General's report (1992),
194
State of Cambodia (SoC), 31, 90,

148, 149, 152, 304
Supreme National Council (SNC),
101, 107, 150, 151
Vietnamese forces in, 152
Vietnamese Khmer and, 102, 151
see also UN Transitional
Authority in Cambodia
Cambodian People's Armed Forces
(CPAF), 152
Cambodian People's Party (CPP), 90,
91, 92, 106, 109, 112, 114
access to safe havens, 107–08
Campaign for a More Democratic
United Nations (CAMDUN),
250
Canada, 16, 55, 218, 221, 225, 309
rapid reaction force and, 69, 311
Carter, Jimmy, 237, 240, 313
Carter Center, 67
Cartwright, Silvia, 38
Center for War/Peace Studies (New
York), 251
Central Treaty Organisation
(CENTO), 222
Chea Sim, 109
Chechnya, 61, 74, 168, 235
Chemical Weapons Convention, 51
Chiang Kai Shek, 217
Childers, Erskine, 317
Chile, 67, 122, 126, 124, 314
China, 51, 131, 147, 212, 219, 221–
22, 223, 225, 242, 283, 284,
286
Gulf War and, 287, 319
India and, 223, 315
Korean War and, 221
Security Council and, 21, 22,
217, 237
Christmas Island, 51
civil conflicts, *see* conflict, internal
Clausewitz, Carl von, 200
Cleveland, Harland, 318
Clinton Administration, 25
Clinton, Bill, 36
Club of Rome, 279
Clyne, Peter, 248
Cold War, 50, 74, 75, 85, 179, 246

collective security, 4, 13, 56, 60,
    202, 272, 285, 288–90
colonialism, 303, 315
colonies, UN and, 251
Comecon, 217
command and control in
    peacekeeping, 138, 196, 197,
    310
    UNPROFOR and, 197
    UNTAC and, 191–92
command structures, 191–94
Commission on Global Governance,
    314
Commission on Human Rights, 258,
    297
Commission on the Status of
    Women, 258
Committee on Disarmament, 50–51
Committee on the Elimination of
    Discrimination Against
    Women, 38
common security, 60
Commonwealth Monitoring Force,
    128
Commonwealth, 96, 115, 116, 117,
    271
comprehensive security, 60
Comprehensive Test Ban Treaty
    (CTBT), 52, 53
confidence-building, 186
conflict resolution, 184
conflict, 7, 61, 62, 67, 74, 75, 84,
    203, 269
    ethnic, 35, 203
    internal, 7–9, 49, 61, 62, 64, 75,
    85, 95, 120, 180, 304
    management of, 77, 85
    responses to, 76, 77, 78, 80
Congress of Vienna, 42, 203
Convention on the Safety of UN and
    Associated Personnel, 59
Conventional Forces in Europe Treaty
    (CFE), 51
Cooperating for Peace, 66, 145, 260
cooperative security, 60
Copenhagen, 122, 123
    Social Summit, 37, 316

Corner, Frank, 305, 307
Crimean War, 42
Croatia, 35, 74
Crough, Greg, 255
CTBT, *see* Comprehensive Test Ban
    Treaty
Cuba, 129, 131, 141, 288
Cuéllar, Javier Pérez de, 287
Cyprus, 246, 308
Czechoslovakia, 218

decentralisation of political systems,
    234, 316
Declaration on Colonialism, 47
decolonisation, 30, 46, 64, 85, 278
democracy, peace and, 64, 95–96, 99,
    115, 232
democratisation, 280
Deng Xiaoping, 219
Denmark, 311
Department of Foreign Affairs and
    Trade (Australia), 70
development, 27, 29, 63, 115, 119,
    120–22, 269, 281, 314
Diplomacy, 43
disarmament, 49–50, 51, 228, 304
Disarmament Commission, 50
Donne, John, 178
Dos Santos, Jose Eduardo, 142
Doyle, Michael, 265
Dumbarton Oaks, 220

Earth Forum, 239
East Timor, 46, 247
EC, *see* European Community
Economic and Social Commission for
    Asia and the Pacific (ESCAP),
    224, 315
Economic and Social Council
    (ECOSOC), 251–53, 258, 293,
    294, 296, 298, 306
Economic Commission for Asia and
    the Far East (ECAFE), 224,
    315
Economic Commission for Latin
    America (ECLA), 314
Economic Security Council, 294

Economist, 3
ECOSOC, *see* Economic and Social
    Council
Egypt, Gulf War and, 287
El Salvador, 6, 265, 266, 270, 286
enforcement action, 4, 9, 10, 13, 154,
    185–88, 197, 273–74, 291
environment conferences, 37, 239,
    296, 316
Eritrea, 6
Estonia, 65, 75
ethnic conflict, 35, 203
ethnic movements, 7, 61
European Community, (EC), 45, 218
European Court of Human Rights, 45
European Economic Community
    (EEC), 52
European Union (EU), 23, 36, 218,
    283, 284, 292, 316, 318
Evans, Gareth, 19, 27, 28, 34, 76,
    103, 145, 260, 261, 302, 304,
    309, 311, 312
expanded Permanent Five, 162
Exxon, 256

failed states, 6, 11, 291
Falk, Richard, 305
Ferencz, Benjamin, 248
Financial Times, 123
Finger, Max, 26
First World, 242
FNLA, *see Frente Nacional de
    Libertacao de Angola*
Food and Agriculture Organisation
    (FAO), 294
Force Commander, 138, 139
Force Communications Unit, 165
force, use of, 9, 69, 183, 184
Ford, 256
Former Yugoslav Republic of
    Macedonia (FYROM), 35, 65,
    266
Fourteen Points of Woodrow Wilson,
    44
France, 14, 44, 49, 51, 217, 221,
    242, 249, 286, 287, 306, 311
    nuclear tests, 51, 52, 304

Rainbow Warrior, 313–14
Security Council and, 21, 55,
    209, 307
Franco–Prussian War, 42
Fraser, Peter, 46
Free University of Berlin, 252
French Polynesia, 51
*Frente Nacional de Libertacao de
    Angola* (FNLA), 130, 131
Friggerio, Paul, 235
FUNCINPEC, *see* National United
    Front for an Independent,
    Neutral, Peaceful and
    Cooperative Cambodia

G7, *see* Group of Seven
General Agreement on Tariffs and
    Trade (GATT), 217, 318
General Motors, 256
Geneva Accords, 221
genocide, 91, 170
Georgia, 14
Germany, 162, 210, 217, 218, 222,
    249, 287, 302
    League of Nations and, 44, 285,
    311
    Security Council and, 21, 22, 55,
    202, 209–11, 243, 286
Ghana, 244
global economy, 281, 292
global governance, 12, 277, 285, 298
globalisation, 30, 123, 230, 316
Golan Heights, 214
Goldwyn, Sam, 318
Goma, 215
Gorazde, 172, 174
Gorbachev, Mikhail, 244, 286
Green, Marshall, 301
Greenpeace, 261
Groom, John, 12, 20, 302, 304, 316,
    317
Group of 77, 30
Group of Seven (G7), 73, 292
Guatemala, 266
Gulf War, 4, 10, 17, 23, 66, 126,
    170, 182, 206, 223, 237, 260,
    287, 319

Haiti, 14, 38, 67, 83, 266, 287, 291,
313
Hambro, Edvard, 261
Hammarskjöld, Dag, 9, 26, 27, 32,
87, 172, 290
Hassan bin Talal, Crown Prince of
Jordan, 268
Hazzard, Shirley, 26
Heine, Jorge, 29, 314
Hercus, Ann, 38
Hiroshima, 224
Hobbes, Thomas, 168
Hong Kong, 219, 225
Howard, John, 261
Huambo, 131, 135, 136
Hudson, Richard, 251, 260
Hufner, Klaus, 252
human rights, 6, 15, 16, 44, 46, 232,
296, 297, 302
UNTAC and, 110–12, 149, 150
Human Rights Conference, Vienna,
239, 316
humanitarian aid, 3, 6, 11, 13, 270,
290, 291
Hun Sen, 90, 106, 109, 148
Hungary, 65
Hussein, Saddam, 48, 66, 288, 289,
319

IBM, 256
ICJ, *see* International Court of Justice
ICRC, *see* International Committee
of the Red Cross
ILO, *see* International Labour
Organisation
IMF, *see* International Monetary Fund
In Retrospect, 95
India, 23, 162, 219, 221, 222, 225,
227, 243, 283, 284, 315
Security Council and, 22, 55,
205, 286
Indochina, 221, 315
Indonesia, 23, 44, 67, 162, 224, 243,
247, 286, 301
intelligence, need for, 141, 193
International Bill of Rights, 15–16
International Committee of the Red

Cross (ICRC), 12, 291
International Conference on Former
Yugoslavia, 36
International Control Commissions
(Vietnam, Laos, Cambodia),
221
International Convention on Civil and
Political Rights, 16, 150
International Convention on
Economic, Social and Cultural
Rights, 16, 150
International Court of Justice (ICJ),
24, 52, 53, 63, 247, 248
International Covenants on Human
Rights, 45
International Institute for Democracy
and Electoral Assistance
(IDEA), 65
International Labour Organisation
(ILO), 31, 56, 224, 259, 294,
295
International Monetary Fund (IMF),
27, 64, 217, 252, 293, 312
International Peace Academy, 263–
268
International Peace Cooperation Law
(Japan), 208, 209, 215
International Research and Training
Institute for the Advancement of
Women (INSTRAW), 38
International Telecommunications
Union, 295
Iran, 73, 286
Iran–Iraq war, 223
Iraq, 1, 7, 73, 75, 223, 272, 286–90,
304
Ireland, 257
Ismail, Razali, 246
Israel, 49, 307
Italy, 235, 311

Jamaica, 257
James, Alan, 10
James, Clive, 310
Japan Socialist Party, 208
Japan, 44, 162, 212–14, 217–19,
222, 225, 228, 249, 283, 284,

Japan (cont'd)
  292, 302, 315
  Article 9 of Constitution, 207,
    208, 213, 308
  Gulf War and, 206, 287
  peacekeeping and, 214, 215, 309
  Security Council and, 21, 22, 55,
    201, 202, 205, 206, 207, 209,
    210, 211, 243, 286
Japanese Self Defense Forces, 209
Jarring, Gunnar, 81
Jenkins, Roy, 268
Jenkins, Simon, 2
Johnson, Lyndon, 221, 228
Johnstone, Ian, 265
Jonah, James, 243
Jordan, Regional Security Centre, 67

Kampong Cham, 106
Kashmir, 222
Kazakhstan, 218
Keating, Colin, 306
Keith, Kenneth, 303
Kennan, George, 57
Kennedy, John F., 221
Khmer Krom, 102
Khmer People's National Liberation
    Front (KPNLF), 90, 150
Khmer Rouge, 31, 90, 91, 102, 107,
    148, 151, 154, 155, 157, 160
  Paris Agreements and, 149, 152,
    158, 187
  see also Party of Democratic
    Kampuchea
Kissinger, Henry, 42, 43, 57, 205
Kiwi Company, 36
Kono, Yohei, 208
Korea, 272, 304
Korean War, 4, 182, 220–21, 315
Kosaka, Zentaro, 205
KPNLF, *see* Khmer People's
    National Liberation Front
Kuomintang (KMT), 217
Kuwait, 1, 7, 48, 126, 206, 244,
    287, 289, 304
Kyrghizstan, 218

La Trobe University, 305
Lagos, Ricardo, 120
Lake, Jennifer, 38
landmines, 31, 96, 129, 141
Laos, 221
Lasso, Jose, 46
Latin America, 237, 243
Latvia, 65
Law of the Sea, 63, 303
leadership, 274, 283, 320
League of Nations, 41, 42, 44, 54,
    204, 246, 285, 302, 311
Lebanon, 222
Lee Kuan Yew, 226
legitimacy, 234
Lehn, Jean-Marie, 63
Liberal Democratic Party (Japan), 208
Liberal Party (Australia), 261
Liberia, 38, 83, 95, 272
Libya, 24
Limits of Growth, 279
Luanda, 142
Luck, Ed, 244
Lusaka Accords, 134, 135

Macedonia, *see* Former Yugoslav
    Republic of Macedonia
    (FYROM)
Mahathir Mohamad, 226
Malaysia, 162
mandates, in peacekeeping, 68, 70,
    97, 133, 143, 184, 186–91,
    198, 310
Mandates, 251
Mandela, Nelson, 117, 320
Mann, Michael, 282
Mao Ze Dong, 217
Marcos, Ferdinand, 234
Marshall Plan, 278
Massachusetts Institute of
    Technology (MIT), 308
McDonald's, 323
McKinnon, Don, 2, 12, 13, 125,
    304, 306, 311, 312
McMillan, Stuart, 57
McNamara, Dennis, 111
McNamara, Robert, 95

McNaught, Helen, 38
Médecins Sans Frontières, (MSF), 12
media, 157, 175, 199, 255, 312
mediation, 80–81, 82, 313–14
    UN and, 83–86
Medical Association for the
    Prevention of War, 261
Mekong River, 315, 316
Mekong Valley Development Plan,
    224
Mexico, 225, 237 243
Mierlo, Hans Van, 69
Milovanovic, Manojlo, 173
Mixed Military Working Group
    Secretariat (UNTAC), 162
MNCs (multinational corporations),
    see transnational corporations
Mobil, 256
Modelski, George, 283, 284
Mogadishu line, 171, 174
Mogadishu, 8
Mortimer, Edward, 123
Mororua, 52
Mountain, Ros, 38
*Movimento Popular de Libertacao de
    Angola* (MPLA), 130, 131
Mozambique, 6, 17, 66, 123, 129,
    134, 214, 315
    humanitarian action and, 270
MPLA, *see Movimento Popular de
    Libertacao de Angola*
multinational corporations (MNCs),
    see transnational corporations
Mutually Assured Destruction
    (MAD), 217
Myrdal, Gunnar, 228

NAFTA, *see* North American Free
    Trade Agreement
Nagasaki, 224
Nagorno–Karabakh, 83
Najman, Dragoljub, 31
Namibia, 2, 6, 93, 95, 113, 128,
    129, 131, 147, 244, 286, 315
Napoleon, 42
Napoleonic Wars, 203
Narang, Nouth, 16

nation-state, 241, 254, 318
National Army of Democratic
    Kampuchea (NADK), 151, 152
National Program to Eradicate
    Poverty (Chile), 124
National Rifle Association, 317
National United Front for an
    Independent, Neutral, Peaceful
    and Cooperative Cambodia
    (FUNCINPEC), 91, 92, 106,
    107, 109, 112, 148, 150
nationalism, 233, 301
NATO, *see* North Atlantic Treaty
    Organisation
Nehru, Jawaharlal, 226
Nestlé, 256
Netherlands, 283, 311, 314
New International Economic Order,
    219
New Strategic Concepts document
    (1991), 172
New York, 244
New York Police Department, 34
New Zealand, 31, 35, 43, 45, 51, 52,
    53, 59, 128, 129, 167, 222,
    224, 244, 263, 304, 306
    Angola and, 132, 133, 142, 143
    Bosnia and, 35, 49
    human rights and, 44, 45–46
    peacekeeping and, 34, 127
    Rainbow Warrior affair, 248, 313–
    14
    Security Council and, 22, 37, 55,
    309
*New Zealand as an International
    Citizen: Fifty Years of United
    Nations Membership*, 33, 37
New Zealand Defence Force (NZDF),
    127, 128–29
Nicaragua, 6, 24, 38, 93
Nigeria, 23, 55, 243, 286
Nixon, Richard, 228
Nobel Peace Prize, 31
Nobel Prize for Chemistry, 63
non-government organisations
    (NGOs), 12, 13, 20, 22, 34,
    37, 39, 67, 116, 125, 155, 188,

non-government organisations
(cont'd)
236, 250, 254, 255, 258–60,
270, 271, 291, 295, 296, 305,
316, 317
nonaligned nations, 211
Norodom Ranariddh, 90, 106, 148
Norodom Sihanouk, 91, 103, 112,
151
North American Free Trade
Agreement (NAFTA), 224,
225, 292
North Atlantic Treaty Organisation
(NATO), 3, 169, 218, 280
Bosnia and, 14, 172, 175, 185
North Korea, 212, 313
Carter Center and, 67
Northern League (Italy), 235
Nuclear Non-Proliferation Treaty
(NPT), 53, 203, 212, 219
nuclear weapons, 50, 279
Nuremberg War Crimes trials, 248

O'Reilly, Tom, 6, 19, 31, 310, 313
One Hundred Years' War, 168
Organisation for Economic
Cooperation and Development
(OECD), 217, 278, 292, 294
Organisation for European Economic
Cooperation (OEEC), 278
Organisation of African Unity (OAU),
23, 117, 266
Mechanism for Conflict
Prevention, Management and
Resolution, 266, 267
Organisation on Security and
Cooperation in Europe (OSCE),
65, 67
Osbaldeston, Michael, 257
Otago, 45, 89
Otunnu, Olara, 11, 22, 23, 28, 30,
304, 305, 310, 312, 317
Our Global Neighbourhood, 314
Owen, David, 313
Pacific island nations, 47
Pakistan, 222, 223, 243, 315
Panama, 287

Paraguay, 237
Paris Agreements, 90, 92, 97, 101,
102, 106, 110, 112, 113, 146,
147, 149, 152, 158, 159, 184,
187, 189, 195
goals of, 163
justice system, 149, 196
Mixed Military Working Group
and, 162
Party of Democratic Kampuchea
(PDK), 90, 91, 150
peace-building, 63, 64, 65, 76, 79–
80, 265–66
as part of peacekeeping, 79
peace-enforcement, 10, 11, 76, 310
peace-maintenance, 76
peacekeeping, 5–7, 14, 15, 18, 32,
34, 48, 69, 79, 94–95, 139,
142, 157, 164, 176, 186, 191,
194, 210, 221, 246, 269, 289,
290
Chile and, 126
command and control, 138, 191–
92, 196, 197, 310
consent and, 70, 71, 154, 185–86
'expanded', 8, 62
failure of, 168, 203
financing, 66, 68, 139, 143
force, use of, 9, 13, 16, 69, 154,
171, 184, 310
human rights abuses by UN
troops, 16, 17
impartiality of, 11, 155, 186
internal conflict and, 8
Japan and, 215, 309
mandates, 68, 70, 97, 133, 143,
184, 186–91, 198, 310
need for clear objectives, 190
planning, 145
rapid reaction force, 14, 35, 56
regional organisations and, 115
self-defence and, 9, 154, 189
stand-by arrangements, 14, 69
standing force, 5, 14, 69, 239,
247
traditional, 10–11, 12, 17, 272,
273

peacekeeping (cont'd)
  transition management, 96, 311
  tribalisation of, 12, 271
  troop contributions, 139, 140,
    156, 310
  UN Charter and, 182, 245, 295
  UN Headquarters, 138, 143
  unity, importance of, 156
peacemaking, 4, 49, 78, 79, 93
  requirements for, 97–99
Philippines, 212
Philips, 256
Phnom Penh, 151, 195
Pol Pot, 112
Poland, 221
Population Conference, Cairo, 37,
  316
Porcell, Gerard, 159
Portugal, 130, 141, 247, 283
post-conflict peace-building, 32
poverty, alleviation of, 120–25
preventive diplomacy, 27, 29, 65, 66,
  77, 312–13
preventive strategies, conflict and, 65,
  269
proliferation, danger of, 202–03

Qatar, 67
Queen Elizabeth II, 97

Radio UNTAC, 157
Rainbow Warrior affair, 53, 248
rapid reaction force, 35, 56, 273, 311
  Canada and, 69
Reagan Administration, 30, 244
refugees, 146, 197, 223, 279
regional conflict, 203
regional organisations, 67, 270
  peacekeeping and, 115
regionalisation, 232
religious fundamentalism, 235
Rhodesia, 95, 128, 315
Rhodesia, Southern, 89
Richelieu, Cardinal, 42
Righter, Rosemary, 1, 21, 26
Rights and Reconciliation: UN
  Strategies in El Salvador, 265

Rikhye, Indar Jit, 263
Rio de Janeiro, 37, 239, 296, 316
Rogers, William, 205
Roosevelt, Eleanor, 318
Roosevelt, Franklin D., 43
Rose, Michael, 3, 11, 12, 13, 310,
  312
Rosenau, James, 19, 89, 124, 301,
  316
Rostow, Walt, 228
Royal Dutch Shell, 256
Russia, 14, 36, 61, 202, 212, 218,
  235, 242, 244, 283, 284, 315
  Security Council and, 205, 308
Rwanda, 2, 7, 12, 14, 38, 46, 83, 97,
  129, 180, 183, 190, 197, 198,
  232, 270, 272, 310

Saar dispute, 311
Sahara, 51
Sakigake Party (Japan), 208
Sam Rainsy, 107
San Francisco, 33, 35, 46, 245, 258,
  302
San Francisco Chronicle, 235
sanctions, Iraq and, 288
Sanderson, John, 11, 13, 14, 29, 30,
  70, 129, 310, 313
Santici, 35
Sarajevo, 3, 25, 168, 172, 174
Saudi Arabia, 15, 287
Savimbi, Jonas, 142
SEATO, *see* Southeast Asia Treaty
  Organisation
Second World War, *see* World War II
self-determination, 291–92
Sen, Katayama, 228
Shields, Margaret, 38
Shinyo, Takahiro, 22, 304, 308, 309
Sinai, 222
Singapore Institute of Strategic
  Studies, 97
Singh, S, K., 23, 314, 315
Sino–Soviet border clashes, 223
SIPRI Yearbook 1994, 60
SIPRI, *see* Stockholm International
  Peace Research Institute

Slovakia, 65
Social Summit, *see* World Summit
    for Social Development
Solzhenitsyn, Alexander, 1
Somalia, 2, 7–9, 12–14, 16, 71, 74,
    75, 83, 97, 129, 145, 167, 171,
    183, 198, 203, 214, 246, 253,
    266, 272, 291
Son Sann, 102
Son Sen, 153
South Africa, 23, 49, 120, 121, 123,
    129, 237, 243, 304
    Angola and, 131, 141
    UNOMSA and, 117
South China Sea dispute, 67
South Korea, 48, 219, 225, 228
South Pacific, nuclear tests and, 304
South Pacific Nuclear Free Zone
    (SPNFZ), 51, 52
Southeast Asia Treaty Organisation
    (SEATO), 222
Southern African Development
    Community (SADC), 67
Southern Rhodesia, 89
Southwest Africa, 129
Southwest African People's
    Organisation (SWAPO), 113
sovereignty, 30, 56, 236–38, 270,
    298, 304, 316, 318
Soviet Union, 44, 50, 131, 217, 221,
    233, 237, 285, 287, 306, 307
    collapse of, 61, 75, 179, 218, 286
specialised agencies, 293, 294
Spratly Islands, 212
Sputnik, 279
Sri Lanka, 75
standing force, 5, 14, 69, 239, 247
Stevenson, Adlai, 306
Stockholm, 296, 316
Stockholm International Peace
    Research Institute (SIPRI), 70
Sudan, 129
Suez, 9, 304
Sullivan, Gordon A., 169
Suter, Keith, 12, 20, 304, 305, 317
SWAPO, *see* Southwest African
    People's Organisation

Sweden, 22, 311
Swiss Federal Council, 253
Swissair, 257
Switzerland, 44, 253
Syria, 287

Taiwan, 217, 219, 225, 228
Tajikistan, 218
technological innovation, 281
Templeton, Malcolm, 302, 303, 304,
    305
Thailand, 162
Thakur, Ramesh, 49
Thimayya, K. S., 221
Third World, 28, 74, 242, 279, 295
Thirty Years' War, 254
Thomson, John, 286
Tiananmen Square, 232
Tlatelolco Treaty, 51
Todd, Edith, 89
Todd, Garfield, 89
Touval, S., 87
transnational corporations (TNCs),
    12, 20, 253, 255–58, 259, 260,
    293, 298, 316
Truman, Harry S., 43
Trust Territories, 251
Trusteeship Council, 251
Tunis, 67
Turkmenistan, 218
Tuzla, 173, 175

U Thant, 221, 263, 264, 313
Uige, 136
UK MEDACT, 250
UK Medical Association for the
    Prevention of War, 250
unemployment, 123
*Uniao Nacional para a Independencia
    Total de Angola* (UNITA), 130,
    131, 133, 135, 141
    Lusaka Accords and, 135, 136
    mistrust of UN, 132, 142
    UNAVEM III and, 137, 138
Unilever, 257
UNITA, *see Uniao Nacional para a
    Independencia Total de Angola*

United Kingdom, *see* Britain
United Nations UN), 1, 3, 4, 7, 18,
    44–45, 56, 74, 108, 115, 177,
    190, 222, 230, 238, 240, 273,
    277, 298, 299, 302, 310
    bureaucracy of, 20, 54, 238, 304,
        310
    Department of Peacekeeping
        Operations (DPKO), 68
    finances, 19, 28, 34, 54, 238,
        243–45, 247, 309
    force, use of, 4, 9, 13–14, 190
    human rights and, 16, 46
    Indonesia's withdrawal, 44
    intervention by, 15, 303
    'legalism', 204
    links with parliaments, 317
    mediation and, 80, 81, 83–86,
        313–14
    membership, 44
    Military Staff Committee, 10,
        198, 199, 246, 247, 310
    moral authority of, 29–30
    neutrality of, 104, 184
    normative standards and, 275, 296
    peacekeeping and, 5, 35, 56, 66,
        69, 139, 143, 319
    'politicism', 204
    preventive diplomacy and, 65–66
    rapid reaction force, 14, 35, 56
    reform of, 20–21, 54
    representative of international
        community, 319
    'selective engagement', 204
    specialised agencies, 253, 293,
        294
    standing force, 5, 14, 69, 239,
        247
    United States and, 17, 260
    women in, 245
UN Advance Mission in Cambodia
    (UNAMIC), 148
UN Angola Verification Mission
    (UNAVEM), 142
    UNAVEM I, 127, 131
    UNAVEM II, 131, 132–36, 139
    lack of resources, 133, 134

UNAVEM III, 128, 136, 137,
    139–41, 143
UN Association of Australia, 261
UN Association (USA), 244
UN Charter, 34, 47, 181–82, 217,
    221, 241–43
    Article 1, 50
    Article 2 (7), 291, 297, 302
    Article 2, 50, 186
    Article 11, 50
    Article 22, 250
    Article 26, 50
    Article 27 (3), 308
    Article 33, 76, 78, 182, 186
    Article 42, 4, 10, 182, 209
    Article 43, 10, 56, 197, 209, 311
    Article 55, 302
    Article 71, 258
    Article 99, 25
    Article 109, 242
    Chapter VI, 3–4, 13, 70, 71, 149,
        182, 183, 185, 186, 190, 198,
        199, 209, 294, 314
    'Chapter VI and a half', 209, 289
    Chapter VII, 4, 13, 70, 71, 182,
        183, 185, 190, 198, 199, 209,
        210, 272, 274, 286, 289, 294,
        308, 309, 314, 319
    human rights and, 15, 46, 296
    moral authority of, 199, 200
    origins, 19, 33
    reform of, 20, 305
    review conference, 242
    Security Council powers, 204
    self-determination and, 47, 291–92
    settlement of disputes, 198
    sovereignty and, 56, 180; *see also*
        UN Charter, *Article 2(7)*
    special conferences and, 316
    structural defects, 55
UN Children's Fund (UNICEF), 31,
    252
UN Conference on Environment and
    Development (UNCED), 37
UN Conference on Trade and
    Development (UNCTAD), 30,
    293, 319

UN Department of Peacekeeping
Operations (DPKO), 68
UN Development Programme
(UNDP), 38, 96, 252, 295, 296
UN Disengagement Observer Force
(UNDOF), 214
UN Educational, Scientific and
Cultural Organisation
(UNESCO), 28, 31, 224, 244,
253, 294
UN Emergency Force (UNEF), 49,
222
UN Environment Programme
(UNEP), 252
UN General Assembly, 4, 20, 22, 47,
50, 52–53, 221, 250, 251, 260,
286, 303, 304, 306
  Resolution A.49/76C, 264
  Resolution A/47/L.26.Rev.1, 206
UN High Commissioner for Human
Rights, 46
UN High Commissioner for Refugees
(UNHCR), 12, 31, 68, 96, 170,
174, 291
UN Industrial Development
Organisation (UNIDO), 293,
319
UN Institute for Training and
Research (UNITAR), 97
UN Interim Force in Lebanon
(UNIFIL), 222
UN Observer Mission in South Africa
(UNOMSA), 117
UN Operation in the Congo (ONUC),
146
UN Peacekeeping in Cambodia:
UNTAC's Civil Mandate, 265
UN Protection Force in Former
Yugoslavia (UNPROFOR), 35,
36, 146, 174, 197, 291, 304
UN Secretariat, 20, 54, 68, 98–99,
163, 199, 249, 309
  relations with UN agencies, 27
  resources, 67
  UNTAC and, 156
UN Secretary-General, 25–26, 48, 57,
63, 92, 94, 114, 247–48, 253,

290, 311
  Special Representative of (SRSG),
  101, 102, 106, 108, 138, 139,
  147, 163, 195
UN Security Council, 18, 20, 68, 98,
116, 197, 201, 204, 246, 271–
72, 286, 287, 290, 303
  Afghanistan and, 223
  Article 45 and, 246
  Cambodia and, 103, 163
  decision-making, 59, 67
  Gulf War and, 10, 223
  mandates, 68, 196
  membership of, 22, 55, 206, 207,
  211, 242, 319
  New Zealand and, 37, 132
  Permanent Five (P5), 21, 156,
  162, 198, 201, 205, 219, 228,
  242, 249, 250, 286, 287, 289,
  291
  permanent members, 21, 49, 156
  reform of, 24, 205, 243, 250,
  305–09
  regional representation, 23, 55,
  287
  Resolution 687, 23, 288, 289
  Resolution 688, 290
  Resolution 748, 24
  role of, 4, 198, 285
  Secretary-General and, 25, 26
  veto power, 55, 62, 202, 209,
  212, 237, 249, 307–08
  Working Group on membership
  of, 211
UN Transitional Assistance Group
(UNTAG), 128, 129
UN Transitional Authority in
Cambodia (UNTAC), 31, 91,
94, 96, 98, 101, 103–10, 145,
146, 150, 188, 195, 311–12
  Civil Administration Component,
  98, 106, 113–14, 153
  Civilian Police, 150, 153, 195
  comprehensive peacekeeping and,
  97, 194
  delay in deployment, 152, 187,
  311–12

UN Transitional Authority in
    Cambodia (cont'd)
  election and, 89, 92, 93, 100,
    109, 159–61
  Electoral Component, 98, 105,
    107, 114, 112, 195
  enforcement and, 153, 183, 187–
    88
  Force Commander, 147
  Force Communications Unit, 165
  Human Rights Component, 111,
    112
  human rights and, 110–12, 149
  Information and Education
    Division, 195
  Khmer Rouge perceptions, 155
  mandate, 112, 196
  media and, 157
  Military Component, 147, 148,
    150, 152, 153, 158
  election and, 188, 195
  internal security and, 154
  Mixed Military Working Group
    Secretariat, 162
  Office of the Legal Adviser to the
    SRSG, 112
  planning problems, 153, 163
  political expediency and, 103–10
  relations with politicians, 113
  role of, 147, 155
  support by Cambodian people,
    158
  unity, importance of, 156, 164
United Nations University, 265
United States, 19, 120, 131, 202,
    217–22, 225, 242, 283, 306
  Gulf War and, 4, 223, 287
  Haiti and, 287
  human rights and UN Charter, 44
  isolationism, 71
  Japan and, 207, 212–13
  League of Nations and, 44, 285
  Panama and, 287
  UN and, 13–14, 17, 19, 48, 238–
    39, 229, 244, 260
  UNESCO and, 294
  veto and, 209, 307, 308

  Yugoslavia and, 36
Uniting for Peace Resolution, 221
Universal Declaration of Human
    Rights, 16, 45, 297
Universal Postal Union, 295
Urquhart, Brian, 69, 317
Uruguay, 147
Uzbekistan, 218

Vance, Cyrus, 313
Vatican, 67
Vernon, Raymond, 257
veto power, 26, 55, 237, 249, 250,
    307–08
Vidal, Gore, 256
Vietnam, 212, 221, 319
violence, 280
Vitez, 35

Waldheim, Kurt, 26
war crimes tribunal, Bosnia, 24
Warhol, Andy, 33, 38
Warsaw Pact, 217, 218
Western European and Other group,
    55, 309
Western Sahara, 95
Westphalian system, 254
Wheelwright, Ted, 255
Whitehouse, Steve, 38
WHO, *see* World Health Organisation
Wilson, Woodrow, 43, 44
Woerner, Manfred, 172
Women's Conference, Beijing, 37,
    239, 316
Women's International League for
    Peace and Freedom, 261
World Bank, 27, 64, 218, 228, 252,
    293, 312
World Chronicle, 244
World Court, *see* International Court
    of Justice
World Health Organisation (WHO),
    170, 245, 252, 294
World Investment Report (1993), 256
World Meteorological Organisation,
    295

World Summit for Social
    Development, Copenhagen, 37,
    122, 123, 316
World Trade Organisation (WTO),
    292, 318
World War II, 182, 220, 242, 278
WTO, *see* World Trade Organisation

Yalta conference, 308
Yemen, 288
Young, Ruth Forbes, 263, 264

Yugoslavia, Former Republic of, 3,
    35, 36, 48, 49, 163, 167, 168,
    169, 170, 184, 203, 212, 218,
    233, 246, 272, 291; *see also*
    Balkans, Bosnia, Croatia,
    Serbia, Macedonia
    UN and, 35, 83

Zaire, 197, 214, 215
Zimbabwe, 93, 95, 128, 134, 271,
    315